Deep Learning Research Applications for Natural Language Processing

L. Ashok Kumar
PSG College of Technology, India

Dhanaraj Karthika Renuka
PSG College of Technology, India

S. Geetha
Vellore Institute of Technology, India

A volume in the Advances in Computational
Intelligence and Robotics (ACIR) Book Series

Published in the United States of America by
IGI Global
Engineering Science Reference (an imprint of IGI Global)
701 E. Chocolate Avenue
Hershey PA, USA 17033
Tel: 717-533-8845
Fax: 717-533-8661
E-mail: cust@igi-global.com
Web site: http://www.igi-global.com

Library of Congress Cataloging-in-Publication Data

Names: Kumar, L. Ashok, editor. I Renuka, D. Karthika, 1981- editor. I
    Geetha, S., 1979- editor.
Title: Deep learning research applications for natural language processing
    / L. Ashok Kumar, Dhanaraj Karthika Renuka, and S. Geetha, editors.
Description: Hershey, PA : Engineering Science Reference, [2023] I Includes
    bibliographical references and index. I Summary: "This book delves into
    issues of natural language processing, a subset of artificial
    intelligence that enables computers to understand the meaning of human
    language using techniques of machine learning and deep learning
    algorithms to discern a words' semantic meanings"-- Provided by
    publisher.
Identifiers: LCCN 2022027508 (print) I LCCN 2022027509 (ebook) I ISBN
    9781668460016 (h/c) I ISBN 9781668460023 (s/c) I ISBN 9781668460030
    (ebook)
Subjects: LCSH: Natural language processing (Computer science) I Machine
    learning. I Human face recognition (Computer science) I Speech
    processing systems.
Classification: LCC QA76.9.N38 D397 2023 (print) I LCC QA76.9.N38 (ebook)
    I DDC 006.3/5--dc23/eng/20220805
LC record available at https://lccn.loc.gov/2022027508
LC ebook record available at https://lccn.loc.gov/2022027509

This book is published in the IGI Global book series Advances in Computational Intelligence and Robotics (ACIR) (ISSN:
2327-0411; eISSN: 2327-042X)

British Cataloguing in Publication Data
A Cataloguing in Publication record for this book is available from the British Library.

All work contributed to this book is new, previously-unpublished material. The views expressed in this book are those of the
authors, but not necessarily of the publisher.

For electronic access to this publication, please contact: eresources@igi-global.com.

Advances in Computational Intelligence and Robotics (ACIR) Book Series

Ivan Giannoccaro
University of Salento, Italy

ISSN:2327-0411
EISSN:2327-042X

MISSION

While intelligence is traditionally a term applied to humans and human cognition, technology has progressed in such a way to allow for the development of intelligent systems able to simulate many human traits. With this new era of simulated and artificial intelligence, much research is needed in order to continue to advance the field and also to evaluate the ethical and societal concerns of the existence of artificial life and machine learning.

The **Advances in Computational Intelligence and Robotics (ACIR) Book Series** encourages scholarly discourse on all topics pertaining to evolutionary computing, artificial life, computational intelligence, machine learning, and robotics. ACIR presents the latest research being conducted on diverse topics in intelligence technologies with the goal of advancing knowledge and applications in this rapidly evolving field.

COVERAGE

- Adaptive and Complex Systems
- Cyborgs
- Robotics
- Agent technologies
- Cognitive Informatics
- Pattern Recognition
- Natural Language Processing
- Intelligent Control
- Machine Learning
- Computational Logic

IGI Global is currently accepting manuscripts for publication within this series. To submit a proposal for a volume in this series, please contact our Acquisition Editors at Acquisitions@igi-global.com or visit: http://www.igi-global.com/publish/.

Titles in this Series

For a list of additional titles in this series, please visit: www.igi-global.com/book-series

Controlling Epidemics With Mathematical and Machine Learning Models
Abraham Varghese (Higher College of Technology, Oman) Eduardo M. Lacap, Jr. (Higher College of Technology, Oman) Ibrahim Sajath (Higher College of Technology, Oman) Kamal Kumar (Higher College of Technology, Oman) and Shajidmon Kolamban (Higher College of Technology,Oman)
Engineering Science Reference • © 2023 • 300pp • H/C (ISBN: 9781799883432) • US $270.00

Handbook of Research on Computer Vision and Image Processing in the Deep Learning Era
A. Srinivasan (SASTRA University (Deemed), ndia)
Engineering Science Reference • © 2023 • 400pp • H/C (ISBN: 9781799888925) • US $325.00

Multidisciplinary Applications of Deep Learning-Based Artificial Emotional Intelligence
Chiranji Lal Chowdhary (Vellore Institute of Technology, India)
Engineering Science Reference • © 2023 • 296pp • H/C (ISBN: 9781668456736) • US $270.00

Principles and Applications of Socio-Cognitive and Affective Computing
S. Geetha (VIT University, Chennai, India) Karthika Renuka (PSG College of Technology, India) Asnath Victy Phamila (VIT University, Chennai, India) and Karthikeyan N. (Syed Ammal Engineering College, India)
Engineering Science Reference • © 2023 • 330pp • H/C (ISBN: 9781668438435) • US $270.00

Revolutionizing Industrial Automation Through the Convergence of Artificial Intelligence and the Internet of Things
Divya Upadhyay Mishra (ABES Engineering College, Ghaziabad, India) and Shanu Sharma (ABES Engineering College, Ghaziabad, India)
Engineering Science Reference • © 2023 • 279pp • H/C (ISBN: 9781668449912) • US $270.00

Convergence of Big Data Technologies and Computational Intelligent Techniques
Govind P. Gupta (National Institute of Technology, Raipur, India)
Engineering Science Reference • © 2023 • 335pp • H/C (ISBN: 9781668452646) • US $270.00

Design and Control Advances in Robotics
Mohamed Arezk Mellal (M'Hamed Bougara University, Algeria)
Engineering Science Reference • © 2023 • 320pp • H/C (ISBN: 9781668453810) • US $305.00

701 East Chocolate Avenue, Hershey, PA 17033, USA
Tel: 717-533-8845 x100 • Fax: 717-533-8661
E-Mail: cust@igi-global.com • www.igi-global.com

Rajamohana S. P., *Pondicherry University, Karaikal, India*
Monorama Swain, *Silicon Institute of Technology, Bhubaneswar, India*
Hemalatha T., *PSNA College of Engineering and Technology, Dindigul, India*
Vairam T., *PSG College of Technology, India*
Srivinitha V., *Bannari Amman Institute of Technology, India*
Asnath Victy Phamila Y., *Vellore Institute of Technology, Chennai, India*

Table of Contents

Section 1
Deep Learning Models for Natural Language Processing

Section 2
Research Applications Using Deep Learning

Detailed Table of Contents

Section 1
Deep Learning Models for Natural Language Processing

Chapter 1

P. Chinnasamy, MLR Institute of Technology, India
K. B. Sri Sathya, KPR Institute of Engineering and Technology, India
B. Jency A. Jebamani, KPR Institute of Engineering and Technology, India
A. Nithyasri, M. Kumarasamy College of Engineering, India
S. Fowjiya, Vivekananda College of Engineering for Women, India

Deep learning has become one of the hottest research topics in the machine-learning world, with tremendous success in several sectors. The summary and inductive reasoning procedures of deep learning are mostly used in this study. It begins by outlining the history and present state of deep learning globally. The second part of the chapter explains the fundamental structure, the traits, and a few types of traditional deep learning techniques, including the stacked auto encoder, deep belief network, deep Boltzmann machine, and convolutional neural network. Thirdly, it discusses the most recent advancements and uses of deep learning in a variety of industries, including speech recognition, machine learning, computational linguistics, and healthcare. Finally, it outlines the issues and potential possibilities for deep learning studies in the future.

Chapter 2

Puneet Mittal, Mangalore Institute of Technology and Engineering, Karnataka, India
Sukhwinder Sharma, Mangalore Institute of Technology and Engineering, Karnataka, India

Automatic speech recognition (ASR) has gained wide popularity in last decade. Various devices like mobile phones, computers, vehicles, and audio/video players are now being equipped with ASR technology. The increasing use and dependence on ASR technology leads to research enhancements and opportunities in this domain. This chapter provides a detailed review of various advancements in

ASR systems development. It highlights history of speech recognition followed by detailed insight into recent advancements and industry leaders providing latest solutions. ASR framework has been discussed in detail which includes feature extraction techniques, acoustic modeling techniques, and language modeling techniques. The chapter also lists various popular data sets available and discusses generation of new data sets. This work will be helpful for the researchers who are new to this field and are exploring development of new speech recognition techniques.

Despite the increased attention and substantial research into it claiming outstanding successes, the problem of misinformation containment has only been growing in the recent years with not many signs of respite. Misinformation is rapidly changing its latent characteristics and spreading vigorously in a multi-modal fashion, sometimes in a more damaging manner than viruses and other malicious programs on the internet. This chapter examines the existing research in natural language processing and machine learning to stop the spread of misinformation, analyzes why the research has not been practical enough to be incorporated into social media platforms, and provides future research directions. The state-of-the-art feature engineering, approaches, and algorithms used for the problem are expounded in the process.

Stance detection systems are built in order to determine the position of text authors using the text that they produce and other contextual information. As the result of the stance detection procedure, the position of the text producer is determined as favor, against, or none. On the other hand, transformer-based technologies are reported to perform well for various natural language processing tasks. These are deep learning-based models that also incorporate attention mechanism. BERT and its variants are among the most popular transformer-based models proposed so far. In this chapter, the authors provide a plausible literature review on stance detection studies that are based on transformer models. Also included in the current chapter are important further research directions. Stance detection and transformer-based models are significant and recent problems in natural language processing and deep learning, respectively. Hence, they believe that this chapter will be an important guide for related researchers and practitioners working on these topics of high impact.

The growing demand for having a conversation amongst people who come from different areas, across the globe, resulting from globalization, has led to the development of systems like machine translations. There are techniques like statistical models, Bayesian models, etc. that were used earlier for machine translations. However, with growing expectations towards better accuracies, neural networks aided systems for translations termed as neural machine translations (NMT) have come up. Models have been proposed by several organizations like Google NMT (G-NMT) that are widely accepted and implemented. Several machine translations are also based on RNN models. This work studies neural machine translations with respect to long short-term memory (LSTM) network and compares them on the basis of several widely accepted accuracy metrics like BLEU score, precision, recall, and F1 score. Further, a combination of two LSTM models is implemented for better accuracy. This work analyzes the various LSTM models on the basis of these metrics.

Suresh Kumar Nagarajan, Presidency University, India
Geetha Narasimhan, Vellore Institute of Technology, Vellore, India
Ankit Mishra, Vellore Institute of Technology, Vellore, India
Rishabh Kumar, Vellore Institute of Technology, Vellore, India

Music is an essential component of a promotional video since it helps to establish a brand's or entity's identity. Music composition and production, on the other hand, is quite costly. The expense of engaging a competent team capable of creating distinctive music for your firm could be prohibitively expensive. In the last decade, artificial intelligence has accomplished feats previously unimaginable to humanity. Artificial intelligence can be a lifesaver, not only in terms of the amount of money a company would have to spend on creating their own unique music but also in terms of the amount of time and work required on the firm's part. A web-based platform that can be accessed from anywhere in the world would help the product obtain customers without regard to geography. AI algorithms can be taught to recognize which sound combinations produce a pleasing melody (or music). Multiple machine learning algorithms can be used to accomplish this.

Vishnu S. Pendyala, San Jose State University, USA
VigneshKumar Thangarajan, PayPal, USA

A picture is worth a thousand words goes the well-known adage. Generating images from text understandably has many uses. In this chapter, the authors explore a state-of-the-art generative deep learning method to produce synthetic images and a new better way for evaluating the same. The approach focuses on synthesizing high-resolution images with multiple objects present in an image, given the textual description of the images. The existing literature uses object pathway GAN (OP-GAN) to automatically generate images from text. The work described in this chapter attempts to improvise the discriminator network from the original implementation using OP-GAN. This eventually helps the generator network's learning rate adjustment based on the discriminator output. Finally, the trained model is evaluated using semantic object accuracy (SOA), the same metric that is used to evaluate the baseline implementation, which is better than the metrics used previously in the literature.

Today's world is full of digital images; however, the context is unavailable most of the time. Thus, image captioning is quintessential for providing the content of an image. Besides generating accurate captions, the image captioning model must also be scalable. In this chapter, two variants of long short-term memory (LSTM), namely stacked LSTM and BiLSTM along with convolutional neural networks (CNN) have been used to implement the Encoder-Decoder model for generating captions. Bilingual evaluation understudy (BLEU) score metric is used to evaluate the performance of these two bi-layered models. From the study, it was observed that both the models were on par when it came to performance. Some resulted in low BLEU scores suggesting that the predicted caption was dissimilar to the actual caption whereas some very high BLEU scores suggested that the model was able to predict captions almost similar to human. Furthermore, it was found that the bidirectional LSTM model is more computationally intensive and requires more time to train than the stacked LSTM model owing to its complex architecture.

Section 2
Research Applications Using Deep Learning

After the proliferation of deep learning technologies in computer vision applications, natural language processing has used deep learning methods for its building steps like segmentation, classification, prediction, understanding, and recognition. Among different natural language processing domains, dubbing is one of the challenging tasks. Deep learning-based methodologies for dubbing will translate unknown language audio into meaningful words. This chapter provides a detailed study on the recent deep learning models in literature for dubbing. Deep learning models for dubbing can be categorized based on the feature representation as audio, visual, and multimodal features. More models are prevailing for English language, and a few techniques are available for Indian languages. In this chapter, the authors provide an end-to-end solution to predict the lip movements and translate them into natural language. This study also covers the recent enhancements in deep learning for natural language processing. Also, the future directions for the automated dubbing process domain are discussed.

    Ashok Kumar L., PSG College of Technology, India
    Karthika Renuka D., PSG College of Technology, India
    Shunmugapriya M. C., PSG College of Technology, India

Tamil question answering system (QAS) is aimed to find relevant answers in in the native language. The system will help farmers to get information in Tamil related to the agriculture domain. Tamil is one of the morphologically rich languages. As a result, developing such systems that process Tamil words is a difficult task. The list of stop words in Tamil has to be collected manually. Parts of speech (POS) tagging is used to identify suitable POS tag for a sequence of Tamil words. The system employs Hidden Markov Model (HMM)-based viterbi algorithm, a machine learning technique for parts of speech tagging of Tamil words. The analyzed question is given to the Google search to obtain relevant documents. On top of Google search, locality sensitive hashing technique (LSH) is utilized to retrieve the five relevant items for the input Tamil question. Jaccard similarity is used to obtain the response from the retrieved document items. The proposed system is modelled using a dataset of 1000 sentences in the agriculture domain.

    Eymen Kagan Taspinar, Marmara University, Turkey
    Yusuf Burak Yetis, Marmara University, Turkey
    Onur Cihan, Marmara University, Turkey

Abstractive summarization aims to comprehend texts semantically and reconstruct them briefly and concisely where the summary may consist of words that do not exist in the original text. This chapter studies the abstractive Turkish text summarization problem by a transformer attention-based mechanism. Moreover, this study examines the differences between transformer architecture and other architectures as well as the attention block, which is the heart of this architecture, in detail. Three summarization datasets were generated from the available text data on various news websites for training abstractive summarization models. It is shown that the trained model has higher or comparable ROUGE scores than existing studies, and the summaries generated by models have better structural properties. English-to-Turkish translation model has been created and used in a cross-lingual summarization model which has a ROUGE score that is comparable to the existing studies. The summarization structure proposed in this study is the first example of cross-lingual English-to-Turkish text summarization.

    Ashok Kumar L., PSG College of Technology, India
    Karthika Renuka D., PSG College of Technology, India
    Raajkumar G., PSG College of Technology, India

Recently, communication via signing acknowledgment has received a lot of attention in personal computer vision. Sign language is a method of conveying messages by using the hand, arm, body, and face to convey considerations and implications. Communication through gestures, like communication in languages, arises and develops naturally within hearing-impaired networks. All the same, gesture-based communication is uncommon. There is no universally perceived and accepted gesture-based communication for all deaf and hard-of-hearing people. Each nation has its own communication via gestures with a significant level of syntactic variety, just as it does when communicating in language. The gesture-based communication utilized is usually known as sign language.

    Shoba S., Centre for Advanced Data Science, Vellore Institute of Technology, Chennai, India
    Chanthini B., Vellore Institute of Technology, Chennai, India
    Sasithradevi A., Centre for Advanced Data Science, Vellore Institute of Technology, Chennai, India
    Manikandan E., Centre for Innovation and Product Development, Vellore Institute of Technology, Chennai, India

Sign language recognition has become a critical research in the field of computer vision as the need of disability solutions grow. Sign language acts as a bridge to reduce the communication gap between normal people and deaf and dumb people. Current sign language identification systems, on the other hand, lack essential characteristics such as accessibility and cost, which are critical for people with speech disabilities to interact with their daily settings. The successful attractive solution is to initiate the sign languages in terms of words and common expressions for daily activities. This will interact the deaf and dumb people by connecting to the outside world more quickly and easily. The sign gestures obtained are processed through popular machine learning and deep learning models for classification accuracy. This chapter discusses the word sign recognition, image processing algorithms for separating the signs from the background, machine learning algorithms, and the complete model set up for sign recognition.

    Suresh Kumar Nagarajan, Presidency University, India
    Geetha N., Vellore Institute of Technology, Vellore, India
    Raghav Talwar, Vellore Institute of Technology, Vellore, India
    Shivoma Ahuja, Vellore Institute of Technology, Vellore, India

MorseEx uses Morse code, which allows partially visually impaired and hard of hearing people to chat with others. In Morse code, letters are represented as a combination of dots and dashes. The person inputs a dot by tapping on the left of the screen, dash by tapping on the center of the screen to form a message, and tapping on the right will separate letters of the message, and tapping it twice sends the message. This message will be saved to the database and then converted to a normal text message to receive by people who do not have any impairments. On the other hand, people with no impairments have to type and send text messages. For this message to be understood by the visually and partially impaired, a dot will be produced as short vibration and a dash will be produced as long vibration. The model will be developing an Android mobile application using Android studio and Firebase database to store user information. The aim is to contribute to society in any way possible.

    Rajkumar S., Vellore Institute of Technology, Vellore, India
    Mary Nikitha K., Vellore Institute of Technology, Vellore, India
    Ramanathan L., Vellore Institute of Technology, Vellore, India
    Rajasekar Ramalingam, University of Technology and Applied Sciences, Sur, Oman
    Mudit Jantwal, Vellore Institute of Technology, Vellore, India

In this chapter, online rental listings of the city of Hyderabad are used as a data source for mapping house rent. Data points were scraped from one of the popular Indian rental websites www.nobroker. in. With the collected information, models of rental market dynamics were developed and evaluated using regression and boosting algorithms such as AdaBoost, CatBoost, LightGBM, XGBoost, KRR, ENet, and Lasso regression. An ensemble machine learning algorithm of the best combination of the aforementioned algorithms was also implemented using the stacking technique. The results of these algorithms were compared using several performance metrics such as coefficient of determination (R2 score), mean squared error (MSE), root mean squared error (RMSE), mean absolute error (MAE), and accuracy in order to determine the most effective model. According to further examination of results, it is clear that the ensemble machine learning algorithm does outperform the others in terms of better accuracy and reduced errors.

Chapter 16

Sanjay V., School of Computer Science and Engineering, Vellore Institute of Technology,
    Vellore, India
Swarnalatha P., School of Computer Science and Engineering, Vellore Institute of
    Technology, Vellore, India

In Alzheimer's disease (AD), memory and cognitive abilities deteriorate, affecting the capacity to do basic activities. In and around brain cells, aberrant amyloid and tau protein accumulation is believed to cause it. Amyloid deposits create plaques surrounding brain cells, whereas tau deposits form tangles inside brain cells. The plagues and tangles harm healthy brain cells, causing shrinkage. This damage seems to be occurring in the hippocampus, a brain region involved in memory formation. There are presently no methods that provide the most accurate outcomes. The current techniques do not identify AD early. The proposed DL-EDAD method achieves excellent clustering using CNN with E-GKFCM (enhanced gaussian kernel fuzzy c-means clustering). The E-GKFCM utilizes an elbow method to determine the number of clusters in a dataset. Unlike other medical pictures, brain scans are extremely sensitive.

Foreword

The fourth industrial revolution, according to the World Economic Forum, is about to begin. This will blend the physical and digital worlds in ways we couldn't imagine a few years ago. Advances in machine learning and AI will help usher in these existing changes. Machine learning is transformative which opens up new scenarios that were simple impossible a few years ago. Profound gaining addresses a significant change in perspective from customary programming improvement models. Rather than recording un-equivocal top guidelines for how programming ought to act deep learning permits your product to sum up rules of tasks. Deep learning models empower the engineers to configure that are characterized by the information have not the guidelines to compose. Deep learning models are conveyed at scale and creation applications, for example, car, gaming, medical services and independent vehicles. Deep learn-ing models employ artificial neural networks, which are computer architectures comprised of multiple layers of interconnected components. By avoiding data transmission through these connected units, a neural network can learn how to approximate the computations required to transform inputs to outputs. Deep learning models require top-notch information to prepare a brain organization to carry out a par-ticular errand. Contingent upon your expected applications, you might have to get thousands to millions of tests. The objective of the book is to provide the readers with the fundamentals, recent trends of deep learning algorithms in the field of natural language processing. This book gives the introduction, ap-plications of deep learning to the academicians, researchers and students who are new to this field. This book produces an evident research outcomes using cutting edge technologies in this field with real time applications. The book provides a refreshing and motivating new synthesis of the field by one of AI's master expositors and leading researchers.

Regards,
Sheng-Lung Peng
College of Innovative Design and Management, National Taipei University of Business, Taiwan

Preface

Humans have the most advanced method of communication which is known as natural language. While humans can use computers to send voice and text messages to each other, computers do not innately know how to process natural language. Natural language processing is a subset of artificial intelligence that enables computers to understand the meaning of human language. Natural language processing uses machine learning and deep learning algorithms to discern a word's semantic meaning. It does this by deconstructing sentences grammatically, relationally, and structurally and understanding the context of use. Natural language processing is broken down into many subcategories related to audio and visual tasks. For computers to communicate in natural language, they need to be able to convert speech into text, so communication is more natural and easy to process. They also need to be able to convert text-to-speech, so users can interact with computers without the requirement to stare at a screen. Deep learning has become the most popular approach in machine learning in recent years. This is due to the high accuracies obtained by deep learning methods in many tasks especially with textual and visual data. Natural language processing (NLP), and computer vision are the research areas that deep learning has demonstrated its impact at utmost level. Natural language processing (NLP) is a crucial part of artificial intelligence (AI), modeling how people share information. In recent years, deep learning (or neural network) approaches have obtained very high performance across many different NLP tasks, and computer vision using single end-to-end neural models that do not require traditional, task-specific feature engineering. This book provides thorough introduction to cutting-edge research in Deep Learning for NLP.

Machine learning is a collection of algorithms and tools that help machines understand patterns within data and use this underlying structure to perform reasoning about a given task. There are many ways that machines aim to understand these underlying patterns. In recent years, deep learning has primarily transformed the perspectives of a variety of fields in artificial intelligence, including vision, natural language processing. In particular, the extensive success of deep learning in a wide variety of applications has served as a benchmark for the many downstream tasks in artificial intelligence. Natural language processing, voice, are some of the most common application domains. Natural language and speech processing applications such as virtual assistants and smart speakers play an important and ever-growing role in our lives. The field of computer vision has taken great leaps in recent years and surpasses humans in tasks related to detecting and labelling objects, thanks to advances in deep learning and neural networks. Self-driving automobiles can use this technology to understand their surroundings. It's used in facial recognition software, which allows computers to match pictures of people's faces to their identities. It is also important in augmented and mixed reality. The technology that enables smart phones, tablets and smart glasses to overlay and embed virtual things on real-world images. In this book, we provide an overview of how deep learning fits into this realm and also discuss some of its applications and challenges.

Even though deep learning algorithms have proven to beat human-level accuracy, there is no clear way to backtrack and provide the reasoning behind each prediction that's made. This makes it difficult to use in applications such as finance where there are mandates to provide the reasoning behind every loan that is approved or rejected.

This book reviews the state of the art of deep learning research and its successful applications to major NLP tasks, including understanding, machine translation, question answering, and computer vision based applications and natural language generation from images. Outlining and analyzing various research frontiers of NLP in the deep learning era, it features self-contained that explains the concepts and state-of-art research in the field of NLP. This book provides an overview research trends and applications of NLP tasks. The application areas are divided into two sections: section 1 discuss deep learning models for NLP, section 2 discusses the research applications for deep learning.

SECTION 1: DEEP LEARNING MODELS FOR NLP

Natural Language Processing is an emerging interdisciplinary field involving deep learning, computational linguistics, and big data. Artificial Intelligence, a field in computer science that aims in giving computers the ability to mimic human-like intelligence, is being heavily deployed in building powerful and highly intelligent machines. Deep learning mimics the human behavior on impersonating human performance and reckoning to provide solutions to complex problems in NLP. The first chapter of this book gives a detailed survey on the recently developed deep learning algorithms such as Recursive neural network, Deep Generative models and transfer learning. It also presents few prominent NLP-Deep learning-based applications, in-depth survey on deep learning frameworks and insights of fruitful ongoing research in optimization techniques.

Automatic speech recognition (ASR) is one of the widely adopted applications. Second chapter of this section focuses on the building blocks of ASR system are acoustic, language and pronunciation model. It also presents few prominent ASR-Deep learning-based applications, in-depth survey on challenges of ASR.

Social media has been subject to plenty of controversies owing to its use for spreading misinformation, sometimes to the extent of manipulating a country's presidential elections. Third chapter explores the misinformation containment based on the recent machine learning and NLP techniques. It also explores language models, few-shot learning, bot detection, graph theoretic approaches to misinformation containment, and using Generative Adversarial Network models for detecting fake multimedia content as well as textual content.

Stance detection has emerged as a significant problem which has its roots in natural language processing (NLP), social media analysis, and information retrieval. Stance detection is related to the problems in affective computing such as sentiment analysis. The fourth chapter discuses transformer-based stance detection.

Fifth chapter explores machine translation using neural network-based system. It mainly focusses on LSTM and RNN based machine translation system by providing plausible results in terms of BLEU score, precision, and recall. More interesting use case of AI is discussed in sixth chapter, AI music generation system using LSTM. It also discusses the effectiveness of LSTM based model against other benchmarking algorithm such as GRU.

Figures capture the latent semantic space of the corresponding text effortlessly using the advent deep learning techniques. Seventh chapter explores generative deep learning-based model to generate figures from text. This provide answer to the research question "to what extent can deep learning systems capture a pictorial representation of a given text and exercise control over the generated image?"

Automatic Image Captioning entails extracting important content from an image and representing it in the form of a meaningful sequence of words. Eighth chapter focusses on building automated image captioning system using LSTM based models and evaluated using accuracy and BLEU score metrics.

SECTION 2: RESEARCH APPLICATIONS FOR DEEP LEARNING

Section 2 of this book discusses cutting edge research applications using deep learning. The deep learning methods prevalent today are very data hungry, and many complex problems such as language translation don't have sophisticated data sets available. Deep learning methods to perform neural machine translation to and from low-resource languages often perform poorly. Deep learning-based application for Indian language automated dubbing is depicted in Chapter 9. Indian language question answering system for agricultural domain is explored in Chapter 10.

Due to the rapid growth of the web, the amount of text data is increasing exponentially which suggests a need for effective techniques and tools to manage this data. Reducing the length of texts while retaining the core meaning, referred to as summarization, has drawn significant attention from researchers in the recent past. Transformers are transforming the landscape of deep learning applications in the research perspective. Chapter 11 shows the Turkish text summarization and cross lingual summarization application using transformer-based models.

Computer vision has recently paid a lot of attention to communicating via signing acknowledgement. The use of the hands, elbow, body, and expression to communicate ideas and implications is known as sign language. Communication through gestures, like communication in languages, arises and develops naturally within hearing-impaired networks. Chapter 12 provides a systematic survey in sign language recognition.

Chapter 13 guides us through the challenges faced by deaf and dumb community people. It also investigates various deep learning models for building and deploying sign language recognizer. Chapter 14 discusses sign language recognition using computer vision-based applications and achieved a good results.

Cloud hosted ensemble learning based rental apartment price prediction model using stacking technique is discussed in Chapter 15. It also executes different machine learning models and boosting methods for house price prediction that have several applications in the real estate industry.

Worldwide, research is underway to detect and diagnose Alzheimer's. The study's goal is to detect and diagnose this disease early. Chapter 16 shows DL-EDAD model for Early Prediction for Alzheimer's disease using deep learning models.

The application areas that have the potential to be impacted significantly by deep learning and that have been experiencing research growth including natural language and text processing, computer vision and multimodal information processing empowered by multi-task deep learning. It explores research ideas in the filed NLP, Recent deep learning methods and state-of-the-art approaches applicable to NLP and computer vision. Provides insights into using the tools and libraries in python for real-world applications. A comprehensive resource that builds up from elementary deep learning, text, computer vision principles

Preface

to advanced state-of-the-art neural architectures. This book provides a single source that addresses the gap between theory and practice using case studies with experiments, and supporting analysis.

The book appeals to advanced undergraduate and graduate students, post-doctoral researchers, lecturers and industrial researchers, as well as anyone interested in deep learning and natural language processing. Target audience and potential users are to identify potential contexts in which this book will be used and to what market this book is appropriate for. The intended audience for this book consists of anyone working in natural language processing, Computer Vision, Computational linguists, machine learning and deep learning. This book attempts to simplify and present the concepts of deep learning in a very comprehensive manner, with suitable, full-fledged examples of deep learning models, for Natural Language Processing and its applications. The book tries to bridge the gap between the theoretical and the applicable. Armed with all the information in this book, you are now ready to go deeper into your journey of deep learning. There are several variations and additions to the artificial neural network that help with achieving unseen levels of accuracy for different applications.

L. Ashok Kumar
PSG College of Technology, India

Dhanaraj Karthika Renuka
PSG College of Technology, India

S. Geetha
Vellore Institute of Technology, India

Acknowledgment

We bow our head before "The God Almighty" who blessed us with health and confidence to undertake and complete the book successfully. We express our sincere thanks to the Principal and Management of PSG College of Technology and VIT for their constant encouragement and support.

We thank our family and friends who always stood beside us and encouraged us to complete the book.

Dr. L. Ashok Kumar is thankful to his wife, Ms. Y. Uma Maheswari, for her constant support during writing. He is also grateful to his daughter, Ms. A.K. Sangamithra, for her support; it helped him a lot in completing this work.

Dr. D. Karthika Renuka would like to express gratitude to her parents, for their constant support. Her heartfelt thanks to her husband, Mr. R. Sathish Kumar, and her dear daughter, Ms. P. S. Preethi, for their unconditional love which made her capable of achieving all her goals.

Dr. Geetha records her gratitude to her parents, to her husband, and to her sons for their unconditional love which made her capable of achieving all her goals.

We would like to acknowledge the help of all the people involved in this project. First, we would like to thank each one of the authors for their contributions. Our sincere gratitude goes to the chapter's authors who contributed their time and expertise to this book. We thank all the authors of the chapters for their commitment to this endeavor and their timely response to our incessant requests for revisions.

Second, the editors wish to acknowledge the valuable contributions of the reviewers regarding the improvement of quality, coherence, and content presentation of chapters. Most of the authors also served as referees; we highly appreciate their double task.

Next, the editors would like to recognize the contributions of editorial board in shaping the nature of the chapters in this book. In addition, we wish to thank the editorial staff at IGI Global for their professional assistance and patience. Sincere thanks to each one of them.

Section 1
Deep Learning Models for Natural Language Processing

Chapter 1
Deep Learning:
Algorithms, Techniques, and Applications — A Systematic Survey

P. Chinnasamy
https://orcid.org/0000-0002-3202-4299
MLR Institute of Technology, India

K. B. Sri Sathya
KPR Institute of Engineering and Technology, India

B. Jency A. Jebamani
KPR Institute of Engineering and Technology, India

A. Nithyasri
M. Kumarasamy College of Engineering, India

S. Fowjiya
Vivekananda College of Engineering for Women, India

ABSTRACT

Deep learning has become one of the hottest research topics in the machine-learning world, with tremendous success in several sectors. The summary and inductive reasoning procedures of deep learning are mostly used in this study. It begins by outlining the history and present state of deep learning globally. The second part of the chapter explains the fundamental structure, the traits, and a few types of traditional deep learning techniques, including the stacked auto encoder, deep belief network, deep Boltzmann machine, and convolutional neural network. Thirdly, it discusses the most recent advancements and uses of deep learning in a variety of industries, including speech recognition, machine learning, computational linguistics, and healthcare. Finally, it outlines the issues and potential possibilities for deep learning studies in the future.

DOI: 10.4018/978-1-6684-6001-6.ch001

INTRODUCTION

Machine learning is becoming increasingly common in recent studies and has already been united into a wide range of applications, namely processing of visual perceptions, analysis of image, audiovisual recommendations, impact of social links, information retrieval, etc. Deep learning, "also recognized as representations learning (Abadi, 2016), is commonly included in these simulations by different machine-learning algorithms." The growth of massively efficient and learning techniques studies has been facilitated by the rapid expansion and accessibility of data as well as the significant advancements in process control. Deep learning significantly outperforms its predecessors and is based on traditional neural networks. To design of multiple-layered learning approaches, it incorporates graph developments with inequalities between neuronal. Some of the new deep learning models were already implemented and significant improvements have been shown throughout numerous applications, like Natural Language Processing (NLP), visual data management, voice recognition and so on (Ossama, 2014, Abel, 2017).

The performance of machine-learning algorithms has historically depended heavily on a consistency of input vectors interpretation. Compared to a standard data visualization, a poor data interpretation sometimes resulting in poorer results. Consequently, for just a long period of time, feature extraction has become a significant research path in machine learning, concentrating on constructing features from the dataset and leading to many studies conducted. In addition, feature extraction is always unique to the environment and involves considerable human work. For example, various types of samples, such as Histogram of Directed Gradients (HOG) (Abel, 2017), Scale Invariant Feature Transform (SIFT), and Bag of Words (BoW), are being investigated and compared in machine vision. When a new function is introduced and works well enough for decades, it will become a standard. Recent incidents, like voice recognition and NLP, also occurred in many other environments.

Relatively speaking, deep learning techniques facilitate faster extraction of information, allowing scientists to extract discriminatory features without limited knowledge of the subject and manual effort (Sami, 2016). These strategies provide a layered data modeling framework where it would be possible to extract the high-level features from upper level of the systems, whereas the lower features are retrieved from bottom layer. Initially, different types of designs are motivated by Artificial Intelligence (AI), which simulated the function of a main brain modalities in the human. Our neurons can derive the description of the data spontaneously through various scenes. The input is the knowledge that the scenario receives from eyes, whereas the confidential images are the result. This review presents an overview of deep learning from various points of view, such as background, obstacles, possibilities, techniques, architectures, implementations, and distributed and cloud-based strategies.

Objectives of the Proposed Survey

This report tries to give an overall picture and communicate scientific knowledge with colleagues, though deep learning is recognized an enormous area of scientific. Whereas other previous report reports concentrated mostly on a specific deep learning scope (Berant, 2013, Leo, 2003), the uniqueness of such a report would be that it emphasizes on numerous perspectives of learning techniques thru the summary of a higher-sensitive documents, the knowledge of a researchers, as well as the scientific advances in neural network-based research and the development.

The primary issue facing by deep learning nowadays would be to practice the vast available information at disposal. Even as dataset becomes broader, increasingly nuanced, and much more difficult, deep learning is becoming a vital method for data analytics. In our survey the major aspects of deep learning which demand 1st-priority attention, especially parallel processing, interoperability, energy, and optimizations. In diverse disciplines, like RNNs for Language processing and CNNs for image analysis, various kinds of neural networks are designed to solve different existing issues. The report includes summarizes and evaluates common deep learning instruments across each deep learning approach, like DeepLearning4j, TensorFlow, Torch, and evolutionary algorithms. In conjunction, various technologies for deep learning are evaluated to encourage many scientists extend their perspective on deep learning.

The remainder of this paper is structured as follows. Advanced deep learning models are momentarily discussed in Section 2. In deep learning, section 3 addresses many algorithms, techniques, and frameworks. As neural networks are being used for voice and image processing and also industry-focused implementations through NLP, Section 4 offers a wide variety of deep learning algorithms. In the future, Section 5 highlights the difficulties and possible study approaches. After that, this episode ended with Section 6.

BACKGROUND

Deep Learning Networks

Throughout this section, we are going to see about some familiar deep learning networks like recursive neural network, recurrent neural network, conventional neural network, and model for deep generative.

Recursive Neural Network

RvNN can categorize outcomes employing constituent vectors and create recommendations in a hierarchy organization. Recursive Auto associative Memory (RAAM) (Davide, 2016), a technology required to handle items with any structures, including such as tree or graphs, is used to construct a RvNN. The technique was to construct a fixed-width probabilistic model from a recursion data structure of various sizes. To apply this technique, the Back - propagation learning Via Framework (BTS) training technique has been proposed (Chen, 2015). BTS uses a stochastic gradient descent technique that is comparable to the traditional learning algorithm, but it can also support a tree-like topology. Auto association is used to communicate the networks toward recreate patterns of the input nodes there at output neuron. A phrase is subdivided into words, but an imagery is unglued into several portions of significance. RvNN computes the scores of a potential pair in order to combine them and construct a syntax tree. RvNN computes a score for the merge's believability for each coupling of subunits. The highest-scoring pair is then concatenated to form a composing vector. RvNN generates (1) a larger zone with numerous units, (2) a composing vector characterizing the territory, and (3) the membership functions after each convergence. The dynamic word representations of the entire continent are at the base of the RvNN tree - like structure.

Figure 1. A Simple Recursive Neural Network (src: https://en.wikipedia.org/wiki/Recursive_neural_network)

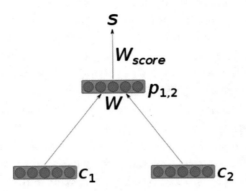

Recurrent Neural Network

RNN (Ting, 2014) seems to be another frequently being used successful neural learning method, particularly in NLP and voice analysis. Unlike standard neural networks, RNN makes use of the channel's consecutive layers. This characteristic is crucial in numerous circumstances when the data sequence's level of preparation conveys valuable knowledge. For instance, understanding a phrase or term requires understanding its context. With input neurons x, concealed (state) parts s, and return vertices y, an RNN can be seen as a group of preferential memory space.

Figure 2. The Generalized architecture of RNN

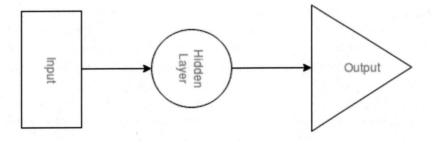

Conventional Neural Network (CNN)

CNN is a well-known and commonly used deep classification technique (Tianqi, 2015). It has been widely used in a variety of applications, including natural language processing (Sharan, 2013), voice recognition (Hsieh, 2013), and machine vision, to mention a very few. Its architecture is modeled by neurotransmitters in humans and other animals' brains, comparable to typical neural network models. It resembles the visual system of a cat's brain, which is made up of a complicated series of neurons

(Timothy, 2016). CNN offers three parts of this activity, as explained in (Hazan, 2010), including prior to distributing, shallow connections, and comparable descriptions.

Model for Deep Generative

Deep generative models (DGMs) are one type of neural based model with a large number of hidden layers that have been accomplished to estimated difficult, high-dimensional prospect disseminations with a large amount of data. Again, when the DGMs have been effectively trained, we could use them to evaluate the every observable and make a sample from its properties. In recent years, evolving DGMs is the recent areas in AI based research. Some breakthroughs have even made it into the public eye, such as recent accomplishments in creating efficient images, multimedia properties. In spite of improvements, a number of mathematical and practical challenges prevent DGMs from being widely used: designing and training a DGM for a specific dataset remains difficult, and determining why a model is or is not useful is much more difficult. We present DGMs and present a clear scientific model for describing the different prominent tactics: normalizing flows (NF), variational autoencoders (VAE), and generative adversarial networks (GAN) to help enhance the theoretical understanding of DGMs (GAN).

BACKGROUNDS AND PROCEDURES FOR DEEP LEARNING

Numerous deep learning processes help to increase learning efficiency, extend the range of applicability, and streamline control procedures. But computational intelligence models' extraordinarily lengthy training times prove to be a significant problem for scientists. Adding extra training examples and prediction models can also significantly boost generalization ability. To expedite deep learning computation, several ground-breaking techniques are developed in the research. Deep learning systems include the deployment of flexible modular deep learning methods as well as analytic applications, dissemination strategies, and infrastructure maintenance. They have been created to facilitate system-level research in this area while also facilitating the integration process. This section introduces a few of these excellent approaches and environments.

Transfer Learning

Some researchers have engrossed on the unsupervised machine learning difficulty in deep learning, given the substantial development into controlled deep learning. However, using unstructured methods to gather repeatable characteristics has recently produced positive results in a number of situations. Over the past ten years, the awareness of a self-taught education model remained passionately contested in the literature (Moataz, 2011). The most well-liked uncontrolled deep learning methods in recent years have been design and project like GANs and VAEs. For process that gives (Rasool, 2013), for instance, trains and employs GANs as a constant feature representation. This network creates a high-level feature extraction technique from unstructured data that can be used for uncontrolled face recognition. The resulting features could also be used to find other elevated objects, such human body parts or wildlife features. A synthetic probabilistic networking for unsupervised classification is presented by (Bengio, 2014) as just a replacement to the parameter estimation depending on transitioning generators of Markov chain.

Optimization Techniques in Deep Learning

a)   Centralized Optimization

In DDLS that employ centralized enhancement, an unique optimizing instances (often known as a parameter server) is in charge of modifying a specific vehicle component. Measurement systems just use concentrations generated by cluster members performing transfer learning (workers). The flow of information in a system throughout retraining is shown in Figure 3. It's important to note that the terms parametric service and workforce describe to application operations rather than actual hardware. We'll assume for the moment term so each functionality works on a separate computer.

Figure 3. Implementation of centralized optimization

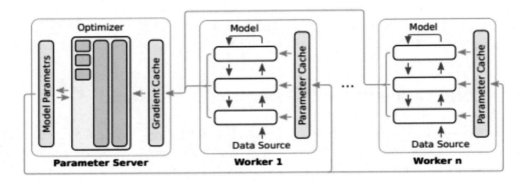

By aggregating all communications at the these should, the simulation may well be maintained attractively while the costly task of determining each variation is distributed amongst some of the clustered devices. This makes it simple to find per-parameter declines for massive number of base classifiers. Whether or not operations among agents are handled statically or dynamically can have a varied impact on the effectiveness. Since a discrete parameter service seems to be the only agent with right access to a particular estimation of parameters, its position continuously represents the quality of the training procedure. Data administration is greatly streamlined as a result, but individuals now have a manufacturer engagement. To ensure that the values the model produces are appropriate, each employee must periodically retrieve it again. In multiple clusters, this ongoing need for interaction concentrated on same networking devices can easily lead to a congestion. In redistributing the variable service responsibility, the majority of centralised performance tuning DDLS employ communication techniques. Flow of information in a cluster with decentralization optimizing is shown in Figure 4. The central server builds the subsequent global modeling state by merging the local model replicates (J- -) that the employees independently teach. searches for stochastic gradient minimum itineraries with strong applicability features by examining the nonlinear function (Feng, 2015). Instead of centralizing the optimization cycle onto to the group like conventional DDLS accomplishes, decentralized systems undertake classification models independently in each employee. To align the different points of view and create a better incentivize, some form of adjudication is necessary (Zisserman, 2016). Decentralized minimization can sometimes be employed if certain workers are unable to satisfy the storage overhead for repeating both the slope computation and the optimizing process. Figure 4 shows the data flow in a distributed structure.

Figure 4. Dataflow in clusters that implements decentralized optimization

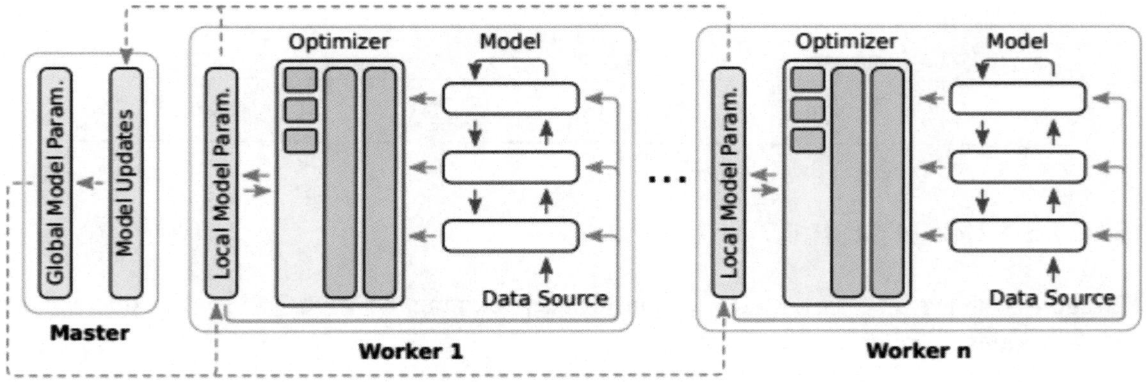

Deep Learning in Distributed System

The development of decentralized deep learning algorithms has helped more to enhance the training time because the performance of feature learning is confined to a single-machine system. Data synchronization and prototype simultaneously are the two basic strategies for the modeling process in a distributed architecture. Each model is built using the specified subset of data, and the modelling is replicated throughout all computational platforms to allow data synchronization. After a specific length of time, the frequencies alteration requires to be synchronized amongst endpoints. Model concurrency, in comparison, uses a single theory to handle all the data, among each nodes in responsible of calculating some of the model's attributes. A model synchronization technique, to the contrary hand, divides the training phase across several GPUs. A simple model-parallel approach evaluates just a portion of the simulation on each GPU. For case, the structures with two GPUs could practice each of them to generate one LSTM erection for a model consisting of two LSTM layers. The model-parallel approach has the benefit of enabling enormous deep neural network learning and predictions (Abadi, 2016).

Deep Learning Frameworks

Table 1 includes information about CNN, RNN, and DBN's licensing, core language, supported interface language, and framework support. From Table 2, it is clear that C++ is frequently utilized to construct deep learning architectures since it speeds up training. The majority of the abovementioned architectures greatly facilitate GPU through the order to speeding up matrices processing.

Table 1. The Comparison of different Deep Learning Models

Background	Authorization	Core Language	Interface Support	CNN & RNN Support	DBN Support
(Abadi, 2016)	Apache 2.0	Python	C/C++, Go	Yes	Yes
(Sami, 2016)	BSD	Python	Python	Yes	Yes
(Tiangi, 2015)	Apache 2.0	C++	C++, Perl, Julia, etc.	Yes	Yes
(Ting, 2014)	BSD	Lua	Lua	Yes	Yes
(Dong, 2014)	MIT	C++	Python, C++, & BrainScript	Yes	No

DEEP LEARNING APPLICATIONS

The Figure 5, shows that, various applications of deep learning in various fields. we explained one by one applications in the below the parts;

Figure 5. Different Applications of Deep Learning

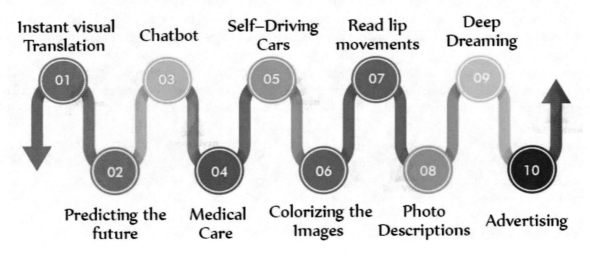

A. AI based Helper

Automated systems are cloud-based applications that understand human language voice recognition and execute them as directed by the client. A few examples of virtual personal assistants are Amazon Alexa, Bing, Cortana, and Google Assistant. They need network devices in order to perform at their best at work is shown in Figure 6.

Figure 6. Applications of AI Assistant

B. **Bots**

The Figure 7 shows that, Bots applications. Bots can quickly resolve customer problems. A bot is an artificial intelligence (AI) application that enables interactive text or text-to-speech communication between users.

Figure 7. Working Architecture of Bots

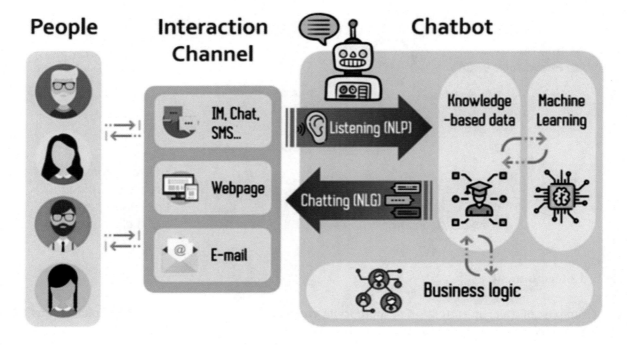

C.   Medical Sector

The medical field has become a stronghold for deep learning. Computers can now help with illness treatment and classification thanks to deep learning. Medical imaging is extensively used in pharmaceutical research, clinical research, and the detection of potentially fatal chronic diseases such as cancer and macular degeneration is clearly shown in Figure 8.

Figure 8. Applications in Medical Field

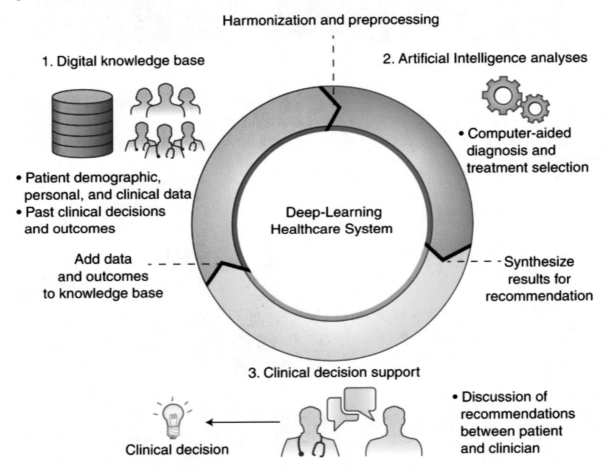

D.   Entertainment

Examples of companies that offer appropriate cinema, music, and television recommendations to their users include Netflix, Amazon, YouTube, and Soundcloud is shown in Figure 9. Everything is the result of deep learning. To help users choose products and services, internet streaming companies generate personalized recommendations on a user's internet activity, hobbies, and behavior (Kavitha, 2010, John, 1993).

Figure 9. Applications in Entertainment

E. Fake News Detection

Utilizing deep learning, you may tailor news to the identities of your viewers. Influenced by social, regional, socioeconomic, and psychological inclinations of users, you can consolidate and analyze news content (Sumathi, 2021). The creation of classifications that can identify and exclude skewed and false news from the newsfeed is made possible with the use of neural nets. Additionally, they alert you to possible security breaches as like shown in Figure 10.

Figure 10. Application in News Feed

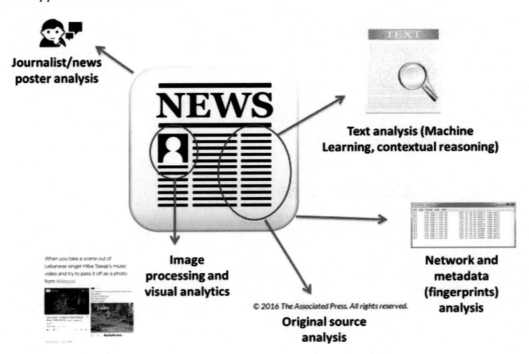

F. Transportation Prediction

The Figure 11 shows that another use for deep learning is the anticipation of road transport. To forecast how the overcrowding in the transportation system would change as a result of the bottleneck in one area, (Ma, 2015) offer a deep learning system that relies on the RNN-RBM architecture.

Figure 11. Application in Transportation

G. Autonomous Vehicle

Many major corporations and unicorns entrepreneurs, such as Google, Tesla, Aurora, and Uber, are working on self-driving automobile innovations. The minimal Deep learning model with convolution layers and one maximum particular thread level to extract feature representations (Samira, 2019, Alom, 2019, Kuutti, 2021, Gidado, 2020). In order to create a classification to distinguish between extracted features in off setting for lengthy perception, they used a self-supervised process of learning. Recently, autonomous vehicle solutions have already been divided into two categories: robotic techniques for identifying drivers aspects and psychological replication techniques for acquiring a mapping function from sensory information to steering behavior is shown in Figure 12.

OPEN CHALLENGES AND OPPORTUNITIES

We had already thoroughly reviewed the state-of-the-art for using deep learning in several areas in the above section. However, the relevant study remains in its early stages, and more work has to be done in this sector in the future. In this part, we first list four significant obstacles to integrating deep learning into Internet of Things applications. We immediately highlight two benefits that come from fusing IoT and deep learning solutions.

Figure 12. Applications in Autonomous Driving

A. Lack of Creativity in System Architecture

In the past, the majority of models were piled on simple models, making it harder to boost data application performance as a result. The creation of a brand-new depth of classification algorithm, either as the contemporary complexity of teaching approach or the other acceptable ways for successful implementation, is needed to deal with the problem, but the complexity of the benefits of learning technology continue to be attained.

B. An Enhancement of Training Models

The two training techniques for the present deep learning models are supervised learning and unsupervised learning. Using numerous training techniques, such as the limited Boltzmann engine, the automatic encoding as the modelling tool, and the usage of supervised training techniques. Unsupervised learning is the method they are also coupled with reinforcement methods to optimize training for learning. Training completely unsupervised makes no practical sense. Therefore, the focus of further research into the deep learning technique will be on how and where to accomplish fully unsupervised training. The following list of difficulties with parameterization estimation in deep neural systems

(i) **Response rate:** A slow learning rate can become stuck in local optimal solution and require a long time to reach the optimal point. Large learning rates, to the contrary hand, could skip the optimal locations yet never convergence.

(ii) **Optimization:** A local optimum is a significant issue for many learning objectives using dimensions. The conjugate gradient solutions to those problems the elements based on the slope of the present position. The ultimate minima may be established for the idealized symmetrical issue because there is simply one lowest or maximal location. While there are numerous minima and maxima places in the case of local minima.

(iii) **Variability that disappears and explode:** One of the major issues encountered during the training of the massive neural networks is this. Deep neural networks have a little more than hidden layer, therefore in terms of implementing the attributes to the top layer, numerous affine translations are applied first, and then training algorithm. As a result, the gradient's value may occasionally grow extremely large or decrease dramatically.

C. **Cut back on training time**

The majority of deep learning model evaluation currently takes place in an ideal setting. The modern technology seems unable to produce the expected results in the complicated respective facilities. Additionally, either a basic model or a number of models make up the deep training algorithm. The quantity of knowledge received increases in proportion to the problem's complexities, necessitating an increase in the deep learning model's preparation time. Scientific investigations on intelligent systems will focus on how to modify the system while modifying the hardware in order to increase computational time and efficiency.

CONCLUSION

A succession of asymmetric levels is used in reinforcement learning, a current hot area in computer vision, to learn multiple issues related to data interpretations. For years, machine learning scientists have been striving to infer structures and analytical models from unstructured data. Representation acquisition is the term used to describe this method. In contrast to conservative machine learning and data mining methods, deep learning can create enormously high data illustrations from vast measurements of original data. As an outcome, it takes suggested an alternative to a variety of issues encountered in the actual world. One of most recent deep learning approaches and strategies are investigated systematically. It starts with an introduction to artificial neural networks and their development since 1940, then continues on to contemporary artificial neural networks and significant achievements in numerous sectors. The main strategies and platforms in this area are then discussed, along with well-known machine learning methods. It starts with a brief explanation of conventional neural network models before moving on to numerous regulated deep learning models, including recurrence, cyclical, and multilayered neural networks, multi - layer perceptron, and Markov engines. The description of more sophisticated deep learning methods including uncontrolled and online activation follows. A variety of optimization algorithms have also been provided. Theano, Caffe, and TensorFlow were amongst of the most widely used technologies throughout this discipline. To solve issues with enormous data, decentralized deep learning algorithms are also briefly presented. The most effective deep learning techniques for several industries, including network analysis, speech and voice recognition, visualization tools handling, and computational linguistics, are then explored.

REFERENCES

Abadi, M., Agarwal, A., Barham, P., Brevdo, E., & Chen, Z. (2016). *Tensorflow: Large-scale machine learning on heterogeneous distributed systems.* https://arxiv.org/abs/1603.04467

Abdel-Hamid, O., Abdel-rahman, M., Jiang, H., Deng, L., Penn, G., & Yu, D. (2014). Convolutional neural networks for speech recognition. *IEEE/ACM Transactions on Audio, Speech, and Language Processing, 22*(10), 1533–1545. doi:10.1109/TASLP.2014.2339736

Abel, J., & Fingscheidt, T. (2017). A DNN regression approach to speech enhancement by artificial bandwidth extension. In *IEEE Workshop on Applications of Signal Processing to Audio and Acoustics.* IEEE.

Abu-El-Haija, Kothari, Lee, Natsev, Toderici, Varadarajan, & Vijayanarasimhan. (2016). *YouTube-8M: A large-scale video classification benchmark.* https://arxiv.org/abs/1609.08675.

Alom, M. Z., Taha, T. M., Yakopcic, C., Westberg, S., Sidike, P., Nasrin, M. S., Hasan, M., Van Essen, B. C., Awwal, A. A. S., & Asari, V. K. (2019). A State-of-the-Art Survey on Deep Learning Theory and Architectures. *Electronics (Basel), 8*(3), 292. doi:10.3390/electronics8030292

Berant, J., Chou, A., Frostig, R., & Liang, P. (2013). Semantic parsing on freebase from question- answer pairs. In Empirical Methods in Natural Language Processing (Vol. 2). Association for Computational Linguistics.

Bharath, M., & Prakash, S., & Chinnasamy. (2021). Detecting Fake News Using Machine Learning Algorithms. *2021 International Conference on Computer Communication and Informatics (ICCCI)*, 1-5. doi: 10.1109/ICCCI50826.2021.9402470

Breiman, L. (2003). Statistical modeling: The two cultures. *Quality Control and Applied Statistics, 48*(1), 81–82.

Castelvecchi, D. (2016). Can we open the black box of AI? *Nature, 538*(7623), 20–23. doi:10.1038/538020a PMID:27708329

Chen, C., Seff, A., Kornhauser, A., & Xiao, J. (2015). Deepdriving: Learning affordance for direct perception in autonomous driving. In *IEEE International Conference on Computer Vision.* IEEE. 10.1109/ICCV.2015.312

Chen, T., & Chefd'hotel, C. (2014). Deep learning based automatic immune cell detection for immunohistochemistry images. In *International Workshop on Machine Learning in Medical Imaging.* Springer. 10.1007/978-3-319-10581-9_3

Chen, T., Li, M., Li, Y., Lin, M., Wang, N., Wang, M., Xiao, T., Xu, B., Zhang, C., & Zhang, Z. (2015). *MXNet: A flexible and efficient machine learning library for heterogeneous distributed systems.* https://arxiv.org/abs/1512.01274

Chetlur, S., Woolley, C., Vandermersch, P., Cohen, J., Tran, J., Catanzaro, B., & Shelhamer, E. (2014). *cuDNN: Efficient primitives for deep learning.* http:// arxiv.org/abs/1410.0759

Chien, J.-T., & Hsieh, H.-L. (2013). Nonstationary source separation using sequential and variational Bayesian learning. *IEEE Transactions on Neural Networks and Learning Systems*, *24*(5), 681–694. doi:10.1109/TNNLS.2013.2242090 PMID:24808420

Dozat, T. (2016). Incorporating Nesterov momentum into Adam. *International Conference on Learning Representations Workshop*, 1–4.

Duchi, J. C., Hazan, E., & Singer, Y. (2010). Adaptive subgradient methods for online learning and stochastic optimization. In *Conference on Learning Theory*. Omnipress.

El Ayadi, M., Kamel, M. S., & Karray, F. (2011). Survey on speech emotion recognition: Features, classification schemes, and databases. *Pattern Recognition*, *44*(3), 572–587. doi:10.1016/j.patcog.2010.09.020

Fakoor, R., Ladhak, F., Nazi, A., & Huber, M. (2013). Using deep learning to enhance cancer diag- nosis and classification. In *International Conference on Machine Learning*. Omnipress.

Feichtenhofer, C., Pinz, A., & Zisserman, A. (2016). Convolutional two-stream network fusion for video action recognition. In *IEEE Conference on Computer Vision and Pattern Recognition*. IEEE. 10.1109/CVPR.2016.213

Feng, M., Xiang, B., Glass, M. R., Wang, L., & Zhou, B. (2015). Applying deep learning to answer selection: A study and an open task. In *IEEE Workshop on Automatic Speech Recognition and Understanding*. IEEE. 10.1109/ASRU.2015.7404872

Fukushima, K. (1980). Neocognitron: A self-organizing neural network model for a mechanism of pattern recognition unaffected by shift in position. *Biological Cybernetics*, *36*(4), 193–202. doi:10.1007/BF00344251 PMID:7370364

Ganesan, K., Zhai, C. X., & Han, J. (2010). Opinosis: A graph-based approach to abstractive summarization of highly redundant opinions. In *23rd International Conference on Computational Linguistics*. Association for Computational Linguistics.

Garofolo, J. S., Lamel, L. F., Fisher, W. M., Fiscus, J. G., & Pallett, D. S. (1993). *DARPA TIMIT acoustic-phonetic continuous speech corpus*. NIST speech disc 1-1.1. NASA STI/Recon Technical Report N 93.

Gidado, U. M., Chiroma, H., Aljojo, N., Abubakar, S., Popoola, S. I., & Al-Garadi, M. A. (2020). A Survey on Deep Learning for Steering Angle Prediction in Autonomous Vehicles. *IEEE Access: Practical Innovations, Open Solutions*, *8*, 163797–163817. doi:10.1109/ACCESS.2020.3017883

Kuutti, S., Bowden, R., Jin, Y., Barber, P., & Fallah, S. (2021, February). A Survey of Deep Learning Applications to Autonomous Vehicle Control. *IEEE Transactions on Intelligent Transportation Systems*, *22*(2), 712–733. doi:10.1109/TITS.2019.2962338

Ma, Yu, Wang, & Wang. (2015). Large-scale transportation network congestion evolution prediction using deep learning theory. *PLoS ONE, 10*(3), e0119044

Pouyanfar, Sadiq, Yan, Tian, Tao, Reyes, Shyu, Chen, & Iyengar. (2018). A Survey on Deep Learning: Algorithms, Techniques, and Applications. *ACM Comput. Surv., 51*(5). doi:10.1145/3234150

Yu, D., Eversole, A., Seltzer, M. L., Yao, K., Guenter, B., Kuchaiev, O., Seide, F., Wang, H., Droppo, J., Huang, Z., Zweig, G., Rossbach, C. J., & Currey, J. (2014). An introduction to computational networks and the computational network toolkit. In *The 15th Annual Conference of the International Speech Communication Association*. ISCA.

Chapter 2
Automatic Speech Recognition Models, Tools, and Techniques:
A Systematic Review

Puneet Mittal

Mangalore Institute of Technology and Engineering, Karnataka, India

Sukhwinder Sharma

Mangalore Institute of Technology and Engineering, Karnataka, India

ABSTRACT

Automatic speech recognition (ASR) has gained wide popularity in last decade. Various devices like mobile phones, computers, vehicles, and audio/video players are now being equipped with ASR technology. The increasing use and dependence on ASR technology leads to research enhancements and opportunities in this domain. This chapter provides a detailed review of various advancements in ASR systems development. It highlights history of speech recognition followed by detailed insight into recent advancements and industry leaders providing latest solutions. ASR framework has been discussed in detail which includes feature extraction techniques, acoustic modeling techniques, and language modeling techniques. The chapter also lists various popular data sets available and discusses generation of new data sets. This work will be helpful for the researchers who are new to this field and are exploring development of new speech recognition techniques.

INTRODUCTION

Since the beginning of human life, communication has been the most important aspect for humans. Speech communication is the easiest and widely popular way of interaction between human to human. But when we interact with a machine, it is often limited to some controls or buttons present on it. Automatic Speech Recognition (ASR) means machine will automatically recognize what a person speaks, i.e., it can convert speech into text, operate based on the spoken command and respond. Communication with machine using speech has given a new dimension for interaction with machines like mobile phones,

DOI: 10.4018/978-1-6684-6001-6.ch002

computers, vehicles and televisions, therefore, gained wide popularity in last few decades. It has made interactions with machine more natural and easier (Neustein, 2010; Kumar et al., 2011; Tan & Lindberg, 2008). Now, humans can talk to machines just like human-to-human communication takes place. The technology is helpful in conditions where a person is busy in some physical tasks like driving a vehicle and cannot operate the machine with hands. Eyes and hands-free communication is quite helpful in such situations. It is proving to be a boon for people with disabilities like blindness and handless, who are struggling to use devices like normal persons. With the advancements in speech technology, controlling various devices is becoming much easier. The execution of an appropriate action depends on the recognition accuracy of underlying ASR system. If the system is unable to clearly identify the spoken words, either no action or some inappropriate action will likely to be taken. Therefore, an accurate ASR system is required.

In latest times, the need to build an efficient interface that provides speech recognition is mounting swiftly due to the increasing use of mobile phones and similar devices. These devices are having a variety of applications such as voice calling, SMS, listening music, setting alarms and reminders, internet surfing, smart home automation, speech based dictation, and control of various devices.

Speech is basically a signal produced by human's speech organs and detected by human ears. Speech articulatory organs are vocal cords, pharyngeal wall, glottis, jaw, soft palate, hard palate, nasal cavity, tongue, alveolar ridge, teeth and lips. The sound is produced when air passes through these organs. Human auditory organs perceive sound in the form of vibrations, and this sound is transduced into nerve impulses, which is further perceived by brain. The brain processes the sound and extracts meaningful words from it or takes action or responds accordingly.

Speech Recognition by machines requires machines to perceive the speech and recognize it. For developing the ASR, various researchers have proposed algorithms, tools, techniques and models in various languages of the world. This paper highlights the contributions made by researchers in the field of ASR. The chapter has been structured in the following order: Section 2 illustrates history of ASR and pioneering work done in this field. Section 3 highlights the recent advancements being done in ASR, while Section 4 elaborates the ASR architecture showcasing various techniques for feature extraction, acoustic modeling, language modeling and pronunciation dictionary modeling. It also gives brief details about various toolkits and decoders available for ASR model generation. Section 5 presents the challenges being faced by ASR technology followed by conclusions in last section.

BACKGROUND

History of Speech Recognition

Researchers have been exploring the ASR field for the past seven decades (Kikel, nd). Research commenced in this field in the year 1952 when Davis et al. developed Aurdey at Bell Labs, which is the first known speech recognizer, which recognizes digits with an accuracy of 97-99%.

IBM shoebox technology (IBM ShoeBox) was introduced in the year 1960. This device recognized digits from 0 to 9 and commands like plus, minus and total. Total 16 words were there in the vocabulary.

In 1975, Baker proposed The Dragon System, which was going to be the basis of modern ASR research. The model was based on the Markov process probabilistic function which has revolutionized modern speech recognition.

Lowerre proposed the HARPY Speech Recognition System developed in 1976 at CMU having capability of recognizing 1011 words. DARPA Speech Understanding Research (SUR) program (Klatt, 1977) was presented in the next year, 1977.

In 1980s, Hidden Markov Model (HMM) became popular. In mid 1980s, IBM Tangora (Averbuch et al., 1986) was released. It was named after world's fastest typist Albert Tangora. It could type what speaker spoke. But it was not very fast and allowed only clean speech with no background noise. It was developed using hidden markov model. Each user had to train it with the recorded speech for 20 minutes. Tangora was able to distinguish 20,000 English words and few sentences. In 1987, a speaking doll was released named 'Julie'. It was trained with children's voice, so that it could respond to speech. But it had one problem that each word had to be spoken with a little break.

As the technology advanced in the field of microprocessors, development of speech software gained pace. In 1989, Dragon Company released 'Dragon Dictate' (Baker, 1989). It was the first known speech recognition software released for consumers. Another improvement, Dragon Naturally Speaking, was released in 1997 which was able to recognize 100 words in a minute (Dragon Dictate, 1997).

A major breakthrough in speech recognition technology came in the year 2001 when Google introduced 'Google Voice Search'. It is used to match user queries with actual human speech.

Speech model with around 230 billion English words was developed by Google in 2010. It recorded users' voice queries to develop voice app for Android devices. Siri was launched in 2010 which relied on cloud computing and works as a great personal assistant.

Recent Advancements in Speech Recognition System

There are number of speech recognition applications and programs (proprietary and free softwares) developed for various platforms, such as Google Voice Search, Windows Speech Recognition, Dragon Naturally Speaking, Tazti etc.

Google Voice Search: Google voice search (Schalkwyk et al., 2010) is developed by Google, which provides speech based search for users. In this, the user can ask question by speaking to it and get answers spoken back. It works on iOS, Android and Chrome browsers for laptops and desktops. More than 110 languages are supported by Google voice search. English (US, Australia, Canada, India, UK New Zealand, and South Africa) was part of it since its inception in 2008. Bengali, Gujarati, Kannada, Hindi, Malayalam, Nepali, Marathi, Tamil, Telugu and Urdu have been recently (in 2017) added to the support list by Google. Still many Indian languages have not found their position in Google's list.

Siri: Siri (Siri - Apple (IN)) is a virtual assistant mobile based application provided by Apple. Various languages supported by Siri are English (American, Australian, British, and Canadian), Chinese, Mandarin, German, Italian, Spanish, French, Japanese, Cantonese, and Korean. No support for any Indian language is currently being provided by it.

Amazon's Alexa: Alexa (Alexa Voice Service Overview) is a virtual assistant provided by Amazon. Currently it supports only three languages- English (Australia, Canada, India, UK and US), German and Japanese. It does not support any Indian language.

Dragon Naturally Speaking: It (Dragon Speech Recognition - Get More Done by Voice) is a speech recognition software provided by Nuance Communications, which uses a minimal user interface. It is currently available in languages like U.S. English, Spanish, UK English, Japanese, Dutch, French, Italian, and German.

Windows Speech Recognition: Windows provides speech recognition application in various operating system versions of Windows- Vista, 7 and 8. It provides speech recognition for English, Spanish, German, Japanese, French and Chinese languages. Users can operate computer by speaking voice commands. It also provides dictation of text where document can be typed using spoken words.

Tazti: Tazti (Voice Recognition Software | Speech Recognition Software | Tazti) is a proprietary speech recognition software. It is developed by Voice Tech Group, Inc. It allows to browse our computer using voice control. One can play songs, play games, control applications, open files and do multiple tasks by voice commands.

Cortana: Cortana is Microsoft's intelligent personal assistant. One can talk to Cortana and set reminders, connect with people, send email, join meetings etc. Its development started in 2009 and it was first showcased in the year 2014 in build conference held in the month of April, 2014.

Above voice recognition applications are widely being used on mobile phones, computers and special dedicated devices as well available for entertainment purposes. They are providing a step forward towards easing the life of humans, especially persons with disabilities.

AUTOMATIC SPEECH RECOGNITION

Automatic Speech Recognition (ASR) can be classified as one pattern recognition branch. Its primary objective is to locate the most likely word sequence during speech recognition. The ASR can be realized with the help of Bayes' theorem. A speech signal is represented as acoustic feature observation, O, derived from the word sequence, W, and the decoder or recognition engine finds the most probable sequence of words based on following equation:

$$\hat{W} = argmax_w P(W \mid O) \tag{1.1}$$

Using Bayes' theorem, it can be written as

$$\hat{W} = argmax_w \frac{P(O \mid W) P(W)}{P(O)} \tag{1.2}$$

$P(O)$ is constant, hence, $\hat{W}$ can be written as

$$\hat{W} = argmax_w P(O \mid W) P(W) \tag{1.3}$$

or

$$\hat{W} = argmax_w \left(logP(O \mid W) \right) + \log \left(P(W) \right) \tag{1.4}$$

$P\left(O|W\right)$ depends upon sequence of observations and evaluated using acoustic model, and P(W) is determined by language modeling which represents the prior knowledge about the words arrangement. Logarithm values are taken to ease the computations. Acoustic modeling consists of two parts: (i) pronunciation modeling i.e., representation of each word in terms of phonemes, and (ii) mapping of phonemes to acoustic observations. Based on observations generated from acoustic model, language model accepts these observations and computes the probability of occurrence of word.

FRAMEWORK FOR ASR

Figure 1. ASR architecture

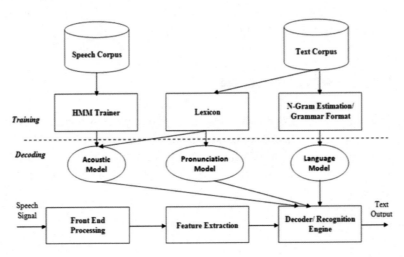

ASR engine accepts input speech signal in the form of sine waves using microphone, mobile phone or any other transducer and converts it into the appropriate text. The process of accepting and converting speech signal involves various tasks like feature extraction, acoustic modeling, language modeling, pronunciation dictionary and decoding. Typical ASR architecture has been presented in Figure 1 (Chou &Juang, 2003). There are two parts of ASR architecture – (i) training, and (ii) decoding of speech to text. Firstly, speech and text corpus is collected and speech transcriptions are prepared for training the model. Based on pronunciation rules of language, pronunciation dictionary is generated. Acoustic Models are generated from speech transcriptions and they undergo Hidden Markov Model training process. Language model is generated using n-gram estimation or grammar rules from text corpus. All words in text corpus must be specified in dictionary. For decoding, speech signal is processed and acoustic and linguistic features are extracted from it. Acoustic model, Pronunciation model and Language model are used by decoder to generate the text.

Speech Corpus Development

Speech corpus comprises of speech audio files along with its text transcription. The speech audio files may be recorded, or standard baseline speech corpus can be used for ASR model development purposes. There are various speech corpus providers like Spoken CORPORA by Clarin (Spoken corpora | Clarin ERIC), National Speech Corpus (National Speech Corpus-Infocomm Media Development Authority), Linguistic Data Consortium (Home| Linguistic Data Consortium), Linguistic Data Consortium for Indian Languages (LDC-IL). LibriSpeech ASR corpus is 1000 hours speech corpus developed for English. The corpus is carefully segmented and aligned (OpenSLR | LibriSpeech). TED-LIUM Release 3 is available under Creative Common License having 452 hours of audio (OpenSLR | TED-LIUM) Corpus can be downloaded from these platforms and be used for model developments. In case, the desired language speech corpus is not available, then speech corpus needs to be developed first. It involves collecting or recording of speech audio files and transcription of speech files into text. The task of collecting/recording speech and transcribing is quite cumbersome and needs to be done with utmost care. Pre-processing of speech signals is also required to remove any extraneous sounds, noise and redundancy. The final model accuracy is highly dependent on the correctness of speech corpus. Various tools are available for recording, processing and transcribing of speech signals i.e, Audacity, Praat, Transcriber, LIUM etc. tools are available.

Feature Extraction

Speech signal contains lot of data like spoken text, emotions, age and gender of speaker. Feature extraction helps in extracting such features from the speech signal. In order to clean the speech signal, pre-processing function is applied for removing unnecessary or redundant data. These pre-processed speech features are further used for modeling purpose. It is one of the important steps in ASR as data reduction is done here. Data generated after removing redundant data from signal is used by upcoming stages. If any lapse is there in extracting useful data from signal, then it cannot be overcome in later stages. Figure 2 shows various feature extraction techniques.

Figure 2. Feature Extraction Techniques

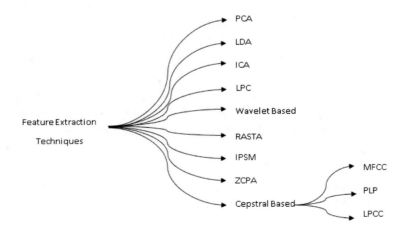

Feature Extraction Techniques

Principle Component Analysis (PCA): PCA is a statistical analytical tool (Pearson, 1901) used for dimensionality reduction. It tries to find out the relations within the data and keeps only those data which are of significance (Shlens, 2014). PCA preserves the variance, i.e., statistical information in the data required for interpretation. The new variables formed after dimensionality reductions are called Principal Components. It also showcases the genetic distance and relationship within the data. PCA first normalizes the data before starting the process so that all variables are in same space. Covariance matrix is prepared to get the pair-wise covariance between different variables. Then, the covariance matrix is decomposed into Eigen values and Eigen vectors. These Eigen vectors represent the principal components. Here, the most significant Eigen vector-value pairs are selected and projection matrix is prepared from these Eigen vectors. PCA is an unsupervised technique due to absence of class labels on extracted features.

Linear Discriminant Analysis (LDA): Originally derived from Fisher's linear discriminant (Fisher, 1936), LDA is used to find the discriminative features of the spectro-temporal input. The method is used to extract linear grouping of features that characterize or separate two or more clusters. It works on the basis of dimensionality reduction i.e. plotting multidimensional data in 2 or 3 dimensions. There are three steps in LDA. The first step is to compute the separability between different clusters. It is defined as the distance between the means of different clusters. Second step is to calculate within-cluster variance, i.e., distance between mean and sample of every cluster. The last step is to construct lower dimensional space that maximizes Step 1 and minimizes Step 2 values. LDA is a supervised learning technique as it retains the class labels and information about output classes. LDA for improved LVCSR was also introduced (Haeb-Umbach& Ney, 1992). The reported error rate for baseline system without LDA was 18.6%. It was claimed to be able to reduce the WER by 5% by employing LDA on it. Probabilistic Linear Discriminate Analysis, an extension of LDA, is based on i-vector extraction. The i-vector is one which is full of information and is a low dimensional vector having fixed length.

Independent Component Analysis (ICA): (Lee, 1998) in his book specifies that ICA is a signal processing method used to extract independent non gaussian signal from multivariate signal.ICA extracts feature vectors based on higher order statistics of speech. It decomposes multivariate signal into independent non-Gaussian signal. It reveals unseen factors that underlie sets of random variables, signal or measurement. It comes under blind source separation technique in which speaker's voice is separated from background noise.

Linear Predictive Coding (LPC): LPC is a technique used for signal source modeling and represents the spectral envelope of speech signal (Atal &Remde, 1982). It encodes the speech at low bit rate and gives highly precise estimates for speech parameters. This technique estimates the formants in speech signal, removes its effect and estimates the intensity and frequency of speech signal left. It requires good quality of speech signal for feature extraction, with poor signals LPC does not work accurately.

Wavelet based techniques: In these techniques, speech signal is divided into various parts. Discrete Wavelet Transform (DWT) provides integrated signal representation at a time and frequency that can be computerized efficiently (Tan et al., 1996). They are known for their efficient localization of time frequency and multi-adjusted, multi-scale analysis of wave representation signals. Wavelet Packet Decomposition (WPD) is an extension of DWT (Gokhale &Khanduja, 2010). Wavelet pack decay provides a breakdown of the frequency with multiple signal levels. The signal is subdivided into low frequency components and high frequency components at each level.

RelAtiveSpecTrAl Filtering (RASTA): RASTA (Hermansky & Morgan, 1994) is a way of improving speech. It is used to improve audio speech. Trajectories of speech signals are a transition band filtered through RASTA. Originally, it was recently used to reduce the impact of sound on speech signal but is now used to enhance signal directly.

Integrated Phoneme Subspace Method (IPSM): The IPSM method collects information on the interrelationships between phonetic spaces and also reconstructs the feature space for better phonetic knowledge (Park et al., 2009). In this process process a verbal vector is generated by displaying a vector hired in the sub-component of an integrated phonetic (IPS) based PCA or ICA.

Zero Crossing with Peak Amplitude (ZCPA): Zero Crossings with Peak Amplitudes (ZCPA) method was proposed by (Kim et al., 1996). In this technique stimulus periodicity in filter sub-band can be taken from zero crossing interval. In noisy environment also, the model performs well due to less effected dominant spectral peaks and valleys. The model is more robust in the presence of noise, as there is less emphasis on dominant spectral peaks and less emphasis on valleys that are usually distorted by noise.

Cepstral based techniques: A cepstrum is a series of numbers that characterize the frame of a speech. A cepstrum is an integral transform computed from a spectrum that can be used to track pitch. (Bogert et al., 1963) described the energy cepstrum. Signal power cepstrum is defined as the square of the inverse Fourier transform of the logarithm of the square of the Fourier transform of the signal. There are various methods for feature extraction based on cepstral analysis. One such method is Mel cepstral frequency coefficients (MFCC) (European **Telecommunications Standards Institute, 2003** In large vocabulary SR systems, MFCC is one of the widely used methods. MFCC uses overlapping triangular windows to represent short-term power spectra of sound waves rendered on the Mel scale. A linear predictive cepstral coefficient (LPCC) (Makhoul, 1975) is computed from a smoothed autoregressive power spectrum instead of estimating the power spectrum from a periodogram. In LPCC, one voice sample at the current time can be predicted as a linear combination of previous voice samples. The bark frequency cepstral coefficient (BFCC) is another method for extracting features from speech signals. It is very similar to MFCC. This method uses a bark scale filter instead of a mel filter (Zwicker, 1961). Perceptual linear prediction (PLP) models were developed by (Hermansky, 1990). The PLP conceptualizes the psychophysical concepts of the human auditory model. It discards unnecessary speech information and speed up speech recognition. PLP is similar to LPC in that it transforms spectral characteristics according to human hearing characteristics. PLP approximates three main aspects of perception: the critical band resolution curve, the equal loudness curve, and the intensity-loudness power law known as the cube root.

Pronunciation Modeling

Pronunciation modeling deals with linguistics of language. In this each word is represented into subwords based on speech to sound rules of language. While decoding, it provides mapping between words and phones (subwords). Acoustic model is built for each phone recognized in pronunciation dictionary. Accuracy of model developed is directly proportional to the pronunciation model built. Figure 3 illustrates various pronunciation modeling techniques.

(Lucassen and Mercer, 1984) presented a decision tree model for nine-character window based phone prediction. Prediction accuracy for phones was observed to be 94%. The accuracy increased to 97% when it was combined with phoneme recognizer.

Figure 3. Pronunciation Modeling Techniques

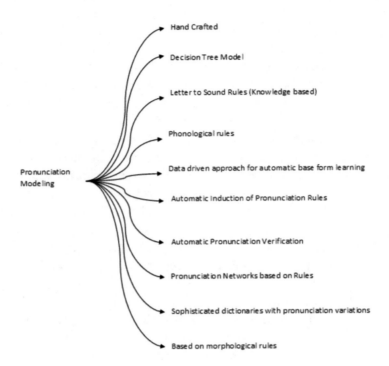

(Fosler-Lussier, 2003) in his tutorial has described role of pronunciation modeling in ASR and how it has progressed in years. He explored several techniques for building pronunciation dictionary. First technique, hand crafted dictionary, is based on knowledge base. In this, linguistic expert prepares pronunciation model for every word. It is drafted manually and is very exhaustive process. Dictionary is developed with utmost care and any confusion or inconsistency in pronunciation of same sound words is resolved. One such dictionary is The PRONLEX pronunciation dictionary provided by Linguistic Data Consortium (LDC) in 1996 and CMU dictionary developed in 1993-2002. Another technique is letter to sound rules. It is also knowledge-based approach. In this pronunciation dictionaries are derived from text to speech systems. (Klatt, 1987) reviewed such system for English. TTS system contains hand compiled dictionary of most common words and rules for pronunciations generation for words, which are not present in dictionary. Rules are generally based on word morphology and orthography. For English hand written rules perform well due to different accents and style of speaking. (Mittal & Singh, 2020) in their research paper presented how words can be represented as subwords. They proposed an algorithm for replacement of least occurring subword with similar sound subword. The next explored technique was based on phonological rules. In this technique, phonological rules are used to model the co articulation and fast speech based phonetic variations. Problem encountered in this technique is that, rules can be over generalized. He also studied techniques which can generate dictionaries automatically i.e., data driven approach for automatic baseform learning. In this technique two components are required: source data, and data variation capturing method. In this method various variants of pronunciation are learnt on word by word basis. Best alternative is determined for each word by aligning between phone-recognition string and canonical-baseform pronunciations given by baseline dictionary. For a word sequence, surface pronunciation and canonical phone sequence can be found. Surface pronunciation can be generated from the recognizer to produce the most likely phonetic sequence and canonical sequence can be engendered by swapping the word sequence with its most probable pronunciation. Alignment can be done on the two phone sequences generated and get the refined pronunciation. Word based techniques suffer from one problem that they cannot model the coarticulation between words and cannot learn word-by-word learning generalizations from words.

Another approach studied is automatic induction of pronunciation rules. In this approach focus changes from pronunciation of word to pronunciation of phoneme. In this decision tree models and various machine learning techniques are used to model. (Cremelie and Martens, 1999) have introduced a method of developing simpler models into a new model that can specify various variations of pronunciation for each word. As the strategy presented is capable of generating a variety of pronunciation and relying on different words automatically, it is a good alternative to hand-coding pronunciation that is often specified in dictionary. The method learns the rules of pronunciation in grammar written in grammar, and then uses these rules to produce a common variety of pronunciation. All forms of the same word are then combined into a combined pronunciation model. The acquired models are neatly integrated into the speech model, which replaces the simpler models previously used. By learning the rules of pronunciation rather than the variety of pronunciations from the data, one can combine the benefits of data-driven and law-based methods. Significant features of the proposed method are that it incorporates interdependence between the rules from the starting of training, that it supports different rules that do not produce different utterances but affect the creation of those methods by other rules (known as production rules), and that it has a reasonable base. Studies have shown that the introduction of such variations in segment-based vision considerably enhances the accuracy of the recognition in TIMIT to reduce the error rate of the related word by up to 17% obtained.

(Rao et al., 2015) suggested verification for automatic pronunciation of speech recognition. It is a data-driven and independent framework for verbal verification in order to improve dictionary quality in ASR. The sound of a new candidate is confirmed by re-seeing historical audio logs and checking the associated recognition costs. They create an additional sound quality feature from word frequencies and logs. The machine-trained section on these features achieves almost 90% accuracy in labeling good v / s bad words in all the languages it has tested. Newly pronounced pronunciation may be added to the dictionary, while incorrect pronunciation may be discarded or sent to a specialist for further testing. They tested 5,000 to 30,000 new pronunciations within a few hours and showed improvements in ASR functionality as a result of the accentuated instability guaranteed by the system.

(Liu and Fung, 2000) proposed production of **rules-based pronunciation networks** instead of the standard decoder dictionary. Networks take into account special Chinese textures and incorporate the acceptable alternatives for each of the Chinese characters. Also, the rules of diversity are found by designing the automatic learning algorithm. Their suggested method was tested on HLTC desk stack and Hub4NE by Mandarin Broadcast News Corpus. The error rate for character recognition has been condensed to 3.20% completely so both internal and intermediate member variations are modeling.

(Westendorf and Jelitto, 1996) have emphasized that in order to recognize the proper functioning of complex dictionaries, the variety of pronunciation is important, i.e.,dictionaries supporting multiple pronunciation variations. Compilation of dictionary by hand is exhaustive process and may contain errors and inconsistencies. The authors demonstrate how to automatically generate appropriate vocabulary dictionaries from the speech website itself. The only sources of information outside the website are signals (without labels) and their translation based on words. The first test to bring hopeful results was done with the DataLab software system, integrating the TU Dresden monitoring system.

(NKosi et al., 2011) discussed the importance of pronunciation dictionaries for the development of ASR systems. They developed pronunciation dictionary for Northern Sotho language based on morphological rules to improve language coverage of the ASR system as compared to data-driven methods of dictionary creation.

(Wei et al. 2022) worked on Pronunciation Error Detection (PED) for Pluricentric languages. They used transfer learning approach to transfer the knowledge from dominant variety to non-dominant variety.

ACOUSTIC MODELING

Acoustic models integrate the features of the generated speech signal with a phonetic or vocabulary dictionary. It is one of the largest ASR modules. Produces a map between speech units and acoustic observation. A phonetically rich and large website is needed to train the acoustic model. There are many variations in speech because of gender, age, environment and other factors. Different mathematical methods have been proposed by various researchers for building ASR model. Figure 4 lists the different acoustic modeling methods.

Hidden Markov Model (HMM): The first work at HMM was started by (Baker, 1973). Introduced the Dragon speech recognition program. He described the key features of the DRAGON speech comprehension system. DRAGON systematically represents each of the sources of information needed for the automatic detection of continuous speech using a common invisible model. The model based on the possible functionality of the Markov process is highly flexible and leads to features that allow DRAGON to work despite the high levels of errors from each data source. Repeated use of a simple invisible model produces a simple system with structure, but powerful capabilities.

(Rabiner, 1989) introduced the theory of Markov models hidden from simple ideas (different Markov chains) to more complex models (flexible lengths, models of continuous congestion). They focus on the physical meanings of basic mathematics and focus on its practical application to real-world systems. They demonstrated the application of HMM theory to speech-recognition and demonstrated application of strategies to more advanced speech recognition problems.

(Juang and Rabiner, 1991) explored role of mathematical methods in this dynamic technology as they are used in speech recognition and discussed the list of theoretical & practical issues, that have not yet been resolved, and their significance and impact on the implementation of various programs. . They pointed out that HMM's strength lies in its mathematical framework and its implementation structure.

Gaussian Mixture Model (GMM): Based upon Gaussian Mixtures, three different acoustic models: continuous (Bahl et al., 1983), semi-continuous (Huang and Jack, 1988; Huang and Jack 1989) and phonetically-tied model (Liu and Fung, 2004) are generally developed. In these models, separate way of building Gaussians mixtures is used to calculate the score for each frame. Continuous models with around 150,000 gaussian mixtures having high processing and storage requirements are not suitable for mobile phones with limited capabilities. Semi-continuous models having only 700 gaussian mixtures, require minimal processing and storage, are suitable for mobile phones to provide fast operations but with less accuracy. PTMs lie between continuous and semi-continuous models with 5000 gaussian mixtures having moderate processing and storage requirements. PTMs are considered as most viable solution for speech based mobile phone applications owing to their fast processing and high accuracy features with moderate requirements.

Deep Neural Network (DNN): (Hinton et al., 1995) proposed Deep Neural Networks for the acoustic modeling in speech recognition. They used feedforward NN which takes multiple frames of co-efficients as their input, and generates background opportunities over the HMM regions as output. Deep neural networks with numerous hidden layers, which are trained using new techniques, have been shown to surpass gaussian mixed models in various speech recognition benchmarks.

(Maas et al., 2017) investigated DNN acoustic models to explore the aspects important for speech recognition system and compared DNN using various metrics to quantify factors which can influence the system performance. They have used switchboard benchmark corpus having 300 hours of conversational telephone speech. In first experiment they developed untied neural networks for acoustic modeling and compared DNN with convolution networks. They combined Switchboard corpus and Fisher corpora to work on larger corpus. They examined the performance of large DNN models. They showed that good results are generated by using simple DNN architecture and optimization techniques.

(Kumar & Aggarwal, 2022) proposed i- vector adaptation based time delay neural network acoustic modeling. They have used TDNN architecture where every hidden layer is having different temporal resolution which increases layer by layer. Thus these networks can learn wider temporal relationships. i-vector extraction has been done during training and decoding. The results show accuracy of 89.9%.

Acoustic Modeling unit

Unit which is to be used for modeling the acoustic characteristics need to be carefully explored. To get a minimum WER, accurate model needs to be generated keeping in mind its features like trainability and generalizability. In word based models, entire word is used to model the acoustic features. Word based acoustic units are very accurate but they are not trainable and general in nature. As only few words can be trained. In phone based models, word to be modeled is split in distinguished small acoustic unit (collectively which comprise the whole word). This approach is usually used for large vocabulary systems. Smaller sound units are trained in this approach and words can be formed from those units.

Figure 4. Acoustic Modeling Techniques

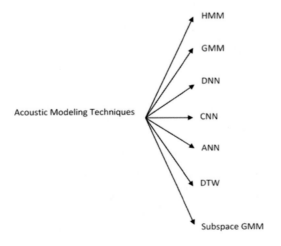

LANGUAGE MODELING

Language model is used for predicting the following word in the given sentence. It generates the occurrences probability of each word and it predicts the upcoming word on the basis of previous words. Figure 5 shows various language modeling techniques. N-gram estimation is one of the popular techniques used in ASR. In this, likelihood of nth word is generated from the preceding *(n-1)* words. Word sequence occurrence probability, *W*, may be calculated as:

$$P\left(W\right) = P\left(w_1, w_2, \ldots\ldots, w_{m-1}, w_m\right) \tag{1.5}$$

$$P\left(W\right) = P\left(w_1\right), P\left(w_2|w_1\right), P(w_3|w_1 w_2)\ldots\ldots, w_{m-1}, P(w_m|w_{m-n+1} w_{m-n+2} \cdots w_{m-2} w_{m-1}) \tag{1.6}$$

Bi-gram (where n = 2) and trigram (where n = 3) are in general used for common ASR applications. Another popular language modeling technique is using grammar format. In this, various grammar-based rules are written and sequence of words is generated using those rules. For example, for the following rule:

<rule1> = (Hello | Hi) (Sir | Madam);

Four sentences can be generated from this rule:

1) *Hello Sir*
2) *Hello Madam*
3) *Hi Sir*
4) *Hi Madam*

This technique of language modeling is generally used where command and control operations are to be done. For small vocabulary, grammar format is a good choice.

N-gram model: (Bahl et al., 1983) described n-gram model. *n*-gram model predicts the next word in the *(n-1)*–order Markov model sequence form. *n*-gram model draws sequences using *n*-grams statistical properties. The probability $P\left(w_1^n\right)$ P (w 1, ..., w m) {\displaystyle P(w_{1},\ldots w_{m})} of observing the sentence (w 1, ..., w m {\displaystyle w_{1},\ldots, w_{m}} $w_1, w_2, \ldots. w_{n-1}, w_n$) in *n*-gram model may be approximated as

$$P\left(w_1^n\right) \cong \prod_{k=1}^{n} P(w_k \mid w_{k-N+1}^{k-1}) \tag{2.1}$$

Where, the $k-1$ time state relates to $N-1$ most recently used words, w_{k-N+1}, w_{k-1}.

(Brown et al., 1992) talked about the problem of guessing the word from the prior sequence of words. They proposed class-based*n* gram models of natural language. The words are grouped together in accordance to statistical similarity of their surroundings.

Factored LM: (Bilmes and Kirchhoff, 2003) present Factored LM and Generalized-Parallel-Backoff (GPB) integration. FLM gives representation to words as plural elements like morphological categories, titles and data-driven collections, and promotes a possible model covering the sequence of piles instead of just words. The GPB extends the general regression to general conditional probability tables carrying various types of variables, without apparent natural regression, allowing multiple dynamic regression strategies. It remarks that bigrams lower than most well-prepared basic triggers can be produced with much lower confusion. These results are highly consistent in context of the multilingual speech recognition, where bigrams are used to create the first bigram letters or N-best lists.

Recurrent Neural Network-based Language Model (RNNLM): (Mikolov et al., 2010) presented RNNLM for speech recognition with simple recurrent neural network or Elman network based architecture. Their results suggest that perplexity can be reduced, in comparison to backoff language model, by 50% when using mixture of several RNN LMs. Further 18% WER reduction has been shown on Wallstreet journal task trained on same amount of data. RNN LM outperformed backoff model even when backoff was trained with more data

Java Speech Grammar Format (JSGF): Sun Microsystems developed JSGF (JSpeech Grammar Format, 2000) to represent grammar text in speech recognition. JSGF is a BNF style language program. It is an independent representation of the forum and the vendor's independent language systems that can be used to identify speech. JSGF embraces the style and language principles of the JavaTM application in addition to the use of standard program notes. It is a legal language grammar that determines what a user can say. (Georgila et al., 2004) has developed an illustrated tool used to produce and demonstrate grammatical grammar in the JSGF format, developed by Generic Environment for Multilingual Interactive Natural Interfaces (GEMINI). The word building component is also included in the tool to produce phonetic spelling of words included in program file. At present, the tool supports grapheme-to-phoneme embedded translation in Greek only SAMPA format. A stand-alone language function is added for allowing the user to write contextual coding rules. Automatic grammar management with tools is compared and evaluated over time to create grammar and efficiency.

(Bringert, 2007) explained how grammar-recognition-systems-based language models can be produced in the Grammatical Framework (GF) language system. The formatting of Non-contextual language programs and standardized models can have numerous formats: GSL, SRGS, JSGF, and HTK-SLF. Additionally, the semantic translation code can be implanted in prepared context-language. It allows faster development of applications for mobile, multi-lingual and flexible speech recognition.

(Karpe et al., 2014) presented a paper on the control device with an ASR. The command-and-control based application performs speech recognition through conversion of an acoustic signal, ingested from microphone, into a set of words. Known names are used as operating system commands. They used the Sphinx 4, JSAPI and JSGF tool kits to build the system. In this language file containing all the words or command words employ the JSGF-Java Speech Grammar Format. The speech applications enabled by Java Speech API provide the default, normal, and independent interactions. In this program the user speaks the command through a microphone and the viewer converts the speech into text. Next, with the help of a dictionary, mapping is done on a word-for-word basis. Now the received text is sent to the run command and action is performed.

Figure 5. Language Modeling Techniques

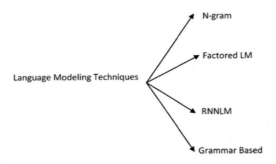

Decoder

Decoder is also called Recognition Engine. Decoder accepts speech signal, extracts feature from it and uses acoustic model and pronunciation dictionary for mapping the speech units with acoustic observations and utilizes language model for prediction of next word. The speech recognition responsibility is taken by the decoder, which converts it into text with acoustic model, language model and pronunciation dictionary support. Variety of ASR toolkits is available in market and can be used for training and testing of models. Few of them are listed below:

HTK: It is a Hidden Markov Model toolkit written in C. As the name suggests it is based on HMM. It is widely popular for tasks like speech processing, character recognition, DNA sequencing etc. It is developed by Machine Intelligence Laboratory and is available freely for download. It encompasses various tools for Data Preparation, Model Training, Speech Recognition and its Analysis. Data preparation tool helps in transcription of data. Training tools help in building the HMM model. Recognition tools help in decoding the speech to text and Analysis tool calculate Word error rate for the model built, it helps in checking the performance and accuracy of the model developed.

CMUSphinx: It is also one of the popular toolkits available in market for free. It provides various packages based on type of application you want to build. It provides following packages:

a)   Pocketsphinx: It is a C programming based lightweight recognizer library. It is widely popular for mobile phones.

b)   Sphinxbase — It is a support library, that is required for Pocketsphinx.

c)   Sphinx4 — It is a Java based modifiable and adjustable recognizer, which is useful for desktop applications. It gives good accuracy but compromises with speed in case of large models.

d)   Sphinxtrain —It provides various training tools for building the acoustic model.

Kaldi: Kaldi is also an ASR toolkit. It is C++ based widely used open source toolkit for speech recognition and signal processing. It is freely available under Apache License. It also provides tools for data preparation, feature extraction, training & performance analysis.

Figure 6 shows the general structure of speech application. The application is installed on device. The application consists of speech user interface, recognition engine or decoder required for decoding the speech, dictionary, acoustic model and language model. Decoder is included in application as a library. Whatever user speaks the interface fetches it and sends it to the decoder. Decoder decodes it and generates the hypothesis with the help of an acoustic model, dictionary and the language model. This hypothesis is the text extracted from speech signal and delivered to the user.

Figure 6. General structure of speech application depicting role of Decoder

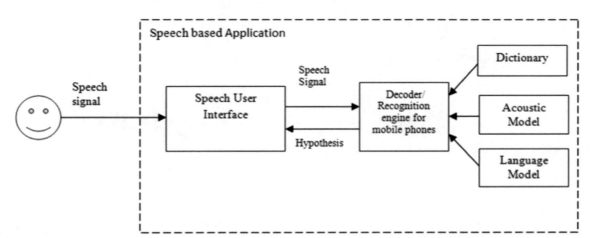

Challenges with ASR Technology

Speech signal contains lot of information in it like linguistic information, coarticulation effects, speaker's gender, age, region, health, emotion, environmental information like noise etc. There are lots of factors which influence the speech signal. Speech produced by every speaker is different in many aspects. So, there is lot of speech variability (Benzeghiba et al., 2007) in speech signals. ASR can be improved by characterization of effect of speech variations. Speech variations are part of speech signal and their presence can affect the overall process of ASR. Speech signal is variable in nature and changes with time. Speech variability can affect the voice signal in different terms. If variability is less the desired information can be retrieved easily with little processing, but if variability is high then special techniques need to be devised to extract the information from it. Behavioral variability can affect the structure and quality of voice signal as voice while crying is different, smoking person's voice changes, and person suffering from some disease or has difficulty in speaking etc. Voice can be modulated at different times to gain attention of someone or to convey any emotion. There are various sources of speech variability like gender, environment, region, speaker physiology, speech rate, style of speaking, age, emotion to name few.

Male and female voices are very different. Males have larger vocal folds than females and so produce low pitched voices. And their vocal tract is also larger resulting in lower sounding timbre. Spectrogram, a picture of sound, shows the frequencies that make up the sound and change in frequencies. The frequencies are shown from low to high, and the change in frequencies is given from left to right. Female voices have denser frequency than male counterparts on spectrogram. The red, green, blue and yellow lines in spectrogram represent the formant frequency. Figure 7 and 8 show that formant frequency of female is higher than that of male, difference is clearer from third and fourth formant. This is due to the shorter length of vocal tract in the females, and formant frequencies are inversely proportional to the length of vocal tract. If any ASR model is trained for male voices only, then that model is not much capable to recognize female voices. Surroundings/ Environment in which speech is being decoded also affects the recognition. Noise is the unwanted signal which is added to speech signal resulting in distorted speech. If user has to use the ASR in noisy environment and ASR is trained for clean speech i.e., noise free environment only then recognition rate given by such model will be quite low. Noise and type of noise i.e., working conditions, need to be taken care while developing the model.

Figure 7. Male speech (a) wave form, and (b) spectrogram for word 'Ikk'

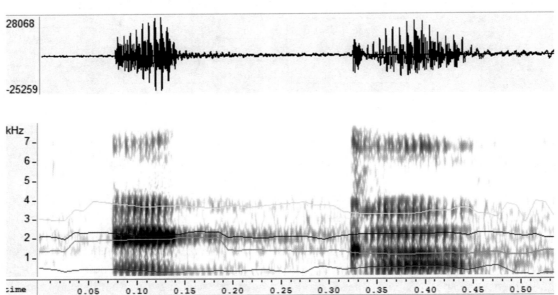
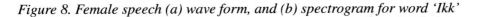

Figure 8. Female speech (a) wave form, and (b) spectrogram for word 'Ikk'

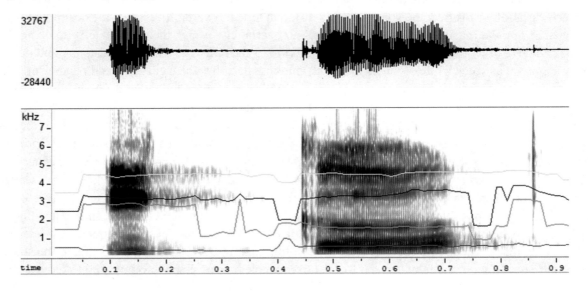

There is lot of variability in speech of native speakers and non- native speakers. Non- native speakers may not catch the correct accent and result in generating incorrect speech, as for any unfamiliar phoneme which is not in their native language, they will try to produce similar phoneme from their native language. Non-native speech is incorrectly handled by the ASR models. State of mind of user, while using any ASR model is also major source of speech variability. If someone is in anger, tensed or depressed they may not produce the sound correctly. Pitch will vary if person is angry and try to be loud. There are some speakers who can modulate their voices, sometimes low or sometimes high. This is generally done by lecturers, presenters or politicians who want to convey information along with emotions to the audience. So, their speech rate changes and leads to variability in speech. Children have high pitched voice as they have shorter vocal length and when they grow up to reach puberty their voice changes and becomes heavier and low pitched. This is more visible in boys than girls. As we grow old speech slows down and words are elongated. Pitch and loudness is also reduced. Every person is having a different speaking style which also results in variability. Some people speak casually and some people give lot of stress on words, many people hesitate to speak, some take pauses while speaking and some stammer, all these factors also give rise to variable speech.

Best ASR model will be the one which can model and recognize speech despite of such variability. But for developing such model corpulent speech and text database is required. For under resourced (Besacier al. 2014) languages it is difficult to collect so much data and develop such models. Researchers' group contribution is the only possible solution for it.

DISCUSSIONS AND CONCLUSION

This chapter primarily focused on various ASR tools and techniques. It also presents the historical aspects of speech recognition and the recent trends being followed in the recognition process. ASR system development depends upon building three models - Pronunciation model, Acoustic model and Language model, which are thoroughly discussed in this work. It covers review of various techniques like hand crafting dictionary to using algorithms for developing automatic pronunciation generation dictionary, which can be streamlined by varying pronunciations by hand. Acoustic model maps the pronunciation of each one phone in a pronunciation dictionary with a sound unit and develops the model. While building acoustic model, features need to be extracted from the speech signal. Various techniques are available for this like LPC, PLP, and MFCC etc. MFCC is widely used technique for feature extraction. Accuracy of model is largely dependent upon speech and text data available. There are various techniques available for developing the acoustic model like HMM, GMM and Neural networks. DNN techniques are becoming widely popular because of their higher accuracy as compared to its counterparts. Language model is used while decoding of speech to generate the likelihood of occurrence of word after the previous word. The most popular technique is statistical modeling technique. This technology has to face various issues and challenges due to varying nature of speech. Lot of factors affect the model accuracy like gender, age, noise, emotions etc. these factors need to be studied before developing an ASR model with good recognition accuracy. This work will be helpful for the researchers who are new to this field and are exploring development of new speech recognition techniques.

REFERENCES

Alexa Voice Service Overview (v20160207) | Alexa Voice Service. (n.d.). Retrieved May 15, 2022, from https://developer.amazon.com/docs/alexa-voice-service/api-overview.html

Atal, B., & Remde, J. (1982, May). A new model of LPC excitation for producing natural-sounding speech at low bit rates. In *Proceedings of the IEEE International Conference on Acoustics, Speech, and Signal Processing (ICASSP'82)* (vol. 7, pp. 614-617). IEEE. 10.1109/ICASSP.1982.1171649

Averbuch, A., Bahl, L., Bakis, R., Brown, P., Cole, A., Daggett, A. G., Das, S., Davies, K., DeGennaro, S., DeSouza, P., Epstein, E., Fraleigh, D., Jelinek, F., Katz, S., Lewis, B., Mercer, R., Nadas, A., Nahamoo, D., Picheny, M., ... Spinelli, P. (1986). An IBM PC based large-vocabulary isolated-utterance speech recognizer. In *Proceedings of the IEEE International Conference on Acoustics, Speech, and Signal Processing (ICASSP'86)* (vol. 11, pp. 53-56). IEEE. 10.1109/ICASSP.1986.1169169

Bahl, L. R., Jelinek, F., & Mercer, R. L. (1983). A maximum likelihood approach to continuous speech recognition. *IEEE Transactions on Pattern Analysis and Machine Intelligence, PAMI-5*(2), 179–190. doi:10.1109/TPAMI.1983.4767370 PMID:21869099

Baker, J. (1973). Machine-Aided Labeling of Connected Speech. In *Working Papers in Speech Recognition--II.* Computer Science Department, Carnegie Mellon University. Retrieved from https://apps.dtic.mil/docs/citations/AD0770633

Baker, J. M. (1989). DragonDictate (TM)-30K: Natural Language Speech Recognition with 30,000 Words. In *Proceedings of the First European Conference on Speech Communication and Technology* (pp. 2161-2163). Academic Press.

Benzeghiba, M., DeMori, R., Deroo, O., Dupont, S., Erbes, T., Jouvet, D., Fissore, L., Laface, P., Mertins, A., Ris, C., Rose, R., Tyagi, V., & Wellekens, C. (2007). Automatic speech recognition and speech variability: A review. *Speech Communication, 49*(10-11), 763–786. doi:10.1016/j.specom.2007.02.006

Besacier, L., Barnard, E., Karpov, A., & Schultz, T. (2014). Automatic speech recognition for under-resourced languages: A survey. *Speech Communication, 56,* 85–100. doi:10.1016/j.specom.2013.07.008

Bilmes, J. A., & Kirchhoff, K. (2003, May). Factored language models and generalized parallel back-off. In *Proceedings of the 2003 Conference of the North American Chapter of the Association for Computational Linguistics on Human Language Technology: companion volume of the Proceedings of HLT-NAACL 2003—short papers-Volume 2* (pp. 4-6). Association for Computational Linguistics. 10.3115/1073483.1073485

Bogert, B. P., Healy, M. J. R., & Tukey, J. W. (1963, June). The quefrency analysis of time series for echoes; Cepstrum, pseudo-autocovariance, cross-cepstrum and saphe cracking. In *Proceedings of the Symposium on Time Series Analysis* (pp. 209-243). Academic Press.

Bringert, B. (2007, June). Speech recognition grammar compilation in Grammatical Framework. In *Proceedings of the workshop on grammar-based approaches to spoken language processing* (pp. 1-8). 10.3115/1626333.1626335

Brown, P. F., DellaPietra, V. J., deSouza, P. V., Lai, J. C., & Mercer, R. L. (1992). Class-Based n-gram Models of Natural Language. *Computational Linguistics*, *18*(4), 467–479.

Chou, W., & Juang, B. H. (2003). *Pattern recognition in speech and language processing*. CRC Press. doi:10.1201/9780203010525

CMU Sphinx download | SourceForge.net. (n.d.). Retrieved May 15, 2022, from https://sourceforge.net/ projects/cmusphinx/

Cremelie, N., & Martens, J. P. (1999). In search of better pronunciation models for speech recognition. *Speech Communication*, *29*(2-4), 115–136. doi:10.1016/S0167-6393(99)00034-5

Davis, K. H., Biddulph, R., & Balashek, S. (1952). Automatic recognition of spoken digits. *The Journal of the Acoustical Society of America*, *24*(6), 637–642. doi:10.1121/1.1906946

Dempster, A. P., Laird, N. M., & Rubin, D. B. (1977). Maximum Likelihood from Incomplete Data via the EM Algorithm. *Journal of the Royal Statistical Society. Series B. Methodological*, *39*(1), 1–38. doi:10.1111/j.2517-6161.1977.tb01600.x

Dragon Speech Recognition - Get More Done by Voice | Nuance. (n.d.). Retrieved May 15, 2022, from https://www.nuance.com/dragon.html

DragonDictate® 2.5. Computer software. (1997). Dragon Systems.

European Telecommunications Standards Institute. (2003). *Speech Processing, Transmission and Quality Aspects (STQ); Distributed speech recognition; Front-end feature extraction algorithm; Compression algorithms*. ETSI ES 202 050 V1.1.5 (2007-01). Retrieved May 15, 2022, from: https://www.etsi.org/ deliver/etsi_es/202000_202099/ 202050/01.01.05_60/es_202050v010105p.pdf

Fisher, R. A. (1936). The Use of Multiple Measurements in Taxonomic Problems. *Annals of Eugenics*, *7*(2), 179–188. doi:10.1111/j.1469-1809.1936.tb02137.x

Fosler-Lussier, E. (2003). A tutorial on pronunciation modeling for large vocabulary speech recognition. In *Text-and Speech-Triggered Information Access* (pp. 38–77). Springer. doi:10.1007/978-3-540-45115-0_3

Freitas, J., Calado, A., Barros, M. J., & Dias, M. S. (2009). Spoken language interface for mobile devices. In *Proceedings of the Language and Technology Conference* (pp. 24-35). Springer.

Georgila, K., Fakotakis, N., & Kokkinakis, G. (2004). A Graphical Tool for Handling Rule Grammars in Java Speech Grammar Format. In *Proceedings of the 4th International Conference on Language Resources and Evaluation (LREC)* (pp. 615-618). Academic Press.

Gokhale, M. Y., & Khanduja, D. K. (2010). Time Domain Signal Analysis Using Wavelet Packet Decomposition Approach. *International Journal of Communications, Network and Systems Sciences*, *3*(03), 321–329. doi:10.4236/ijcns.2010.33041

Haeb-Umbach, R., & Ney, H. (1992, March). Linear discriminant analysis for improved large vocabulary continuous speech recognition. In *Proceedings of the 1992 IEEE International Conference on Acoustics, Speech, and Signal Processing (ICASSP-92)* (vol. 1, pp. 13-16). IEEE. 10.1109/ICASSP.1992.225984

Hermansky, H. (1990). Perceptual linear predictive (PLP) analysis of speech. *Journal of Acoustica. Society of America, 87*(4), 1738–1752. PMID:2341679

Hermansky, H., & Morgan, N. (1994). RASTA processing of speech. *IEEE Transactions on Speech and Audio Processing, 2*(4), 578–589. doi:10.1109/89.326616

Hinton, G. E., Dayan, P., Frey, B. J., & Neal, R. (1995). The wake-sleep algorithm for unsupervised neural networks. *Science, 268*(5214), 1158–1161. doi:10.1126cience.7761831 PMID:7761831

Home| Linguistic Data Consortium. (n.d.). Retrieved May 15, 2022, from https://www.ldc.upenn.edu/

HTK speech Recognition Toolkit. (n.d.). Retrieved May 15, 2022, from https://htk.eng.cam.ac.uk/

Huang, X. D., & Jack, M. A. (1988). Hidden Markov modelling of speech based on a semicontinuous model. *Electronics Letters, 24*(1), 6–7. doi:10.1049/el:19880004

Huang, X. D., & Jack, M. A. (1989). Semi-continuous hidden Markov models for speech signals. *Computer Speech & Language, 3*(3), 239–251. doi:10.1016/0885-2308(89)90020-X

JSpeech Grammar Format. (2000). Retrieved May 15, 2022, from https://www.w3.org/TR/jsgf/

Juang, B. H., & Rabiner, L. R. (1991). Hidden Markov Models for Speech Recognition. *Technometrics, 33*(3), 251–272. doi:10.1080/00401706.1991.10484833

Kaldi-ASR. (n.d.). Retrieved May 15, 2022, from https://kaldi-asr.org/

Karpe, V., Kabadi, S., Mutgekar, A., & Pokharkar, M. (2014). Controlling Device through Speech Recognition System. *International Journal of Advanced Research in Computer Science and Software Engineering, 4*(2), 1020–1024.

Kikel, C. (2022). A *Brief History of Voice Recognition Technology | Total Voice Technologies.* Retrieved May 15, 2022, from https://www.totalvoicetech.com/a-brief-history-of-voice-recognition-technology/

Kim, D. S., Jeong, J. H., Kim, J. W., & Lee, S. Y. (1996, May). Feature extraction based on zero-crossings with peak amplitudes for robust speech recognition in noisy environments. In *Proceedings of the 1996 IEEE International Conference on Acoustics, Speech, and Signal Processing* (vol. 1, pp. 61-64). IEEE. 10.1109/ICASSP.1996.540290

Klatt, D. (1987). A review of text-to-speech conversion for English. *The Journal of the Acoustical Society of America, 3*(3), 737–793. doi:10.1121/1.395275 PMID:2958525

Klatt, D. H. (1977). Review of the ARPA speech understanding project. *The Journal of the Acoustical Society of America, 62*(6), 1345–1366. doi:10.1121/1.381666

Kohler, T. W., Fugen, C., Stüker, S., & Waibel, A. (2005). Rapid porting of ASR-systems to mobile devices. In *Proceedings of the Ninth European Conference on Speech Communication and Technology* (pp. 233-236). 10.21437/Interspeech.2005-116

Kumar, A., & Aggarwal, R. K. (2022). Hindi speech recognition using time delay neural network acoustic modeling with i-vector adaptation. *International Journal of Speech Technology, 25*(1), 67–78. doi:10.100710772-020-09757-0

LDC-IL. (n.d.). Retrieved May 15, 2022, from https://www.ldcil.org/resourcesSpeechCorp.aspx

Lee, T. W. (1998). Independent component analysis. In *Independent component analysis* (pp. 27–66). Springer. doi:10.1007/978-1-4757-2851-4_2

Liu, Y., & Fung, P. (2000). Rule-based word pronunciation networks generation for Mandarin speech recognition. In *Proceedings of the International Symposium of Chinese Spoken Language Processing (ISCSLP'00)* (pp. 35–38). Academic Press.

Liu, Y., & Fung, P. (2004). State-dependent phonetic tied mixtures with pronunciation modeling for spontaneous speech recognition. *IEEE Transactions on Speech and Audio Processing*, *12*(4), 351–364. doi:10.1109/TSA.2004.828638

Lowerre, B. T. (1976). *The Harpy Speech Recognition System* [Unpublished doctoral dissertation]. Carnegie Mellon University, Pittsburgh, PA, United States.

Lucassen, J., & Mercer, R. (1984). An information theoretic approach to the automatic determination of phonemic baseforms. In *Proceedings of the IEEE International Conference on Acoustics, Speech, and Signal Processing (ICASSP'84)* (vol. 9, pp. 304-307). IEEE. 10.1109/ICASSP.1984.1172810

Maas, A. L., Qi, P., Xie, Z., Hannun, A. Y., Lengerich, C. T., Jurafsky, D., & Ng, A. Y. (2017). Building DNN acoustic models for large vocabulary speech recognition. *Computer Speech & Language*, *41*, 195–213. doi:10.1016/j.csl.2016.06.007

Makhoul, J. (1975). Linear prediction: A tutorial review. *Proceedings of the IEEE*, *63*(4), 561–580. doi:10.1109/PROC.1975.9792

Meisel, W. (2010). "Life on-the-Go": The Role of Speech Technology in Mobile Applications. In A. Neustein (Ed.), *Advances in Speech Recognition* (pp. 3–18). Springer. doi:10.1007/978-1-4419-5951-5_1

Mikolov, T., Karafiát, M., Burget, L., Černocký, J., & Khudanpur, S. (2010). Recurrent neural network based language model. In *Proceedings of the Eleventh annual conference of the international speech communication association* (pp. 1045-1048). Academic Press.

Mittal, P., & Singh, N. (2020). Subword analysis of small vocabulary and large vocabulary ASR for Punjabi language. *International Journal of Speech Technology*, *23*(1), 71–78. doi:10.100710772-020-09673-3

National Speech Corpus-Infocomm Media Development Authority. (n.d.). Retrieved May 15, 2022, from https://www.imda.gov.sg/programme-listing/digital-services-lab/national-speech-corpus

Neustein, A. (2010). *Advances in speech recognition: mobile environments, call centers and clinics*. Springer Science & Business Media. doi:10.1007/978-1-4419-5951-5

Nkosi, M., Manamela, M., & Gasela, N. (2011). Creating a Pronunciation Dictionary for Automatic Speech Recognition - a Morphological approach. In *Proceedings of the Southern Africa Telecommunication Networks and Applications Conference (SATNAC)* (pp. 1-5). Academic Press.

OpenSLR.org- LibriSpeech. (n.d.). Retrieved August 20, 2022 from https://www.openslr.org/12

OpenSLR.org- TED-LIUM. (n.d.). Retrieved August 20, 2022 from https://www.openslr.org/51

Park, H., Takiguchi, T., & Ariki, Y. (2009). Integrated phoneme subspace method for speech feature extraction. *EURASIP Journal on Audio, Speech, and Music Processing, 2009*, 1–6. doi:10.1155/2009/690451

Pearson, K. (1901). On Lines and Planes of Closest Fit to Systems of Points in Space. *Philosophical Magazine, 2*(11), 559–572.

Quach, T., & Farooq, M. (1994). Maximum Likelihood Track Formation with the Viterbi Algorithm. In *Proceedings of the 33rd IEEE Conference on Decision and Control* (pp. 271–276). 10.1109/CDC.1994.410918

Rabiner, L. R. (1989). A tutorial on Hidden Markov models and selected applications in speech recognition. *Proceedings of the IEEE, 77*(2), 257–286. doi:10.1109/5.18626

Rao, K., Peng, F., & Beaufays, F. (2015, April). Automatic pronunciation verification for speech recognition. In *Proceedings of the 2015 IEEE International Conference on Acoustics, Speech and Signal Processing (ICASSP)* (pp. 5162-5166). IEEE. 10.1109/ICASSP.2015.7178955

Schalkwyk, J., Beeferman, D., Beaufays, F., Byrne, B., Chelba, C., Cohen, M., & Strope, B. (2010). Your word is my command. In *Google search by voice: A case study. Advances in speech recognition* (pp. 61–90). Springer. doi:10.1007/978-1-4419-5951-5_4

Shlens, J. (2014). *A tutorial on principal component analysis.* arXiv preprint arXiv:1404.1100.

Siri - Apple (IN). (n.d.). Retrieved May 15, 2022, from https://www.apple.com/in/siri/

Spoken corpora | Clarin ERIC. (n.d.). Retrieved May 15, 2022, from https://www.clarin.eu/resource-families/spoken-corpora

Tan, B. T., Fu, M., Spray, A., & Dermody, P. (1996, October). The use of wavelet transforms in phoneme recognition. In *Proceeding of the Fourth International Conference on Spoken Language Processing (ICSLP'96)* (vol. 4, pp. 2431-2434). IEEE. 10.1109/ICSLP.1996.607300

Tu, S. (2014). *Pattern Recognition and Machine Learning (Information Science and Statistics)*. Retrieved May 15, 2022, from https://people.eecs.berkeley.edu/~stephentu/writeups/hmm-baum-welch-derivation.pdf

Voice Recognition Software | Speech Recognition Software | tazti. (n.d.). Retrieved May 15, 2022, from https://www.tazti.com/

Westendorf, C. M., & Jelitto, J. (1996, October). Learning pronunciation dictionary from speech data. In *Proceedings of the Fourth International Conference on Spoken Language Processing (ICSLP'96)* (vol. 2, pp. 1045-1048). IEEE. 10.1109/ICSLP.1996.607784

Zwicker, E. (1961). Subdivision of the audible frequency range into critical bands. *The Journal of the Acoustical Society of America, 33*(2), 248. doi:10.1121/1.1908630

Wei, X., Cucchiarini, C., van Hout, R., & Strik, H. (2022). Automatic Speech Recognition and Pronunciation Error Detection of Dutch Non-native Speech: Cumulating speech resources in a pluricentric language. *Speech Communication, 144*, 1–9. doi:10.1016/j.specom.2022.08.004

Chapter 3

Misinformation Containment Using NLP and Machine Learning:
Why the Problem Is Still Unsolved

Vishnu S. Pendyala
https://orcid.org/0000-0001-6494-7832
San Jose State University, USA

ABSTRACT

Despite the increased attention and substantial research into it claiming outstanding successes, the problem of misinformation containment has only been growing in the recent years with not many signs of respite. Misinformation is rapidly changing its latent characteristics and spreading vigorously in a multi-modal fashion, sometimes in a more damaging manner than viruses and other malicious programs on the internet. This chapter examines the existing research in natural language processing and machine learning to stop the spread of misinformation, analyzes why the research has not been practical enough to be incorporated into social media platforms, and provides future research directions. The state-of-the-art feature engineering, approaches, and algorithms used for the problem are expounded in the process.

INTRODUCTION

Social media has been subject to plenty of controversies owing to its use for spreading misinformation, sometimes to the extent of manipulating a country's presidential elections (Pendyala et al., 2018). The objective of this chapter is to explain some of the recent machine learning and natural language processing approaches for misinformation containment and provide reasons why, despite the large quantity of research in the area, the problem is still unsolved. Modeling domains using math has time and again proven to yield solutions to some of the toughest problems in the past. Machine learning, for the most part, has evolved from applied math. There has been an upsurge in the literature on the topic of trust in social media using machine learning models in recent times. This chapter starts with a survey of some

DOI: 10.4018/978-1-6684-6001-6.ch003

of the machine learning models, methods, and techniques that have been used to address the problem of the trustworthiness of the information on the Internet, which helps in misinformation containment.

The techniques are discussed under various sub-heads such as language models, few-shot learning, bot detection, graph theoretic approaches to misinformation containment, and using Generative Adversarial Network models for detecting fake multimedia content as well as textual content. As Table 1 shows, the corpus of articles on this topic is tremendous. A comprehensive survey of the existing literature is beyond the scope of this work. The survey is mainly intended to convey the underlying techniques and the resulting success that is reported in the literature and then to show why despite the claimed success, the problem is largely unsolved. The selection of the survey sub-topics in this chapter is based on the author's perception of what is indicative of the emerging literature.

As can be seen in the following sections, researchers have reported substantial success in misinformation containment (MC). However, even the layman can see that the problem is far from resolved. Information platforms such as WhatsApp have adopted means that are far from satisfactory to control the spread of lies on the Internet. For instance, by limiting the number of times a post can be forwarded, WhatsApp is curtailing useful information as well and not just malicious posts. Google search engine still returns web pages with a significant amount of misinformation and does not always indicate or quantify its belief in the fetched search results. Platforms such as Facebook depend on social media community standards to police the usage and are often a cause for grief for users who have genuine interests in posting information. Using formal methods such as First-Order-Logic can prove to be effective as well (Pendyala, 2018) but for focus and brevity, this chapter discusses only trends in machine learning and particularly in deep learning that seem promising. This chapter addresses the challenges in solving the misinformation containment problem and suggests some future directions.

BACKGROUND

Fake news continues to be a major problem. It is undoubtedly a complex problem to solve and appropriately attracted plenty of attention from the research community. A wide variety of machine learning algorithms such as support vector machines and logistic regression (Patel & Meehan, 2021), ensemble techniques like random forest (Antony Vijay et al., 2021) and Adaboost, deep learning frameworks such as LSTM (Rajalaxmi et al., 2022) and GAN (Xie et al., 2022), language models like BOW / TF-IDF (Mondal et al., 2022) and BERT (Palani et al., 2022), and many more have been tried out in the attempts to solve the problem. In terms of feature engineering as well, no stone has been left unturned. Manual feature extraction, graph embeddings (Karpov & Glazkova, 2020), and other approaches to representation learning (ElSherief et al., 2021) have all been tried. Not just supervised and unsupervised learning, but various other types of learning such as few-shot learning (Lo et al., 2022), meta-learning (Kozik & Chora's, 2022), transfer learning (Ghayoomi & Mousavian, 2022), meta-transfer learning (Shen, 2022), self-supervised learning (Huh et al., 2018), semi-supervised learning (Li et al., 2022), reinforcement learning (Mosallanezhad et al., 2022) (He et al., 2022), and active learning (Sahan et al., 2021) have been explored extensively for the problem. Figure 1 illustrates some of the approaches explored for misinformation containment. Despite the voluminous research literature purporting to solve the problem using machine learning methods, misinformation containment is largely unsolved and is growing by the day. The chapter provides some insights into the current state-of-the-art solutions and analyzes why they are not helping enough. The chapter will present some future directions that can help.

Figure 1. Some of the approaches for Misinformation Containment that have been explored in the literature

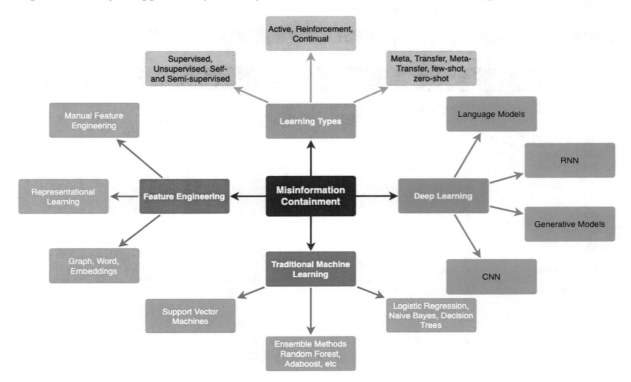

A Google search for "fake news" on July 23, 2022, returned 81.5 million results, including a fake news item relating to the Ukrainian President. The results also show that the Seattle times runs a section titled, "This week in fake news." To illustrate the problem further, Figure 1 is a screenshot of the metadata of a fraudulent upload on YouTube faking as the popular Indian movie, "Kashmir Files." It received tremendous attention from gullible viewers who seem to have believed that it is indeed the real movie. This is just one instance of how fake posts are largely uncontained.

Table 1. Google Scholar results listing articles purporting to solve the fake information problem

Search String	Article Count
"Machine learning" fake	103,000
"Deep learning" fake	48,800
"Language model" fake	6,830
"LSTM" fake	17,300
"graph neural networks" fake	17,800

Figure 2. A fake upload not matching the actors or attributes of the real movie gets ~19 million views, 289,000+ likes, and 15,250 genuine comments in 2 months (screenshot taken on July 23, 2022)

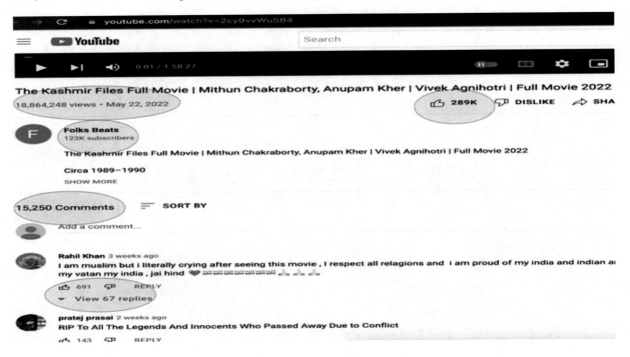

On the other hand, Table 1 shows the number of articles indexed by Google scholar that apparently use the popular technologies given in the search string to tackle the fake news problem. Depending on the underlying Google's search algorithm, the numbers may or may not be accurate, but the search results are quite indicative. The problem has attracted tremendous interest from the research community. Several articles that the author surveyed report outstanding successes. A "Fake News Challenge (FNC-1)[1]" was organized in 2017 to seek Machine Learning, Natural Language Processing, and Artificial Intelligence solutions to combat fake news and there are plans to organize FNC-2. The problem is still largely unsolved in the real world. It is therefore pertinent to research this huge disconnect between what is claimed in research and the actual reality.

Misinformation containment has been proven to be NP-hard more than a decade ago (Budak et al., 2011), which makes it a good candidate for approximate models such as the ones generated by machine learning. Given that artificial neural networks serve as universal function approximators, misinformation containment can be framed as a function of the features of the information that outputs whether the information is true or false or a degree of truthfulness. Deep learning that uses deep neural networks is rapidly expanding its scope of applications to the extent of prompting a debate in some corners as to whether traditional machine learning techniques are even relevant today. Deep learning generalizes better and performs better when the classification is nonlinear as in this case. Researchers (Wanda & Jie, 2020) used a deep learning architecture called Convolutional Neural Network (CNN) to detect fake profiles in online Social Networks. They achieve high accuracy in doing so. Like for any supervised machine learning classification problem, the authors extract features, train a model, handle overfitting issues by using regularization and apply the model to test data. They compare the results obtained using the CNN architecture with the conventional machine learning models such as Logistic Regression and SVM and confirm that CNN performs better. We, therefore, focus more on deep learning approaches in the following sections. Figure 3 summarizes the flow of the rest of the chapter.

Figure 3. Misinformation Containment: Methods and challenges

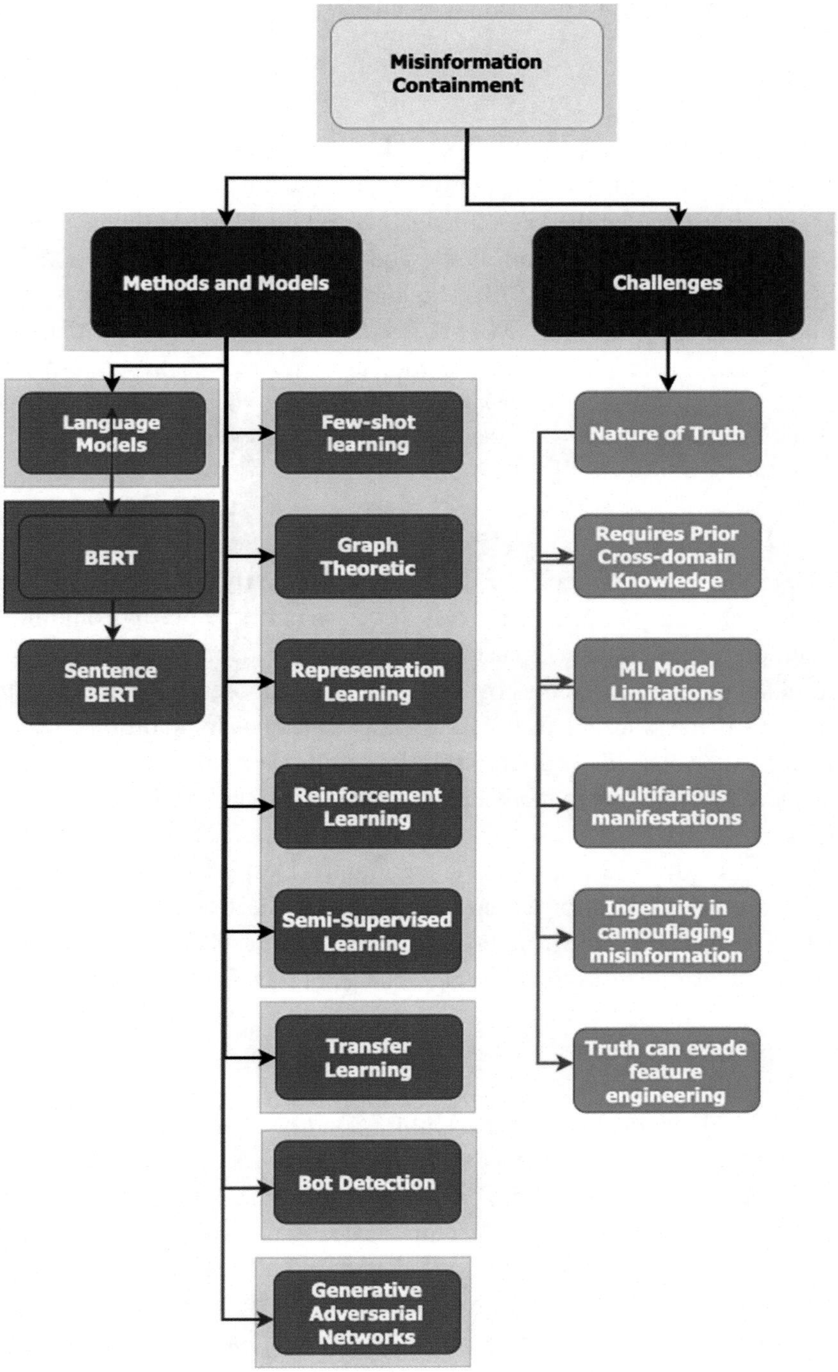

Methods and Models

In the following paragraphs, although there is a reference to both deep learning and traditional machine learning-based approaches as they relate to the misinformation containment problem, most of the discourse is on deep learning. The purpose again is not for an exhaustive survey, which is almost infeasible given the amount of literature but to provide a high-level overview of some of the emerging trends not covered in other surveys on the topic.

Few-Shot Learning

The problem of misinformation detection has been addressed using meta-algorithms in traditional machine learning such as random forest and extra tree classifier with substantial reported success (Hakak, et al., 2021). The authors claim that the experiments resulted in 100% training and test accuracy on one dataset but training and testing accuracy of 99.8% and 44.15% respectively on a different training set (Hakak, et al., 2021). Few-shot learning (FSL) uses meta-learning that can work with fewer training examples. Model-agnostic meta-learning (MAML) is one such FSL technique that has been shown to result in better performance on fake news classification as compared to a host of other machine learning models (Salem, et al., 2021). Authors (Lwowski & Najafirad, 2020) propose identifying a latent space using self-supervised learning for few-shot learning and claim good results.

Language Models

Language models like BERT and Sentence BERT are quite popularly used for misinformation classification and efforts have been made to improve the classification performance by combining with enhanced attention-based methods (Paka, Bansal, Kaushik, Sengupta, & Chakraborty, 2021). When even human beings are not good at detecting fake news by just reading them, merely generating embeddings using NLP techniques is not sufficient for the task. Mining a wider corpus for additional features related to the information that needs to be classified can improve the results (Deepak & Chitturi, 2020). However, the secondary features so added are metadata like domain name and author details, which may not make a substantial difference. A similar approach is taken in (Braşoveanu & Andonie, 2019), but the augmented features include relations extracted from knowledge graphs. Despite the successes reported, language models based classification of misinformation in the form of short sentences is fundamentally flawed (Mifsud et al., 2021). It has been confirmed (Guderlei & Aßenmacher, 2020) that pre-trained BERT-based language models are good to start with for a subsequent transfer learning task for stance detection.

Graph Theoretic Approaches

Social media is often used synonymously with Online Social Networks. social media can be modeled as a network or a graph of users, and artifacts from the user posts. Such a model can then be used to predict the trust or credibility in the media. If we know the credibility of the nodes of a subset of this graph, that information can then be used by machine learning algorithms to estimate the credibility of the remaining graph. Researchers (O'Brien et al., 2019) prove that graph dependencies play an important role in credibility estimation in social media. We can relate this to the real world, where the credibility of a well-connected person can be much more easily established than a completely isolated person. The idea can be related to the concept of homophily in psychology, where similar people are expected to bond with each other. Graph theoretic techniques can be used to model connections in social media and then exploit these homophily tendencies. The authors (O'Brien et al., 2019) use traditional machine learning algorithms such as Logistic Regression and Decision trees on the local and relational features based on the graphical structures, to achieve reasonably good accuracies in estimating credibility.

Learning from the neighborhood of a graph node using deep learning and generalizing the function learned to unseen nodes in the graph has many applications. Authors (Ghafari et al., 2019) use and extend Stanford University's GraphSAGE (Hamilton et al., 2017), which does exactly this to predict the trust between a pair of reviewers on an online review website such as Epinions. The authors use two datasets, one of which is from Epinions to do their experiments. This is an improvement over the Web-of-trust approach for Epinions like websites surveyed earlier (Pendyala, 2019) because it takes context into account. Trust is often contextual; an entity can be trusted in certain contexts but not all. As the authors (Ghafari et al., 2019) point out, most trust computing frameworks ignore this fact, whereas this work (Ghafari et al., 2019) leverages it. The system developed extracts contextual features from user demographics and reviews and uses them for the classification of the pairwise trust.

The work discussed above extracts a graphical structure from the social media entities and components to predict trustable relationships. Work has also been done the other way around to create a graphical framework in which entities are assured of trustable exchanges even in the presence of malicious players. Using several trust-based parameters and math around them, authors (Urena et al., 2020) create a robust framework for reputation-based communication. The authors run simulations to evaluate its performance and obtain good results. The Online Social Network (OSN) view of social media brings out the need for graph theoretic approaches for analyzing trust and credibility relationships between the entities in the social media space. We discussed only a few such approaches in this section, but until the problem of distrust is entirely solved, which probably is unlikely, we can expect to see a growth in the graph-theoretic-based approaches to address the problem.

Representation Learning

Manual feature engineering is increasingly getting replaced by representation learning. The goal of representation learning is to derive (or learn) a representation of the data automatically. The representation is usually in the form of an embedding, typically a vector. The embeddings can then be processed like any other feature vectors, possibly as the input layer for artificial neural networks. Representation learning is particularly effective with natural language and graphs. From the literature survey, we present a case study each, for natural language and graphs in the context of misinformation containment. Researchers (Borges et al., 2019) have used representation learning for stance detection as described in the "Fake News Challenge – 1 (FNC-1)" problem description1. Stance detection determines if two pieces of information agree with each other. In the FNC-1 case, the agreement is between the headline and the body of a news snippet. Using word embeddings from the pre-trained model, bi-directional RNNs such as LSTM and GRU, maxpooling, and attention mechanism, the researchers (Borges et al., 2019) model long news articles. Representation learning comes in handy when the data is a large graph. Social network graphs are large and evolving. New nodes can get added rapidly. Node embeddings for the new nodes need to be computed rapidly as well. Using the entire graph structure in a transductive manner to compute the embeddings may not scale well. Researchers (Rath, et al., 2020) therefore used an inductive approach inspired by the GraphSAGE work (Hamilton et al., 2017) to compute embeddings based on the inductive representation learning. The graph models how fake news spreads on microblog sites like Twitter.

Reinforcement Learning

A predominant assumption in most machine learning models is that the data is i.i.d, Independent and Identically Distributed. Most of the machine learning solutions presented in the literature for the misinformation containment problem focus on a dataset from a single domain such as politics (Pendyala et al., 2018) or healthcare (Pendyala & Figueira, 2015), the embeddings for which are i.i.d. However, misinformation often covers multiple domains. Reinforcement learning can be used for cross-domain modeling (Mosallanezhad et al., 2022). Users' comments, interactions, and information in two disparate domains are used to learn a domain-agnostic representation of the information to aid in its classification. Reinforcement learning is used to convert the representations in the source domain into a representation in the target domain. Reinforcement learning has also been used to increase the availability of labeled data (Wang, et al., 2020). Annotating information is an expensive process and requires manual expertise. An automatic annotator assigns the labels based on user reports. This initial labeling is weak and not entirely accurate. Reinforcement learning is then used to select the best-labeled instances from the weakly labeled data.

Semi-Supervised Learning

Similar to the above reinforcement learning approach to augment the labeled data, researchers (Li, et al., 2022) introduced a "confidence network layer" into a bidirectional LSTM to filter out the data that is confidently labeled. The neural network is initially trained on a limited labeled dataset in a supervised manner. The confidence network layer adds the confidently labeled data to this initial dataset in an iterative manner, quite along the lines of semi-supervised learning. Semi-supervised learning is often used in conjunction with graphs. Typically, each data item is a node, and the weighted edges connecting them indicate the similarity between the nodes. Labels can then propagate from labeled nodes to unlabeled ones. A graphs-based semi-supervised learning approach has also been used for fake news detection (Benamira, 2019). A graph is constructed from the GloVe embeddings of the documents. Each node is a document. Some of the nodes are already labeled as genuine, some others are labeled fake, and several others are unlabeled. The nodes are interconnected based on the k-nearest neighbors algorithm. Graph convolution network approach is used to classify the unlabeled nodes.

Transfer Learning

Pretrained language models like BERT, RoBERTa, GPT2, and Funnel generate embeddings that can be used subsequently as inputs to Artificial Neural Networks (ANN) or Convolutional Neural Networks (CNN) to determine the veracity of a given text (Samadi, Mousavian, & Momtazi, 2021). Capsule networks can also be used with word embeddings in the process of transfer learning (Goldani, Momtazi, & Safabakhsh, 2021). The datasets used for the problem are well-known and limited in scope. The literature survey confirms that there have not been any attempts to generate embeddings exclusively from misinformation.

DETECTING BOTS

Misinformation spread often happens on social media using accounts owned by software. The trend has given rise to the growth of companies that even offer Bot-as-a-service (BAAS). During the 2016 US Presidential elections, about 20% of the social media discussions on the topic happened using bots (Wu et al., 2018). A wide spectrum of various types of machine learning algorithms can be used to detect bots. Algorithms vary, but the overall process of classification of the user as a bot or not is somewhat similar when the machine learning is supervised. Various features such as the screen name, description, and the number of followers are extracted from the user profiles. Parametric, supervised machine learning algorithms such as logistic regression determine the weights for each of these features from already classified data. The algorithms model the classification as a function of the weighted features. The model can then be applied to new user data, based on which the user needs to be classified as a bot or human.

Obtaining user profile data that is already classified as belonging to a bot or a human being may pose challenges. In the absence of such a training set, unsupervised learning algorithms can be used to cluster the data into those belonging to bots and others to real humans. Researchers (Wu et al., 2018) use several clustering algorithms on network traffic to detect if a host is infected by bots. Similar techniques can be used on social media profiles as well. Hegelich and Janetzko (Hegelich & Janetzko, 2016) apply k-means and hierarchical clustering algorithms to the posts made by social bots in Ukraine elections to draw interesting conclusions about the behavioral patterns of the social bots. Clustering algorithms still work with the features extracted from the data and group the data into clusters based on similarity.

For certain classification problems, deep learning can achieve better classification accuracy, as noted in the preceding section on fake profile identification. Authors (Kudugunta & Ferrara, 2018) have proven that the problem of classifying accounts as bots or humans can be solved with superlative accuracies using deep neural networks, but this time, using a different architecture than CNNs. Using Long Short-Term Memory (LSTM) architecture, the authors bring out the advantage of using deep learning techniques over conventional machine learning algorithms. The LSTM architecture can be applied even when the feature set is small and the size of the dataset is limited, as the authors show. LSTM networks are a type of Recurrent Neural network (RNN), which provide for information to persist. RNNs have been extensively used to come up with outstanding solutions to challenging problems.

Generative Adversarial Networks

Machine learning and deep learning particularly have been central to some of the techniques discussed earlier. One area of deep learning that requires special mention in the context of trusting social media is Generative Adversarial Network or GAN. GAN models have helped create unbelievably realistic fake content that includes images and text. The website, ThisPersonDoesNotExist.com displays several faces generated using GANs that look amazingly realistic but are completely synthesized. The fake facial images created using GAN models are used on social media to create fake accounts to propagate malicious agendas. Since the fake content generated by GAN is close to real, it becomes a challenge to differentiate the fake ones from the real images. GAN can be used for addressing the problem of trust in social media in two ways: (a) to generate a dataset of fake content for training the model used to detect new fake content and (b) to detect fake content itself.

Multiple techniques have been developed to deal with the problem of detecting fakes generated by GAN and one of them is using part of GAN itself. A GAN has two parts – a generator and a discriminator, both implemented as neural networks, typically convolutional or recurrent. The generator creates fake content and the discriminator keeps rejecting it until it is convinced that the content from the generator is real. The function of the discriminator is really to reject fake content. Hence, GAN discriminators can potentially be used to detect fake content (Marra et al., 2018). The authors use the same GAN discriminator that was used in the process of generating fake images to train various other models described in the paper, as a baseline algorithm to detect fake content. To make sure that the discriminator is not biased because it has already gone through the training samples, the discriminator needs to be retrained. The work uses several other models as well and compares the results with those obtained by using the GAN discriminator.

Given that majority of the social media is still in text format, a major development in detecting misleading content is to apply the powerful GAN models to text data (Aghakhani et al., 2018). Here too, the discriminator part of the GAN does the job of determining fake content, this time, textual reviews on TripAdvisor with an accuracy of 89.1%. Since Convolutional Neural Network (CNN) works better with text, the discriminator is implemented as a CNN. The authors use two discriminators, both CNN, instead of just one that the GAN model originally proposed. Based on the experiments and results obtained from them, they confirm that using two discriminators works better in this case of textual reviews.

Interpretable models, which can explain the classification done by the model are the need of the hour. Explanations provide transparency and better confidence in the model. Authors (Carton et al., 2018) use the GAN philosophy to develop "Extractive Adversarial Networks" to go a step further, beyond text classification, to provide explanations for the classification decisions. Their work detects comments on social media that are personal attacks and points out the words in those comments that are the reason the model classified the comment as a personal attack. The key difference between their model from the original GAN is that their model extracts a modified sample from an existing sample instead of generating one, as done in GAN. The generation function is thus replaced by extraction, hence the name they chose for the model.

MISINFORMATION CONTAINMENT IS STILL UNSOLVED: WHY?

As the previous sections indicate, substantial research and success have been reported in the literature so far. However, there is no ambiguity in stating that the problem is largely unsolved. To understand the reasons, there is a need to understand the nature of misinformation. Unlike spam, which can be detected based on the occurrence of certain word patterns, misinformation is highly complex. It is hugely a challenge even for human beings to detect misinformation. For instance, it can take years for the truth to be established in a court of law. The following paragraphs discuss a few points to consider when designing solutions to misinformation containment.

Truth is Temporal, Subjective, and Relative

There were times when the truth about the earth was that it is flat, people who believe that the truth is that God does not exist, and objects that are small only when compared to other relatively large objects.

On the other hand, machine learning models used in the current literature are fixed and cannot handle the dynamic variations in subjectivity or relativity.

Determining Truth can Require a huge Corpus of Prior Knowledge

Often, the truth can be determined only after cross-checking against a huge corpus of facts, evidence, and reasoning. Machine learning models are incapable of such cross-checking as compared to First-Order-Logic (FOL) and other formal methods that have the implements to reason and inference from prior statements.

Truth can evade Feature Engineering

The same source of information with their features intact can produce conflicting statements. For instance, there are several cases where a user on Twitter posted conflicting tweets. Merely extracting the features, whether manually engineered or automatically generated by the hidden layers via deep learning are unlikely to flag the misinformation. The feature set used in a substantial part of the literature is limited to temporal or contextual or content-based, whereas the need is for much more comprehensive and exhaustive information.

Ingenuity in Camouflaging Misinformation

Misinformation is often seamlessly interwoven with truth in ingenious ways. Even the intent and purport can sound genuine. Latent space mapping and self-supervised learning approaches can help only to some extent but are not always accurate or exhaustive.

Limitations of the Machine Learning Models

RNNs, CNNs, and other language models that are often used for Natural Language Understanding (NLU) in the process of misinformation detection cannot capture long-term dependencies in large texts. Even the latest transformer-based models like BERT are only good for 512 tokens in the text and efforts were made to increase it to 2048 tokens (Yang, et. al., 2020).

There is no Silver Bullet

Misinformation containment is not a single problem to have a single do-it-all solution. Misinformation is manifested in many modalities and forms. Each manifestation needs to be addressed in one or more ways. The current approaches address the problem by experimenting with a sample dataset, which is usually identically distributed, report the results from the same dataset and portray general success based on those results. On the other hand, misinformation is far from being identically distributed.

FUTURE RESEARCH DIRECTIONS

Despite its limitations and extensive use, it does not appear that machine learning has been fully used in addressing the misinformation containment problem. For instance, unsupervised and semi-supervised techniques do not seem to have been used in areas they can be used, such as pointed out in the subsection on "Detecting Bots". Given that most of the available data in the social media space cannot easily be classified with certainty into bot-generated or genuinely generated by humans, unsupervised and semi-supervised methods should show substantial promise. State-of-the-art deep learning frameworks in general are computationally expensive and require humongous data. Once trained, the essential parameters are fixed, so newer patterns are not modeled if the data is still evolving. Static feature extraction for subsequent classification using parametric methods does not model the evolving nature of misinformation either. On the other hand, Misinformation Containment (MC) needs to be continuous, instantaneous, evolve with the changing patterns in the data, and use fewer resources so that users can deploy the models on edge devices such as smartphones. Future research needs to address these characteristics.

The research needs to focus on both applications of the existing machine learning frameworks and changing the underlying methodologies to suit the needs of misinformation containment. Graph theoretic approaches hold substantial promise because they can capture dependencies in a long sequence substantially well and can serve as the long-term memory that RNNs fail to provide. Inductive approaches to compute embeddings such as GraphSAGE (Hamilton et al., 2017) can scale well. The problem indeed needs to be solved in multiple stages as pointed out in the Fake News Challenge -1 (FNC-1)1 problem description.

CONCLUSION

Misinformation containment is a complex problem. The problem has been addressed using several techniques, algorithms, and frameworks available in machine learning, but the problem remains unsolved. Similar problems such as spam, viruses, cyberattacks, and other malicious implements are in reasonable control, but not misinformation, which is a reflection of the complexity of the problem. This chapter presented a brief survey of the trends in misinformation containment using machine learning and explained why the current approaches have not been effective. Future research directions should go beyond the traditional dataset collection, train, validate, and test cycle, and use frameworks that can model the characteristics of misinformation better.

ACKNOWLEDGMENT

This research received no specific grant from any funding agency in the public, commercial, or not-for-profit sectors.

REFERENCES

Aghakhani, H., Machiry, A., Nilizadeh, S., Krügel, C., & Vigna, G. (2018). Detecting Deceptive Reviews Using Generative Adversarial Networks. *2018 IEEE Security and Privacy Workshops (SPW)*, 89-95.

Antony Vijay, J., Anwar Basha, H., & Arun Nehru, J. (2021). A Dynamic Approach For Detecting The Fake News Using Random Forest Classifier And Nlp. In *Computational Methods And Data Engineering* (pp. 331–341). Springer. doi:10.1007/978-981-15-7907-3_25

Benamira, A., Devillers, B., Lesot, E., Ray, A. K., Saadi, M., & Malliaros, F. D. (2019, August). Semi-supervised learning and graph neural networks for fake news detection. In *2019 IEEE/ACM International Conference on Advances in Social Networks Analysis and Mining (ASONAM)* (pp. 568-569). IEEE. 10.1145/3341161.3342958

Borges, L., Martins, B., & Calado, P. (2019). Combining similarity features and deep representation learning for stance detection in the context of checking fake news. *Journal of Data and Information Quality, 11*(3), 1–26. doi:10.1145/3287763

Braşoveanu, A. M., & Andonie, R. (2019). *Semantic fake news detection: a machine learning perspective*. International Work-Conference on Artificial Neural Networks.

Budak, C., Agrawal, D., & El Abbadi, A. (2011). Limiting The Spread Of Misinformation In Social Networks. *Proceedings Of The 20th International Conference On World Wide Web*, 665–674. 10.1145/1963405.1963499

Carton, S., Mei, Q., & Resnick, P. (2018). *Extractive Adversarial Networks: High-Recall Explanations For Identifying Personal Attacks In Social Media Posts*. doi:10.18653/v1/D18-1386

Deepak, S., & Chitturi, B. (2020). Deep neural approach to Fake-News identification. *Procedia Computer Science, 167*, 2236–2243. doi:10.1016/j.procs.2020.03.276

Elsherief, M., Sumner, S. A., Jones, C. M., Law, R. K., Kacha-Ochana, A., Shieber, L., Cordier, L., Holton, K., & De Choudhury, M. (2021). Characterizing And Identifying The Prevalence Of Web-Based Misinformation Relating To Medication For Opioid Use Disorder: Machine Learning Approach. *Journal of Medical Internet Research, 23*(12), E30753. doi:10.2196/30753 PMID:34941555

Ghafari, S. M., Joshi, A., Beheshti, A., Paris, C., Yakhchi, S., & Orgun, M. (2019). Dcat: A Deep Context-Aware Trust Prediction Approach For Online Social Networks. *Proceedings Of The 17th International Conference On Advances In Mobile Computing & Multimedia*, 20–27. 10.1145/3365921.3365940

Goldani, M. H., Momtazi, S., & Safabakhsh, R. (2021). Detecting fake news with capsule neural networks. *Applied Soft Computing, 101*, 106991. doi:10.1016/j.asoc.2020.106991

Ghayoomi, M., & Mousavian, M. (2022). Deep Transfer Learning For Covid-19 Fake News Detection In Persian. *Expert Systems: International Journal of Knowledge Engineering and Neural Networks, 39*(8), E13008. doi:10.1111/exsy.13008 PMID:35599852

Guderlei, M., & Aßenmacher, M. (2020, December). Evaluating unsupervised representation learning for detecting stances of fake news. In *Proceedings of the 28th International Conference on Computational Linguistics* (pp. 6339-6349). 10.18653/v1/2020.coling-main.558

Hakak, S., Alazab, M., Khan, S., Gadekallu, T. R., Maddikunta, P. K., & Khan, W. Z. (2021). An ensemble machine learning approach through effective feature extraction to classify fake news. *Future Generation Computer Systems*, *117*, 47–58. doi:10.1016/j.future.2020.11.022

Hamilton, W., Ying, Z., & Leskovec, J. (2017). Inductive Representation Learning On Large Graphs. *Advances in Neural Information Processing Systems*, 30.

Hasani, R., Lechner, M., Amini, A., Rus, D., & Grosu, R. (2021). Liquid time-constant networks. *Proceedings of the AAAI Conference on Artificial Intelligence*, *35*(9), 7657–7666. doi:10.1609/aaai.v35i9.16936

He, Q., Lv, Y., Wang, X., Huang, M., & Cai, Y. (2022). Reinforcement Learning-Based Rumor Blocking Approach In Directed Social Networks. *IEEE Systems Journal*, 1–11. doi:10.1109/JSYST.2022.3159840

Hegelich, S., & Janetzko, D. (2016). Are Social Bots On Twitter Political Actors? Empirical Evidence From A Ukrainian Social Botnet. *Tenth International Aaai Conference On Web And Social Media*.

Huh, M., Liu, A., Owens, A., & Efros, A. A. (2018). Fighting Fake News: Image Splice Detection Via Learned Self-Consistency. *Proceedings Of The European Conference On Computer Vision (Eccv)*, 101–117. 10.1007/978-3-030-01252-6_7

Karpov, I., & Glazkova, E. (2020). Detecting Automatically Managed Accounts In Online Social Networks: Graph Embeddings Approach. *International Conference On Analysis Of Images, Social Networks And Texts*, 11–21.

Kozik, S., Kula, S., Choraś, M., & Woźniak, M. (2022). Technical Solution To Counter Potential Crime: Text Analysis To Detect Fake News And Disinformation. *Journal of Computational Science*, *60*, 101576. doi:10.1016/j.jocs.2022.101576

Kudugunta, S., & Ferrara, E. (2018). Deep Neural Networks For Bot Detection. *Information Sciences*, *467*, 312–322. doi:10.1016/j.ins.2018.08.019

Li, X., Lu, P., Hu, L., Wang, X., & Lu, L. (2022). A Novel Self-Learning Semi-Supervised Deep Learning Network To Detect Fake News On Social Media. *Multimedia Tools and Applications*, *81*(14), 19341–19349. doi:10.100711042-021-11065-x PMID:34093070

Lo, K.-C., Dai, S.-C., Xiong, A., Jiang, J., & Ku, L.-W. (2022). Victor: An Implicit Approach To Mitigate Misinformation Via Continuous Verification Reading. *Proceedings Of The Acm Web Conference 2022*, 3511–3519. 10.1145/3485447.3512246

Lwowski, B., & Najafirad, P. (2020). *Covid-19 surveillance through twitter using self-supervised and few shot learning*. Academic Press.

Marra, F., Gragnaniello, D., Cozzolino, D., & Verdoliva, L. (2018). Detection Of Gan-Generated Fake Images Over Social Networks. *2018 IEEE Conference On Multimedia Information Processing And Retrieval (Mipr)*, 384–389.

Mondal, S. K., Sahoo, J. P., Wang, J., Mondal, K., & Rahman, M. (2022). Fake News Detection Exploiting Tf-Idf Vectorization With Ensemble Learning Models. In *Advances In Distributed Computing And Machine Learning* (pp. 261–270). Springer.

Mosallanezhad, A., Karami, M., Shu, K., Mancenido, M. V., & Liu, H. (2022). Domain Adaptive Fake News Detection Via Reinforcement Learning. *Proceedings Of The Acm Web Conference 2022*, 3632–3640. 10.1145/3485447.3512258

O'Brien, K., Simek, O., & Waugh, F. (2019). *Collective Classification For Social Media Credibility Estimation*. Academic Press.

Paka, W. S., Bansal, R., Kaushik, A., Sengupta, S., & Chakraborty, T. (2021). Cross-SEAN: A cross-stitch semi-supervised neural attention model for COVID-19 fake news detection. *Applied Soft Computing*, *107*, 107393. doi:10.1016/j.asoc.2021.107393

Palani, B., Elango, S., & Viswanathan, K. (2022). Cb-Fake: A Multimodal Deep Learning Framework For Automatic Fake News Detection Using Capsule Neural Network And Bert. *Multimedia Tools and Applications*, *81*(4), 5587–5620. doi:10.100711042-021-11782-3 PMID:34975284

Patel, A., & Meehan, K. (2021). Fake News Detection On Reddit Utilising Countvectorizer And Term Frequency-Inverse Document Frequency With Logistic Regression, Multinominalnb And Support Vector Machine. *2021 32nd Irish Signals And Systems Conference (Issc)*, 1–6.

Pendyala, V. S., & Figueira, S. (2015, October). Towards a truthful world wide web from a humanitarian perspective. In *2015 IEEE Global Humanitarian Technology Conference (GHTC)* (pp. 137-143). IEEE. 10.1109/GHTC.2015.7343966

Pendyala, V. (2018). *Veracity of Big Data: Machine Learning and Other Approaches to Verifying Truthfulness*. Apress. doi:10.1007/978-1-4842-3633-8

Pendyala, V. S., Liu, Y., & Figueira, S. M. (2018). A Framework For Detecting Injected Influence Attacks On Microblog Websites Using Change Detection Techniques. *Development Engineering*, *3*, 218–233. doi:10.1016/j.deveng.2018.08.002

Pendyala, V. S. (2019). Securing Trust In Online Social Networks. *International Conference On Secure Knowledge Management In Artificial Intelligence Era*, 194–201.

Rajalaxmi, R., Narasimha Prasad, L., Janakiramaiah, B., Pavankumar, C., Neelima, N., & Sathishkumar, V. (2022). Optimizing Hyperparameters And Performance Analysis Of Lstm Model. In *Detecting Fake News On Social Media*. Transactions On Asian And Low-Resource Language Information Processing.

Rath, B., Salecha, A., & Srivastava, J. (2020, December). Detecting fake news spreaders in social networks using inductive representation learning. In *2020 IEEE/ACM International Conference on Advances in Social Networks Analysis and Mining (ASONAM)* (pp. 182-189). IEEE. 10.1109/ASONAM49781.2020.9381466

Sahan, M., Smidl, V., & Marik, R. (2021). Active Learning For Text Classification And Fake News Detection. *2021 International Symposium On Computer Science And Intelligent Controls (Iscsic)*, 87–94. 10.1109/ISCSIC54682.2021.00027

Salem, F. K., Al Feel, R., Elbassuoni, S., Ghannam, H., Jaber, M., & Farah, M. (2021). Meta-learning for fake news detection surrounding the Syrian war. *Patterns*, *2*(11), 100369. doi:10.1016/j.patter.2021.100369 PMID:34820650

Samadi, M., Mousavian, M., & Momtazi, S. (2021). Deep contextualized text representation and learning for fake news detection. *Information Processing & Management*, *58*(6), 102723. doi:10.1016/j.ipm.2021.102723

Shen. (2022). Mdn: Meta-Transfer Learning Method For Fake News Detection. *Ccf Conference On Computer Supported Cooperative Work And Social Computing*, 228–237.

Urena, R., Chiclana, F., & Herrera-Viedma, E. (2020). Decitrustnet: A Graph Based Trust And Reputation Framework For Social Networks. *Information Fusion*, *61*, 101–112. doi:10.1016/j.inffus.2020.03.006

Wanda, P., & Jie, H. J. (2020). Deepprofile: Finding Fake Profile In Online Social Network Using Dynamic Cnn. *Journal Of Information Security And Applications*, *52*, 102465. doi:10.1016/j.jisa.2020.102465

Wang, Y., Yang, W., Ma, F., Xu, J., Zhong, B., Deng, Q., & Gao, J. (2020, April). Weak supervision for fake news detection via reinforcement learning. *Proceedings of the AAAI Conference on Artificial Intelligence*, *34*(01), 516–523. doi:10.1609/aaai.v34i01.5389

Wu, W., Alvarez, J., Liu, C., & Sun, H.-M. (2018). Bot Detection Using Unsupervised Machine Learning. *Microsystem Technologies*, *24*(1), 209–217. doi:10.100700542-016-3237-0

Xie, J., Chai, Y., & Liu, X. (2022). An Interpretable Deep Learning Approach To Understand Health Misinformation Transmission On Youtube. *Proceedings Of The 55th Hawaii International Conference On System Sciences*. 10.24251/HICSS.2022.183

Yang, L., Zhang, M., Li, C., Bendersky, M., & Najork, M. (2020, October). Beyond 512 tokens: Siamese multi-depth transformer-based hierarchical encoder for long-form document matching. In *Proceedings of the 29th ACM International Conference on Information & Knowledge Management* (pp. 1725-1734). 10.1145/3340531.3411908

ENDNOTE

[1]   http://www.fakenewschallenge.org

Chapter 4
A Survey of Transformer-Based Stance Detection

Dilek Küçük

TÜBİTAK Marmara Research Center, Turkey

ABSTRACT

Stance detection systems are built in order to determine the position of text authors using the text that they produce and other contextual information. As the result of the stance detection procedure, the position of the text producer is determined as favor, against, or none. On the other hand, transformer-based technologies are reported to perform well for various natural language processing tasks. These are deep learning-based models that also incorporate attention mechanism. BERT and its variants are among the most popular transformer-based models proposed so far. In this chapter, the authors provide a plausible literature review on stance detection studies that are based on transformer models. Also included in the current chapter are important further research directions. Stance detection and transformer-based models are significant and recent problems in natural language processing and deep learning, respectively. Hence, they believe that this chapter will be an important guide for related researchers and practitioners working on these topics of high impact.

INTRODUCTION

Stance detection has emerged as a significant problem which has its roots in natural language processing (NLP), social media analysis, and information retrieval (Küçük and Can, 2020; Küçük and Can, 2021; Küçük and Can, 2022). Stance detection is also closely related to the problems in affective computing such as sentiment analysis. In stance detection, the main objective is to automatically infer the position (stance) of the text author towards a target where the output of this procedure is usually 'favor' or 'against' (Küçük and Can, 2020).

On the other hand, deep learning approaches dominate the methods used in many application domains including NLP, speech processing, and computer vision. Transformer-based methods are among these popular deep-learning methods (Yay et al., 2020). As is the case for many tasks related to NLP, a high percentage of recent work on stance detection employ transformer-based deep learning approaches,

DOI: 10.4018/978-1-6684-6001-6.ch004

including but not limited to Bidirectional Encoder Representations of Transformers (BERT) (Devlin et al., 2018).

In this book chapter, we present a survey of transformer-based stance detection studies. We also address future research opportunities and provide pointers to related outstanding issues. Stance detection is an important research problem and is beneficial in many application settings including polling, predictions for elections and referendums, and Web search. Hence, a survey of transformer-based stance detection studies will have both theoretical and application-oriented contributions to the related literature.

Stance Detection

Stance detection is commonly considered as a classification task requiring two inputs, a piece of text and a target, and the stance (position) of the text author towards the target is expected at the end of the stance detection procedure (Küçük and Can, 2020). Stance detection is usually considered within the scope of *affective computing* and sometimes considered as a subproblem of *sentiment analysis*.

There are several subproblems of stance detection including *multi-target stance detection, cross-target stance detection*, and *contextual stance detection* (Küçük and Can, 2021; Küçük and Can, 2022). In multi-target stance detection, there is a set of (usually interrelated) targets instead of a single one. In cross-target stance detection, the training dataset is available for one target although the test dataset is about another target (Küçük and Can, 2020). In contextual stance detection, in addition to the text under consideration, contextual features can also be used such as retweets, user information and other inter-relationships in case of social media posts (Cignarella et al., 2020). Another relevant research problem is *stance quantification* (Küçük, 2022), where the percentages of pieces of text items classified as *favor, against, neutral*, or *none* are expected instead of the individual classification results for the input text items.

Other and more application-specific subproblems of stance detection are *fake news stance detection* and *rumour stance detection*. In fake news stance detection, a news headline and news body are provided and the stance of the body towards the headline is expected, usually in the form of a class label as *agrees, disagrees, discusses*, and *unrelated* (Küçük and Can, 2020; Umer et al., 2020). On the other hand, in rumour stance detection, we have a piece of text and a rumour as input, and the position of the text towards the rumour is expected, usually as *supporting, denying, querying*, and *commenting* (Zubiaga et al., 2018).

Stance detection research problem and its subproblems are shown schematically in Figure 1, based on the related figure given in (Küçük and Can, 2020).

There are a number of stance detection competitions that have been carried out (Küçük and Can, 2020). The initial and most prominent of these competitions is *SemEval-2016 Shared Task on Stance Detection* (Mohammad et al., 2016) performed on English tweets. This competition and its followers for other languages help stance detection researchers by providing annotated datasets and up-to-date information about the performance rates of various approaches applied to the problem.

Various approaches have been applied to the stance detection problem so far, such as rule-based methods, machine learning-based models, deep learning-based models, and hybrid approaches (Küçük and Can, 2022). Transformer learning models fall under the deep-learning methods. Since they are central to main topic of our current survey, they are described in details in the following subsection.

Important machine learning models tested for stance detection include SVM (Mohammad et al., 2016) and neural networks (). Ensemble models such as random forest are also tested for the problem. Considering deep learning approaches, RNN, LSTM, CNN, and transformer-based models are also utilized to solve the stance detection problem. Figure 2 below is taken from (Küçük and Can, 2020) and displays a world cloud of the models used for stance detection, as of 2020.

Figure 1. Stance Detection and Its Subproblems, Mostly Based on the Related Work Given in (Küçük and Can, 2020)

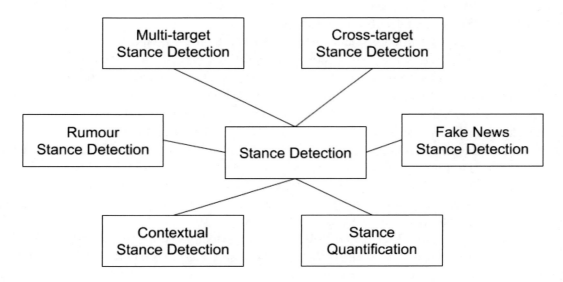

Figure 2. Approaches Used for Stance Detection until 2020 (as Excerpted from (Küçük and Can, 2020))

TRANSFORMER LEARNING MODELS

Transformer learning models are considered a specific type of deep learning models and they are known to be first introduced in (Vaswani et al., 2017). Due to the importance of these learning models and their successful application on different text processing tasks, several recent survey papers have been published on this topic (Tay et al., 2020; Gruetzemacher and Paradice, 2022). We will present a brief overview of these models below and interested readers are referred to (Tay et al., 2020; Gruetzemacher and Paradice, 2022) for more details on transformers.

Transformers are deep learning architectures that are based on the attention mechanism (Vaswani et al., 2017). They are defined as deep neural network architectures which do not use recurrence or convolution mechanisms but instead make use of the attention mechanism (Vaswani et al., 2017). In the original work, they are tested for the machine translation task and achieve better results than the state-of-the-art (Vaswani et al., 2017). Yet, they are employed for many other text and speech processing tasks since their introduction and achieve favorable results (Tay et al., 2020; Gruetzemacher and Paradice, 2022).

Bidirectional Encoder Representations of Transformers (BERT) is one of the most popular transformer learning models (Devlin et al., 2018). Due to the widespread use of BERT, there exist survey papers dedicated to BERT including (Rogers et al., 2020; Xia et al., 2020). BERT is a transformer-based architecture that has pre-training and fine-tuning stages, and during the pre-training stage masked language modeling and next sentence prediction tasks (Rogers et al., 2020).

An improved version of BERT called RoBERTa is described in (Liu et al., 2019) where different decisions are taken to improve the model during the pre-training stage. It is reported that the performance gains obtained from BERT can be increased considerably through changes such as training for longer periods, with bigger chunks of data, among others.

Another transformer-based multilingual language model called XLM-R is described in (Conneau et al., 2020). It is stated in the related study that XLM-R is trained on one hundred languages and the corresponding evaluation results show that XLM-R outperforms multilingual BERT on different cross-lingual benchmarks (Conneau et al., 2020).

Survey of Transformer-Based Stance Detection

Transformer-based architectures have been employed by various studies related to stance detection. The focus of some of these studies is generic (single-target) stance detection, while other studies address particular subproblems of stance detection, such as fake news stance detection and rumour stance detection.

In (Ghosh et al., 2019), a stance detection approach based on BERT is tested along with other deep learning-based and machine learning-based models. Based on the evaluation results reported, the BERT-based approach surpasses the other approaches to the stance detection problem.

The work by Cignarella et al. (2020) describes a shared task (competition) on stance detection on Italian tweets about a specific target (Sardines movement). When analyzing the results of this competition, it is emphasized that four different participants have used different versions of BERT (such as AlBERTo, GilBERTo, UmBERTo) during stance detection on tweets. This work by Cignarella et al. (2020) signifies the prevalence of the use of BERT-based transformer architectures for the stance detection task by different researchers. For instance, among the participants of this shared task, Giorgioni et al. (2020) combine transformer-based models and transfer learning for stance detection.

A multilingual stance detection dataset is proposed in (Vamvas and Sennrich, 2020) and multilingual BERT is tested on this dataset resulting in moderately successful performance rates. This dataset comprises texts in French, German, and Italian.

The study by Calleja and Mendez (2021) is carried our within the scope of a stance detection competition on tweets in Spanish and Basque where the tweets are all about the topic of the vaccines. This study concludes that the best stance detection results for the Spanish tweets are obtained using multilingual BERT (Calleja and Mendez, 2021).

Dulhanty et al. (2019) have used the modified BERT version, called RoBERTa (Liu et al., 2019), in order to achieve improved results for the fake news stance detection task. They report that they obtain state-of-the-art performance rates on the *Fake News Challenge-1* (*FNC-1*) dataset[1] about fake news stance detection.

Fake news stance detection using transformers is also studied in (Slovikovskaya, 2019). First, BERT sentence embeddings are used as an additional feature for the problem and secondly, fine-tuned versions of BERT, XLNet, and RoBERTa are used where state-of-the-art results for the fake news stance detection task are obtained.

Karande et al. (2021) have also tackled with the problem of fake news detection. While doing so, they have considered fake news stance detection and employed BERT embeddings for this purpose. The authors of the study (Karande et al., 2021) claim that their approach based on BERT embeddings achieves state-of-the-art performance rates for fake news stance detection. Rizky and Suyanto (2021) have also used BERT for fake news stance detection problem, and reported their results, where they also employ data augmentation techniques.

Matero et al. (2021) employ a transformer based learning architecture which they call message-level transformer (MeLT) for the stance detection task. They test their approach on the annotated stance dataset from SemEval-2016 shared task on stance detection (Mohammad et al., 2016) and achieve favorable results.

There also exist significant work that apply transformer learning models to the problem of rumor stance detection. These studies include the works by Fajcik et al. (2019), Tian et al. (2020), and Wang et al. (2021). As mentioned in the previous section, rumor stance detection (or, classification) is a particular type of stance detection and is usually considered an indispensable stage in rumour detection and resolution (Zubiaga et al., 2018).

FUTURE RESEARCH DIRECTIONS

Future research directions on transformer-based stance detection can be listed as follows:

1. Stance detection studies are performed for a number of languages including English, Spanish, Italian, Czech, and Turkish (Küçük and Can, 2020). Transformer-based architectures such as the variants of BERT or XLM-R could be employed and evaluated on stance detection datasets in these different languages. The corresponding findings will help better compare the contributions of these models.
2. Comprehensive studies can be performed using transformer learning models for different subproblems of stance detection. The research problems that can be considered as subproblems of stance detection (see Figure 1 in the previous section) can all benefit from transformer-based models.

Hence, future research for these subproblems will contribute to both stance detection research and transformer learning research.

CONCLUSION

Automatic determination of stances from textual content is important for various application domains. The areas that can benefit from automatic stance detection systems include surveys/polls, recommendation systems, and information retrieval systems, among many others. On the other hand, deep learning-based approaches are reported to achieve successful results for many text processing problems. Transformers constitute a specific type of deep learning methods that make use of the attention mechanism. Hence, in this book chapter, we present a brief review of the literature on stance detection studies that utilize transformer-based approaches. Moreover, we list a number of future research directions on our survey topic. We believe that this survey will be helpful for researchers and practitioners that are interested in stance detection and transformer learning methods.

REFERENCES

Calleja, J., & Mendez, A. (2021). SQYQP@ Vaxxstance: Stance detection for the antivaxxers movement. In *Proceedings of the International Conference of the Spanish Society for Natural Language Processing (IberLEF 2021)* (pp. 202-209). Academic Press.

Cignarella, A. T., Lai, M., Bosco, C., Patti, V., & Paolo, R. (2020). Sardistance@EVALITA2020: Overview of the task on stance detection in Italian tweets. In *Proceedings of the Seventh Evaluation Campaign of Natural Language Processing and Speech Tools for Italian (EVALITA 2020)*. 10.4000/books.aaccademia.7084

Conneau, A., Khandelwal, K., Goyal, N., Chaudhary, V., Wenzek, G., Guzmán, F., . . . Stoyanov, V. (2019). *Unsupervised cross-lingual representation learning at scale.* arXiv preprint arXiv:1911.02116.

Devlin, J., Chang, M. W., Lee, K., & Toutanova, K. (2018). *BERT: Pre-training of deep bidirectional transformers for language understanding.* arXiv preprint arXiv:1810.04805.

Dulhanty, C., Deglint, J. L., Daya, I. B., & Wong, A. (2019). *Taking a stance on fake news: Towards automatic disinformation assessment via deep bidirectional transformer language models for stance detection.* arXiv preprint arXiv:1911.11951.

Fajcik, M., Burget, L., & Smrz, P. (2019). *BUT-FIT at SemEval-2019 task 7: Determining the rumour stance with pre-trained deep bidirectional transformers.* arXiv preprint arXiv:1902.10126. doi:10.18653/v1/S19-2192

Ghosh, S., Singhania, P., Singh, S., Rudra, K., & Ghosh, S. (2019). Stance detection in web and social media: A comparative study. In *Proceedings of the International Conference of the Cross-Language Evaluation Forum for European Languages* (pp. 75-87). Springer. 10.1007/978-3-030-28577-7_4

Giorgioni, S., Politi, M., Salman, S., Basili, R., & Croce, D. (2020). UNITOR@Sardistance2020: Combining transformer-based architectures and transfer learning for robust stance detection. In *Proceedings of the Seventh Evaluation Campaign of Natural Language Processing and Speech Tools for Italian (EVALITA 2020)*. 10.4000/books.aaccademia.7092

Gruetzemacher, R., & Paradice, D. (2022). Deep transfer learning & beyond: Transformer language models in information systems research. *ACM Computing Surveys*, *54*(10s), 1–35. Advance online publication. doi:10.1145/3505245

Karande, H., Walambe, R., Benjamin, V., Kotecha, K., & Raghu, T. S. (2021). Stance detection with BERT embeddings for credibility analysis of information on social media. *PeerJ. Computer Science*, *7*, e467. doi:10.7717/peerj-cs.467 PMID:33954243

Küçük, D. (2021). *Stance quantification: Definition of the problem.* arXiv preprint arXiv:2112.13288.

Küçük, D., & Can, F. (2020). Stance detection: A survey. *ACM Computing Surveys*, *53*(1), 1–37. doi:10.1145/3369026

Küçük, D., & Can, F. (2021). Stance detection: Concepts, approaches, resources, and outstanding issues. In *Proceedings of the 44th International ACM SIGIR Conference on Research and Development in Information Retrieval* (pp. 2673-2676). ACM.

Küçük, D., & Can, F. (2022). A tutorial on stance detection. In *Proceedings of the Fifteenth ACM International Conference on Web Search and Data Mining* (pp. 1626-1628). 10.1145/3488560.3501391

Liu, Y., Ott, M., Goyal, N., Du, J., Joshi, M., Chen, D., . . . Stoyanov, V. (2019). *RoBERTa: A robustly optimized BERT pretraining approach.* arXiv preprint arXiv:1907.11692.

Mohammad, S., Kiritchenko, S., Sobhani, P., Zhu, X., & Cherry, C. (2016). SemEval-2016 Task 6: Detecting stance in tweets. In *Proceedings of the 10th International Workshop on Semantic Evaluation (SemEval-2016)* (pp. 31-41). 10.18653/v1/S16-1003

Matero, M., Soni, N., Balasubramanian, N., & Schwartz, H. A. (2021). *MeLT: Message-level transformer with masked document representations as pre-training for stance detection.* arXiv preprint arXiv:2109.08113. doi:10.18653/v1/2021.findings-emnlp.253

Ren, Y., Zhang, Y., Zhang, M., & Ji, D. (2016). Context-sensitive Twitter sentiment classification using neural network. *Proceedings of the Thirtieth AAAI Conference on Artificial Intelligence.* 10.1609/aaai.v30i1.9974

Rizky, L. M. R., & Suyanto, S. (2021). Improving stance-based fake news detection using BERT model with synonym replacement and random swap data augmentation technique. In *Proceedings of the IEEE 7th Information Technology International Seminar (ITIS)* (pp. 1-6). 10.1109/ITIS53497.2021.9791600

Rogers, A., Kovaleva, O., & Rumshisky, A. (2020). A primer in BERTology: What we know about how BERT works. *Transactions of the Association for Computational Linguistics*, *8*, 842–866. doi:10.1162/tacl_a_00349

Slovikovskaya, V. (2019). *Transfer learning from transformers to fake news challenge stance detection (FNC-1) task.* arXiv preprint arXiv:1910.14353.

Tay, Y., Dehghani, M., Bahri, D., & Metzler, D. (2020). *Efficient transformers: A survey.* arXiv preprint arXiv:2009.06732.

Tian, L., Zhang, X., Wang, Y., & Liu, H. (2020). Early detection of rumours on twitter via stance transfer learning. In *Proceedings of the European Conference on Information Retrieval (ECIR)* (pp. 575-588). Springer. 10.1007/978-3-030-45439-5_38

Umer, M., Imtiaz, Z., Ullah, S., Mehmood, A., Choi, G. S., & On, B. W. (2020). Fake news stance detection using deep learning architecture (CNN-LSTM). *IEEE Access: Practical Innovations, Open Solutions*, 8, 156695–156706. doi:10.1109/ACCESS.2020.3019735

Vamvas, J., & Sennrich, R. (2020). X-stance: A multilingual multi-target dataset for stance detection. In *Proceedings of the 5th SwissText & 16th KONVENS Joint Conference* (p. 9). Academic Press.

Vaswani, A., Shazeer, N., Parmar, N., Uszkoreit, J., Jones, L., Gomez, A. N., ... Polosukhin, I. (2017). Attention is all you need. *Advances in Neural Information Processing Systems*, 30.

Wang, X., Feng, W., & Wang, F. (2021). Determining the rumour stance with ensemble method based on BSAF model. In *Proceedings of the 4th International Conference on Computer Science and Software Engineering (CSSE 2021)* (pp. 6-12). 10.1145/3494885.3494887

Xia, P., Wu, S., & Van Durme, B. (2020). *Which* BERT? A survey organizing contextualized encoders.* arXiv preprint arXiv:2010.00854. doi:10.18653/v1/2020.emnlp-main.608

Zubiaga, A., Aker, A., Bontcheva, K., Liakata, M., & Procter, R. (2018). Detection and resolution of rumours in social media: A survey. *ACM Computing Surveys*, 51(2), 1–36. doi:10.1145/3161603

ENDNOTE

1 http://www.fakenewschallenge.org/

Chapter 5
Study of Neural Machine Translation With Long Short–Term Memory Techniques

Mangayarkarasi Ramaiah

https://orcid.org/0000-0003-3088-6001

Vellore Institute of Technology, Vellore, India

Debajit Datta

Vellore Institute of Technology, Vellore, India

Vanmathi C.

Vellore Institute of Technology, Vellore, India

Rishav Agarwal

Columbia University, USA

ABSTRACT

The growing demand for having a conversation amongst people who come from different areas, across the globe, resulting from globalization, has led to the development of systems like machine translations. There are techniques like statistical models, Bayesian models, etc. that were used earlier for machine translations. However, with growing expectations towards better accuracies, neural networks aided systems for translations termed as neural machine translations (NMT) have come up. Models have been proposed by several organizations like Google NMT (G-NMT) that are widely accepted and implemented. Several machine translations are also based on RNN models. This work studies neural machine translations with respect to long short-term memory (LSTM) network and compares them on the basis of several widely accepted accuracy metrics like BLEU score, precision, recall, and F1 score. Further, a combination of two LSTM models is implemented for better accuracy. This work analyzes the various LSTM models on the basis of these metrics.

DOI: 10.4018/978-1-6684-6001-6.ch005

INTRODUCTION

Evolution has always been a constant change over time. The ability to communicate amongst humans is one such evolution that changed the world for the better. As the ability to communicate developed, so did the way to communicate. Now communication can be anything ranging from simple sign language to a telephonic conversation from miles away. But speech, speech is the most efficient and the most used for this activity. Using eleven thousand to around twenty-five thousand words per day, it is evident that for any human being this is the go-to method to facilitate any kind of communication amongst them. A meeting, a discussion, an event, or any such activities require the ability to speak. Now, these speeches may not be comprehensible by all the participants. With evolution, humans have managed to develop different languages and different dialects. Each is similar to the others as they are different. So, how does the world continue the constant exchange of words, of dialects when the involved participants are unable to understand each other? That's when Speech-to-Speech translation comes into play. In this information-driven world, intercommunal exchanges of information are unavoidable. Thus, breaking this language barrier by a digitized medium is very important and necessary using a framework or machine. The innovation that was observed in the Speech Translation machinery is the onset of one speech dialect getting converted naturally to another speech dialect. The difficulty of learning a new language or even remotely understanding the countless languages all around the globe will always be a tedious task for humans, thus, a Speech Translation framework might just be the way out of this difficulty.

Speech Translation can be described in layman's terms by specifying that it takes the voice of the user as an input and provides the output with the same semantic meaning in the language required by the end-user. Google has a framework called the Google Neural Machine Translation (GNMT) that has its algorithm using the Artificial Neural Network (ANN), An improvement over this will be the use of the Recursive Neural Network (RNN) framework. Now, RNN is an architecture that works on the set of a data sequence, assumed to be like a time series, and each of the current samples is dependent on the one before it. RNN has also shown application with an amalgam with the Convolutional layers used in image processing. Machine translation is one of the benchmark use cases of NLP (Natural Language processing). Machine translation (MT) has been complemented with various categories of techniques in the past decades. The ability to communicate amongst humans is one such evolution that changed the world for the better. Machine translation is the automation of converting the textual information in one human language to another human language. While solving the translation problem the Human and the computer both have their inherent challenge. Two human translators can produce matching translations of the same given text in the same language possibly to a certain good extent. The machine needs to face e greater challenge, compared to a human translator. The difficulty of learning a new language or even remotely understanding the countless languages all around the globe will always be a tedious task for humans, thus, a precise Machine Translation framework might just be the way out of this difficulty. The first category of technical approaches to the machine translation problem is the rule-based approach (were to convert a piece of textual information the needs need a lexicon for all the morpheme's morphological, syntactic, and semantic information in both source and target language. Steps to implement RBMT (rule-based machine translation) can be found in Huang et al (2020), and Alvarez et al (2020), and also the authors, discuss the pros and cons of the same. Another category of technique to accomplish Machine Translation is using statistical models. Statistical Machine Translation was presented by Warren Weaver in 1947. Model parameters of SMT are obtained from the analysis of bilingual text corpora. Such type of translation activity is heavily dependent on corpus features, especially the size of the corpus. Decoder

Qiao et al (2020) play a crucial role in the statistical machine translation approach and present various approaches to improvising the decoder along with that the author discusses the solution to overcome the sparse data problem. A new dynamic programming kind of algorithm by Xia et al (2019) is introduced to reduce the computational cost of the algorithm through an alignment-based pruning technique. In trend, Machine translation complemented the development of neural network models. So there comes another category of techniques called Neural Machine Translation (NMT) has emerged and received substantial attention.

A neural network shows similarity to the structure of neurons in the human brain. Neural Networks have different layers (the input layer, the hidden layer, and the output layer). Neural Networks execute works based on finding the connection and the patterns amongst datasets that might be too cast or difficult for humans to work upon Tufano et al (2019) Recurrent Neural Network is that branch of the neural network that works with series input rather than many inputs, that is, each node has some dependency on the previous nodes. It can be devised that RNN words as with the concept of feedback series, that is, it bases its decision on the output of the past. A neural network works on the applied weights that have been given to it, and the output is dependent on that particular weight. RNN has the concept of the hidden layer as well, thus, allowing the algorithm to get the output based on weights and prior knowledge of adjacent outputs encountered in the past. The "recurrent" nature of the network is shown when the change taking place or the function that has been applied to a particular input set is continuously applied and the subsequent output is formulated sequentially. There is no limitation as to the size of the entire vector of the dataset. The noteworthy aspect of this algorithm is that the hidden state, which is based on the previous state, also gets updated by the output of the previous nodes, thus, making the current output dependent upon the current input, the weights, and the previous states Nishimura et al (2019) Artificial Neural Network can be defined as a self-learning system which tries to mimic the neurons of the biological brain. This connectionist system takes other examples as the training dataset and formulates the output without the requirement of extensive programming. It has a fully connected or a complete graph structure, thus, each neuron can receive the inputs and then pass them on to every node in the structure, to get the desired output. Although ANN seems a desirable algorithm for Speech Translation, it begs the question as to why use RNN. The advantages of RNN over ANN can be attributed to its feedback or the constant backpropagation technique. RNN takes into account the previous state or sample and the current one is always dependent on the previous one. The number of states or the number of times the recurrent process will be taking place is not fixed, that is unlimited states can be dealt with, unlike the case in Finite State Automats or hidden Markov Models, thus, giving the work a more well-developed algorithm for computation.

The motive of this work is to get the speech of a particular language as an input and produce a spoken dialect in the required language with the same semantic meaning. The entire work is summarized into a three-stage model-Speech Recognition, Machine Translation, and Speech Synthesis. Once the user gives the framework the input as speech (voice), the input is converted to text (of that particular language), the text is then converted to the text of the required language, and then the subsequent output is formulated as speech (voice) of the converted language. The use of Google APIs is done for speech-to-text and text-to-speech, while the Recurrent Neural Network framework is used for machine translation, that is, text-to-text from one language to another. The paper goes on to elaborate on the concept of RNN that is used for translation. The architecture showcasing the communication protocols and the client-server mechanism has also been portrayed. The entire research works on elaborating the field of Speech Translation keeping in mind that the semantic meaning is preserved while the change takes place. The annotations and the ambiguity in the speeches are disregarded (ambiguities like sarcasm, idioms, and such). The basis of this paper is that it focuses on the data available to it in a spoken interactive format. This work brings out the requirement of such a speech translation mechanism in an overly-connected world and brings out the advantages in doing so. The increase in efficiency is also kept in mind to avoid most errors that may be encountered during the translation process. There are NSR models Soltau et al (2016) that have a deep LSTM RNN architecture built by stacking multiple LSTM layers, similarly, some works propose attention-based NMT Luong et al (2015). Though there are a reasonable amount of techniques proposed in the literature using NMT, Still there is a demand for the best translation system with better accuracy. In this paper, a Machine translation system is demonstrated using RNN, and LSTM Models and a combination of bidirectional LSTM with the LSTM encode-decode model is proposed to obtain the best possible results. The rest of the paper is organized as follows –section 2 of this work discusses some of the benchmark approaches presented in the literature against Machine translation. Section 3 drafts the insight into the proposed work along with the steps used for designing the hybrid model for machine translation using LSTM. Section 4 provides the implementation of the system and section 5 discusses the experimental results. Finally, in section 6 of this work, the conclusion is drawn along with the possible extension of this work.

RELATED WORK

Machine translation and recurrent neural networks have both been the subject of several studies. To develop procedures that can improve machine translation, researchers have developed several ways and approaches. They have also examined several variables that are pertinent to the development of machine translation systems in the future.

Soltau et al. (2016) claim that the NSR model's deep LSTM RNN architecture was built by stacking different LSTM layers. Because the bidirectional RNN models have better accuracy and are used for offline voice recognition on the system, they have used two LSTM layers at each depth, one acting in the forward direction in time over the input sequence and the other acting in the backward direction. Their study used the Vocabulary corpus, a collection of 296 films from 13 different genres with an average runtime of 5 minutes. The system would have been fantastic if they had been able to resolve concerns like the error rates. Because the references are in text, working with the CTC spoken word model is difficult. Even so, because the output of the model is spoken, it occasionally makes fake errors such as substituting "three" for "3." The entire architecture of the voice recognizer is replaced with a single neural network. However, accuracy can be increased with statistical machine translation based on deep neural networks, as proposed by Xia (2020). The method uses a binary convolutional neural network whose weights are applied to the input sequence iteratively until it generates a single fixed-length vector, according to research by Cho et al (2014). The UN (421M words), press commentary (5.5M words), Europarl (61M words), and two crawling corpora are among the large datasets used to build the model (90M and 780M words, respectively). This study shows that neural machine translation performs rather well on short phrases without unknown terms, but that performance swiftly degrades as sentence length and the percentage of unfamiliar words increase. The model has received good testing and training. It does an excellent job of translating words accurately. By using techniques based on encoder-decoder technology, the work may successfully highlight the properties of a neural machine translation system. The system has to look into various neural designs, especially for the decoder. The performance of neural machine translation is significantly hampered by the length of phrases. Additionally, Senrich et al. (2016)'s study incorporates recurrent neural networks along with an encoder-decoder network to build the neural machine translation system. The dataset used in this study is from WMT 2015 and contains about 100 million tokens or 4.2 million phrase pairings. The study examines the applicability of several word segmentation techniques, such as segmentation based on the byte pair encoding compression algorithm and straightforward character n-gram models. Their research suggests that neural machine translation systems can translate words from an open vocabulary by encoding uncommon and unknown words as a series of sub-word units. According to a study by Kumar et al., these systems can also be extended to more languages in the future (2020). The system has several flaws that need to be considered and fixed, thus it is not ideal. Bilingually informed segmentation algorithms have a greater chance of creating more alignable sub-word units even when they cannot rely on the target text at runtime.

Wu et al (2016) .'s research focuses on a model that closely adheres to the conventional sequence-to-sequence learning paradigm. Its three components are an encoder network, a decoder network, and an attention network. Since the work is based on a range of datasets from numerous language pairs, no linguistic adjustments are necessary. The project is comprehensive and is centered on the GNMT, or Google Neural Machine System, that is anticipated. The results that GNMT generates for the English-to-German and English-to-French standards of the WMT'14 are competitive and cutting edge. The Word piece modeling successfully solves open vocabularies and the issue of morphologically rich languages in terms of translation quality and inference time. There are certain issues with the proposed system, but these can be fixed going forward. The translation is reduced by the GNMT technology by about 60%. The system is separated into distinct modules according to Chen et al(2017) .'s research for better deployment, recovery, and development. The system is based on the LDC dataset for ZH-EN, which deals with translations between Chinese and English. The paper uses the NN joint model based on the Dependency-based Bilingual Context Sequence (DBiCS) (DNNJM). The DNNJM that the authors of the research have proposed is made up of two parts: the first is based on an out-layer feed-forward NN, and the second is an in-layer BiCNN for improving accuracy. The phrase-based translation job is done with the created DNNJM. The experiment's findings are remarkably accurate. With this approach, SMT performance can be improved. The filter can be replaced with the suggested DNNJM in addition to the decoding of PBT and HPBT using k-based rescoring. The method can be enhanced for better translation prediction, including ambiguous translations and word form translations, according to the proposed work's limits.

According to the work of Zhang et al (2017), the most important factor on which the model depends is sentence length. When the disjoint sentences were grouped according to their length, it was noticed that the system resulted in better performance when it came to shorter sentences. They have worked with NIST 2005 dataset for the Chinese dataset and WMT2014 data for the English-German words as their dataset. Thus, the system is capable of translations of English-Chinese and English-German. In the paper, the authors have discussed that context representation is learned from right to left for creating a context-aware recurrent encoder. The CA Encoder is capable of assembling the context from the past as well as predicting the future. The proposed experiments on Chinese-English and English-German translation using FCA Encoder and BCA Encoder are capable of portraying the efficiency of the model that has been proposed. There is a major drawback of the paper that can be considered in the future. The drop in BLEU points for larger sentences is a big limitation of the system proposed. The model fails to integrate sequence-to-sequence tasks. Optimization of the model can be further done extending it to document-level translations.

In the research work of Wang et. al. (2018) the coverage information is very important as the SMT model cannot record which source words are covered. Alignment information also plays an important role in understanding the SMT approaches. The system is built on the NIST dataset for Chinese-to-English which consists of 1.25 million data. In the work, the system is built on attention-based neural machine translation. The attention-based neural machine translations are used for fetching the target word. A statistical machine on the other hand is implemented within the log-linear framework. Incorporating SMT knowledge into NMT encoder-decoder architecture has improved the NMT translation performance. There is only one big enhancement that can be implemented for future work. The proposed method in the paper can be extended for a larger size word-based STM and NMT model. The proposed model ignores the feature values of STM word recommendation which are useful in NMT and can be considered in future work. In the research work of Singh et al (2017) the authors propose that joint translation is one of the important aspects where the prediction of the target word is carried out. Binary tree for creating target language finite state automata and implementing context-free grammar. The dataset used in the work is English-Hindi bilingual corpus containing 120,000 words with their feature values. The paper deals with machine-based translations using deep neural networks which are nothing but neural networks with more than one hidden layer in the model. Words are aligned within the corpus to generate meaningful sentences. Various models like the Skip-gram and CBOW are used for word2vec processing. Recursive and recurrent neural networks are used for selecting the rules and reordering sentences Nishimura, et al (2019). Language modeling is carried out in FNN for optimizing the score. They concluded that the system worked properly. The authors have proposed that RNN and RAE have been used provide a better result in text processing and GPU solves complex computation problems. The system has several reconstruction and reordering errors present, which can be concentrated on and worked on in the future. Also, LSTM can be implemented along with the existing system to optimize the whole thing for better accuracy. The work of Wang et al (2018) authors have proposed in the work that dynamic sentence weighting plays a vital role in the model, where every sentence is associated with an in-domain ratio, which keeps increasing gradually. The dataset associated with their work is vast and not just a single one. Along with the IWSLT-2014 EN-FR dataset and IWSLT-2015 EN-DE dataset, publicly available EN-FR parallel corpora from JRC-Acquis, Gnome, KDE, European Central Bank, United Nations documents, OpenOffice, PHP, and Ubuntu have been used as a dataset. The authors in this paper have talked about the role of sentence selection in neural machine translations. In the system, sentence embedding is taken place where annotations are vectorized. Sentence Scoring is carried out after which sentences are selected based on the scores that are obtained. Sentences are given weight based on their domain and batch weighting is also given. The work, as proposed by the authors, is compared to the existing work presented for machine translations. It has been observed that the method proposed by the authors has outperformed most of the approaches, making it highly useful for future work. Although the work is appreciable, at the same time, it should be considered that the proposed method is based on the translation of EN to FR (English – French) or EN to DE (English – German), but it can be broadened to other languages too in future works.

The work of Luong et al (2015) is on the different approaches to attention-based Neural Machine Translation. This paper takes two models, the NMT, and the Attention-based model, and combines both to get a higher BLEU value and to make the combined model a more effective one. The purpose of this paper is to improve the NMT (neural machine translation) using the attention-based model, specifically, the local attention-based model. The results, as showcased by this paper, are that the local attention-based NMT had an increase in efficiency of up to 5.0 BLEU over the non-attentional models. The work of Cho, et al (2014) the paper proposes the use of a novel neural network model, the Recurrent Neural Networks (RNN) Encoder-Decoder. The work that this paper address is the performance analysis of Statistical Machine Translation (SMT) using the RNN Encoder-Decoder. The model has been described to work simultaneously, that is they are trained together to gain the most efficient probability of a target output based on a source input. The work of Ott et al (2018) explores approaches to improve training on a single machine and effectiveness. They minimize training time by 65% while maintaining accuracy by using training with lower floating-point precision. The WMT'14 English-German and WMT'14 English-French data sets were used in the presented work. According to Koehn et al. (2017), the researchers used standard toolkits for classical phrase-based statistical machine translation and neural machine translation with standard data sets taken from WMT and OPUS. The experiment used the WMT English-Spanish and German-English datasets. In their 2016 study, Kalchbrenner et al. introduced the ByteNet, a neural translation model that decouples translation from memory, has linear running time, and has short signal propagation channels for tokens in sequences. The research by Chaudhary and Patel (2018) compares how several neural networks, including CNN, FNN, RNN, RAE, and attention-based neural networks, are created. To enhance the effectiveness of machine translation, various models, such as the splicing model and similarity models, are explained. The proposed algorithm, according to Chaudhary and Patel's (2018) research, consists of four main steps: gathering all the Japanese-English vocabulary data; developing a recurrent neural network for text encoding using Python; training the model using a language corpus, and translating Japanese into English. The choice of the translation rule is done after the language has been translated.

According to the work of Artetxe et al (2017), the shared encoder uses fixed cross embeddings with monolingual data to reconstruct its input. The model also incorporates the use of back-translation into the training procedure for improving performance. The encoder uses a two-layer bidirectional RNN whereas the decoder uses a 4-layer RNN. The single RNN contains GRU cells with 600 units and the dimensions of the embedding are set to 300. Understanding the original message from the proposed translation is greatly hampered by fluency and adequacy issues that the suggested model fails to address. The research work of Tu et al (2016) advocated a coverage mechanism for neural-based translation to solve the issues of under-translation and over-translation. The coverage vector is appended to the intermediate representation of an NMT model, which is sequentially updated after each attentive iteration of the decoding process. The coverage vector can improve the over-alignment between the source and target sentences by adjusting the future attention. According to the work of Lample et al (2018)], The unsupervised machine translation model consists of three components: initialization of translation models, language modeling, and iterative back-translation. In the initialization stage, instead of considering the words, they considered byte-pair encodings. Instead of explicit mapping, the byte-pair encodings can be considered by jointly processing both monolingual pairs. The language modeling stage is attained by denoising autoencoding. Since it makes sense to integrate parallel corpora and monolingual corpora to develop bidirectional NMT translation models in a semi-supervised situation, Cheng (2019) uses autoencoders to reconstruct the monolingual corpora. The dataset for Chinese-English experiments was used. Our joint model was trained by the authors using mini-batch stochastic gradient descent. It is intriguing to investigate the more accessible, abounding monolingual corpora to enhance NMT. A machine translation system from English to French that is built on various RNN models is the subject of Datta et al (2020) .'s research. The dataset utilized in this system contains the GitHub datasets "small_vocab_en" and "small_vocab_fr." However, the approach that is suggested does not take into account different assessment techniques.

PROPOSED FRAMEWORK

Proposed Framework Using Hybridization

The juxtaposition of the Artificial Neural Network (ANN) and the Recurrent Neural Network (RNN) is immaculate. The advantages, that are observed, are of using ANN as the widely-used algorithm in the concepts of learning the model and solving non-linear and complex relationships amongst the datasets. The less popular algorithm is the Recurrent Neural Network (RNN) which has clear advantages over ANN like its dependent nature over the previous nodes, and the backpropagation of the samples, all of these allows for the validation of the assumption as it works for modeling of a sequence of data, like the time series model. The Long Short Term Memory (LSTM) networks, which are based on RNN, can also be used for neural machine translation, however, when it comes to providing a gap in lengths, LSTM overpowers RNN in having insensitivity that helps it in recalling from any interval.

This work aims to compare the performances of the various LSTM and RNN models that are widely used and visualize the various accuracy metrics associated with them including the precision score, recall score, F1 score, and BLEU score. This work, after analyzing the various accuracy metrics scores of the different models, finally creates a hybrid model by combining the models with higher accuracies, to test the final accuracy of the system. In this work, the final model is obtained by the combination of the Bidirectional LSTM model and the LSTM that is facilitated with embeddings.

System Architecture

The application facilitating language conversion is not scarce. Several mobile-based and web-based applications can be found online which convert the written text in some language to some other required language. Google Translator is also highly capable of doing such translation processes; however, it again takes a text in a particular dialect and converts it to the text format of another dialect. In this scenario, the purpose of this system can be made very clear. It takes in the input of a sentence and processes it by word of mouth, that is, it listens to an input in a particular language and then gives an output in the required language.

The components that are being used in this work are the Google Text-to-Speech, a Python library, the CLI tool (gTTS API) and the Google Speech Recognition API along with the RNN model which will help in the text conversion from one language to another. This system proposes a study of several LSTM networks in successfully translating from one particular language, here English, to another, here French. Be it the Google Translation application or other iOS or Android mobile applications, Artificial Neural Network dominates the market when it comes to such translations between texts. Google also has its own neural machine translation system called Google Neural Machine Translation (G-NMT) which can provide very high accuracy.

This work skirts from using ANN and RNN, and goes on with LSTM because of its inevitable advantage over ANN when using a series of data that can be and are dependent upon each other and also over RNN by being insensitive in nature when it comes to considering gap lengths. The architecture of the system is shown in Figure 1 which clearly shows that the entire system is broadly divided into three parts – it begins with recognition of speech that is aided by Google API, a translation module that has several LSTM models and RNN model, and the last section that generates speech, which is also aided with Google Text-To-Speech API. Despite the advantages of LSTM over RNN and ANN, it still lacks the consideration of several parameters that are considered by the widely accepted G-NMT. This work studies several different models of LSTM as shown in Figure 1, which is benchmarked with the GNMT translations, to compare the reach of these models.

Figure 1. Architecture diagram of proposed Neural Machine Translation system

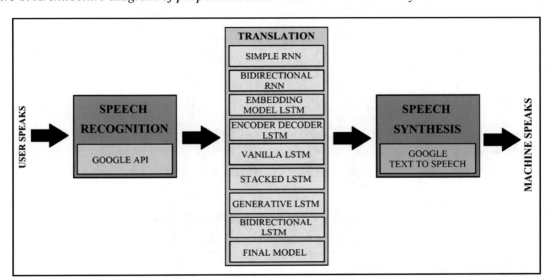

LSTM Architecture

Various LSTM models have been used in this work, ranging from simple LSTM model to bidirectional LSTM model, LSTM with embeddings as well as LSTM with encoder and decoders.

The architecture of the simple LSTM model is shown in Figure 2, where the sigma denotes the sigmoid layer that generates numbers between zero and one, to let a fraction of input through the component to the next layer. The tanh shown in Figure 2 represents the hyperbolic tangent layer, that creates a vector of values for the new candidates Olah (2018). Finally, the most likely word, corresponding to the highest value, is given as output and forwarded to the next step.

Figure 2. Simple LSTM Architecture

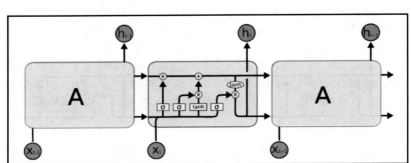

The simple LSTM model is also known as the Vanilla LSTM model. The different models are compared based on their accuracy metrics scores. The final model that has been used in this system merges the bidirectional LSTM and LSTM that are facilitated with embeddings since they have been observed to provide higher accuracies, as specified in further sections.

Figure 3. Bidirectional LSTM Architecture

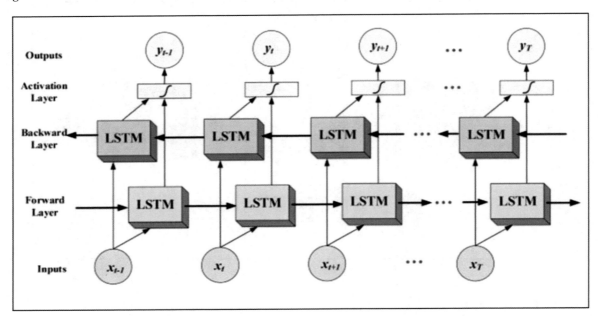

The bidirectional LSTM as shown in Figure 3, in addition to the simple LSTM, considers the input in backward sequences too, which experimentally gives higher accuracies. Further, the outputs of the layers are passed on to the next layer, by either adding the results or multiplying them, or simply concatenating them or the average values are considered.

The architecture for the LSTM model with embeddings is shown in Figure 4, which works on embeddings, along with the usual LSTM Agrawal (2019). The tokens of words are converted into embeddings of a specific size, considering the overall size of vocabulary and the dimension of the embedding. A data structure like the look-up table or the weight matrix is maintained, and accordingly, weightage is given to individual embeddings to the overall vocabulary. In other words, an embedding can be compared with that of any representation in vector form of words that are nearly similar to the words in a multidimensional space. The multidimensional is decided by the size of the vectors with embedding.

The encoder-decoder LSTM, as shown in Figure 5, has a unique ability to input and output sequences of random lengths. The sequence of current input along with the summary of the sequence of past input is taken into account by Park et al (2018). The LSTM model takes the summary of the input sequence into account which makes it able to work with variable lengths of the input sequence.

Figure 4. LSTM with embeddings Architecture Agrawal (2019)

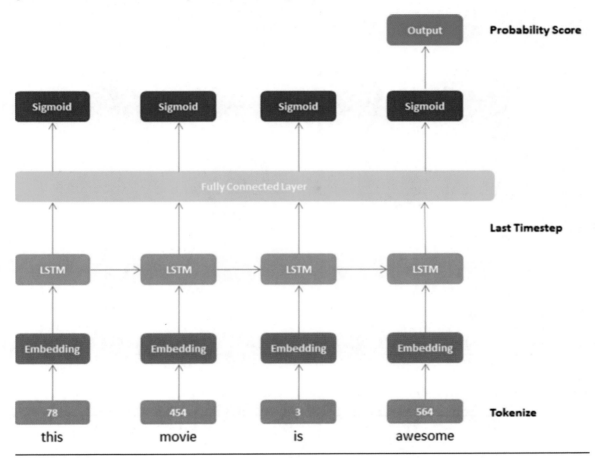

Hybrid LSTM Architecture

After considering the accuracy metrics into account, the hybrid model is designed by taking into account the bidirectional LSTM model as well as the LSTM model with embeddings. The two models are merged Al-Sabahi et al (2018) such that the embeddings are added onto the vectors and then the bidirectional LSTM concept is applied to it.

The architecture as shown in Figure 6, has an embedding layer additional to that of the normal bidirectional layer and the activation layer that has been used is SoftMax. The hybridization of the LSTM model increases the accuracy and provides better scores for the accuracy metrics as discussed in the further sections.

Figure 5. Encoder-Decoder LSTM Architecture Park et al (2018)

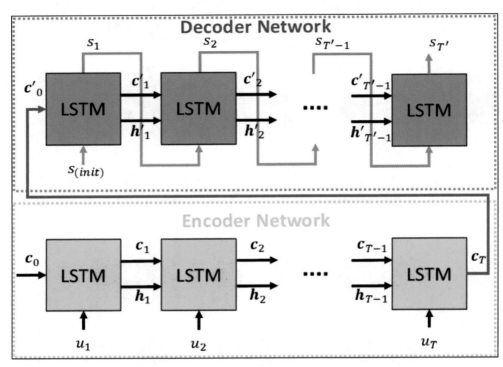

Figure 6. Hybrid LSTM with Bidirectional and Embedding Architecture

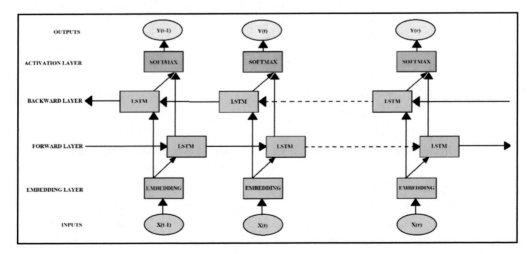

Module-Wise Distribution of The System

The Module for Speech Recognition

This is the first module of this work and it deals with taking the auditory input (speech) and converting it into the corresponding text. The input is given by the user in the speech format, that is, audio format. The module takes in the said input, and using certain libraries extracts the required sentence from the audio, and correspondingly converts it into the required text of the same language as the speech. To carry out the conversion from speech to text, the Google Speech Recognition API has been used. This is a prominent application programming interface that allows for speech-to-text conversion. It can recognize more than 120 languages and different dialects. It automatically recognizes the language that is spoken and correspondingly converts it into accurate text. This API has a real-time no-latency ability, that is, it provides the text as the user is speaking the time gap is reduced tremendously. This API also can automatically recognize proper nouns and convert the word accordingly, giving an accurate text with context.

The system required downloading of certain other python libraries as well to get specific features apart from speech recognition, which is essential for providing proper working of this module in a Python environment. The 'Speech Recognition' library and 'Pyaudio' library were installed for further support. Pyaudio library is used by the system to access or facilitate the use of the microphone via which the input speech can be given to the system. The 'Speech Reognition' library is used for background subtraction of noises to gain the actual speech that has to be evaluated. Noises like whispering, or redundant voices of other people, noises like footsteps or construction sounds, all these ambient noises are canceled out by this library and the foreground audio is extracted. This extracted audio is actual user-inputted speech, which is then further converted into the required text using the API, as mentioned previously. This converted text goes as the input for the next module, the Machine Translation module, which is the main focus of this research.

The Module for Machine Translation

The second module of this work is termed the Machine Translation module. It is the crux of this research work, as the implementation of the RNN and LSTM models takes place in this module, and the main result is obtained here to get synthesized in the next module. This module receives its input from the Speech Recognition module, in the form of the text converted from the speech by the proposed API. Before the text, which is used as input in this module, can be converted to the subsequently required language, certain prerequisite steps need to be followed. The preprocessing of the text is required before it can be converted to the required language. The entire text, which is fed as input into the module, is in the form of a sentence or a group of words. These words are required to be tokenized so that the unique identification of the sentence can be successfully carried out. After the process of tokenization on the sentences, each word or token is padded, to make each of them of the same length.

Once the pre-processing of the input text is implemented without any flaw, the flow of the system moves to the conversion of the text from one language to the required language using several models. This process is entirely carried out on the RNN and the LSTM models, like the Simple RNN model, the bidirectional RNN model, the LSTM with embedding, the encoder-decoder LSTM, the vanilla LSTM, the stacked LSTM, the generative LSTM, and the bidirectional LSTM. Based on the accuracies that are obtained, the system is also trained using a final model that combines other models for giving better accuracies.

The process of encoder-decoder is an important aspect of this LSTM implementation since it consists of two LSTM networks that act as a pair to encode and decode the input or the given state. The encoder maps the sequence, which is of variable length, into a fixed-length vector by the padding of the tokens. The decoder, on the other hand, does the reversal of the encoder by mapping it back to its variable length, to get the actual output in the correct format. In between the working of the encoder-decoder pair, the model works on converting the encoded tokens into the subsequent output based on the dataset that was used to train the same.

The sequence-to-sequence aspect is used where the current state gets its output based on what the current state is and what the previous state's output was. Taking an example into consideration, the English sentence, "we are a computer program" roughly translates into "nous sommes un program Informatique" in the French language. Translation of sentences is different compared to translating words, like if one word is changed, an entire frame of sentence can change because of it – for example, if "we" in "we are a computer program" is changed to "they", forming the sentence "they are a computer program", then the subsequent output becomes "c'est un program Informatique". The change of a single word changes how the word "are" is converted, which shows that the word "are" is not only dependent on itself but is also dependent on the previous word, and the reason our model can predict it is that it takes into consideration the previous words too. If that would not have been the case, then "are" would have simply been converted to its French counterpart, based on the dataset, and both the above sentence would have had the same text for that particular token. This is a prime example of why the LSTM and RNN models and their feature of having a feedback loop are important for this work.

This entire work demonstrates and compares the accuracy of the translation between two languages, English and French, based on the premise but using different models conjugated with the RNN and LSTM models. Once the output from this module is generated it is passed on to the next module, which is the Speech Synthesis module, as its input.

The Module for Speech Synthesis

This module is the final module of this system that deals with the synthesis of speech, hence the name, the Speech Synthesis module. The module takes translated text as an input from the Machine Translation module and gives the output to the user as a speech. It takes different inputs from the different models of RNN and LSTM that do the translation process in the previous module and it provides the subsequent speech output for the same. The main function of this module is to convert the text that is already converted from one language to another, into the speech of the same destination language. Unlike the previous modules, the output from this module is an audio output. The machine is made to "speak" the converted text in the required language, having been translated from the source language, thus, providing the user with the required speech or output.

For the conversion of text-to-speech, a Google Text-to-Speech API has been used, which allows for the users to get a near-to-human speech in an audio format in a particular language (MP# or LINEAR16) of a text input provided to it in that very language. This software allows for the selection of different voices with different accents belonging to different genders to get varying modes of the audio files or the auditory outputs. The use of this API allows the system to easily get the speech format of the translated speech to the user.

These three modules comprise the entirety of this research, however, the main focus is given to the translation part. The chain of the input-output goes from the speech of the source language to the text of the same language to the text of the destination language and finally, to the speech of that language. This provides users with an efficient way to get the required translation of their speech. This work goes on to evaluate the result and analysis of the accuracy of all the different RNN and LSTM models that have been implemented, and showcases as to which model trumps the accuracy and efficiency of the others.

IMPLEMENTATION

Hardware and Software Requirements

The system is implemented on the Kaggle platform, which is a platform that is open to all. It is widely popular amongst data science and machine learning enthusiasts since the platform provides really good CPU and GPU along with Python3-enabled notebooks, with access to several Python libraries that can be installed as well. This platform also has a huge collection of datasets that can be downloaded and used for research purposes. The work has been carried out in the Python environment, and several Python libraries and APIs have been used for coming up with a successful machine translation system.

Dataset Used for The System

The entire premise of this work is wildly dependent upon the dataset that has been employed. The translation that is facilitated by this work is from English to French. The system requires the datasets of English and French sentences to train the various models, and then get the required result once the data has been inputted. The dataset that is chosen for this work has been taken from the 'statmt.org' website of the dataset from WMT Workshop 2014.

The dataset has been presented in the ninth workshop on statistical machine translation of English-French and French-English. The dataset has been compared and evaluated using the G-NMT model provided by Google which is widely accepted. The English corpus comprises several English words along with the French corpus with many French words.

Methodology

This system works with the Long Short Term Memory (LSTM) network along with a few Recurrent Neural Network (RNN) models, for training the dataset. Both LSTM and RNN work with a looping mechanism, which allows for the current state to be dependent on the current node as well as the previous nodes, to recollect data from any instance of time. This work is broadly divided into three fine-grain modules, which are interdependent, following this very feedback loop of RNN structure. The first part or module is the Speech Recognition module, which takes in the input as an auditory input, in English, in this case. This module converts the speech to text of the particular language which will then be processed further. Thus, for the first module, the input is the speech that is given by the user, in a particular language, and the output is the text of the same speech in the same language. Further, in the next module, the output from the first module is used as the input for the second. In simple words, the text that is formulated in the first module becomes the input for the second module, Machine Translation. This is the most important module of this work because this is where the main translation between one language to another takes place using several different models for training the dataset. The probability calculation for input sequence $(x_1,..., x_T)$ is provided in equation (1), where $x_1,..., x_T$ are the input sequence and $y_1,..., y_{T'}$ is its corresponding output sequence, and $p(y_1,..., y_{T'} \mid x_1,..., x_T)$ is the conditional probability.

$$p\left(y_1,\ldots,y_{T'}|x,\ldots,x_T\right) = \prod_{t=1}^{T'} p\left(y_1|v,y_1,\ldots,y_{t-1}\right)$$

In this module, a simple RNN model, a bidirectional RNN model with several LSTM models and concepts is used to convert the text of a particular language to a text of a different language, in the case of this system it is English to French. The third and final module is the Speech Synthesis module which takes in the output from the previous module, that is, the translation module. Here the translated text is further converted into the speech of the destination language, in this case, it is French. This model synthesizes or formulates speech from the given text using a text-to-speech API.

$$d = argmax_T P(T \mid S) \tag{2}$$

The most likely translation Ť, as shown in equation (2), is calculated according to the LSTM, where T is the correct translation and S is the source sentence, and P is the probability function.

Accuracy Metrics

The system provides four accuracy measures – BLEU score, Precision, Recall and F1 score. These metrics help in evaluating the system, that is benchmarked with the G-NMT translations.

Precision

Precision is a widely accepted metric that is used for evaluating the accuracy of a machine learning model. It is defined as the ratio of relevant information that has been retrieved from the model versus all the information that has been retrieved by the model as shown in equation (3), where correct is the count of words that are translated correctly, and the length is the length of the output of the translation, in other words, it is the total number of words in the output. However, when it comes to machine translation, it is calculated as the ratio of the number of translated words that are identical to the translation done by the benchmark model, to the total number of words in the translated sentence Maučec et al (2019).

$$precision = \frac{correct}{length_o} \tag{3}$$

The value of precision lies between 0 to 1, the value is 1 when all the retrieved information is relevant and identical to that of the translated sentence by the benchmark model, while a 0 signifies that there is no similarity at all.

Recall

Recall measure is defined as the ratio of the relevant information that is retrieved versus all the relevant information that exists in the input as shown in question (4), where correct is the count of words that are translated correctly, and length is the length of the reference of the translation, in other words, it is the total number of words in the desired or reference output.

$$recall = \frac{correct}{length_r} \tag{4}$$

In terms of machine translation, it is calculated as the relevant meaning of the output speech, as compared to all relevant meaning that could have been retrieved - in other words, it is calculated as the ratio of the number of translated words that are identical to the translation done by the benchmark model, to the total number of words in the sentence that is translated using the benchmark model Maučec et al (2019). The value of recall ranges from 0 to 1, where 0 signifies that different information has been retrieved from the model, whereas,1 signifies that a completely similar sentence has been retrieved.

F1 Score

The F1 score is a better measurement tool as it allows for the balance between precision and recall measures. It is calculated as the harmonic mean of precision and recalls Maučec et al (2019). which is simplified as the ratio of twice the product of precision and recall, to that of the sum of precision and recall as shown in equation (5).

$$F_1 = \frac{2 * \left(precision\right)\left(recall\right)}{precision + recall} \tag{5}$$

In an uneven distribution of large negative values, the measure of accuracy might fail to give appropriate results, this is where the F1 score comes in, as it considers that anomaly and provides the most accurate value of the models. Its value also ranges from 0 to 1 just like precision and recall.

BLEU Score

The BLEU score corresponds directly to how efficient a particular model is when it comes to machine translation. By definition, the BLEU score evaluates the quality of the text output that is received via a machine translation. Its value ranges from 0 to 1, and it depicts how similar the output of the speech in a different language is to the input of the speech in a particular language. The BLEU score is used for calculating the total overlap of a unigram and the high-order n-grams Maučec et al (2019) between the output that is obtained from machine translation and that of the reference translations, as shown in equation (6), where the length is the length of the reference of the translation and length is the length of the output of the translation.

$$BLEU = \min\left(1, \frac{length_o}{length_r}\right)\left(\prod_{i=1}^{4} precision\left(i\right)\right)^{\left(\frac{1}{4}\right)} \qquad (6)$$

A value of 0 signifies that the sentence is entirely different, and the value of 1 signifies that the sentence is completely similar which is very challenging to attain, thus, very few translations will have a value very close to 1. A good value would be anything above 0.5 which signifies that it is highly similar.

RESULTS AND ANALYSIS

To get the best result and to come up with a better algorithm to facilitate the machine translation work, the system worked on several models including the simple RNN model, the LSTM with embedding, the bidirectional RNN, LSTM with embedded encoder and decoder, vanilla LSTM, stacked LSTM, generative LSTM, and bidirectional LSTM. Inbuilt functions of Keras have been used for implementing the models. The accuracy measures that have been collected, after the successful implementation of models, are tabulated and the plots are done using the matplotlib library of Python.

The plots result in proper visualization of the accuracy measures and help in comparison which helps in having a better analysis. All the graphs display a juxtaposition of different models, showing how each model fairs when subjected to different outlooks. A final model has been created by combining the bidirectional LSTM along with the LSTM with embedding. The combination of the two models results in better accuracy of the entire system along with better bleu score, precision, recall, and F1 score.

Table 1 displays a tabular representation of all the different parametric values, associated with accuracies of different models, that have been observed while building the final model for the system. All the different models show varying degrees of value showcasing how various models trump over another, and how accurate the final model is that has been used to create the system.

Table 1. Various accuracy parameters of the models used in NMT

Model	Accuracy	Bleu Score	Precision	Recall	F1 Score
Simple RNN	40.87	0.01	0.00	0.00	0.00
Bidirectional RNN	61.64	38.86	0.63	0.50	0.56
Embedding model LSTM	80.01	41.20	0.84	0.65	0.74
Bidirectional LSTM	66.55	41.20	0.72	0.54	0.61
Vanilla LSTM	58.73	30.43	0.66	0.50	0.57
Stacked LSTM	61.04	29.10	0.65	0.50	0.56
Generative LSTM	63.89	29.38	0.43	0.34	0.38
Encoder-Decoder LSTM	54.67	40.00	0.70	0.50	0.58
Final model	95.8	53.48	0.89	0.70	0.78

The visualization of several accuracy metrics like precision, recall, F1-score and BLEU score is shown in Figure 7, where M1 is the simple RNN model, M2 is the bidirectional model, M3 is the LSTM model with embedding, M4 is the bidirectional LSTM model, M5 is the vanilla LSTM model, M6 is the stacked LSTM, M7 is the generative LSTM model, M8 is the encoder-decoder enabled LSTM model and M9 is the final model that is formed using a combination of bidirectional LSTM along with LSTM model that is facilitated with embedding. As highlighted from the tabulated data and plotted graphs, the importance of the Long Short Term Memory network outperforms several RNN models; the Long Short Term Memory network model, as the name suggests, is a model which can "remember" information for an arbitrary amount of time, that is, from any instance, the data can be recalled. LSTM works based on feedback connections, where instead of working on a single data point it takes in a whole stream of data, thus, making it very useful in the field of text analysis, or speech analysis. The use of different LSTM models in this system brings out a good contrast to show how much a simple LSTM model like the vanilla LSTM model can outperform the RNN models. The entire system has been benchmarked with the translation provided by G-NMT since it is widely accepted and implemented these days.

Figure 7. Visualization of measured metrics on various models (t.l.) precision (t.r.) recall (b.l.) F1 score (b.r.) BLEU score

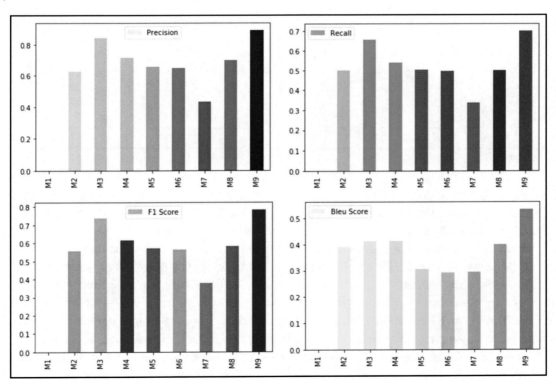

The line chart shown in Figure 8, can be referred to come up with a better analysis of different models based on the various accuracy metrics – BLEU score, Precision, Recall and F1 score. The BLEU score is normalized within the range of 0-1 for easier visualization of data with other accuracy metrics.

From Figure 3 the accuracy of all the various models can be observed, which have been compared to tune it down to a final model. This accuracy is termed as how accurate the machine translation system is when it converts one speech input, in a language, to another speech output, in a different language. It can be seen that a simple RNN model has the least accuracy of 40.87%, which is aggressively low for a machine translation system. The bidirectional RNN model provides an accuracy of 61.64%, which is higher than that of a simple RNN. However, getting the LSTM network models into the mix, different accuracies can be seen which range from 54.67% accuracy for bidirectional LSTM to 80.01% accuracy for LSTM with embedding. In the LSTM model, the most promising one apart from the LSTM model with embedding is the encoder-decoder LSTM, with a value of 66.55. Vanilla LSTM, being a very basic and classic model provides a value of 58.73% accuracy, which is not a very promising result. Finally, it can be observed that the final model created by combining bidirectional LSTM with the LSTM model with embedding, provides a tremendous value of 95.80% accuracy.

Figure 8. Visualization of (l.) all the metrics for different models (r.) accuracy of different models

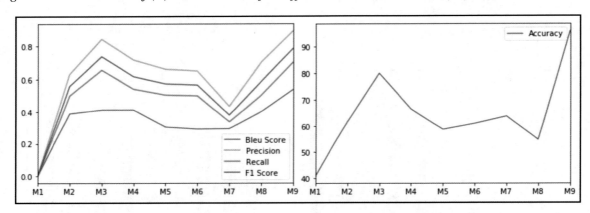

According to the bar plots shown in Figure 7, Figure 8, and Table 1, it is observed that simple RNN has a value very small that multiple of 10^{-7}, which is negligible and approximately equal to 0. This signifies that simple RNN gives no apparent relevant value for the machine translation. All the models give moderately comprehensive values, the generative LSTM has the least value that of 0.4, besides the simple RNN. However, the LSTM model with embedding presents a promising value that of 0.84. All the other models show a small range of values around 0.6 to 0.7. Comparing the final model to the rest, it can be seen that the final model provides the highest precision value of 0.89 which is pretty close to perfect precision. The BLEU score is normalized within the range of 0-1 for easier visualization of data with other accuracy metrics. For this work, the simple RNN model gives a value of around 10^{-8} which is negligible. The LSTM model with embedding shows a promising value of 0.65. Besides the Simple RNN, Generative LSTM displays the least value of 0.3, while the rest of the models range from a value of around 0.4 to 0.5. The final model shows a promisingly high value that of 0.699 which can be approximated to 70 percent, which is a high value for recall for neural machine translations.

About Table 1 values along with Figure 7 and Figure 8, simple RNN fails to have an acceptable value for the F1 score as well – it has an F1 score value of the order 10^{-8}, which is approximately 0. A promising value is shown by the LSTM model with embedding that has a value of 0.7, while the rest models have values ranging from 0.5 to 0.6. The final model which includes the LSTM model with embedding along with bidirectional LSTM produces a high F1 score of 0.78, which is approximately 80 percent. It can be observed that the simple RNN model has a value of 0.00013 which is approximately equal to 0, thus, it is least useful compared to other models when it comes to machine translation. The LSTM model with embedding and the encoder-decoder model of LSTM, both have a decent BLEU score value of 0.412038 and the bidirectional LSTM has a value of 0.4. However, the final model that is formed by combining the bidirectional LSTM model and the LSTM model with embedding provides a pretty high BLEU score of more than 0.5.

CONCLUSION

The system provides a machine-aided neural network-based translation module that facilitates the recognition of speech, translation of speech using several neural network models, and the synthesis of speech. The speech recognition module and the speech synthesis module are supported by various APIs, but translations are done with different models. This work focuses mainly on the study of several neural network-aided machine translations that are based on LSTM and RNN - the simple RNN model, the LSTM with embedding, the bidirectional RNN, LSTM with embedded encoder and decoder, vanilla LSTM, stacked LSTM, generative LSTM, and bidirectional LSTM and the final model that has been created by adding the bidirectional LSTM along with the LSTM model with embedding. The work compares all the neural machine translation models based on several accuracy parameters that include precision, recall, F1 score, and BLEU scores. When it comes to individual models, the least-performing model is the simple RNN model that succeeds in having negligible values for all the metrics. However, overall, the LSTM models have considerably higher values compared to that the RNN models. For the accuracy parameters, there are still several ongoing research works, although the standard definition of precision, recall, F1 score, and BLEU score have been followed in this work for overall evaluation purposes. The data that is tabulated in its raw form is many a time difficult to analyze, so visualization of the accuracy metric data is done using different plots like bar charts and line plots.

This work can be extended in the future by adding several new models for better comparison and analysis. The models can also be improved and optimized to limit time complexity and improve the overall system performance. Other accuracy measures and metrics can be used for the analysis of the different models. Moreover, this system has only considered unigram-based precision and recall measures, which can be improved in the future that considering higher orders of n-grams for calculating the precision and recall metrics, while comparing the performances of the different models.

REFERENCES

Huang, J. X., Lee, K. S., & Kim, Y. K. (2020). Hybrid Translation with Classification: Revisiting Rule-Based and Neural Machine Translation. *Electronics (Basel)*, 9(2), 201. doi:10.3390/electronics9020201

Alvarez, S., Oliver, A., & Badia, T. (2020, November). Quantitative Analysis of Post-Editing Effort Indicators for NMT. In *Proceedings of the 22nd Annual Conference of the European Association for Machine Translation* (pp. 411-420). Academic Press.

Qiao, Y., Hashimoto, K., Eriguchi, A., Wang, H., Wang, D., Tsuruoka, Y., & Taura, K. (2020). Parallelizing and optimizing neural Encoder–Decoder models without padding on multi-core architecture. *Future Generation Computer Systems, 108*, 1206–1213. doi:10.1016/j.future.2018.04.070

Xia, Y., He, T., Tan, X., Tian, F., He, D., & Qin, T. (2019, July). Tied transformers: Neural machine translation with shared encoder and decoder. *Proceedings of the AAAI Conference on Artificial Intelligence, 33*, 5466–5473. doi:10.1609/aaai.v33i01.33015466

Tufano, M., Pantiuchina, J., Watson, C., Bavota, G., & Poshyvanyk, D. (2019, May). On learning meaningful code changes via neural machine translation. In *2019 IEEE/ACM 41st International Conference on Software Engineering (ICSE)* (pp. 25-36). IEEE. 10.1109/ICSE.2019.00021

Nishimura, Y., Sudoh, K., Neubig, G., & Nakamura, S. (2019). Multi-source neural machine translation with missing data. *IEEE/ACM Transactions on Audio, Speech, and Language Processing, 28*, 569–580. doi:10.1109/TASLP.2019.2959224

Soltau, H., Liao, H., & Sak, H. (2016). *Neural speech recognizer: Acoustic-to-word LSTM model for large vocabulary speech recognition.* arXiv preprint arXiv:1610.09975.

Luong, M. T., Pham, H., & Manning, C. D. (2015). *Effective approaches to attention-based neural machine translation.* arXiv preprint arXiv:1508.04025. doi:10.18653/v1/D15-1166

Xia, Y. (2020). Research on statistical machine translation model based on deep neural network. *Computing, 102*(3), 643–661. doi:10.100700607-019-00752-1

Cho, K., Van Merriënboer, B., Bahdanau, D., & Bengio, Y. (2014). *On the properties of neural machine translation: Encoder-decoder approaches.* arXiv preprint arXiv:1409.1259. doi:10.3115/v1/W14-4012

Sennrich, R., Haddow, B., & Birch, A. (2015). *Neural machine translation of rare words with subword units.* arXiv preprint arXiv:1508.07909.

Kumar, K. C., Aswale, S., Shetgaonkar, P., Pawar, V., Kale, D., & Kamat, S. (2020, February). A Survey of Machine Translation Approaches for Konkani to English. In *2020 International Conference on Emerging Trends in Information Technology and Engineering (ic-ETITE)* (pp. 1-6). IEEE.

Wu, Y., Schuster, M., Chen, Z., Le, Q. V., Norouzi, M., Macherey, W., . . . Klingner, J. (2016). *Google's neural machine translation system: Bridging the gap between human and machine translation.* arXiv preprint arXiv:1609.08144.

Chen, K., Zhao, T., Yang, M., Liu, L., Tamura, A., Wang, R., Utiyama, M., & Sumita, E. (2017). A neural approach to source dependence based context model for statistical machine translation. *IEEE/ACM Transactions on Audio, Speech, and Language Processing, 26*(2), 266–280. doi:10.1109/TASLP.2017.2772846

Zhang, B., Xiong, D., Su, J., & Duan, H. (2017). A context-aware recurrent encoder for neural machine translation. *IEEE/ACM Transactions on Audio, Speech, and Language Processing, 25*(12), 2424–2432. doi:10.1109/TASLP.2017.2751420

Wang, X., Tu, Z., & Zhang, M. (2018). Incorporating statistical machine translation word knowledge into neural machine translation. *IEEE/ACM Transactions on Audio, Speech, and Language Processing*, *26*(12), 2255–2266. doi:10.1109/TASLP.2018.2860287

Singh, S. P., Kumar, A., Darbari, H., Singh, L., Rastogi, A., & Jain, S. (2017, July). Machine translation using deep learning: An overview. In *2017 International Conference on Computer, Communications and Electronics (Comptelix)* (pp. 162-167). IEEE. 10.1109/COMPTELIX.2017.8003957

Wang, R., Utiyama, M., Finch, A., Liu, L., Chen, K., & Sumita, E. (2018). Sentence selection and weighting for neural machine translation domain adaptation. *IEEE/ACM Transactions on Audio, Speech, and Language Processing*, *26*(10), 1727–1741. doi:10.1109/TASLP.2018.2837223

Cho, K., Van Merriënboer, B., Gulcehre, C., Bahdanau, D., Bougares, F., Schwenk, H., & Bengio, Y. (2014). *Learning phrase representations using RNN encoder-decoder for statistical machine translation*. arXiv preprint arXiv:1406.1078. doi:10.3115/v1/D14-1179

Ott, M., Edunov, S., Grangier, D., & Auli, M. (2018). *Scaling neural machine translation*. arXiv preprint arXiv:1806.00187. doi:10.18653/v1/W18-6301

Koehn, P., & Knowles, R. (2017). *Six challenges for neural machine translation*. arXiv preprint arXiv:1706.03872. doi:10.18653/v1/W17-3204

Kalchbrenner, N., Espeholt, L., Simonyan, K., Oord, A. V. D., Graves, A., & Kavukcuoglu, K. (2016). *Neural machine translation in linear time*. arXiv preprint arXiv:1610.10099.

Chaudhary, J. R., & Patel, A. C. (2018). Machine translation using deep learning: A survey. *International Journal of Scientific Research in Science, Engineering and Technology*, *4*(2), 145–150.

Chaudhary, J. R., & Patel, A. C. (2018). Bilingual machine translation using RNN based deep learning. *International Journal of Scientific Research in Science, Engineering and Technology*, *4*(4), 1480–1484.

Artetxe, M., Labaka, G., Agirre, E., & Cho, K. (2017). *Unsupervised neural machine translation*. arXiv preprint arXiv:1710.11041.

Tu, Z., Lu, Z., Liu, Y., Liu, X., & Li, H. (2016). *Modeling coverage for neural machine translation*. arXiv preprint arXiv:1601.04811. doi:10.18653/v1/P16-1008

Lample, G., Ott, M., Conneau, A., Denoyer, L., & Ranzato, M. A. (2018). *Phrase-based & neural unsupervised machine translation*. arXiv preprint arXiv:1804.07755. doi:10.18653/v1/D18-1549

Cheng, Y. (2019). Semi-supervised learning for neural machine translation. In *Joint Training for Neural Machine Translation* (pp. 25–40). Springer. doi:10.1007/978-981-32-9748-7_3

Datta, D., David, P. E., Mittal, D., & Jain, A. (2020). Neural Machine Translation using Recurrent Neural Network. *Regular Issue*, *9*(4), 1395–1400. doi:10.35940/ijeat.D7637.049420

Olah, C. (2018). *Understanding LSTM Networks-Colah's Blog*. https://colah. github. io/posts/2015-08-Understanding-LSTMs/

Agrawal, S. (2019). *Reading between the layers (LSTM Network)*. Retrieved 31 March 2020, from https://towardsdatascience.com/reading-between-the-layers-lstm-network-7956ad192e58

Park, S., Kim, B., Kang, C. M., Chung, C. C., & Choi, J. W. (2018). Sequence-to-Sequence Prediction of Vehicle Trajectory via LSTM Encoder-Decoder Architecture. *2018 IEEE Intelligent Vehicles Symposium (IV)*, 1672-1678. 10.1109/IVS.2018.8500658

Al-Sabahi, K., Zuping, Z., & Kang, Y. (2018). *Bidirectional attentional encoder-decoder model and bidirectional beam search for abstractive summarization*. arXiv preprint arXiv:1809.06662.

Maučec, M. S., & Donaj, G. (2019). Machine Translation and the Evaluation of Its Quality. In Natural Language Processing-New Approaches and Recent Applications. IntechOpen.

Chapter 6
Long Short–Term Memory–Based Neural Networks in an AI Music Generation Platform

Suresh Kumar Nagarajan
Presidency University, India

Geetha Narasimhan
Vellore Institute of Technology, Vellore, India

Ankit Mishra
Vellore Institute of Technology, Vellore, India

Rishabh Kumar
Vellore Institute of Technology, Vellore, India

ABSTRACT

Music is an essential component of a promotional video since it helps to establish a brand's or entity's identity. Music composition and production, on the other hand, is quite costly. The expense of engaging a competent team capable of creating distinctive music for your firm could be prohibitively expensive. In the last decade, artificial intelligence has accomplished feats previously unimaginable to humanity. Artificial intelligence can be a lifesaver, not only in terms of the amount of money a company would have to spend on creating their own unique music but also in terms of the amount of time and work required on the firm's part. A web-based platform that can be accessed from anywhere in the world would help the product obtain customers without regard to geography. AI algorithms can be taught to recognize which sound combinations produce a pleasing melody (or music). Multiple machine learning algorithms can be used to accomplish this.

DOI: 10.4018/978-1-6684-6001-6.ch006

INTRODUCTION

Music theory is a term used by artists and academics to describe what they heard in a musical work. The fundamentals of music theory will help us better understand which sounds join together to create lovely songs. Melody, Harmony, and Rhythm are the most essential terms encountered when learning Music Theory. The emphasis, however, would be on the fundamentals of music theory. Scales, Chords, Keys (or Notes), and Notation are the rudiments of music theory. Notes (or Keys) and Chords would be our primary focus. Let's take the example of a Piano, a piano has something we call octaves, every octave has a set of 7 Musical Keys - C, D, E, F, G, A & B. Between every note, there is another Note, these notes are- C#, D#, E#, F#, G#, A# & B# Every single note has a distinct sound. When multiple notes are played together in harmony, it is called a Chord. Chords can alternatively be defined as individual units of harmony.

A combination of chords and/or notes, which has a certain degree of Melody, Harmony, and Rhythm is known as music. We aim to extract sequences of chords and notes, which sound harmonious. Neural Network can help achieve a Machine Learning model, capable of the task of comprehending the music and producing music. Neural Networks can be understood with a human example, when shown a drawing of a cat, even though it might be just a doodle, we can almost instantly recognize it as a cat. This is because we focused on the "features" of the cat. The features of the cat include it having a couple of eyes, four legs, a couple of ears with a typical shape, and so on. We cannot always be certain that an object is what the ML Algorithm predicted; thus, we assign a probability to the same. Thus, every feature of the cat is given a probability, which is later on converted into a percentage. These features however aren't all equally important. After we find the relative importance of these features in terms of percentage, we call it weight. Now, we multiply the percentage of features with the probability of each of the features to get a value. We apply the sigmoid function on this obtained value to get the value of the probability of the object being a cat.

A neuron is a single unit or function that takes inputs, multiplies them, then adds them together and applies the activation function to the whole. The purpose of a Neuron is to modify the weight depending on a large number of input and output samples. Based on inputs and desired outputs, Neuron learns about weights. Neural Network is a network of such neurons, neurons might have their input as the output of another neuron or vice versa, and this makes a neural network. As human beings, we don't think the same thing again and again. Rather we use our previous knowledge and try to understand it. Traditional neural networks can't do this; they can't refer to the previous information. So, to address this issue recurrent neural networks come into play where the information forms a network of loops so the same information is accessible again. There are times when we need more information to understand things like predicting the last word of a sentence, while we're typing a sentence, naturally, it's not sure what it would be without more context. So that is when the difference between the actual word required and the point where it is required become more.

Long Short-Term Memory Network is a different type of RNN capable of learning those long gaps (Gers et al., 2000). LSTM is a chain-like structure but with a different structure. It has four neural networks interacting in a special way rather than a single neural network. Long Short-Term Memory Network can remember patterns of chords that sound harmonious. This in turn helps generate music, the Machine Learning Algorithm would be integrated with the Web Platform. The Website starts by helping the users understand the purpose of the application and help users navigate to a page, where selecting their preferable instrument and certain associated configurations, the configurations are fed into the Machine

Learning Model, which then churns out the music using those parameters. The Machine Learning Model would already have been trained and deployed on a cloud platform. Music is generated and is turned to the user, who can then listen to it and decide whether they want to purchase the same.

BACKGROUND

Music language models can be used for several musical signals and symbolic music processing applications, such as music composition, symbolic music classification, and automated music transcription (AMT) (Ycart, & Benetos, 2020). The author of this research investigates Long Short-Term Memory (LSTM) networks for polyphonic music prediction using binary piano rolls. The need for more musical assessment criteria is demonstrated by an early experiment evaluating the impact of piano roll timestep on machine output. The author conducts a series of experiments in anticipating polyphonic music (intrinsic evaluation) and its predictive model as a language model for AMT (extrinsic evaluation). The author demonstrates that intrinsic output (as measured by cross entropy) has little bearing on extrinsic performance, underlining the significance of customizing training losses for each application. Furthermore, this model outperforms MLMs that have previously been developed. This paper aids us in gaining a better grasp of music language models, which is extremely beneficial in the field of music development. The set of tests increases our understanding of the value of Long Short-Term Memory (LSTM) and makes it one of the Music Generator's potentially key aspects.

The paper presents a method for polyphonic piano music transcription using a supervised neural network model (Sigtia et al., 2016). An acoustic model and a music language model are what build the basic architecture of the proposed model. Estimating the probabilities of pitches in the radio frame is the acoustic model's essential function. A recurrent neural network is used to model the correlations between pitch combinations over time, this is the language model. Convolution Neural Networks yield the best result. From this paper, we get a deeper understanding of which algorithms perform better for Music Transcription. We also get a deeper understanding of Musical Theory, which will help us build our neural work for the production of melodious songs.

Deep neural networks (DNNs) have been used for music classification and tagging with great success (Choi et al., 2018). However, there are several unanswered questions about DNN preparation, assessment, and review. To better understand the properties of neural networks, the author explores particular aspects of them, such as the effects of noisy labels, in this paper. To examine the efficiency of training and assessment, the author evaluates and (re-)validates the abroad music dataset. The author shows that networks can be successful in ground truth datasets despite relatively high error rates while hypothesizing that label noise could be the cause of varying tag-wise output differences. Finally, the qualified network's analysis reveals important information about the relationships between music tags. These findings demonstrate the value of addressing automated music tagging with data-driven approaches.

This paper helps us in understanding that even though Deep Convolutional Neural Networks might have certain errors, and sometimes these errors may be high in number, it is still one of the best algorithms to use while dealing with Music and its understanding. This also helps us understand the importance of Deep Learning in the overall implementation.

Symbolic music generation is still an unsolved issue that faces several obstacles (Zhang, 2020).

The entire music score is a lengthy note sequence made up of several tracks with repeating elements and variations at different stages. The transformer model has shown benefits in modeling long sequences due to its self-attention. Some attempts have been made to apply the transformer-based model to music production. Despite the apparent variations in the pattern of texts and music, previous works have trained the model using the same technique as the text generation mission. These models are unable to reliably generate high-quality music samples. In this paper, the author proposes a novel adversarial transformer for generating musically rich music bits. The self-attention networks and generative adversarial learning are creatively mixed.

The author has very intelligently built a model using the transformer-based approach and has shown due diligence to enhance the performance of the model using REGS and MC. The approach that the author has taken helped us understand that seemingly small changes can help to produce largely better results.

Adaptive Music Composition for Games (Hutchings & McCormack, 2019)

Music that familiarizes vigorously with content and behavior is essential for creating more immersive, memorable, and emotional game experiences. The design of real-time music generation algorithms, as well as the restricted simulation of player behavior, game-world background, and emotion in present games, have hampered the creation of adaptive music systems (AMSs) for video games to date.

The author believes that these problems must be tackled in parallel to greatly increase the consistency and versatility of adaptive game music. To create a novel AMS, cognitive models of information organization and emotional impact are combined with multimodal, multiagent composition techniques. The system is used in two games that are stylistically different. The author helped us understand that adaptive dynamic music generation has a very appropriate application in games. The concepts used in parallel computing have also been discussed in the paper, which also helped us understand how we can build our application that runs in parallel to another application.

Relationships between music training, neural networks, and speech processing (Elmer, 2016)

Numerous studies have found that trained musicians and youngsters who have received music instruction have an advantage in transferring speech sounds of various spectral and temporal dimensions. Previously, these beneficial effects were frequently connected to improvements in local functional and anatomical aspects of the auditory cortex (AC). However, because it ignores the human brain's natural organization, which includes neuronal networks and rhythmic dynamics, this viewpoint is simplistic. As a result, the research provides a new method that combines multimodal imaging, electrophysiology, and neuronal oscillations to extend earlier findings to a network level. The research demonstrates how functional and structural connections may be utilized to construct basic brain circuits that modulate AC activity. The paper also demonstrates how a network method may be utilized to better understand the benefits of music training on more sophisticated speech processes such as word learning.

This paper helps us understand the various ways in which Neural Networks work and how they are similar to a brain. It helps us to establish a relationship between music theory, neural networks, and speech processing. Concepts relating to Music theory are also explained in the paper, which would be beneficial in the actual project.

This study investigates the effects of AI-based facial and music biometrics on customers' cognitive and emotional states, as well as how these effects affect their behavioral responses in terms of value building (Rodgers et al., 2021).

The findings reveal that in a high-involvement AI purchasing scenario, music-recognition biometric-induced emotion modulates cognition and behavioral intentions for utilitarian-type customers.

This paper gives us deeper insights into Music Theory. In addition to that, we also understand how various types of AI-produced melodies affect the brains of people.

Quantum approaches to music cognition (Beim & Blutner, 2019)

During the last two decades, quantum cognition has grown in importance as a branch of mathematical psychology. The Author's research, which is based on Guerino Mazzola's pioneering work on tonal symmetries, aims to explain and reconcile static and dynamic tonal attraction phenomena in music psychology using a quantum cognition system.

Based on the fundamental concepts of tonal music's octave equivalence, fifth similarity, and transposition symmetry, which are expressed by the structure of the circle of fifths, the Author constructs several wave function definitions over this underlying tonal space. In musicology, we compare and contrast traditional computational models with quantum models for static and dynamic tonal attraction. Our method, which is based on symbolic models of music interpretation, replicates and reinforces predictions. This paper dives deep into the concept of Tonal Symmetries, using various wave functions. This subsection of Music Theory helps develop tones from chords and also deepens the understanding of Music Theory.

Model architectures, training methods, and datasets are typically proposed in machine learning research in music modeling and creation, as well as quantitative and qualitative metrics of system output, such as sequence likelihoods and/or qualitative listening assessments (Sturm et al., 2019). Rarely is such research actively challenged and analyzed for its utility to and influence on real-world practitioners, then used to inform machine learning growth and deployment. This article tries to accomplish these goals in the context of music production using machine learning. We create and use many machine learning algorithms for music development in collaboration with practitioners, and we present the findings in a public concert. We focus on the whole experience to come up with a few ideas about how to advance these and another machine learning-based music production application. This paper amplifies our understanding of music creation using machine learning algorithms with the research done to analyze its utility in the real world.

PopMNet: Generating structured pop music melodies using neural networks (Wu et al., 2020)

Many deep learning models for generating symbolic melodies have recently been proposed. Creating music of pop melodies with well-prepared structures, on the other hand, remains a challenge. We present PopMNet, a model of melody structure for generating organized pop music melodies, in this paper. Pairwise connections, specifically recurrence and series, between melodies determine the melody structure. PopMNet is made up of a Structure Generation Net (SGN) based on Convolutional Neural Networks (CNN) and a Melody Generation Net (RNN) based on Recurrent Neural Networks (RNN) (MGN). The first creates melody structures, while the second creates melodies based on the structures and chord progressions. Attention RNN, Lookback RNN, MidiNet, and Music Transformer are four existing models that are compared to the proposed model. According to the findings, the melodies produced by the model have far stronger structures than those produced by existing models, as evidenced by human behavior experiments.

This paper helps us to understand how we can create well-structured melodies with Pairwise connections, specifically repetition and series. To create a more meaningful melody.

RNNs are powerful AI models that have proven to be useful in a wide range of tasks, including music composition, speech recognition, and machine translation (Mittal & Umesh, 2021). RNN computations have both intra-timestep and inter-timestep dependence. Because of these qualities, the hardware acceleration of RNNs is more difficult than that of CNNs.

RNN hardware architectures have lately been proposed by several academics. Deep-learning algorithm developments have always been closely linked to hardware accelerator advancements. However, even more synergy between these two domains is needed and possible. The goal of this survey is to bring together deep learning, computer architecture, and chip design researchers. This paper helps us understand the various improvements one may make in the RNN as well as the Hardware architectures, to ensure they perform with more efficiency.

For various complicated tasks such as Machine Translation, Natural Language Processing, and time series forecasting, several architectures for Deep Neural Networks (DNNs) have been developed (Vijay-aprabakaran & Sathiyamurthy, 2020). With noteworthy results, the Long-Short Term Model (LSTM), a deep neural network, has become the most prevalent architecture for tackling sequential and time series problems.

When building the LSTM model, many hyper-parameters, such as the activation function, loss function, and optimizer, must be set in advance. DNN efficiency is heavily influenced by these hyper-parameters. The goal of this study is to create a new LSTM activation function that can replace existing activation functions like sigmoid and tanh.

The comb-H-sine (comb-H-sine) function is a newly discovered activation function in this research based on the DEA approach. MNIST and IMDB, and UCI HAR datasets, the proposed comb-H-sine activation feature outperform standard functions in LSTM with an accuracy of 98.83 percent, 93.49 percent, and 78.38 percent, respectively.

This paper helps us understand the importance of hyper-parameters such as activation function, loss function, and optimizer, which can be altered to enhance the accuracy of the existing LSTM Model, which is a suitable model for AI Music Generation.

In recent years, neural networks have been utilized to construct symbolic music (Wu et al., 2019). However, due to the melody's long-term structure, creating an effective model has been difficult. In this research, the author introduces a hierarchical recurrent neural network (HRNN) for melody generation that consists of three long-short-term-memory (LSTM) subnetworks that operate in a coarse-to-fine manner over time. The output of the high-level subnetworks is passed into the low-level subnetworks, where it acts as guidance for the low-level subnetworks to generate the finer time-scale melody components. This structure outperforms the single-layer LSTM, which tries to learn all hidden melodic patterns, according to two human behavior experiments.

The HRNN generates stronger melodies than the recently proposed models MidiNet and MusicVAE, according to human evaluation. This paper deepens our understanding of the Recurrent Neural Network, which seems the most relevant to the project. This paper helped us understand that a Recurrent Neural Network is appropriate for Music Generation

MAIN FOCUS OF THE CHAPTER

Problem Statement

Music is an essential need of various industries for a variety of needs like advertisements, social media handles, digital marketing, etc. However, the production of music is rather expensive and takes some time. Artificial Intelligence generated music could help small businesses, start-ups, etc. who want quality music within a certain time frame. This project aims to build a platform that can help people across the globe to generate their music, using instruments of their choice and, later purchase it. The person/company has sole rights over the music they produce, thus, they can build their brand reputation with it.

Analyzing the existing work on AI Music generation, certain things could be deduced from them. All the papers dealing with AI Music generation, first deal with Music Theory. A deep understanding of Music theory is necessary to work on the platform. Another point to be noted is that machine learning-based approaches are required to generate music. Beyond this point, all the papers vary in their approaches. A majority of papers use the concepts of Convolution Neural Networks (CNN) in their implementation. However, a paper mentions that a combination of Deep Learning techniques and LSTM networks improves the overall accuracy of the model (Hizlisoy et al., 2021). In addition, the results show that the LSTM + DNN classifier improves music emotion recognition accuracy by 1.61, 1.61, and 3.23 points.

This helps us understand that Neural Networks are an appropriate fit for Models involving Music Theory. Some Papers also use different methods like complex-valued neural network (CVNN), K-Means Clustering, Multi-Layer Perceptron (MLP) neural network, and Support Vector Machines (SVM) neural networks as a sub-task of the entire Model. However, research indicates that the most efficient model for our AI Music generator is a combination of Deep Learning Algorithms and Long Short-Term Memory, which is based on recurrent neural networks (RNN).

There may be certain challenges involving the usage of DNN+LSTM based on RNN, the first one being the One-to-Many Sequence Problem where the input data comprises a single time step and the output is a vector of several values or time steps. One of the solutions has been discussed in the research paper that has been analyzed. It stated that by using Stacked LSTM, the One-to-Many Sequence problem may be avoided. Many-to-Many sequence problems may also be faced, which may be avoided in similar ways as the One-to-Many Sequence Problem.

The Overall Aim is to build a platform, and it can be retrieved across the world. The platform shall let the users pick their customizations, the instrument, and certain other factors from Music Theory, which then will be used to run the Machine Learning Model built on Deep Learning Algorithms and Long Short-Term Memory. The Model would be trained before this, using sounds of various instruments. The ML model would produce music after learning the various combinations of chords that sound melodious. The users may then purchase the music, which would then belong to the user or the company and may be used by them in various commercials, their social media handles, and Digital Marketing.

Research Framework

The existing research has successfully given a deeper understanding of how to develop an AI Music Generation platform. It has also given me better knowledge & crisp understanding of the various machine learning available for the task. The platform is built on the web, which would make it easily accessible to people across the globe. The platform would guide users through the simple and intuitive user interface, which would help users select their choice of musical instrument, then proceed to fine-tune certain parameters, which would be chosen by the user. The parameters selected by the user and the instrument are then fed into the machine learning algorithm. The algorithm then processes the data, to produce a song. The song is returned to the client, and the client then has the option to first listen to the song and then, buy the same, if it hasn't already been bought.

The Machine Learning component of the platform needs a significant amount of research, due to the variety of approaches available for the same. After analyzing a variety of ML Models, which are available for the generation of music and looking at the pros and cons of a variety of methods, it is decided that the concept of Neural Networks would be used. Recurrent Neural Networks would be required, these Neural Networks perform the same function at every step, the input of every single neuron however is dependent on the output of the previous neuron. LSTM, which is a type of Recurrent Neural Network can help in remembering patterns or sequences of chords, which sound melodious one after the other. Let us understand how the components work independently & in combination using a detailed architecture diagram.

Figure 1. Architecture Diagram of AI Music Generator

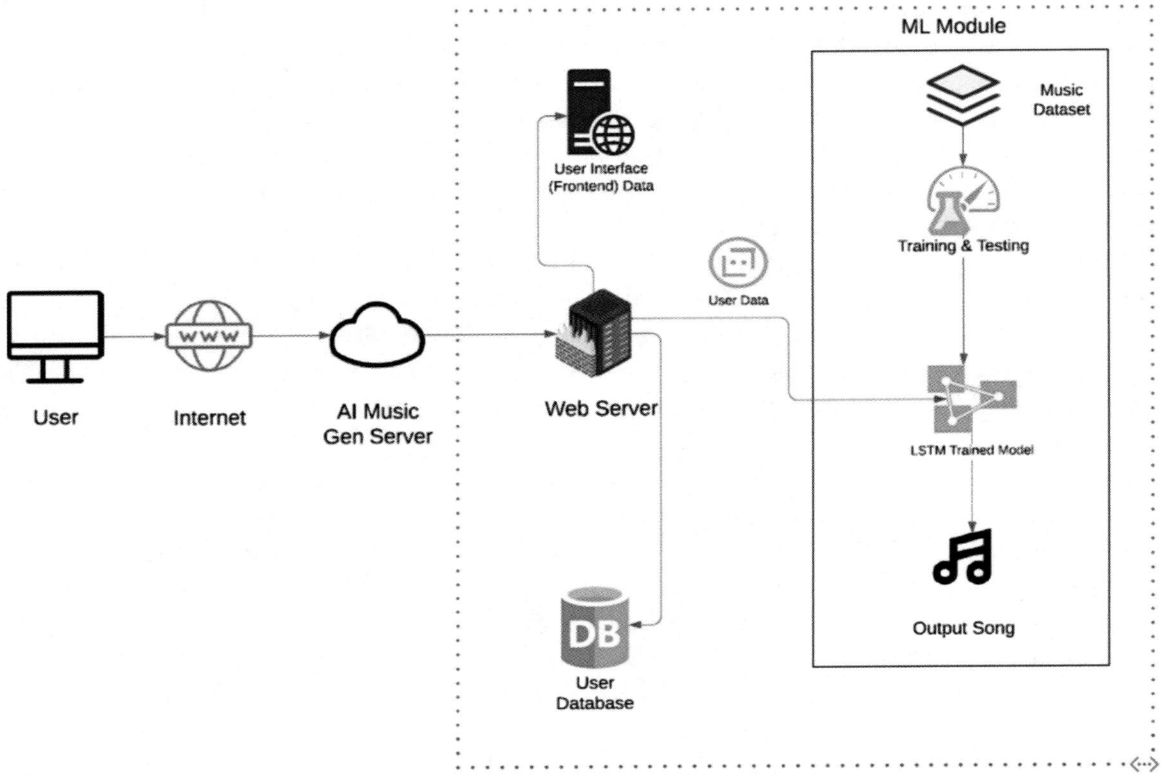

METHODOLOGY

The architecture diagram shows how the various modules function together, an in-depth understanding of the same is presented in this section. The overall description of the function is done first, after which every module is covered in great depth. The user, who is connected to the internet sends a request to the server module of our application, and the server module sends back the website data to the user after it fetches the same from the frontend module. The user can now send their credentials & fine-tune their instrument along with a certain parameter to generate data. The user again sends back data to the server module, which firstly checks the user's identity and then goes ahead to send the parameters to the ML Module. The ML Module runs the LSTM Algorithm which has been trained on data of various musical instruments. The ML Algorithm returns the newly generated music to the user & the user is given an option to purchase the same. The entire system can be divided into the following modules.

ML Module

The ML Module, which is run on a cloud-based server, is the component that produces music. It produces the music using the Long Short-Term Memory Network (LSTM) Algorithm, which is based on neural networks. Neural Networks are built with the basic building block of neurons. Neural Networks can be understood with a human example, when shown a drawing of a dog, even though it might be just a doodle, we can almost instantly recognize it as a dog. This is because we focused on the features of the dog. The features of the dog include it having a couple of eyes, four legs, a couple of ears with a typical shape, and so on. We cannot always be certain that an object is what the ML Algorithm predicted; thus, we assign a probability to the same. Thus, every feature of the dog is given a probability, which is later on converted into a percentage. These features however aren't all equally important. After we find the relative importance of these features in terms of percentage, we call it weight. Now, we multiply the percentage of features with the probability of each of the features to get a value. We apply the sigmoid function on this obtained value to get the value of the probability of the object being a dog. This single unit or function can be called A neuron essentially multiplies the inputs, then adds them up and applies the activation function to the total. The purpose of a Neuron is to modify the weight depending on a large number of input and output samples.

Neuron learns about weights depending on inputs and desired outputs. Neural Network is a network of such neurons, neurons might have their input as the output of another neuron or vice versa, and this makes a neural network. As human beings, we don't think the same thing again and again. Rather we use our previous knowledge and try to understand it. Traditional neural networks can't do this; they can't refer to the previous information. So, to address this issue recurrent neural networks come into play where the information forms a network of loops so the same information is accessible again. There are times when we need more information to understand things like predicting the last word of a sentence, while we're typing a sentence, naturally, it's not sure what it would be without more context. So that is when the difference between the actual word required and the point where it is required become more.

Figure 2. LSTM Network

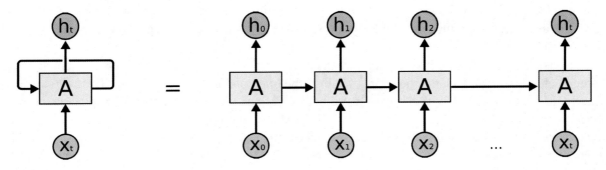

LSTM is a chain-like structure but with a different structure than traditional neural networks. It has four neural networks interacting in a special way rather than a single neural network. LSTM can remember patterns of chords that sound harmonious. The ML Module is first trained using existing instrumental music. After the Module has been trained, we input certain parameters into the ML Module, the parameters are there to ensure that every time the ML Model is run, the results do not come out to be the same. The ML Module after being run produces certain music, which is sent back to the server, which then sends the data back to the User.

Server Module

Server Module helps coordinate all the activities happening in the entire system, it keeps a track of the user requests, and on receiving the requests, it replaces them with the appropriate information. The Server module here is a cloud-based platform, upon which all the services like the database, the entire user interface (frontend) & the ML Module are running. The server is to be built on a cloud-based platform. Some of the most popular cloud-based platforms are Google Cloud Platform & Amazon Web Services. A JavaScript-based server module would be built to help coordinate all the tasks.

The user initially requests data from the web server, which then returns the user interface of the website to the user. The user further interacts with the user interface & enters his/her credentials. The credentials are then sent back to the server module. The server module checks the credentials from the database module & returns a response accordingly. Once the user has logged in, he/she gets the option to generate music with certain parameters, the parameters are again sent to the Server Module, which then invokes the ML Module to produce music with these specific parameters. The ML Module produces music, which is then sent to the server, the server stores the music file temporarily & also sends the music back to the user, the user may listen to the music using their user interface, if the user wants to proceed, the user may purchase the music. If the user requests the server to purchase the music with digital rights, the user is redirected to the payment portal, the server fetches the payment portal from the frontend module & sends it back to the user's frontend. The user may enter his payment details & purchase the digital rights from that point on.

Frontend Module

The module helps the user interact with the server, which further coordinates the various functionalities of the entire system. The front end would be built on the latest technologies in the field of web development. HTML5, CSS3 & JavaScript would be used to build the entire user interface, which would help give the user interface a modern look. The website would also be made responsive using the popular Bootstrap framework.

The user receives the Frontend module when he/she sends the request to the server. The landing page would help the user understand the entire system & the functionalities of the website. The user can navigate to the page where he/she requests an instrument & defines certain parameters. This parameter might be any random number, which is fed into the ML Model through the server module to produce unique music every single time. Once the Music is produced, the user is asked to either log in or register. The credentials of the user are then sent over to the server. The server cross-verifies the credentials with the backend module & then sends back a response accordingly. The user can then redirect himself/herself to the payments page & purchase the digital rights to the newly generated music.

Database Module

The Database module stores the credentials of the users. The database also holds an account of the digital rights of the music with the parameters associated with it like the instrument & its generation parameters. The records help in ensuring that the same music cannot be sold twice to another organization or individual.

When the user enters the login page, the credentials are sent over through the user interface to the server using REST Protocols, the sent data is cross-verified by the server using the records of the user database. Once the user is authenticated, the success message is sent, otherwise, an error code is generated & the user is told to retry the authentication process. Thus, the Database module helps in maintaining a record of all the consumers & works on the REST-based protocol service.

The following illustration helps us in understanding how the data flow throughout the application & how the modules work together to perform the various functionalities of the system.

Figure 3. Data Flow Diagram of AI Music Generator

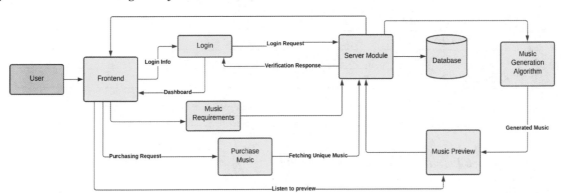

The user interacts with the website through the front end from the browser which is accessed from the database where the website is stored in the cloud on some hosting platform. Now, through the website, the user will have to log in with his/her username and password which are in the database on the cloud, now this Login information will be verified from it and the user will be allowed to access the content which he already purchased, his previous generated music preview and other information.

Now for generating the music, the user needs to define his requirements like the type of instrument, type of melody, and certain other factors which will be sent to the server over the cloud and will be fed to the Music Generating Machine Learning Algorithm on the cloud which will generate the music according to the pre-trained model present on the cloud. On generating the required music, Now the generated music will be stored in the database through the server which will enable the user to listen to it whenever he wishes and then can decide to buy it or not. This music will remain in the database till someone else or the initial user doesn't buy it with a unique copyright id. Suppose, the user decides to purchase the music then the user can go to the payment option where and will be redirected to a payment portal through the server. Now as the payment gets completed the music with a unique copyright ID will be assigned to the user and the user will be allowed to download the final version of the music for this personal or commercial purposes.

TESTING

The AI Music Generator generates music by recognizing the pattern of Notes & Chords of the Dataset that is used as the training set. The dataset does not have any output variable or "prediction" as such.

The testing of the model is done by varying the various parameters, which are used in the training, testing & prediction phase of Machine Learning. The parameters for the deployment (or the flask app) do not have any effect pronounced, which is worth noting.

This section deals with the various interrelated parameters of the Machine Learning Model & finding a relationship between them. Graphical analysis using suitable kinds of plots has further been done, to establish a relationship between the two parameters being analyzed.

Sequence Length & No. of Unique Notes (or, Chords) being produced on average by the Machine Learning Algorithm shown in Table 1.

To interpret this result, the meaning of Sequence Length shall be understood.

Table 1. Sequence Length V/S No. of Unique Notes

Sequence Length	Unique Notes/Chords (Average Value)
100	35
200	43
300	27
400	26
500	32

Figure 4. Sequence Length V/S No. of Unique Notes

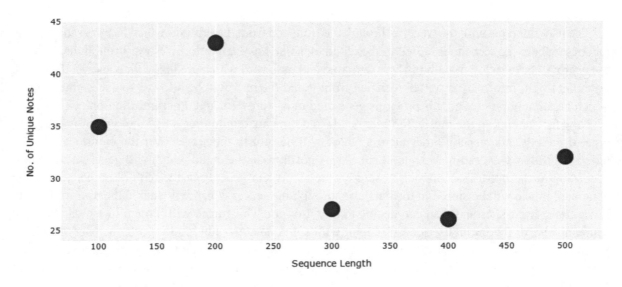

Sequence length is the length of Elements, that would be fed into the LSTM Algorithm in one iteration, looking at the pattern of a certain number of elements, the Algorithm produces a Music Note/ Chord. One can imagine this as a window of 'n' elements. The Window keeps moving, removing one note from the rear end & taking in the new note it produced.

The greater the value of sequence length, the better the result should be. However, Analysis shows that the Most no. of unique notes are produced, when the sequence length is 200. The greater the number of unique Notes (or chords) in the music of fixed length, the better it sounds revealing the primary analysis for this particular algorithm. This means, given that a system is having sufficient Computing resources, 200 shall be the Idea Sequence length to run the Algorithm.

The analysis also shows that the Time (t) to run the algorithm is directly proportional to the Sequence Length, the same is shown in the next subsection.

The conclusion from all the information above is, that the algorithm shall Ideally be using the Sequence Length of 200, however, the Sequence Length of 100 produces music, which is rough of the same quality & would give users half the waiting time. Thus, the AI Music Generator uses a sequence length of 100.

Time to Execute the Algorithm varying with the Sequence Length

As mentioned in the previous sub-section, Time to execute the algorithm increases with the Sequence Length. This section shall justify the reason for taking up the sequence length of the Algorithm as 100, in numeric terms shown in Table 2.

Table 2. Execution Time (in seconds) V/S Sequence Length

Sequence Length	Execution Time (in seconds)
100	37.65
200	66.49
300	93.32
400	121.14
500	160.5

The Execution time increases by almost 60 seconds when the sequence length increases by 100. Sequence length of 100 produces a sufficient number of unique notes (or chords), which is enough to make the music harmonious.

Sequence length is the number of elements (notes or chords) from the training dataset (or input music), which are taken inside one iteration of the Algorithm. This can be imagined as an algorithm where the 'n' number of elements are taken inside a window to produce one element.

A survey by Brafton shows the average duration of a session of a user on a website is close to 2 Minutes and 17 seconds, thus, optimizing both the Execution Time & the quality of the music produced is a must.

After considering all the parameters, it is concluded that the AI Music Generator would be generating music using the sequence length of 100.

Varying the No of elements to be produced (in a single iteration) to change the duration of music produced.

Increasing the No. of Elements to be produced in the Prediction Algorithm leads to an increase in the duration of the music generated. The same has been noted in the following Table 3.

Figure 5. Execution Time (in seconds) V/S Sequence Length

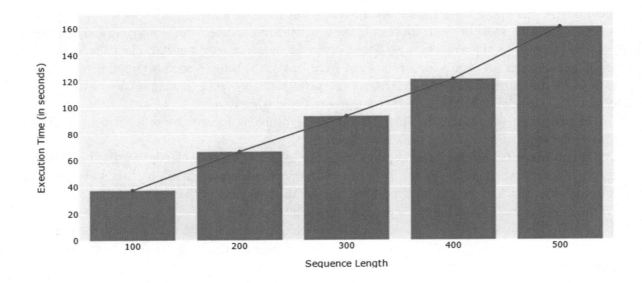

Execution Time (in seconds) V/S Sequence Length

Table 3. Duration (in seconds) V/S No. of Elements

No of Elements	Duration (Seconds)
100	26
200	51
300	76
400	101
500	126

The AI Music Generator was built to provide users with short music for promotions, the average length of Social Media commercials is around 60 seconds, thus, we set the no of elements as 200.

Varying the Offset to change the duration of Music

The offset is the amount of time, that each note or chord should be played from the predicted output. Analysis shows that the offset is directly proportional to the duration of the generated music has been shown in Table 4.

Changing the offset not only changes the duration of the music but also changes how long every single note/chord is played. Thus, increasing or decreasing the Offset beyond a certain value distorts the music. Primary analysis shows, that the suitable range of the Offset value is between 0.5-0.9.

The Music produced when keeping the Offset value as 0.5 is also an idea for Social Media promotions & sounds harmonious. Thus, the offset value is set as 0.5.

Figure 6. Duration (in seconds) V/S No. of Elements

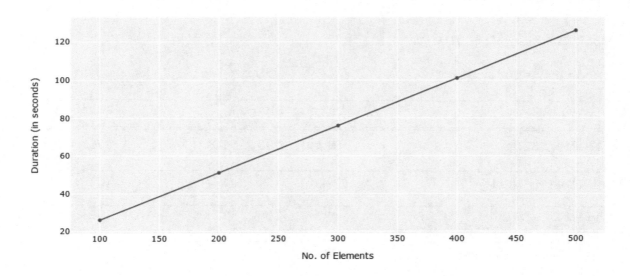

Table 4. Duration of Generated Music (in seconds) V/S Offset

Offset	Duration (Seconds)
0.5	51
0.6	61
0.7	71
0.8	81
0.9	91

Figure 7. Duration of Generated Music (in seconds) V/S Offset

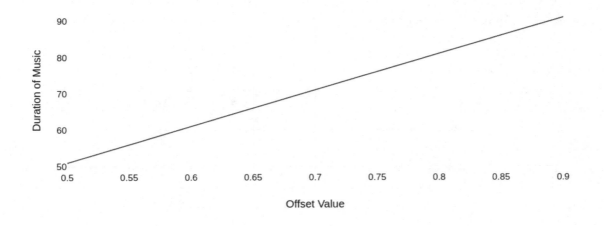

Summary of Model Generated

A summary of the model generated is shown in Table 5. No. of Epochs compared against the Training Time

Table 5. Summary of the ML Model

```
Model: "sequential"

Layer (type)                Output Shape              Param #
=================================================================
lstm (LSTM)                 (None, 100, 512)          1052672

dropout (Dropout)           (None, 100, 512)          0

lstm_1 (LSTM)               (None, 100, 512)          2099200

dropout_1 (Dropout)         (None, 100, 512)          0

lstm_2 (LSTM)               (None, 512)               2099200

dense (Dense)               (None, 256)               131328

dropout_2 (Dropout)         (None, 256)               0

dense_1 (Dense)             (None, 201)               51657
=================================================================
Total params: 5,434,057
Trainable params: 5,434,057
Non-trainable params: 0
```

Epoch is a single iteration where the ML Model processes the entire training set, the more the number of Epochs, the better result is obtained shown in Table 6.

Table 6. Epochs V/S Training Time (in milliseconds)

Epochs	Training Time (in milliseconds)
2	235
10	1175
50	5,875
100	11,750
180	21,150

Since the training phase happens before the Users are allowed to use a particular Model to produce music, thus, The Model has been trained at 180 Epochs. The use of such high Epochs enabled the production of high-quality music.

Figure 8. Epochs V/S Training Time (in milliseconds)

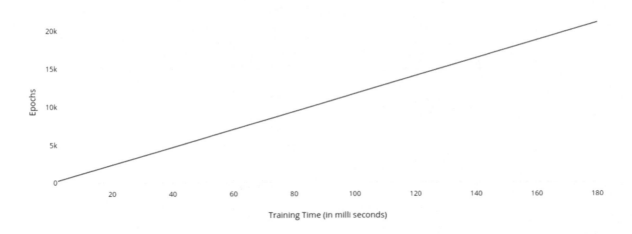

The Optimal settings as specified in every subsection have been used to generate the Music as per the LSTM Algorithm.

Word Cloud of the Notes (and Chord) Generated using the Model on the Optimal Settings

The Testing section is aimed at ensuring that all the individual components of the entire algorithm are optimized to ensure that the Music generated is harmonious and, that the User does not have to wait for too long to hear the generated music either. Numerical & graphical analysis was used to test all the possible configurations to ensure that all the aspects of the algorithm are verified thoroughly. The result is a set of parameters with their optimized value, which is well suited to the Algorithm.

SOLUTIONS AND RECOMMENDATIONS

Comparison of LSTM Model with other Models

Previous work on the various algorithms which aimed to generate music using AI Algorithms shows that a variety of approaches have worked to generate music. The literature survey section of the paper can give insights into the previous work done in the domain. This section aims to compare the previously existing work with the algorithm discussed in this paper. An interesting approach had been taken by Li, H in the paper Piano Automatic Computer Composition by Deep Learning and Blockchain Technology. Here the approach discussed to generate music uses the concept of the GRU-RNN Algorithm. The metrics of a few other algorithms have also been discussed in the paper.

Figure 9. Word Cloud of Generated Music Using Optimal Settings

Figure 10. Comparison of Music Generation Algorithms

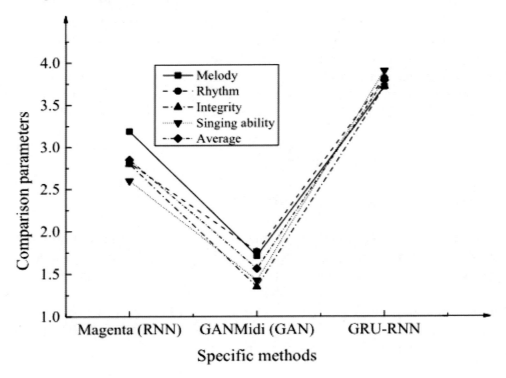

LSTM Algorithm used by this paper can be compared to the GRU-RNN Algorithm used by the paper above in terms of various parameters (time, accuracy, etc.)

The following graph shows the comparison between GRU-RNN & LSTM Algorithms based on

The above graph shows clearly, that the time required for each step decreases with an increase in EVS, however, the time required by the LSTM Algorithm is lesser than the GRU-RNN Algorithm.

LSTM Algorithm also takes a slightly higher time to train as compared to GRU, however, it outperforms GRU, especially when the dataset is large.

Figure 11. Explained Variance Score (EVS) Compared against Time Step (h)

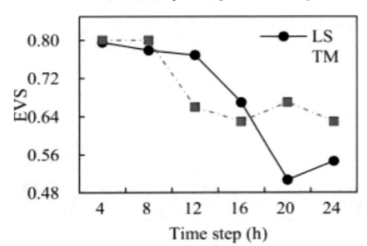

Input and Output

The Users interact with the Website built on Flask. This interaction primarily lets the user understand the use of the website & navigating the user to generate the music. The Music is generated once the user has entered all the relevant details. The user has to select his/her choice of instrument. The algorithm starts processing the request the moment the user has selected the relevant choices.

The parameters other than the instrument of the user's choice are chosen and set to their optimum value by default. The Dropout parameter plays an important role in this portion, as the dropout is selected randomly by the algorithm. This ensures that the music generated every time the algorithm is executed is different.

The output generally takes around 60 seconds to get processed with the pre-defined parameters. This time may however depend on the system being used to run the algorithm. The output of the algorithm is music, that has been generated by the algorithm. The music generated on running the algorithm again would be different, due to the Dropout parameter being randomized.

Consensus

The optimum values of the algorithm were found using analysis. The previous work suggested that the greater the value of Epochs, the better the output is. The following survey with 148 unbiased candidates validates the same.

The Algorithm was trained on a different number of epochs. The models built on different numbers of epochs were then used to produce music. The following are the responses of the candidates on a scale of 1 to 5. Here, 1 denotes that the music produced was Discordant (Unpleasant) and, 5 denotes that the music was Melodious.

Figure 12. User's Response to Music trained on 180 epochs

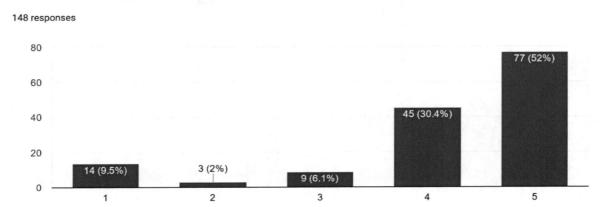

The graph indicates that a large number of people found the music to be melodious. With over 80% of the users selecting options 4 & 5.

Figure 13. User's Response to Music trained on 120 epochs

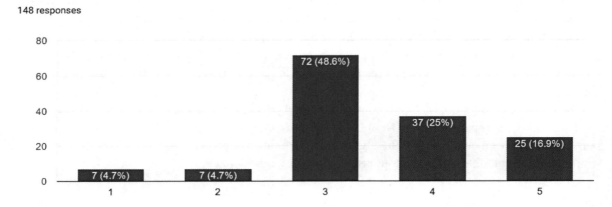

While the users liked the music produced by training the algorithm on 120 epochs, the trend shows that a majority of the users rated the music mediocre (option 3). Thus, the people preferred music trained on 180 epochs.

Figure 14. User's Response to Music trained on 80 epochs

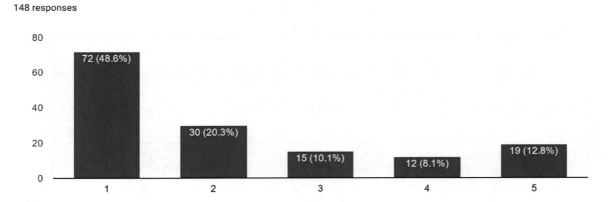

148 responses

The trend of the graph above clearly shows that the majority of the people found the Music trained on 80 epochs unpleasant.

The above results are in line with the concepts of previously researched work, which suggests that increasing the number of epochs leads to better output.

Discussion

The rise of the internet has led to more services available on the internet due to the rising demand & a larger pool of audience. Music being an identity of a brand is essential for small businesses and start-ups. The production of cost of music however can overwhelm a lot of companies that have a lower amount of financial resources. AI Music Generator can be an asset for such companies. The Service is made more reachable by building a flask app, which can be scaled into a deployable website. The website has a simple user interface, which helps the user to understand how the website works and then navigates the users to the webpage where the instrument available is displayed. The user is free to pick the instrument of his/her choice.

The Algorithm generating the music is run, as soon as the user selects the choice of his/her instrument. The Algorithm here producing music is the LSTM algorithm. The Long-short term algorithm remembers patterns of notes or chords of the dataset of music that has been fed into the algorithm. The LSTM Algorithm then produces to generate a sequence of notes or chords based on a variety of parameters. The LSTM Algorithm is pre-trained with a dataset containing music of a particular instrument. The pre-training helps the algorithm to produce the music quicker, as the training time for the model can be as high as 2 days. The algorithm builds a sequence of notes & chords based on the model. The sequence of notes & chords is fed into the music21 library, which produces the music. The user is redirected to another page, where the generated music can be played. The user can then choose to purchase the digital rights of the produced music.

CONCLUSION

The paper proposed an approach to generating music using the concept of LSTM, based on Neural Networks. The idea of music generation is further extended, to build a complete platform on the web. The concepts of music theory are first understood. The ideas are then expanded to understand how music can be generated by understanding which sequences of notes & chords sound harmonious. Various algorithms are analyzed, before choosing the LSTM algorithm, depending on recurrent neural networks. LSTM can remember patterns of chords that sound harmonious. The ML Module compromises the LSTM algorithm, along with the code for cleaning and extraction of data from the dataset. The ML Module is first trained using existing instrumental music.

The users interact with the UI compromising of a web-based platform built on Flask, which is connected to the ML Module. The ML Module, which has been trained using an existing set of music starts running as soon as the user selects their choice of instrument. The Music produced by the LSTM algorithm can then be heard by the user on the webpage. The comparison of the LSTM algorithm has been done with a variety of algorithms on various factors. LSTM algorithm performs significantly better than the traditional approaches to generating music. The algorithm has also been tested thoroughly to optimize the various parameters of the algorithm. This analysis ensures, that the quality of the song produces & the waiting time is equally optimized. The parameters of the algorithm are further checked, by surveying music produced using different parameters in the same algorithm. The users are told to rate the music they hear. The most optimum parameters can be concluded using the combination of the above two analyses.

There are certain aspects of the paper, which can be enhanced in the future. The first one is, that the time for which each note or chord plays remains constant. Although the parameter has been optimized, there is still scope for a wider variety of music. The model can also be trained with a greater number of instruments.

REFERENCES

Bagui, S. C., Mehra, K. L., & Vaughn, B. K. (1997). An M-stage version of the k-RNN rule in statistical discrimination. *Journal of Statistical Planning and Inference*, *65*(2), 323–333. doi:10.1016/S0378-3758(97)00055-4

Beim Graben, P., & Blutner, R. (2019). Quantum approaches to music cognition. *Journal of Mathematical Psychology*, *91*, 38–50. doi:10.1016/j.jmp.2019.03.002

Choi, K., Fazekas, G., Cho, K., & Sandler, M. (2018). The effects of noisy labels on deep convolutional neural networks for music tagging. *IEEE Transactions on Emerging Topics in Computational Intelligence*, *2*(2), 139–149. doi:10.1109/TETCI.2017.2771298

Dong, S., & Ni, N. (2021). A method for representing periodic functions and enforcing exactly periodic boundary conditions with deep neural networks. *Journal of Computational Physics*, *435*, 110242. doi:10.1016/j.jcp.2021.110242

Elmer, S. (2016). Relationships between music training, neural networks, and speech processing. *International Journal of Psychophysiology*, *100*(108), 46. doi:10.1016/j.ijpsycho.2016.07.152

Feng, J., Chai, Y., & Xu, C. (2021). A novel neural network to nonlinear complex-variable constrained nonconvex optimization. *Journal of the Franklin Institute, 358*(8), 4435–4457. doi:10.1016/j.jfranklin.2021.02.029

Gao, S., Huang, Y., Zhang, S., Han, J., Wang, G., Zhang, M., & Lin, Q. (2020). Short-term runoff prediction with GRU and LSTM networks without requiring time step optimization during sample generation. *Journal of Hydrology (Amsterdam), 589*, 125188. doi:10.1016/j.jhydrol.2020.125188

Gers, F. A., Schmidhuber, J., & Cummins, F. (2000). Learning to forget: Continual prediction with LSTM. *Neural Computation, 12*(10), 2451–2471. doi:10.1162/089976600300015015 PMID:11032042

Han, Y., Kim, J., & Lee, K. (2016). Deep convolutional neural networks for predominant instrument recognition in polyphonic music. *IEEE/ACM Transactions on Audio, Speech, and Language Processing, 25*(1), 208–221. doi:10.1109/TASLP.2016.2632307

Herremans, D., & Chew, E. (2017). MorpheuS: Generating structured music with constrained patterns and tension. *IEEE Transactions on Affective Computing, 10*(4), 510–523. doi:10.1109/TAFFC.2017.2737984

Hizlisoy, S., Yildirim, S., & Tufekci, Z. (2021). Music emotion recognition using convolutional long short-term memory deep neural networks. *Engineering Science and Technology, an International Journal, 24*(3), 760-767.

Hutchings, P. E., & McCormack, J. (2019). Adaptive music composition for games. *IEEE Transactions on Games, 12*(3), 270–280. doi:10.1109/TG.2019.2921979

Jiao, M., Wang, D., & Qiu, J. (2020). A GRU-RNN-based momentum optimized algorithm for SOC estimation. *Journal of Power Sources, 459*, 228051. doi:10.1016/j.jpowsour.2020.228051

Kolozali, Ş., Barthet, M., Fazekas, G., & Sandler, M. (2013). Automatic ontology generation for musical instruments based on audio analysis. *IEEE Transactions on Audio, Speech, and Language Processing, 21*(10), 2207–2220. doi:10.1109/TASL.2013.2263801

Li, H. (2020). Piano automatic computer composition by deep learning and blockchain technology. *IEEE Access: Practical Innovations, Open Solutions, 8*, 188951–188958. doi:10.1109/ACCESS.2020.3031155

Liu, F., Zhang, L., & Jin, Z. (2020). Modeling programs hierarchically with stack-augmented LSTM. *Journal of Systems and Software, 164*, 110547. doi:10.1016/j.jss.2020.110547

Mittal, S., & Umesh, S. (2021). A survey on hardware accelerators and optimization techniques for RNNs. *Journal of Systems Architecture, 112*, 101839. doi:10.1016/j.sysarc.2020.101839

Mukherjee, H., Dhar, A., Ghosh, M., Obaidullah, S. M., Santosh, K. C., Phadikar, S., & Roy, K. (2020). Music chord inversion shape identification with LSTM-RNN. *Procedia Computer Science, 167*, 607–615. doi:10.1016/j.procs.2020.03.327

Qi, Y., Liu, Y., & Sun, Q. (2019). Music-driven dance generation. *IEEE Access: Practical Innovations, Open Solutions, 7*, 166540–166550. doi:10.1109/ACCESS.2019.2953698

Rodgers, W., Yeung, F., Odindo, C., & Degbey, W. Y. (2021). Artificial intelligence-driven music biometrics influence customers' retail buying behavior. *Journal of Business Research, 126*, 401–414. doi:10.1016/j.jbusres.2020.12.039

Schiller, I. S., Morsomme, D., & Remacle, A. (2018). Voice use among music theory teachers: Voice dosimetry and self-assessment study. *Journal of Voice, 32*(5), 578–584. doi:10.1016/j.jvoice.2017.06.020 PMID:28754577

Sigtia, S., Benetos, E., & Dixon, S. (2016). An end-to-end neural network for polyphonic piano music transcription. *IEEE/ACM Transactions on Audio, Speech, and Language Processing, 24*(5), 927–939. doi:10.1109/TASLP.2016.2533858

Sturm, B. L., Ben-Tal, O., Monaghan, Ú., Collins, N., Herremans, D., Chew, E., Hadjeres, G., Deruty, E., & Pachet, F. (2019). Machine learning research that matters for music creation: A case study. *Journal of New Music Research, 48*(1), 36–55. doi:10.1080/09298215.2018.1515233

Vijayaprabakaran, K., & Sathiyamurthy, K. (2020). Towards activation function search for the long short-term model network: a differential evolution based approach. *Journal of King Saud University-Computer and Information Sciences.*

Wang, S., Zhao, J., Shao, C., Dong, C., & Yin, C. (2020). Truck traffic flow prediction based on LSTM and GRU methods with sampled GPS data. *IEEE Access: Practical Innovations, Open Solutions, 8*, 208158–208169. doi:10.1109/ACCESS.2020.3038788

Wu, J., Hu, C., Wang, Y., Hu, X., & Zhu, J. (2019). A hierarchical recurrent neural network for symbolic melody generation. *IEEE Transactions on Cybernetics, 50*(6), 2749–2757. doi:10.1109/TCYB.2019.2953194 PMID:31796422

Wu, J., Liu, X., Hu, X., & Zhu, J. (2020). PopMNet: Generating structured pop music melodies using neural networks. *Artificial Intelligence, 286*, 103303. doi:10.1016/j.artint.2020.103303

Ycart, A., & Benetos, E. (2020). Learning and Evaluation Methodologies for Polyphonic Music Sequence Prediction With LSTMs. *IEEE/ACM Transactions on Audio, Speech, and Language Processing, 28*, 1328–1341. doi:10.1109/TASLP.2020.2987130

Zhang, N. (2020). Learning adversarial transformer for symbolic music generation. *IEEE Transactions on Neural Networks and Learning Systems*, 1–10. doi:10.1109/TNNLS.2020.2990746 PMID:32614773

Chapter 7
Reconnoitering Generative Deep Learning Through Image Generation From Text

Vishnu S. Pendyala

https://orcid.org/0000-0001-6494-7832

San Jose State University, USA

VigneshKumar Thangarajan

PayPal, USA

ABSTRACT

A picture is worth a thousand words goes the well-known adage. Generating images from text understandably has many uses. In this chapter, the authors explore a state-of-the-art generative deep learning method to produce synthetic images and a new better way for evaluating the same. The approach focuses on synthesizing high-resolution images with multiple objects present in an image, given the textual description of the images. The existing literature uses object pathway GAN (OP-GAN) to automatically generate images from text. The work described in this chapter attempts to improvise the discriminator network from the original implementation using OP-GAN. This eventually helps the generator network's learning rate adjustment based on the discriminator output. Finally, the trained model is evaluated using semantic object accuracy (SOA), the same metric that is used to evaluate the baseline implementation, which is better than the metrics used previously in the literature.

INTRODUCTION

The objective of this chapter is to explore generative deep learning through the specific example of generating images from text with some control over the placement of objects in the generated image. Expressing ideas in text is often much easier than doing the same in pictures or figures. Coming up with figures is an important skill that is often a formidable challenge even for human beings. In a sense, figures capture the latent semantic space of the corresponding text. Deep learning has been quite ef-

DOI: 10.4018/978-1-6684-6001-6.ch007

fective in processing natural language by capturing its latent space in the language models. With this background, we framed our research question: *to what extent can deep learning systems capture a pictorial representation of a given text and exercise control over the generated image?* We went on to search the literature to survey the existing work in this area and tried to leverage some of it as detailed in the following sections. In general, synthesizing high-quality photo-realistic images is a challenging computer vision problem and has a plethora of practical applications. Generating multiple objects in an image is an even more challenging problem, as there are high chances of missing out on the objects and overlapping of created objects in the image.

Generative Adversarial Networks (GANs) have shown major improvements and capabilities in generating photo-realistic images given an input of textual description. GANs have achieved superlative performance in synthesizing images containing a single object given the textual descriptions as input to the model. Figure 1 shows real-looking images of fictitious people that were generated using a GAN on the website, https://thispersondoesnotexist.com/. As can be seen, it is hard to tell the images are fake. The generator and the discriminator are neural networks that play a minmax game, acting as adversaries (Karras et al., 2020) to produce the astoundingly real-looking images. The generator starts with random Gaussian noise and improves in generating

Figure 1. Images of fictitious people generated on https://thispersondoesnotexist.com using a GAN

real-looking images over several iterations of feedback from the discriminator. The generator tries to make the discriminator believe that the image is that of a real person, while the discriminator acts as an adversary by denying the generator's claim as much as possible. Eventually, when the generator produces images like in Figure 1, the discriminator agrees with the generator's claim and the cycle stops. Given the outstanding performance of GANs combined with the advances in using pretrained deep learning models at text understanding, generating images conditioned on a given textual description seems feasible.

Generating images conditioned on textual description has many applications such as generating a quick visual summary for a text paragraph to enhance the learning experience for students and real-time image generation in sports for a commentary text. The images generated can depict anything from anywhere imagination can take one. For instance, images of flying lions, four-eyed tigers, and flowers that can see with eyes can all be generated by specifying the appropriate words in the text. There were attempts in the past to generate images from directed scene graphs, but they did not achieve significant results. In addition to that, the existing evaluation metrics like Inception Distance do not align with human eye evaluation. Although GANs are successful in these tasks, they are difficult to train, are unstable, and are sensitive to hyperparameters. Previous models like StackGAN faced challenges in generating images that are related to text description as they were using the same text embedding throughout the training process. In addition, these models suffer in the image refinement process, if the image generated at the first attempt is of poor quality.

Object Pathway GAN (OP-GAN) is often the baseline model, which generates photo-realistic images consisting of multiple objects described in the text description. For example, if the textual description is, "two skiers are posing on a snowy slope", the objects expected in the image are "two skiers" and the "snowy slope". The generator network takes labels and other images' metadata like bounding box location as input to generate fine-grained images and the discriminator network feeds on the real image and fake image to classify them into the right bucket. For evaluating the model, we use Semantic Object Accuracy (SOA) (Hinz et al., 2020), which the original implementation in the current literature also uses. SOA is more practical in evaluating the synthetic images compared to other metrics like the Inception score (IS) (Salimans et al., 2016), which fails to significantly indicate the semantic content hidden in the images.

BACKGROUND

In earlier research literature, the process of creating new images from text-based natural language descriptions also known as image synthesis heavily relied upon analysis of a word-to-image correlation. However, recent advancements in deep learning methods and deep generative models can create real-looking images using neural network models and can be extended to generate captivating images based on descriptions in natural language. A successful approach to generate realistic images based on text descriptions uses StackGAN (Stacked Generative Adversarial Network) (Zhang, et al., Stackgan: Text to photo-realistic image synthesis with stacked generative adversarial networks, 2017), and defines a model with two stages. StackGAN++, which is the second version of StackGAN has a noise vector that is introduced along with the conditioning variables, which is input to the first generator. A novel approach that is like StackGAN++ is AttnGAN, Attentional Generative Adversarial Network (Xu, et al., 2018).

In addition to generating text, embedding with conditional variables like previous work (Zhang, Tu, & Cui, 2017), (Reed, et al., 2016), and (Zhang, et al., Stackgan: Text to photo-realistic image synthesis with stacked generative adversarial networks, 2017), AttnGAN's text encoder component generated an additional separate text embedding based on individual words. In addition to the attentional generative network, Deep Attentional Multimodal Similarity Model abbreviated DAMSM (Zhang, et al., Stackgan++: Realistic image synthesis with stacked generative adversarial networks, 2018) is also the major contribution of AttnGAN (Xu, et al., 2018). It tends to add "attentional" details region by region on specific regions of the image independently. After the final stage outputs its high-resolution image, DAMSM is used to compute the closeness of the generated image embedding and the text embedding at both sentence and word level.

Most of the existing text-to-image synthesis models/methods tend to depend heavily on the quality of the initial image (Reed, et al., 2016), (Zhang, et al., Stackgan: Text to photo-realistic image synthesis with stacked generative adversarial networks, 2017), (Zhang, et al., Stackgan++: Realistic image synthesis with stacked generative adversarial networks, 2018) and then refine the initial generated images to a high-resolution one. If the initial image is not well generated, then the quality of images from the refinement process will not be of acceptable quality. Despite the recent advancement in Generative Adversarial Networks to synthesize synthetic images, there are some challenges presented. Visual realism is hard to achieve. The standard of the image quality has scope for improvement. The image generated should precisely illustrate the given textual summary. The model is unlikely to produce the expected result when it is evaluated with a previously unseen scenario.

We set out to look for ways to resolve these challenges by combining the technique of text embedding and the capabilities of Generative Adversarial Networks to synthesize images. Several research articles discussed in the last one or two years have focused on text-image pairing. A taxonomy and timeline of various approaches to generating images from text (Agnese et al., 2020) shows that the enhancements in the approaches can be categorized into semantic, resolution, diversity, and motion. However, the work described in this chapter is predominantly based on the key idea of using object pathways in GANs (Hinz, et al., 2018), which is not covered in the taxonomical survey (Agnese et al., 2020). To generate specified object at the specified locations in an image, an object pathway is added to the generator and discriminator of the GAN. The essential terms in the caption are captured to develop individual objects in the image, which are then combined once the background is generated, forming images with fine-grained details. We use multiple discriminators to produce images with high resolution. This work tries out an efficient deep learning model that demonstrates the capability to generate multiple objects in an image with in-depth details that are seemingly plausible.

State of the Art

A significant breakthrough in connecting visual images with natural language descriptions is CLIP (Radford et al., 2021). The images generated using CLIP have an artistic value (Smith, 2021). CLIP stands for Contrastive Language–Image Pre-training. Using two encoders, one for text and the other for images, the framework can zero-shot learn to associate images with textual descriptions. The idea is to maximize the similarity between the embeddings generated by the two encoders. However, optimizing the similarity between the embeddings is formidable and off-the-shelf packages are not good at it (Liu, et al., 2021). The authors use a pipeline and newer optimization techniques available in the literature to implement zero-shot text-to-image generation without needing extensive training infrastructure. CLIP has been used for zero-shot generation of text from images and vice versa (Galatolo, et al., 2021). A genetic algorithm has been used in the work to maximize the similarity of the embeddings generated by the CLIP framework. The DALL.E system from OpenAI (Ramesh, et al., 2021) is an exhaustive work using an autoregressive transformer with 12 billion parameters that is trained on 250 million pairs of images and the corresponding text description. The images generated can be tuned to match a user-given textual description.

Datasets

CUB (Wah et al., 2011), Oxford, and COCO (Lin et al., 2014) are a few of the datasets used for image synthesis with GAN models. The CUB dataset contains 200 bird images along with text descriptions. The COCO (Common Objects in Context) dataset contains 328k images with 91 different object types. The objects in each image are at unique locations and are annotated in multiple ways. The annotations help with tasks such as object detection, keypoint detection, and semantic segmentation. The images come with five captions each. The annotations for object detection are in the form of bounding boxes. The bounding boxes and captions make the COCO dataset ideal for training the GAN models in this project.

The Oxford dataset contains 102 categories of flowers with 40-258 images each and text descriptions. Additionally, the COCO dataset contains images with multiple objects whereas the CUB and Oxford datasets have images with only a single main object with its text descriptions.

Evaluation Metrics

GAN models are assessed based on certain evaluation metrics, each of which has its own advantages and disadvantages (Borji A., 2022) (Borji A., 2019). Out of the many evaluation metrics used in the literature, Fréchet Inception Distance (FID) (Heusel, Ramsauer, Unterthiner, Nessler, & Hochreiter, 2017) is commonly used as an evaluation metric, which compares the images generated with the real images from the data distribution. A low FID (Zhu, Pan, Chen, & Yang, 2019) is better as this means there is more relationship between the synthetic images being generated by the GAN models and real images. Inception Scores (IS) (Salimans et al., 2016) calculate the randomness of the conditional distribution of images along with the marginal distribution of generated images, which are supposed to be low and high respectively. Both low and high randomness of conditional distribution and marginal distribution respectively are desired features as low randomness means the images are of the same data distribution and high randomness means that the images generated are diverse. The performance of different GAN models used for Text-to- Image synthesis for datasets discussed above along with the evaluation metrics is reported in Table 1.

Table 1. Model comparison sorted by SOA-C

Rank	Model	FID	SOA-C	IS
1	OP-GAN	24.70	35.58	27.88
2	DM - GAN		33.44	30.49
3	AttnGAN		25.88	25.89
4	StackGAN + OP	55.30		12.12

Image Synthesis from Text

The primary objective of this work is to develop a GAN model which can generate images containing multiple objects conditioned on text descriptions. The model is aimed to demonstrate semantic intelligence to decipher what part of the text should be used to generate the corresponding parts of images. The model aims to develop realistic images that are closely related to the description. . In Figure 1, random Gaussian noise is converted into photos that look genuine. Similarly, for this project, text description that can be converted into vectors, which embed the meaning of the words can be converted into images that capture the meaning of the text description. The multi-modal transformation in Figure 1 was from meaningless numbers from a random Gaussian distribution to photo-realistic images. The multi-modal transformation we are targeting for this project is from meaningful text to images that represent the meaning of the text.

Architecture

At a high level, the architected system transforms one kind of numbers to another kind of numbers. Recurrent Neural Networks (RNN) used in the transformer architecture are used to convert the given text description into vectors of numbers that capture the word meanings. Images are essentially numbers – a set of pixel values. Convolutional Neural Networks (CNN) are used to extract the features of the images using a mathematical operation called convolution on the pixel values. The GAN architecture used for this project essentially converts the vectors of numbers representing the given text description into the vectors of numbers that represent the generated image. At a high level, this is primarily done by backpropagating the loss to adjust the weights of the neural networks. The numerical transformations need to go through a stack of GANs that pay attention to different parts of the text description, while improving the resolution of the image. The attention to different words in the text description is staged through a series of GANs.

The architecture of our work is predominantly based on the object pathway GAN (Hinz et al., 2018) and AttnGAN (Xu et al., 2018). In general, like mentioned earlier, GANs have two different networks: a generator that eventually generates images similar to the one given in input samples and a discriminator to differentiate between the real and generated images. AttnGAN architecture (Xu, et al., 2018) is used as a base architecture for our project. It works based on conditional GAN where attention and additional information are conditioned on the generator and three discriminators. Attention is giving importance to different words from the caption to the specific regions of the image. The architecture is illustrated in Figure 2. Captions are converted into word embeddings and bounding boxes are converted into labels. For instance, if the bounding box is around a dog in the image, the label for the bounding box is "dog," which is then converted into a number by using one-hot encoding. The one-hot encoding of the label and the word embeddings for the caption are then combined using a fully connected layer to produce a label. These labels are passed to the first generator, which works with its corresponding discriminator to produce the inputs to the second generator, and so on.

Figure 2. High-Level Architecture

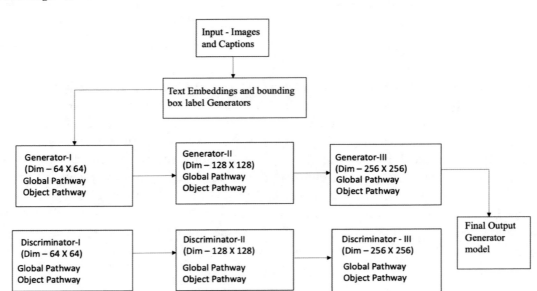

Generator Network

Generators perform up-sampling of the latent space, in this case, the word embeddings of the text description to data in real space, in this case images that capture the intent of the text description. The generator network consists of two different pathways – the global pathway and the object pathway. The generator architecture is illustrated in Figure 3. As their names indicate, the object pathway generates individual objects based on the labels from the pre-trained encoder network. The global pathway generates the "global" scenario - other surrounding common areas of the image which is also conditioned on the text input (Hinz et al., 2018).

Figure 3. Low-level Generator Architecture

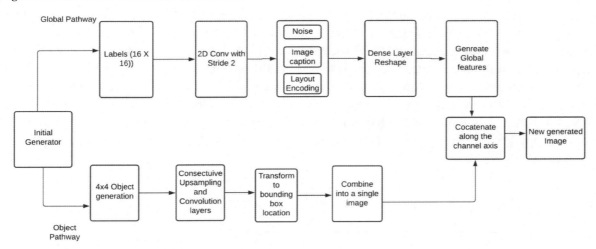

Objects that are associated with the caption are represented in a one-hot vector and the bounding box provides the object's location and size. Object pathway is initialized as an empty zero tensor, after processing all the objects and extracting features, it will have specific features at specific locations and others are marked as zero. A conditioning label is calculated using the one-hot vectors, text embeddings, and noise vector. This label is consumed by the first object pathway in the generator to extract the features and transform them around the bounding box location using a spatial transformer network (STN). Global pathways generate the features by receiving the individual object's location and size and applying a convolutional layer to get layout encoding. At each higher level, objects are conditioned, and features are extracted repeatedly in the same way as from the previous level for each respective resolution. In the process, features are reconditioned by applying several convolutional layers and an up-sampling technique.

Discriminator Network

The discriminator can be thought of as a teacher and the generator, its student who learns from the feedback that the former provides. If the discriminator is trained incorrectly, the generator will be incorrect as well. If the discriminator is trained on incorrect text to image mappings, the generator produces incorrect images for the given text descriptions as well. It is therefore logical that the discriminator also contains the global pathway and object pathway. The object pathway extracts the fine-grained details of individual objects using a Spatial Transformer Network (STN). In the global pathway, an input image is processed by applying a convolutional layer several times with stride two to reduce the resolution of the image, and the process is repeated continuously until it reaches 4 X 4 resolution. It consists of a 2D convolution layer with stride 2, to extract the common global features of the image. Conditional and unconditional losses are calculated for both the generator and discriminator and are optimized by comparing the extracted features with the text embeddings of the image. Thus, the output is a fine-grained image of multiple objects with high resolution.

Web Application Architecture and Deployment

For better usability and comprehensive implementation, we deployed the entire application to be accessible from a web browser. Figure 4 shows the deployment schematic. In a browser client, when the deployment URL is requested, an HTTP request is sent to the web server, where the trained model is deployed. The web server sends back the responses to the web browser, which will be handled by the web browser and display the requested web content. We used the Starlette web application framework for designing the web application for our project. This follows a micro-framework pattern. It is a lightweight WSGI web application framework that provides rapid development, reliability, and scalability to build complex applications. It provides server-side rendering which enables a faster response from the web application when a request is made.

Figure 4. Deployment Diagram

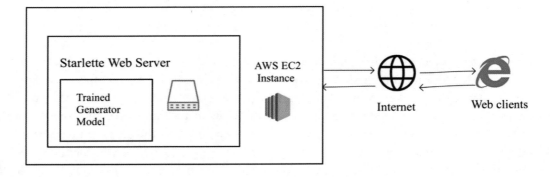

Natural Language and Image Correlation

We use an encoder model for representing fine-grained visual descriptions. The fine-grained visual description denotes how well we can model the words in the caption that describes a particular section of the image. Each part of the caption text contains information about some parts of an image which is why it is crucial to model this before we can construct a generator and discriminator model. Text-based CNN is very similar to the standard image-based CNN. The difference is that the image width is 1 pixel (for a character) and the channel width is the number of unique characters (26 in the case of English). This is followed by a temporal max-pooling layer and a RELU activation layer. Text inputs are characterized by temporal dependencies which are not always captured by CNN models. To address this problem, the hidden layers of the network are constructed with CNN and the top layers are designed to be an RNN to capture the temporal structures in text data. The architecture is illustrated in Figure 5.

Figure 5. Char-CNN-RNN Encoder

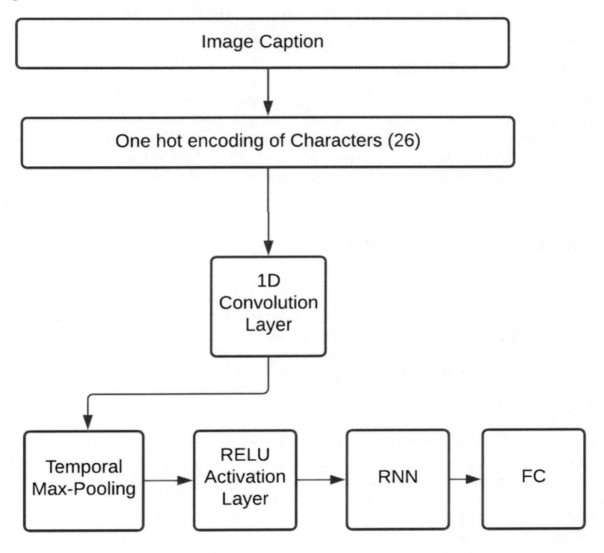

CLIENT IMPLEMENTATION

Starlette

We implemented the Starlette framework for loading the saved model and rendering the output of the model to the users. Starlette is useful as it deals with a synced service. We developed a web application that deploys the GAN model and servers the request for generating the images. We made the model accessible to the user in the browser by utilizing the capabilities of the deep learning model, by abstracting the model itself.

HTML, CSS, and Bootstrap

The HTML web page contains a text box for getting the input as a textual description from the user. On clicking the submit button, the input from the user is sent to the GAN model for generating the images. A list of images is displayed to the user as the result. Cascading Style Sheets are used for stylizing the web page by providing the color of the form and setting the size of the font, text box, etc., Bootstrap framework is implemented to make the web page responsive and make the web page uniform with the existing template.

MIDDLE-TIER IMPLEMENTATION

PyTorch

The entire GAN model is developed using PyTorch. This open-source package provides various utilities for faster development of code and gives fine-grained model implementation functional APIs. We utilized libraries such as transforms for image transformations, "auto grad" for auto differentiations, "nn" for creating the neural networks, "optim" for optimization of training of the models.

Shell Scripting

We developed a shell script for both model training and evaluation. These scripts are the entry point for code invocation. They also support program arguments to the main python file. Some of the model hyperparameters during training and evaluation are defined inside the respective YAML files. The scripts are also responsible for setting up the necessary system path variables. For example, the CUDA_VISIBLE_DEVICES needs to consist of a list of available GPU device indices. These indices will then be referenced by CUDA drivers.

Model Training and Objective function

The model training is initiated from a shell script. The model is trained on a single Nvidia Tesla V100 machine. The objective function of a GAN model is typically a min-max game between the generator and discriminator. However, one difference here is that it is not vanilla GAN but a conditional GAN, conditioned on captions. AttnGAN is used as a baseline model. AttnGAN has achieved significant results in conditional-GAN domain datasets like CUB. The reason being the generator pays more attention to the keywords that describe the image which is spatially and temporally important.

To make the model robust, the discriminator is fed with multiple combinations of text and image pairs. This includes (real text, real image), (fake text, real image), (fake text, fake image), and (real text, fake image). Equation (1) is the overall objective function of the model (Hinz et al., 2018).

$$\underset{G}{min}\,\underset{D}{max}V\left(D,G\right)=\mathbb{E}_{(x,c)\sim p_{(data)}}\left[\log D\left(x,c\right)\right]+\mathbb{E}_{z\sim p(z),c\sim p_{data}}\left[log\left(1-\,\mathrm{D}\left(\mathrm{G}\left(\mathrm{z,c}\right),\;\mathrm{c}\right)\right)\right]$$

IMPLEMENTATION

Natural Language and Image Correlation

We used a pre-trained text encoder model for this task. The pre-trained model is trained on CUB-200 and Oxford Flower dataset. The model is a Char-CNN-RNN encoder model, which is why it captures fine-grained details of the dependency relationship between the text and image. The pre-trained model is trained for 100 epochs after which the model's accuracy has not improved substantially.

Generator Network

The Generator model is constructed using multiple python classes. Figure 6 shows the class-level relationships. The G_NET class is the main class for the generator. It consists of several attributes like CA_NET, h_net1, h_net2, and h_net3. CA_NET is the comprehensive Attention Network. H_net1 is the object of the INIT_STAGE_G class which consists of a bounding box net as its first layer. It also consists of several subsequent up-sampling layers. NEXT_STAGE_G class is used for h_net2 and h_net3 objects. We have also used Gated Linear Unit (GLU) as one of the activation layers in CA_NET to selectively train the model on what part of data to be given attention to.

The implementation of the Global and Object Specific Pathway is similar to the one in the literature (Hinz, et al., 2018).

Discriminator Network

Like the generator, the discriminator is also implemented using a set of python classes. The class diagram of the discriminator is shown in Figure 7. The main class is D_GET_LOGITS which consists of objects like COND_DNET and UNCOND_DNET. These objects are of type D_NET64 (64x64), D_NET128 (128x128) and D_NET256 (256x256). The D_NET128 and D_NET_256 reuse the class attributes of D_NET64. In class D_NET64, we have accommodated the changes for the discriminator network from the original implementation. Spectral normalization is a type of weight normalization helpful in cases where batch normalization does not help much in model performance. Another reason is while training using GPUs, due to low GPU memory, many times we are forced to give lesser batch size. Lesser batch size in training causes random movement in gradient descent and takes a longer time to converge.

Hence, the 2D batch normalization layer is replaced by Spectral normalization. The implementation of the Global and Object Specific Pathway for the discriminator is similar to the one in the literature (Hinz, et al., 2018).

Figure 6. Generator Class Diagram

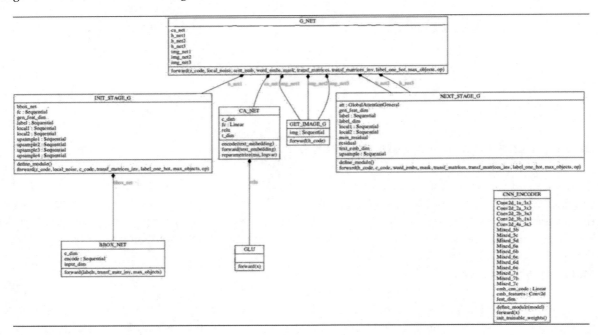

Figure 7. Discriminator Class Diagram

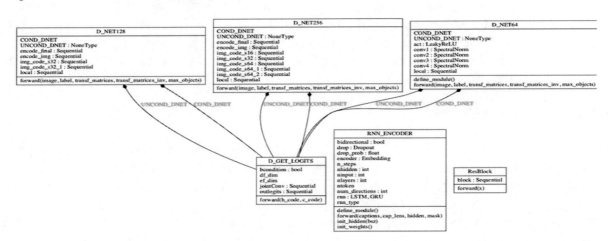

Model Training

The model is trained in Paperspace (https://www.paperspace.com/) cloud provider. We provisioned a machine of type Nvidia Tesla V100. We also used a 100GB SSD hard drive to store the MS-COCO dataset. The SSD drive helps in I/O performance. We have also disabled the Optimized data loading flag from the original implementation to keep the static batch size for every training iteration. Figure 8 shows the snapshot of the machine from Paperspace.

Figure 8. Paperspace NVIDIA Tesla V100 Instance

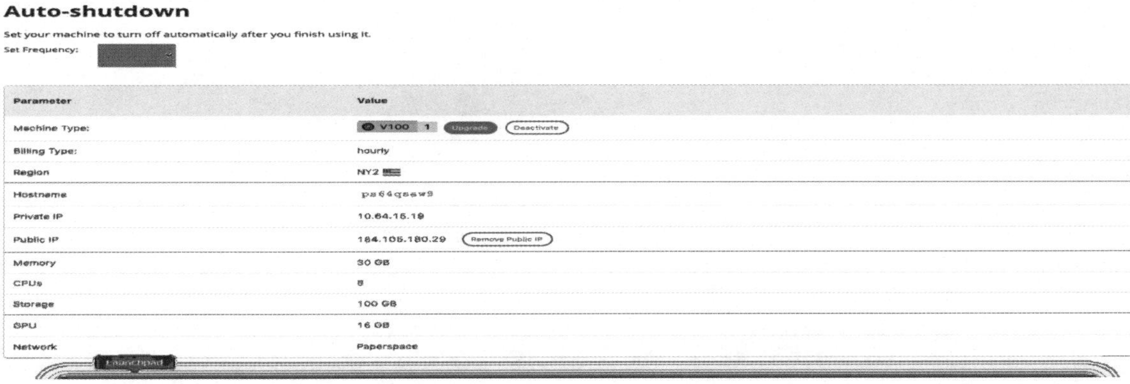

MODEL EXPERIMENTS

Machine Learning Operations with MLflow

We used MLflow for ease of managing our entire Machine Learning project's lifecycle. As per the official website of MLflow, it is an open-source platform for machine learning lifecycle management. It offers four components - MLflow tracking, projects, models, and registry. We leveraged MLflow's tracking component for tracking/logging our GAN model's Generator loss and Discriminator loss. We created a script for auto-logging of the required parameters (batch size, epochs, etc.) for our model. In addition to that, we also tracked metrics such as loss for our generator and discriminator network. Figure 9, 10, and 11 show various screenshots from MLflow.

Performance and Benchmarks

Inception Score (IS) and Fréchet Inception Distance (FID)

For performance metrics and evaluation, we have used the Fréchet Inception Distance score (FID) (Heusel, Ramsauer, Unterthiner, Nessler, & Hochreiter, 2017). FID score takes the feature vector of both real and generated images and calculates the distance between them. The lower the score, the more the similarity between the real and generated/synthetic. That is, FID, evaluates the quality of images generated by the

Generator network and correlates with higher-quality images. The real and generated images are said to be similar, if the FID score is a perfect score of 0.0, indicating identical real and generated images.

Figure 9. Landing page of Mlflow experiments

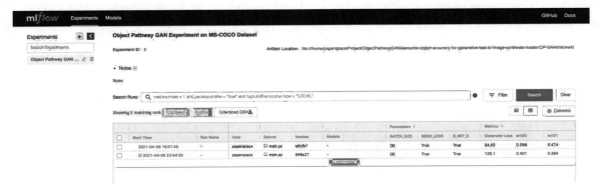

Figure 10. Experiment Parameter

Figure 11. Visualization of Generator loss over time

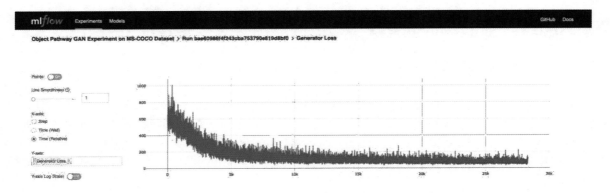

Table 2. CUB Dataset by Inception Score (IS)

Rank	Model	FID	IS
1	DM-GAN	-	4.75
2	Attention-Driver Generator	-	4.58
3	MirrorGAN	-	4.56
4	AttnGAN	-	4.36
5	StackGAN-V2	15.30	3.82
6	StackGAN-V1	51.89	3.70
7	StackGAN	-	3.7

In addition to FID, we have also used the Inception Score (IS) (Salimans et al., 2016), as a metric for evaluating performance in terms of the diversity of the images generated and their quality. The inception score specifically evaluates the quality of the generated/synthetic images generated by the generator network of the GAN model. The inception score captures the image quality and image diversity of the generated / synthetic images. In other words, the Inception score captures, how the images look in terms of a specific object as well as the wide range of objects which are generated in the generated images. The range of the inception score lies between 0.0 to the number of classes supported in the model.

Semantic Object Accuracy (SOA)

SOA (Semantic Object accuracy) is a novel evaluation metric that will evaluate the generated images from the OP-GAN model, given textual description. SOA evaluates if the object in the generated images matches the image caption. For instance, given the caption "A person driving a car" SOA will evaluate if the generated image consists of objects like a person and car. SOA outperforms the two most common evaluation methods: Inception Score (IS) and Fréchet Inception Distance (FID) because they do not take image captions into account when evaluating images.

In the MS-COCO data set, all the text descriptions in the validation set are filtered out based on the keywords which are specified in the labels. There are 80 labels available, and for each label, all the captions are discovered, and three images are generated for each caption. The object detector that we used is the YOLOv3 network, pre-trained on the COCO dataset. It is used to evaluate the given objects on each of the generated images. The process can be simplified using two approaches which are class average SOA-C and image average SOA-I (Hinz et al., 2020). SOA-C gives us the average number of images per class that the given object is detected and SOA-I gives us the average of the number of images in which the desired object was detected. The formula for SOA-I and SOA-C is given below (Hinz et al., 2020),

$$SOA - C = \frac{1}{|C|} \sum_{c \in C} \frac{1}{|Ic|} \sum_{i_c \in I_C} YOLOv3 \left(ic \right)$$

$$SOA - I = \frac{1}{\pounds_c \epsilon C |I_c|} \sum_{c \in C} \sum_{i_c \in I_c} YOLOv3 \left(i_c \right)$$

Table 3. Oxford dataset by Inception Score (IS)

Rank	Model	FID	IS
1	StackGAN-V2	48.68	3.26
2	StackGAN-V1	55.28	3.20
3	StackGAN		3.2

Deployment, Operations, Maintenance

To serve our model on the web, we used the Starlette ASGI web framework. When the end-user clicks on "generate images", our model serves the request by using our trained GAN model. This process of generating the images is done by passing the text input through the text encoder. This text encoder extracts the semantic features. The saved weights of our model are used to serve the user request and based on these weights and the semantic meaning of text describing the images is generated. Figure 12 below illustrates the deployment architecture.

Figure 12. Deployment Architecture

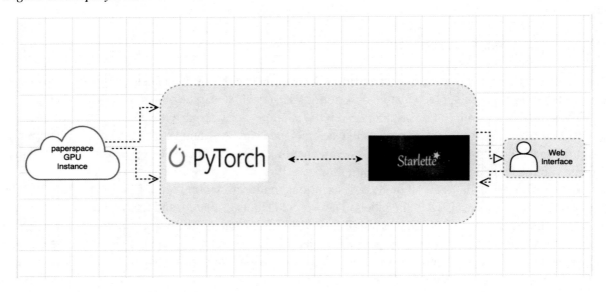

CONCLUSION

The area of generative deep learning is vast and expanding. This chapter gave a focused and comprehensive view of the various aspects, including the deployment of generative deep learning for creating synthetic images from descriptions in natural language. We evaluated our work using multiple relevant evaluation metrics. The task has plenty of potentials and is still evolving. From our assessment, currently, the textual descriptions from which images can be generated are limited by their length and scope. With more powerful models trained on humongous datasets on the horizon, a future direction can be to generate more extensive images from longer texts. Such a possibility opens up a plethora of applications such as illustrating children's story books, generating animated movies from screenplay, and adding figures to research manuscripts. Editing software such as Microsoft Word may be able to provide these services as a value-add, similar to how designer ideas are incorporated into Microsoft powerpoint.

ACKNOWLEDGMENT

The authors are grateful to Sivaranjani Kumar, Akshaya Nagarajan, and Pooja Patil for their contribution to this project.

This research received no specific grant from any funding agency in the public, commercial, or not-for-profit sectors, but was supported by San Jose State University.

REFERENCES

Agnese, J., Herrera, J., Tao, H., & Zhu, X. (2020). A survey and taxonomy of adversarial neural networks for text-to-image synthesis. *Wiley Interdisciplinary Reviews. Data Mining and Knowledge Discovery*, *10*(4), e1345. doi:10.1002/widm.1345

Borji, A. (2019). Pros and cons of gan evaluation measures. *Computer Vision and Image Understanding*, *179*, 41–65. doi:10.1016/j.cviu.2018.10.009

Borji, A. (2022). Pros and cons of GAN evaluation measures: New developments. *Computer Vision and Image Understanding*, *215*, 103329. doi:10.1016/j.cviu.2021.103329

Galatolo, F., Cimino, M., & Vaglini, G. (2021) Generating Images from Caption and Vice Versa via CLIP-Guided Generative Latent Space Search. *International Conference on Image Processing and Vision Engineering*. 10.5220/0010503701660174

Heusel, M., Ramsauer, H., Unterthiner, T., Nessler, B., & Hochreiter, S. (2017). Gans trained by a two time-scale update rule converge to a local nash equilibrium. *Advances in Neural Information Processing Systems*, 30.

Hinz, T., Heinrich, S., & Wermter, S. (2018, September). Generating Multiple Objects at Spatially Distinct Locations. *International Conference on Learning Representations*.

Hinz, T., Heinrich, S., & Wermter, S. (2020). Semantic object accuracy for generative text-to-image synthesis. *IEEE Transactions on Pattern Analysis and Machine Intelligence*. PMID:32877332

Karras, T., Laine, S., Aittala, M., Hellsten, J., Lehtinen, J., & Aila, T. (2020). Analyzing and improving the image quality of stylegan. In *Proceedings of the IEEE/CVF conference on computer vision and pattern recognition* (pp. 8110-8119). 10.1109/CVPR42600.2020.00813

Lin, T. Y., Maire, M., Belongie, S., Hays, J., Perona, P., Ramanan, D., ... Zitnick, C. L. (2014, September). Microsoft coco: Common objects in context. In *European conference on computer vision* (pp. 740-755). Springer.

Liu, X., Gong, C., Wu, L., Zhang, S., Su, H., & Liu, Q. (2021). *Fusedream: Training-free text-to-image generation with improved clip+ gan space optimization.* arXiv preprint arXiv:2112.01573.

Radford, A., Kim, J. W., Hallacy, C., Ramesh, A., Goh, G., Agarwal, S., ... Sutskever, I. (2021, July). Learning transferable visual models from natural language supervision. In *International Conference on Machine Learning* (pp. 8748-8763). PMLR.

Ramesh, A., Pavlov, M., Goh, G., Gray, S., Voss, C., Radford, A., ... Sutskever, I. (2021, July). Zero-shot text-to-image generation. In *International Conference on Machine Learning* (pp. 8821-8831). PMLR.

Reed, S., Akata, Z., Yan, X., Logeswaran, L., Schiele, B., & Lee, H. (2016). Generative adversarial text to image synthesis. *International conference on machine learning* (pp. 1060–1069). Academic Press.

Salimans, T., Goodfellow, I., Zaremba, W., Cheung, V., Radford, A., & Chen, X. (2016). Improved techniques for training gans. *Advances in Neural Information Processing Systems, 29.*

Smith, A., & Colton, S. (2021). Clip-guided gan image generation: An artistic exploration. *Evo, 2021, 17.*

Wah, C., Branson, S., Welinder, P., Perona, P., & Belongie, S. (2011). *The Caltech-UCSD Birds-200-2011 dataset.* Academic Press.

Xu, T., Zhang, P., Huang, Q., Zhang, H., Gan, Z., Huang, X., & He, X. (2018). Attngan: Fine-grained text to image generation with attentional generative adversarial networks. *Proceedings of the IEEE conference on computer vision and pattern recognition, 1316–1324.* 10.1109/CVPR.2018.00143

Zhang, G., Tu, E., & Cui, D. (2017). Stable and improved generative adversarial nets (GANS): a constructive survey. *2017 IEEE International Conference on Image Processing (ICIP), 1871–1875.* 10.1109/ICIP.2017.8296606

Zhang, H., Xu, T., Li, H., Zhang, S., Wang, X., Huang, X., & Metaxas, D. N. (2017). Stackgan: Text to photo-realistic image synthesis with stacked generative adversarial networks. *Proceedings of the IEEE international conference on computer vision, 5907–5915.* 10.1109/ICCV.2017.629

Zhang, H., Xu, T., Li, H., Zhang, S., Wang, X., Huang, X., & Metaxas, D. N. (2018). Stackgan++: Realistic image synthesis with stacked generative adversarial networks. *IEEE Transactions on Pattern Analysis and Machine Intelligence, 41*(8), 1947–1962. doi:10.1109/TPAMI.2018.2856256 PMID:30010548

Zhu, M., Pan, P., Chen, W., & Yang, Y. (2019). Dm-gan: Dynamic memory generative adversarial networks for text-to-image synthesis. *Proceedings of the IEEE/CVF Conference on Computer Vision and Pattern Recognition, 5802–5810.* 10.1109/CVPR.2019.00595

KEY TERMS AND DEFINITIONS

AttnGAN: Attentional Generative Adversarial Network. A machine learning model, generating images from textual description allowing attention-driven, multi-stage refinement to generate images.

COCO: Common Objects in Context. A large-scale dataset used for applications like captioning, object detection, and segmentation.

CUB: Caltech-UCSD Birds. An image dataset of two hundred bird species.

GAN: Generative Adversarial Network. A machine learning model which has two neural networks, namely Generator responsible to generate realistic images, and a Discriminator responsible to discriminate real and fake images generated by Generator.

OPGAN: Object Pathway Generative Adversarial Network. A machine learning model, which specifically models individual objects based on text description to generate images.

STACKGAN: Stacked Generative Adversarial Network. A machine learning model which consists of two stages to generate images from text.

Chapter 8
Automatic Image Captioning Using Different Variants of the Long Short-Term Memory (LSTM) Deep Learning Model

Ritwik Kundu

https://orcid.org/0000-0001-5666-8833

Vellore Institute of Technology, Vellore, India

Shaurya Singh

Vellore Institute of Technology, Vellore, India

Geraldine Amali

Vellore Institute of Technology, Vellore, India

Mathew Mithra Noel

https://orcid.org/0000-0002-3442-1642

Vellore Institute of Technology, Vellore, India

Umadevi K. S.

Vellore Institute of Technology, Vellore, India

ABSTRACT

Today's world is full of digital images; however, the context is unavailable most of the time. Thus, image captioning is quintessential for providing the content of an image. Besides generating accurate captions, the image captioning model must also be scalable. In this chapter, two variants of long short-term memory (LSTM), namely stacked LSTM and BiLSTM along with convolutional neural networks (CNN) have been used to implement the Encoder-Decoder model for generating captions. Bilingual evaluation understudy (BLEU) score metric is used to evaluate the performance of these two bi-layered models. From the study, it was observed that both the models were on par when it came to performance. Some resulted in low BLEU scores suggesting that the predicted caption was dissimilar to the actual caption whereas some very high BLEU scores suggested that the model was able to predict captions almost similar to human. Furthermore, it was found that the bidirectional LSTM model is more computationally intensive and requires more time to train than the stacked LSTM model owing to its complex architecture.

DOI: 10.4018/978-1-6684-6001-6.ch008

INTRODUCTION

Artificial Intelligence, a field in computer science that aims in giving computers the ability to mimic human-like intelligence, is being heavily deployed in building powerful and highly intelligent machines. Nowadays, Machine learning has become quite popular in the field of Artificial Intelligence; and is often used interchangeably with the term 'Artificial Intelligence'. One of the most studied sub-domains of machine learning is Deep Learning, which provides high accuracy in its results, so its performance is high too through its output. One such field of work where artificial intelligence can be applied is image captioning. The idea of being able to explore more about perceptual tasks like image recognition or object detection has enabled researchers to take up more complex tasks which are much above and beyond image recognition (Ivašić-Kos et al., 2019). Image captioning has a huge positive impact on society, for instance it can be used for facilitating ones with visual impairment in understanding the different types of imagery data available on the internet without any external support. Image captioning entails extracting important content from an image and representing it in the form of a meaningful sequence of words. The key idea behind image captioning is to recognise and analyse objects, the relationships between them and the actions performed by the objects from a given input image (Hossain et al., 2019). In simple terms, the process of automatically describing the contents of an image by the use of deep learning and natural language sentences is called Image Captioning. This technique is used for the conversion of images, which are a sequence of pixels into a sequence of words. This can be considered as an end-to-end and sequence-to-sequence (seq2seq) problem. The authors of this chapter aim to build a model that can provide the caption for any image presented to it accurately and quickly.

In order to achieve their purpose of building a sustainable Image Captioning software, the concepts of Deep Learning will be implemented. A rapidly growing and researched domain, Deep Learning is gradually getting into all of our daily lives. It involves the use of ANN (artificial neural networks) using robust and high performing, premium and up-to-date hardware. Deep learning facilitates the development, training, and application of neural networks while keeping the time constraint required for the same as minimum. One such neural network is Convolution Neural Network (CNN). The Convolutional Neural Networks were designed for the purpose of mapping the input image data to an output variable. CNNs have proved to be very effective in these applications and thus they are very commonly used in a variety of prediction problems that involve images as an input. Long Short-Term Memory model (LSTM) is another such neural network. A variant of the Recurrent Neural Networks, it is used frequently with problems involving images. It is a distinct type of network, which has the capability of learning long-term dependencies within the data.

The primary objective of this chapter is to design a neural network that when trained can recognize real as well as synthetic images. It should be able to generate the most accurate caption for a given image in the matter of a few seconds. By combining the advantages of CNN and LSTM models, the aim has been to develop a novel Image Captioning model.

BACKGROUND

The complexity of images can vary widely from being described by a single word to requiring multiple phrases to describe a single image. The authors of this chapter have conducted a detailed analysis of different related studies conducted across the world in order to understand the different models used in similar applications of ML (machine learning) and DL (deep learning). The following table comprises of a summary of some of the existing work in this domain:

Table 1. Literature review for existing models of image captioning

Author/Year	Title	Contribution	Drawbacks
Imtinan Azhar, Imad Afyouni, Ashraf Elnagar (2021)	Facilitated Deep Learning Models for Image Captioning	Facilitated deep learning models provide superior performance as compared to the non-facilitated deep learning models; Facilitated methodology enabled the authors to distil responsibility while simultaneously removing a single point of failure.	The facilitated deep learning model proposed by the authors in this paper did not succeed in providing good quality captions for the basic generator.
Jyoti Aneja, Aditya Deshpande, Alexander G. Schwing (2018)	Convolutional Image Captioning	This model developed by the authors was faster and had a lower training time per number of parameters without affecting the performance when compared to a LSTM baseline.	In many cases the captions generated were semantically incoherent as the model focused more on important objects like man, bike, table, etc. and less on words unrelated to image content like a, of, an, etc.
Nikhil Patwari, Dinesh Naik (2021)	En-De-Cap: An Encoder Decoder model for Image Captioning	Gated recurrent units or GRU has a simpler architecture and is much easier to train in comparison to LSTM; Attention Mechanism in the proposed model helps in increasing the accuracy of the model.	BLEU - 2,4 scores were still higher for the framework using the LSTM model.
Jieh-Ren Chang, Tsung-Ta Ling, Ting-Chun Li (2020)	A Research on Image Captioning by Different Encoder Networks	The proposed model has better description from a human viewpoint and has a higher R-BLEU score.	Accuracy of the model drops with longer sentences because the Seq2Seq model fits all input into a semantic vector of fixed length.
Prashant Giridhar Shambharkar, Priyanka Kumari, Pratik Yadav, Rajat Kumar (2021)	Generating Caption for Image using Beam Search and Analyzation with Unsupervised Image Captioning Algorithm	This paper gives a comparative usage analysis of the Argmax and Beam search method; The model designed using an unsupervised algorithm provides enhanced accuracy with 28.9%.	Higher batch sizes of datasets are needed to improve the accuracy and memory efficiency.
Jacob Devlin, Saurabh Gupta, Ross Girshick, Margaret Mitchell, C. Lawrence Zitnick (2015)	Exploring Nearest Neighbour Approaches for Image Captioning	The authors have made use of the nearest neighbour approaches for providing a high performing model for similar images.	Not suitable for highly dissimilar images. Further tests are required for determining the overall effectiveness of the nearest neighbour approach in image captioning.
Md. Zakir Hossain, Ferdous Sohel, Md. Fairuz Shiratuddin, Hamid Laga, Mohammed Bennamoun (2021)	Text to Image Synthesis for Improved Image Captioning	This paper shows that the combination of real and synthetic images in a model helps it achieve a performance boost compared to other methods; Synthetic Images increase the effectiveness of any image-captioning model.	Image synthesis can be done only from text but not from real images.
Jacob Devlin, Hao Cheng, Hao Fang, Saurabh Gupta, Li Deng, Xiaodong He, Geoffrey Zweig, Margaret Mitchell (2015)	Language Models for Image Captioning: The Quirks and What Works	RNN language model achieves better BLEU performance than a ME (Maximum Entropy) model; The MRNN is outperformed by the ME language model significantly, in terms of human quality judgments.	The improved BLEU score does not translate to improved human quality judgments.

Image captioning algorithms can be primarily categorised into two types, one is based on the template method, whereas the other one is dependent on the encoder-decoder structure (Wang et al., 2021). As a part of this survey of existing work, some popularly used models in this domain have been identified, namely Encoder Decoder Model for Image Captioning, Image Captioning using Beam Search method, Unsupervised Image Captioning algorithms, and Image Captioning using Nearest Neighbour Approach.

In the Encoder Decoder Model for Image Captioning, the approach used is to caption an image using CNN network. The integration of attention-based Gated Recurrent Unit (GRU) helps generate better and vivid text for a given image. However, some limitations have been identified in this model. The model was trained only on one dataset to avoid a computationally intensive process. BLEU - 2,4 scores obtained were still higher for the framework using the LSTM model (Patwari et al., 2021). Some models use the Statistical Language model as a decoder, which converts the caption generation problem into an optimization problem and solves it by finding the most optimal sequence for the same (Wang et al., 2020).

The Image Captioning using Beam Search and Analyzation technique involves the use of supervised as well as unsupervised learning techniques in the building phase of the model. For developing the model discussed in this chapter, pre-trained models have been used for feature extraction. The output from these models is fed to the RNN/LSTM as input vector model for generating the final captions (Shambharkar et al., 2021). However, higher batch sizes of datasets are needed to improve the accuracy and memory efficiency.

In the Image Captioning using Nearest Neighbour approach, the caption for a given input image is generated by finding the most suitable caption representing the accordion of the set of candidates obtained from the nearest neighbouring images. However, it is not suitable for highly dissimilar images. Further tests are required for determining the overall effectiveness of the nearest neighbour approach in image captioning using this model (Devlin et al., 2015).

The various different models have disadvantages of their own. Some deep learning models fail to provide satisfactory results even after overcoming single-point failure and facilitation issues. Some models have used techniques like GRU (Patwari et al., 2021), Beam search method (Shambharkar et al., 2021), Argmax method, etc., which are easier to train but fail to furnish an increase in accuracy over the existing models. Some LSTM based models have a higher focus on salient objects, which leads to an increase in semantic errors (Devlin et al., 2015). A semantic error in terms of a machine learning algorithm means that there is no error in the syntactical structuring of the model but the results produced by the model doesn't make much sense in terms of the model of computation used. Whereas some models having better accuracy and overall performance fail to show consistency when it comes to longer sentences. Another common issue is the non-availability of larger datasets. Most of the models fail to provide satisfactory results with limited data. A unique problem seen in one of the papers is that the technical accuracy scores obtained in machine learning models isn't directly proportional to enhanced human perception (Cheng et al., 2015). Identifying all the drawbacks helps bridge the gap in study and suggests a suitable model for the task.

The chapter is organized as follows: The CNN – LSTM based image captioning model is presented followed by the different pre-processing steps in detail along with the necessary contributions of every step in the machine learning pipeline, the relevant datasets and so on. This has been followed by a demonstration and visualisation of the model, its outcome on the dataset and a discussion of the results and future research directions.

PROPOSED MODEL

The previous section gives a clearer understanding of the premises of image captioning and helps choose a model suitable for the purpose with higher efficiency and lower overheads.

A hybrid model based on the Encoder-Decoder framework with the combination of CNN layers (for feature extraction on input images) in conjunction with LSTM (an artificial RNN for supporting sequence prediction and classification) is proposed. An evaluation of different flavours of LSTM, namely Stacked LSTM and Bi-LSTM will also be conducted to analyse their performance. Finally, the model will be trained and tested on the Flickr 8k dataset taken from Kaggle.

Model For Automatic Image Captioning

The proposed system consists of two primary models, which are as follows:

I.   Convolutional Neural Network (CNN)

This model is used to perform automatic feature extraction. It detects the significant features on its own without any human supervision. Feature extraction involves converting raw data to numerical features while retaining the information available in the original dataset. A pre-trained VGG16 model, excluding the outer layer (since this model is not being used for object classification but only feature extraction) will be used for developing the model in the scope of the problem.

II.   Long Short-Term Memory (LSTM)

It is a kind of artificial recurrent neural network (RNN) model designed for solving sequence prediction problems. It has the ability to store previous information. Considering a novel task, LSTMs require more careful engineering (Aneja et al., 2018). Followed by activation using ReLU (Rectified Linear Activation Function), two different variants of LSTM will be used for prediction of the captions. The two different models of LSTM that will be used are Stacked LSTM and Bidirectional LSTM (Bi-LSTM).

The process of image captioning falls in the domain of Natural Language Processing (NLP) and Computer Vision. In simple terms, it is nothing but the process of converting input images to their corresponding output captions. The most popular approach in this domain is an Encoder-Decoder framework. The Convolutional Neural Network (CNN) used for the purpose of feature extraction can be thought of as an encoder. The Recurrent Neural Network (RNN) connected from the last layer of the CNN used for modelling and sequence prediction can be thought of as the decoder. In the Encoder-Decoder framework, an encoder is supposed to convert the information present within the image to some intermediate representation and the decoder is supposed to convert that intermediate representation to an output text sequence (Hossain et al., 2021).

I.   Feature extraction using CNN

With the increasing size of data, it is common to encounter hundreds of features in a dataset. A machine learning model suffers from overfitting when the number of features in the dataset is the same or more than the recognition number stored in the database. This can be avoided in two different ways, namely by regularisation and dimensionality reduction (or, feature extraction) to obtain numerical features from raw data that can be processed. Feature extraction has some advantages over regularisation, which are as follows:

Figure 1. High-level diagram representing the proposed framework for caption generation

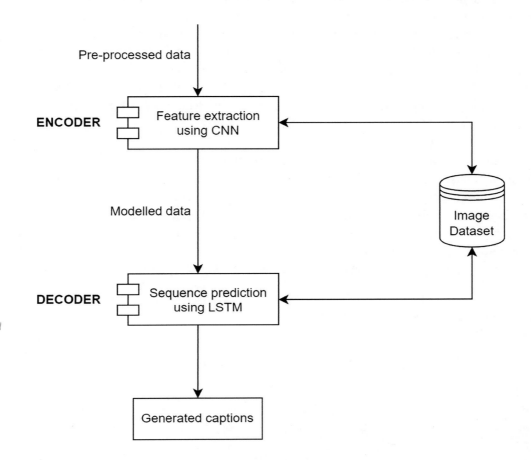

- Improvement in accuracy
- Reduction in overfitting
- Improvement in the speed of training
- Improvement in the visualisation of data
- Improvement in the explainability of the model

There are different techniques that can be used for feature extraction based on the type of data, features to be extracted and model of data to be developed. Some of the popular techniques are ICA (Independent Component Analysis), PCA (Principal Component Analysis), LDA (Linear Discriminant Analysis), LLE (Locally Linear Embedding), etc.

Feature extraction can be achieved in two ways, manually or automatically. Manual extraction requires identifying and defining the relevant features of a particular problem and using a method to remove those features. In most cases, a clear understanding of the background is required to make informed decisions about which factors are most relevant. Automatic feature extraction uses special algorithms or deep neural networks to automatically extract features from signals or images without any human intervention. This is useful in building machine learning algorithms from raw data.

Feature extraction for image data identifies parts of an image into a compact feature vector to represent relevant and meaningful parts of the image. In modern days, deep learning is prevalent in image and video analysis in comparison to the specialised detection, extraction and matching algorithms used in the past.

Convolutional Neural Network – Also called ConvNet or CNN, it is a variant of deep neural network used on data with a grid-like structure, that is, structured arrays like images. A digital image is represented as an array of pixel values, which makes CNN suitable for processing images. CNN is a multi-layered feed-forward neural network with a sequential design to learn hierarchical attributes. It has three main layers:

- Convolutional layer – This layer is used for performing a dot product between two matrices, representing the set of learnable parameters and the restricted portion of the receptive field, respectively. This carries most of the computational load of the neural network.
- Pooling layer – This layer is responsible for replacing the output of the network with a statistical summary of the nearby outputs. It helps in reducing the spatial size of the entire representation and subsequently the computational complexity.
- Fully connected layer – This layer maps the complete representation between input and output.

Figure 2. Convolutional Neural Network
Source: Towards Data Science, 2018

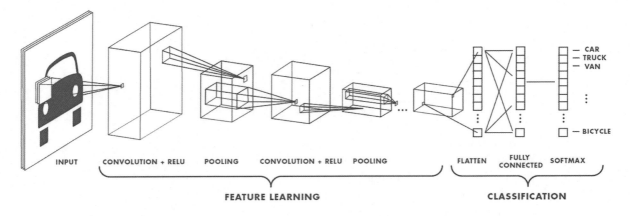

The advantages of using CNN are as follows:

- It does not require human intervention.
- It achieves very high accuracy by seamless feature extraction.
- It performs weight sharing.

As a result of all these, it has found a variety of applications in a number of domains. It is being used in the fields of object detection in various industries, like facial detection, autonomous vehicles, etc. It is also being used in semantic segmentation applications and image captioning models recently.

II. Sequence prediction using LSTM

Sequence prediction is a well-known method of machine learning, which involves predicting the following signs based on the sequence of previously seen signs, which can be a number, alphabet, name, event, word, etc. It is different from supervised machine learning tasks and is used in various industries and real-life applications.

Automatically generating natural language captions based on visual content has attracted many researchers in the field of artificial intelligence. This is challenging because it combines computer-assisted visualisation and natural language processing, which involves object detection and the relationship of objects to an image and the study of grammar to make descriptive texts. LSTM is the most popular model used for sequence prediction.

Long Short-Term Memory or LSTM in short is an advanced version of recurrent neural network architecture – an artificial RNN that was designed for the use case of modelling of sequences timed chronologically along with their long-range dependencies better than the conventional RNNs were capable of doing. Recurrent neural networks find their applications in NLP tasks such as modelling and text generation problems, creating translation machines, voice recognition problems and so on. RNN is a type of neural network where the output from the previous step is used as input to the current step. The advantages of using a recurrent neural network are:

- It is suitable for forecasting time series because it retains information through time.
- It gives a high effective pixel neighbourhood when used with a convolutional layer.

LSTMs, unlike the conventional feedforward neural networks, have feedback connections. They have the capability to process both single data points (like images), as well as continuous arrays of data (audio, video, etc.). LSTMs are explicitly designed to solve the long-term dependency issue that arises in NLP tasks. All recurrent neural networks have a similar architecture in the pattern of a series of repeating neural network modules (generally four neural networks). Standard RNNs have a simple structured repeating module, such as a single 'tanh' layer. LSTMs like all other RNNs also have this chain-like structure, however, the repeating module has a much more complex structure opposed to a standard repeating module. There are four neural networks in an LSTM model, which have a unique interactive mechanism. The fundamental of LSTMs is their cell state. It works more like a conveyor belt, running straight through the entire chain with minimum linear interactions. Information can flow along this easily without being changed. LSTM can remove or add information to the cell state, which is regulated by structures called gates. Gates are an optional way to let information pass through cells. They comprise of a sigmoid neural net layer and a pointwise multiplication operation.

The advantages of using LSTM are as follows:

- They are able to find, understand and model long-term sequence dependencies.
- They are more powerful as compared to Vanilla RNNs in the problem of short memory.
- They can bridge the gap in unknown duration of time series, thus are a good fit for time-series based classification, processing and prediction.
- They have a wide range of parameters, including biases (input and output), learning rates, etc. Therefore, there is no need for fine-tuning.

- They are tolerant to noise, distributed representations and continuous values in long delay (time lag) problems.

Figure 3. Long Short Term memory (LSTM)
Source: Analytics Vidhya, 2021

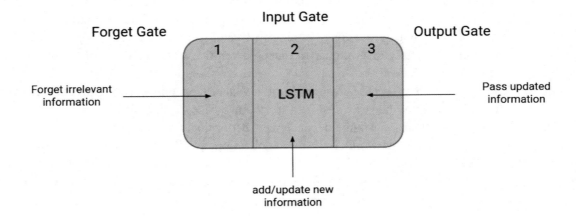

LSTM has three main parts: an input gate, an output gate and a forget gate. The values are recollected over arbitrary time intervals and influx and outflux of data in the cell are regulated by each of the three gates. The input gate adds or updates new information; the forget gate forgets irrelevant and outdated information, whereas the output gate is used to pass on updated information.

In the modern world, LSTMs are being used in a whole host of different domains. Ranging from robot control, time series prediction, speech recognition to handwriting recognition, sign language translation, market prediction and even airport passenger management.

There are different variants of univariate LSTM. The following section discusses about some of them:

- **Vanilla LSTM** – This is the simplest univariate LSTM model. With one feature for every variable, this model comprises of a single hidden layer composed of LSTM units, and an output layer. The hidden layer is functional in making a prediction.
- **Stacked LSTM** – This is another univariate LSTM model, which has multiple hidden layers of LSTM stacked one above the other. Since LSTMs require a three-dimensional input, the two-dimensional output from the previous LSTM layer is converted to three-dimensional by adding a layer of time-step data from the return sequence.
- **Bidirectional LSTM** – This is another univariate LSTM model, which allows the model to learn in both directions, forward and backward. It involves duplicating the first layer in the network, so that there are two identical layers parallel to each-other. The input is fed in-order. The original input sequence is given to the first layer and a reversed copy of the same is given as input to the second layer.
- **CNN LSTM** – This is a hybrid univariate LSTM model, which uses CNN to interpret sub-sequences before the data is provided as an input to the LSTM layer.

- **ConvLSTM –** This is an advanced version of the CNN LSTM model, which consists of the convolutional reading obtained from the input directed into the LSTM model.

Apart from this, there are different variants of multivariate models as well, like multiple input and multiple parallel models, along with different types of multi-step models, like encoder-decoder and vector output model. The hybrid of these two types of models have also resulted in models like "multiple input multi-step output", and "multiple parallel input and multi-step output".

Figure 4. Detailed flow diagram representing the complete model for caption generation

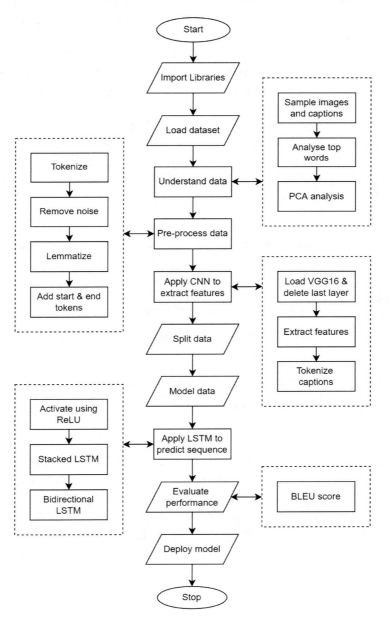

Detailed Description of Model

The different components of the system are described below:

I. Import libraries – Some basic libraries like numpy, pandas, matplotlib, tensorflow, keras, sys, time, os, warnings, copy have been used for basic functions like importing dataset, visualisations, etc. Along with these, libraries like sklearn, collections, PIL, nltk, etc. have also been imported. Some classes like load_img & img_to_array are imported from the sub-package image of keras package to pre-process the image files. The Input, Flatten, Dropout, Activation, Bidirectional classes are imported from the layers sub-package of keras. Classes like stopwords, WordNetLemmatizer, bleu_score are imported from sub-packages of the nltk package for different functions.

The environment has been set up to use up to ninety-five percent of the available GPU memory to boost the processing speed. This has been done using the config argument of Tensorflow sessions. This acts as a hard upper bound on the GPU memory being used by the model while executing.

II. Load dataset – The respective image (.jpg) and corresponding captions (.txt) files are loaded on the system and indexed for further usage from the Flickr 8K dataset downloaded from Kaggle. The captions are converted into a pandas dataframe along with the name of the file it describes.

III. Understand data – This is a data exploratory stage where the dataset is explored by analysing some vital statistics and displaying some samples from the dataset.

Figure 5. Sample data point from the Flickr 8K dataset with the five human annotated captions for the given image

man on a bicycle riding on only one wheel .

asian man in orange hat is popping a wheelie on his bike .

a man on a bicycle is on only the back wheel .

a man is doing a wheelie on a mountain bike .

a man does a wheelie on his bicycle on the sidewalk .

This also includes analysing the count of the top five words used in the cleaned dataset (after performing all pre-processing steps). The frequency of the top twenty most frequently and top twenty least frequently used in the dataset are also plotted.

The similar images from the dataset are plotted together by forming clusters followed by dimensionality reduction performed using PCA analysis. Similar images are grouped together and a colour code is assigned to them.

Figure 6. Bar chart showing the twenty most frequently used words in the dataset along with their frequency of usage

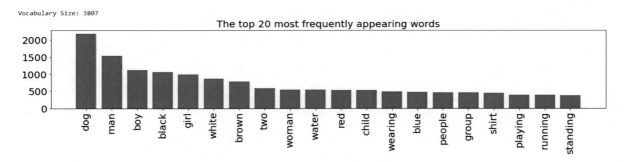

Figure 7. Similar images from the Flickr 8K dataset obtained using PCA analysis

Principal Component Analysis (PCA) – It is an orthogonal transformation technique used to obtain linearly uncorrelated variables from a set of correlated variables (higher dimensional data to lower dimensional data). It is an unsupervised tool, which has many applications, including data exploration and predictive analysis.

PCA finds many applications in day-to-day life, for example in movie recommendation systems, image processing applications etc. It is also used in the domains of finance, data mining, psychology and more.

Principal components are the new features obtained as output of PCA, retaining as much data as possible. Some properties of the principal components are:

- They are a linear combination of the actual features.
- They are perpendicular to each other.
- The significance of the components decreases in order from 1 to n.

PCA can be used to visualise higher dimensional data by clustering. The PC1 and PC2 scores are plotted to find the clusters. The advantages of using PCA are as follows:

- It improves time efficiency by removing multi-collinearity, i.e., removing features that are correlated.
- It boosts the efficiency of the machine learning model due to a reduction in the number of features.
- It removes overfitting by removing unnecessary features in the dataset.

IV. **Pre-process data** – Data pre-processing is the first step in any machine learning or natural language processing application. This includes a set of methods to clean the data and make it ready to be fed to the model. Different steps included in data pre-processing, are as follows:

- **Tokenize** – This is the technique of dividing the text into shorter and meaningful entities of text, known as tokens. Tokens can be words, sub-words, phrases, sentences, etc.
- **Convert to lower case** – The entire text is converted to lowercase in order to simplify the text processing, since upper case and lower case text are interpreted differently by the computer. This helps in reducing the no. of dimensions by unifying words with the same spelling.
- **Remove punctuations** – The punctuations are removed from any piece of text to increase the efficiency because punctuations have a very high frequency of occurrence.
- **Remove tokens with digits** – The combination of digits with words poses difficulty for the system to process the text. Thus, any unnecessary digits or digits combined with letters in any token are removed to clean the data.
- **Remove stop words** – The most commonly used words in any text, which don't carry a significant meaning, are called stop words. Thus, the words like *a, an, the* - are removed.
- **Stemming** – It is the technique of reducing a word to its root by removing the prefix and suffix added to it.
- **Lemmatize** – It is the process of resolving a word to its lemma, i.e. the root form of the word matching to a language dictionary.
- **Remove extra spaces** – The extra spaces at the beginning or end of a text, or extra spaces in between the text are removed in order to reduce the space complexity.

This is followed by the addition of start and end sequence tokens. Since this is an encoder-decoder model, end-of-sequence (EOS) is being used by the authors, termination is required to finalise embedding for the encoder. Similarly, the start-of-sequence (SOS) tokens are required by the decoder to start processing before emitting any input.

V. **Apply CNN to extract features** – As discussed previously, CNN or Convolutional Neural Network has been used for feature extraction. Convolutional Neural Network is a type of deep neural network specially used in the processing of data that have a grid-like structure, for example structured arrays like images. The VGG16 pre-trained network has been used.

VGG 16 – VGG16 is a popularly used Convolutional Neural Network (CNN) architecture. It is used for ImageNet, which is a large visual database project in the domain of object recognition. It achieved 92.7% top-5 test accuracy in ImageNet. The ImageNet dataset consists over 14 million images belonging to 1000 different categories. It finds its applications in various deep learning-based classification algorithms, especially in the domain of image processing. It is widely used because of its ease of implementation. The advantages of using VGG16 are as follows:

- It has a very good architecture for benchmarking on a particular task.
- It is readily available, since this is a pre-trained CNN model.

VGG-16 model gives out 4096 features and the size of the input image is 224*224 pixels. The captions are tokenized for further processing using the *tokenizer* library.

VI. **Split data** – The entire dataset is divided into the training set and the testing set in terms with the Pareto principle of 80:20 split.
VII. **Model data** – The captions and images are processed as per the shape required by the input of the model. The captions are padded to make them of the same length and tuples of iterable items are created as per the required shape.
VIII. **Apply LSTM to predict sequence** – As discussed previously, RNN has been used for sequence prediction in the form of LSTM or Long Short-Term Memory.

Activation function – This function decides whether a neuron should be activated or not, depending on its weight and bias. Activation function enables back propagation in a neural network. Any neural network without an activation function would essentially become a linear regression function. Some popular activation functions used are:

- **Linear function** – This is a straight-line function having a range of activations. The activation function is proportional to the input, and it is taken from the weighted sum of neurons.
- **Sigmoid function** – The output of this function lies between 0 and 1 on giving a real number as input. The Sigmoid function plots an S-shaped graph and the function is non-linear, continuously differentiable and monotonic. This is suitable for a classifier.
- **Tanh function** – The output lies in the range of [-1, 1] on giving a real number as input. Also known as tangent hyperbolic function, it is a non-linear function with gradient stronger than sigmoid function.
- **ReLU function** – The Rectified Linear Units has a simple function max(0,z), for the function variable z. This is a piecewise linear function and does not activate all the neurons simultaneously together time. This solves the vanishing gradient problem. It has lower complexity in comparison to tanh and sigmoid functions.
- **Softmax function** – The probability of dividing a bigger event into 'n' different sub-events is given by this function. In other words, the probability of each target class is calculated over the set of possible target categories.

The ReLU activation function has been used in our model.

Stacked LSTM – Stacked LSTM is a univariate LSTM model, which has multiple hidden layers of LSTM stacked one above the other. The layer of LSTM above generates a sequential output (not a single value output) for the layers of LSTM below.

Figure 8. Model summary for Stacked LSTM showing all layers of the model

```
Model: "model_1"
_____
 Layer (type)                 Output Shape          Param #     Connected to
=========================================================================================
 input_3 (InputLayer)         [(None, 22)]          0           []

 embedding (Embedding)        (None, 22, 64)        243840      ['input_3[0][0]']

 CaptionFeature (LSTM)        (None, 22, 256)       328704      ['embedding[0][0]']

 dropout (Dropout)            (None, 22, 256)       0           ['CaptionFeature[0][0]']

 input_2 (InputLayer)         [(None, 1000)]        0           []

 CaptionFeature2 (LSTM)       (None, 256)           525312      ['dropout[0][0]']

 ImageFeature (Dense)         (None, 256)           256256      ['input_2[0][0]']

 add (Add)                    (None, 256)           0           ['CaptionFeature2[0][0]',
                                                                 'ImageFeature[0][0]']

 dense (Dense)                (None, 256)           65792       ['add[0][0]']

 dense_1 (Dense)              (None, 3810)          979170      ['dense[0][0]']

=========================================================================================
Total params: 2,399,074
Trainable params: 2,399,074
Non-trainable params: 0
_____
None
```

Bi- Directional LSTM – This is another univariate LSTM model, which allows the model to learn in both directions, forward (past to future) and backward (future to past). In bidirectional LSTM, the input is driven into two directions, which makes it different from regular stacked LSTM. Unlike vanilla LSTM, in the bi-directional model, the input can be made to flow bi-directionally to retain the past and the future information.

IX. **Evaluate performance** – The performance of the model has been evaluated using BLEU score for each of the predictions.

BLEU score – BiLingual Evaluation Understudy or BLEU is a metric used in the evaluation of machine-translated texts. It gives a numerical value in the range of zero to one, which represents the coherence between the machine-translated text and its high quality reference translation counterparts. The highest score obtained is one where the translated text is identical to its reference. The higher the value, the better the prediction. The advantages of using BLEU score are as follows:

Figure 9. Model summary for Bi-LSTM showing all layers of the model

```
Model: "model_1"

_____
 Layer (type)                 Output Shape         Param #     Connected to
=================================================================================
 input_3 (InputLayer)         [(None, 22)]         0           []

 embedding (Embedding)        (None, 22, 64)       243840      ['input_3[0][0]']

 CaptionFeature (LSTM)        (None, 22, 256)      328704      ['embedding[0][0]']

 dropout (Dropout)            (None, 22, 256)      0           ['CaptionFeature[0][0]']

 input_2 (InputLayer)         [(None, 1000)]       0           []

 bidirectional (Bidirectional) (None, 512)         1050624     ['dropout[0][0]']

 ImageFeature (Dense)         (None, 512)          512512      ['input_2[0][0]']

 add (Add)                    (None, 512)          0           ['bidirectional[0][0]',
                                                                'ImageFeature[0][0]']

 dense (Dense)                (None, 256)          131328      ['add[0][0]']

 dense_1 (Dense)              (None, 3810)         979170      ['dense[0][0]']

=================================================================================
Total params: 3,246,178
Trainable params: 3,246,178
Non-trainable params: 0
_____

None
```

- It is fast and not at all expensive to compute.
- It is intuitive.
- It is language independent.
- It has significantly high correlation with human evaluation.
- It has been in practice widely in different domains.

X. **Deploy model** – The next step would include the deployment of this model by integrating it into an existing product environment and putting it to real-life usage.

DATASETS

The availability of datasets greatly affects a data-intensive model like this. The datasets required for this process are datasets containing images with corresponding descriptions. The accuracy of the model depends on the quality of the captions.

Crowdsourcing is the most preferred way for collecting data for large-scale datasets owing to constraints like high cost and low speed. The datasets suitable for this model are as follows:

- **Microsoft Common Objects in Context (MSCOCO/COCO)** – It is a collection of more than 300 thousand images with descriptions. It is a large-scale dataset for applications like object segmentation and detection with 5 captions per image and 80 object categories. It has complex images of everyday objects and scenes. This can be downloaded for free from the official website.

- **Flickr 8K** – It is a collection of 8,000 images and 5 clear descriptive captions of each of the images taken from Flickr. The captions highlight the notable features of the image. It is a benchmark collection for sentence-based image description and is available for free on Kaggle.com.

- **Flickr 30K** – It is a collection of 30,000 images and 5 clear descriptive captions of each of the images taken from Flickr. The captions highlight the notable features of the image. This includes and extends the previous Flickr 8K dataset. Both the datasets are crowdsourced and are available for free on Kaggle.com.

- **Dataset for Question Answering on Real-world images (DAQUAR)** – It is a significant virtual question answering dataset, consisting of more than twelve thousand human question-answer pairs, where each image consists of around nine QA pairs. This can be downloaded for free from Kaggle.com.

- **UIUC PASCAL Sentence** – It is one of the earliest crowdsourced datasets with image captioning data. It comprises 1,000 images with five descriptions for each image collected. This was originally created for the study of sentence generation from images but has a limited domain size with relatively simpler captions.

The most popular datasets out of these are MSCOCO and Flickr 30K (Ivašić-Kos et al., 2019). They have been widely accepted as standard benchmarking datasets and the results obtained from these datasets are considered to be standard for performance evaluation.

Flickr 30K has become a standard in sentence-based image caption data. Both Flickr 30K and Flickr 8K have reference images with five reference sentences each provided by human annotators. In order to avoid computational complexity and quicker training of models, the Flickr 8K dataset has been used.

Demonstration

The clusters obtained after PCA analysis to find the similar types of images highlights the different groups with an indicator colour and shows the distribution of all the data points in the entire dataset.

Here, the images labelled 2720, 4250, 4983, 5862, and 4079 have been marked as red, which shows one or more players participating in some kind of sport. The images labelled 6320, 3432, 1348, 7472, and 1518 have been marked as magenta, which represents one or more dogs playing around. Similar, different clusters have been represented by green, blue, yellow, etc.

The model has been prepared by performing a two-step process of encoding and decoding. The model accuracy has been assessed by using BLEU score. The samples having BLEU score equal to 1 are good examples whereas, samples having BLEU score equal to 0 or nearly equal to 0 are bad examples. The second step of decoding has been performed using two different models, namely Stacked LSTM and Bidirectional LSTM.

Figure 10. PC1 vs PC2 values plotted for the entire dataset

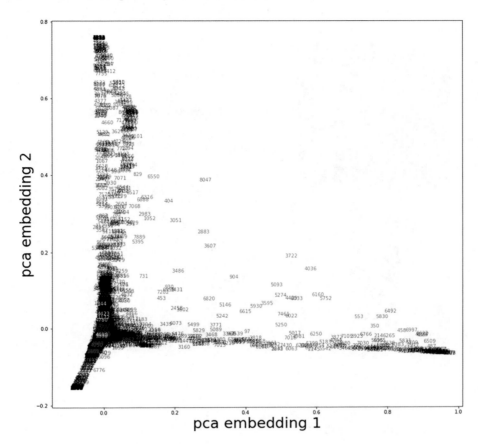

I.   CNN with Stacked LSTM:

Figure 11. Examples of bad captions generated by the Stacked LSTM model

true: child pink dress climbing set stair entry way

pred: boy wearing shirt blue shirt walking along

BLEU: 0

true: black dog spotted dog fighting

pred: black dog running grass

BLEU: 7.422680762211792e-155

Figure 12. Examples of good captions by the Stacked LSTM model

Good Caption

true: black dog running water

pred: black dog running water

BLEU: 1.0

true: black dog running snow

pred: black dog running snow

BLEU: 1.0

II. CNN with Bidirectional LSTM:

Figure 13. Examples of bad captions generated by the Bidirectional LSTM model

Bad Caption

true: man lay bench dog sits

pred: black dog wearing shirt walking

BLEU: 1.2183324802375697e-231

true: man orange hat starring something

pred: man woman standing front

BLEU: 1.0032743411283238e-231

Figure 14. Examples of good captions by the Bidirectional LSTM model

Good Caption

true: black dog running water

pred: black dog running water

BLEU: 1.0

true: black dog running snow

pred: black dog running snow

BLEU: 1.0

RESULTS AND DISCUSSION

The model has been developed completely using Python with the use of different libraries. As it is evident from the results above, during the testing phase, BLEU scores on both ends of the spectrum have been obtained. There were some really low BLEU scores (approximately 0) suggesting that the predicted caption was not at all similar to the actual caption. However, there were some very high BLEU scores as well which suggested that the model was able to predict captions almost similar to what humans would have predicted. The integration of an attention mechanism to the recurrent neural network in the decoder can further enhance the performance of the model by deeper similarity analysis (Azhar et al., 2021).

Compatibility with Other Models

- **BERT Model** – BERT (Bidirectional Encoder Representations from Transformers) will not be suitable for this purpose. BERT is not directly replaceable with LSTM. This is because the BERT model requires a text vector as an input but after applying CNN model on the images, an integer vector is obtained, which cannot be used as an input in the BERT model. It has been tried to use the BERT encoder as a tokenizer for the text data and use the LSTM model for caption generation, but the same problem persisted that the BERT encoder gives an output in the form of text vector but the LSTM model requires an integer vector as an input. Thus, it can be used for text classification but not with images. A BERT-like transformer is utilised by VisualBERT for the preparation of embeddings for image-text pairs but it still cannot be applied with images directly.

- **LSTM variations** – LSTM models are mainly of two types – univariate and multivariate. Since only a single three-dimensional integer vector (size - 5x24x24) is given as input to the LSTM, any type of multivariate LSTM cannot be used in this case. Furthermore, Vanilla LSTM cannot work with three-dimensional vectors, and the same goes for Convolutional LSTM. Thus, here the authors have evaluated the Stacked LSTM and Bidirectional LSTM models only.

Figure 15. This diagram shows a comparative study of the percentage of loss to the number of epochs in Stacked LSTM

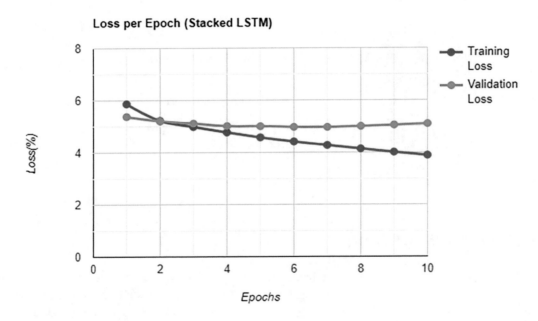

FUTURE RESEARCH DIRECTIONS

- This model can be integrated with Google Images search to give a synopsis of information and assist in searching by an image.
- This can enable visually impaired people to get to know the scene in front of them by listening to the caption generated in an audible format by integrating text to speech conversion.
- This can be useful in improving accuracy of caption generation in videos.
- This can generate insights about an image by application of NLP techniques.
- Social media platforms can infer the location, dress and activity of a person directly from an image and provide more related feed.
- This can help identify a given scenario and provide valuable insights about any image.

The model must aim at analysing images by incorporating image processing techniques, which would enhance the accuracy of the model manifold. The generated captions must be accurate and should be able to convey the message depicted by the images clearly.

Figure 16. This diagram shows a comparative study of the percentage of loss to the number of epochs in Bidirectional LSTM

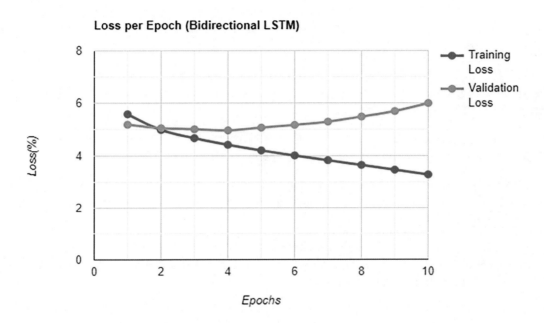

CONCLUSION

Image captioning is a challenging problem, which finds its usage in the domain of image identification, analysis and text generation. It has received copious attention over the last decade due to its applications in a variety of domains. This chapter studies and compares existing models used for image captioning in great depth and conveys the limitations of existing models and their inoperability in analysing images and generating suitable captions. This chapter also demonstrates an image captioning model built using Long Short Term Memory (LSTM) and Convolutional Neural Network (CNN). In order to assess the performance of models built, BLEU score obtained on the generated captions has been considered. Simulation result indicated that the proposed model was able to suggest captions on the images from test set with a very good accuracy. It did extremely well for some images hitting a perfect BLEU score. The proposed model can be used with confidence to generate captions which can then be converted into audible format for visually impaired people in future. It can be implemented for video captioning as well. From the results obtained, it has been concluded that the models worked best for images containing a single object in focus. To overcome this problem and identify multiple objects in an image with equal accuracy and precision, it is suggested to use some pre-processing on images, like passing images through filters to bring into focus only the important features of an image, followed by feature extraction. The accuracy can be further enhanced by computing the complexity of images using their entropy (Chang et al., 2020). The use of a larger dataset like Flickr 30K or MSCOCO for training the model will be considered for future work.

REFERENCES

Ivašić-Kos, M., & Hrga, I. (2019, May). Deep image captioning: An overview. In *2019 42nd International Convention on Information and Communication Technology, Electronics and Microelectronics (MIPRO)* (pp. 995-1000). IEEE.

Azhar, I., Afyouni, I., & Elnagar, A. (2021, March). Facilitated Deep Learning Models for Image Captioning. In *2021 55th Annual Conference on Information Sciences and Systems (CISS)* (pp. 1-6). IEEE. 10.1109/CISS50987.2021.9400209

Aneja, J., Deshpande, A., & Schwing, A. G. (2018). Convolutional image captioning. In *Proceedings of the IEEE conference on computer vision and pattern recognition* (pp. 5561-5570). IEEE.

Patwari, N., & Naik, D. (2021, April). En-de-cap: An encoder decoder model for image captioning. In *2021 5th International Conference on Computing Methodologies and Communication (ICCMC)* (pp. 1192-1196). IEEE.

Chang, J. R., Ling, T. T., & Li, T. C. (2020, November). A Research on Image Captioning by Different Encoder Networks. In *2020 International Symposium on Computer, Consumer and Control (IS3C)* (pp. 68-71). IEEE. 10.1109/IS3C50286.2020.00025

Shambharkar, P. G., Kumari, P., Yadav, P., & Kumar, R. (2021, May). Generating Caption for Image using Beam Search and Analyzation with Unsupervised Image Captioning Algorithm. In *2021 5th International Conference on Intelligent Computing and Control Systems (ICICCS)* (pp. 857-864). IEEE. 10.1109/ICICCS51141.2021.9432245

Devlin, J., Gupta, S., Girshick, R., Mitchell, M., & Zitnick, C. L. (2015). *Exploring nearest neighbour approaches for image captioning.* arXiv preprint arXiv:1505.04467.

Hossain, M. Z., Sohel, F., Shiratuddin, M. F., Laga, H., & Bennamoun, M. (2021). Text to image synthesis for improved image captioning. *IEEE Access: Practical Innovations, Open Solutions*, 9, 64918–64928. doi:10.1109/ACCESS.2021.3075579

Cheng, H., Devlin, J., Fang, H., Gupta, S., Deng, L., He, X., & Mitchell, M. (2015). *Language models for image captioning: The quirks and what works.* arXiv preprint arXiv:1505.01809.

Wang, H., Zhang, Y., & Yu, X. (2020). An overview of image caption generation methods. *Computational Intelligence and Neuroscience.* doi:10.1155/2020/3062706 PMID:32377178

Hossain, M. Z., Sohel, F., Shiratuddin, M. F., & Laga, H. (2019). A comprehensive survey of deep learning for image captioning. *ACM Computing Surveys*, 51(6), 1–36. doi:10.1145/3295748

Wang, C., Zhou, Z., & Xu, L. (2021). An integrative review of image captioning research. Journal of Physics: Conference Series.

Saha, S. (2018). *A Comprehensive Guide to Convolutional Neural Networks — the ELI5 way*. Retrieved June 28, 2022, from https://towardsdatascience.com/a-comprehensive-guide-to-convolutional-neural-networks-the-eli5-way-3bd2b1164a53

Saxena, S. (2021). *Introduction to Long Short Term Memory (LSTM)*. Retrieved June 28, 2022, from https://www.analyticsvidhya.com/blog/2021/03/introduction-to-long-short-term-memory-lstm

KEY TERMS AND DEFINITIONS

Artificial Intelligence: The field of computer science that aims to give computers the ability to have human-like intelligence.

Computer Vision: A subfield of Artificial Intelligence that allows computers to derive meaningful insights from visual inputs like images, videos, etc.

Deep Learning: A subfield of Machine learning that enables computers to learn and enhance themselves with the help of neural networks.

Feature Extraction: The process used to convert raw data to numerical format to make it easier to process the data while retaining the information in the original dataset.

Image Captioning: The process of creating a meaningful and coherent vector of words that best describes an input image is known as image captioning.

Machine Learning: A subfield of Artificial Intelligence that enables systems to learn and improve based upon previous experience and data without the need of explicit programming.

Natural Language Processing: A subfield of Artificial Intelligence and Computer Science that deals with how computers perceive natural languages. It involves giving computers the capability to process large amounts of natural language data.

Sequence Prediction: A popular problem in the field of Machine Learning that deals with predicting the next value in a given sequence based on all the values that have occurred in the sequence until now.

Section 2
Research Applications Using Deep Learning

Chapter 9
Advancements in Deep Learning for Automated Dubbing in Indian Languages

Sasithradevi A.

Centre for Advanced Data Science, Vellore Institute of Technology, Chennai, India

Shoba S.

Centre for Advanced Data Science, Vellore Institute of Technology, Chennai, India

Manikandan E.

Centre for Innovation and Product Development, Vellore Institute of Technology, Chennai, India

Chanthini Baskar

Vellore Institute of Technology, Chennai, India

ABSTRACT

After the proliferation of deep learning technologies in computer vision applications, natural language processing has used deep learning methods for its building steps like segmentation, classification, prediction, understanding, and recognition. Among different natural language processing domains, dubbing is one of the challenging tasks. Deep learning-based methodologies for dubbing will translate unknown language audio into meaningful words. This chapter provides a detailed study on the recent deep learning models in literature for dubbing. Deep learning models for dubbing can be categorized based on the feature representation as audio, visual, and multimodal features. More models are prevailing for English language, and a few techniques are available for Indian languages. In this chapter, the authors provide an end-to-end solution to predict the lip movements and translate them into natural language. This study also covers the recent enhancements in deep learning for natural language processing. Also, the future directions for the automated dubbing process domain are discussed.

DOI: 10.4018/978-1-6684-6001-6.ch009

INTRODUCTION

Dubbing is an intelligent phenomenon or process which is majorly used in film industry. Major companies are getting involved in this dubbing project where there is a need for multilingual. This process involves an audio-video translation which helps in adding new sound effects or audio during the production stage. Also, in translating the other language films (i.e. The dialogues) to the required language dubbing is being done. Not only for the translation, also in the original film adding sound tracks in synchronization with the situation dubbing helps. For example, in other language films translation, the subtitles are given in addition to the dubbing so that the viewers can get the full recipe of the motion picture. But there are some concerns to be addressed in the dubbing process. (Akman et al., 2022) The basic problem in the dubbing process is with the equipment quality used by the dubbing artist. It is suggested to use an efficient microphone which is a one-time investment helps in making profitable in the later stage. Another point is, the environment where the process is getting done. Use of proper noise cancellation system is required for avoiding this kind error. These basic problems can be resolved by using proper environmental setup.

The major issues come in the technical part where proper synchronization is required in audio-video i.e. the timing issue. In another way, the dubbing artist audio timing should get matched with the actor visual where the actor opens mouth for dialogue delivery etc. So the lip synchronization and also the facial expressions matching should be taken care in the dubbing. Next, the lip synchronization system and the importance of deep learning for the automated system are discussed Kunchukuttan, A. et.al. (2017), In short, the following challenges are present in the system.

- Context absence
- Spatial – temporal features extraction
- Difficulty in understanding more expression actors and its synchronization to be done by the artist
- Generalization among people
- Speaker accent such Guttural sounds
- Speakers sound level example: mumbling

So, the automated lip reading system has to be developed which should be able to address these concerns. The generalized flow of the automated lip synchronization model is depicted in Figure 1. The major components of this system are feature extraction and classification. Initially, the videos of speakers will be captured with the proper vision setup. Then the videos will be converted into image frames which represent the data to be decoded. The next step in this is very important where pre-processing will be done. Our objective here is to capture the proper lip movements which helps in identifying the right speech. At this point, the lip locations are our Region of Interest (ROI). So the lip locations are extracted from video images. Some basic transformation and manipulations will be applied which reduces the number of steps involved in the later stage. After this, the feature extraction which is the front-end of the system is being done. This process helps in obtaining the required features effectively from the redundant features. Then, the backend of the system comes which is nothing but a classification process. In the classification, the obtained images are being compared with the database where facial movements corresponding to the input speech is done. Finally, the decoded speech is encoded into in a form of spoken words or sentences.

Figure 1. Generic block diagram of lip synchronization model

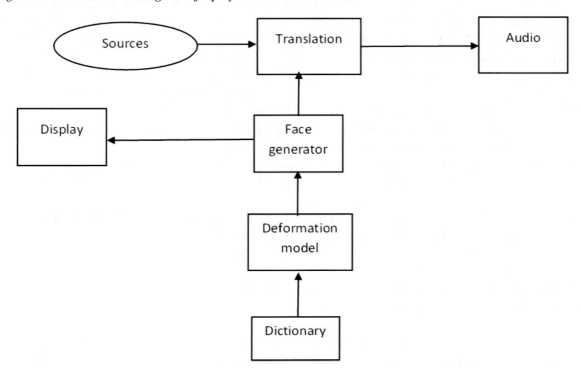

Previously, many traditional techniques like Hidden Markov Model (HMM) is used for the synchronization in the automatic lip synchronization system Also, many conventional techniques like discrete cosine transform, principal component analysis etc. are used for features extraction. Nowadays, in speech and video processing system the advanced machine/deep learning techniques are received attraction that are possible because of large amount of available dataset. The next section discusses the latest work done in the deep learning domain for lip synchronization process.

In dubbing, both audio and visual translation are important. For example, when a person open mouth for speaking the facial expression also varies based on that. So an attempt is made to obtain face to face translation from the input audio-video format using neural machine. Given the video of a speaker speaking in one language A and the aim is to produce a lip synchronized video of another speaker in another language B. A LipGAN model was developed for obtaining the face translation image sequences from the input videos and without any labelling of data lip synchronization was done another language Federico, M. et. al. (2020a), This LipGAN model works for any face and support multilingual.

Next, a Wav2Lip model was developed which works well for real time videos too. The proposed model supporting lip synchronization for any talking faces for speech extraction without any constraints. The changes made in the discriminator helped in improving the performance of the system. The grey scale images usually fed to the model for the lip synchronization process. Instead, colour images were utilized for the training process. In addition, the level was very deeper and also included the residual skip connections. This led to generating the accurate lip-sync by using lip-sync expert Federico, M. et, al. (2020b), The system outperformed both in the quantitative evaluation and also in the human evaluation.

A LipType was proposed for features extraction and classification using deep neural network. It has involved repair model for correcting the background lighting conditions and silent speech enhancement and its recognition. This LipType model is an extended version of LipNet. Compared to LipNet, the LipType has obtained less error rate during the recognition process (Öktem, A. et. al, 2019). Lip-sync effort was taken for translating the lecture videos of speakers in education system mainly from English to Indian languages. The other aspect to be addressed is the new language translation might be shorter or longer compared to the original language. A combination of HMM and GMM is used for this automatic speech translation process. It was observed that syllable segmentation provides better accuracy compared to word alignment process.

This book chapter is organized as follows: section 2 describes the different NLP based deep architecture variants introduced so far in literature to enhance the automated dubbing process. Section 3 gives the details about the performance metrics needed to evaluate the automated dubbing model. Section 4 discusses the applications, advantages of the automated dubbing process. Section 5 provides the challenges and future research directions. Section 6 concludes the book chapter.

NLP BASED DEEP ARCHITECTURE VARIANTS FOR AUTOMATED DUBBING PROCESS

The goal of any automated dubbing process is to translate the audio signal from one language to another desired language of requirement. Automated dubbing process involves two basic processes namely video recreation (face-to-face translation) and Lip synchronization.

LIPGAN Architecture for NLP

A generative adversarial network is created by Federico, M. et. al. (2020b), to generate talking faces for translated speech. The idea was to compute the degree of lip synchronization in the given frames produced by the generator. The model was developed to be invariant of different poses and input language. The prime advantage is that the LipGan model can automatically generate talking faces of target language with lip synchronization. It generates real talking faces and the method was analysed subjectively too. It was designed for English to Hindi translation purpose. The work analysed the research gaps in the previous solutions Liu, N. (2020) and Taylor, S. et. al. (2017), and reported that the reconstruction loss defined in existing work and the GAN are not sufficient to provide an accurate lip synchronization. Owing to those issues, lip synchronization is achieved through the expert knowledge i.e, pretrained lip sync network. A modified network of lipsync expert network is used and it accepts both visual and audio data as input. The designed generator to minimize the reconstruction error is given by:

$$L_{recon} = \frac{1}{N} \sum_{i=1}^{N} \left| L_g - L_G \right|_1 \qquad (1)$$

Where L_g is the generated frames and L_G is the ground truth frames. The generator generates each frame separately and the window size is chosen as 5. This model is validated on three datasets and a different evaluation method is followed. Few drawbacks in the previous evaluation strategy is identified and they are: inappropriate to the real world scenario, inconsistent evaluation, lack of temporal consistency and evaluation metrics.

Lip Synchronization Efforts on Education Videos

Most of the works proposed in lip synchronization Cooke, M. et. al. (2006), used separate techniques for aligning audio and visual content. A prosodic synchronization module based automatic dubbing is introduced which provides synchronization between source and target audio. An attention module is used at the end to add the audio track with faces Mukhopadhyay, R. et. al. (2019), the speed of word delivery plays a crucial role in the automated dubbing algorithms. A huge data is trained to attain a end to end module Aharon, M. et. al. (2006), for audio-video data. An initial attempt to translate the educational video was taken by Yuan, J. et. al. (2008), It was highly challenging due to the duration difference between target and synthesized audio. Also, the lecture video will have more silences compared to others like entertainment. The other factors to be considered are lip movement for technical words, head poses, hand movements and gestures of the resource person. Hence, a word level alignment process is used for the recreated audio. They have attempted to attain a good synchronization between lip movement and the target audio. The developed system is validated based on subjective evaluation and mean opinion score. A sample of alignment process between audio and video in educational video is shown in figure 2.

Figure 2. A sample alignment process after silence detection

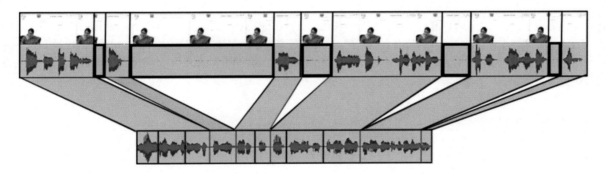

    The long silence in the original video is detected and mapped to the audio segments of source. The final audio is segmented according to the silence duration in the original audio. The issue arises when there is short silence period between words. A good trade off should be there between word clarity and lip synchronization is also stressed. Post processing is also done using the factors spectral flux and group delay. The entire pipeline is validated using mean opinion score and the higher score denotes a better system.

Auto Encoder-Based Lip Synchronization

Even though there is huge proliferation of deep learning technology, it suffers from difficulties like enormous training data and memory resources. Hence capturing the facial details and making the audio to be synchronized with lip movement using deep learning is an open issue. Extensive research is done to alleviate issues like shaky talking heads, quality of synthesized audio and video. A convolutional neural network is developed to automatically synthesize faces and audio. To achieve the task, local facial features are derived and parts are extracted. The facial landmarks are extracted using optical flow A low dimensional part-based auto encoder is designed to encode the face frames. A sequence-to-sequence network is used to introduce the relation between frames. Instead of a fully connected layer based 1D phenome features, convolution based deep regressor is used. The temporal characteristics is captured by deep regressor. Hence, the entire module is based on two folds: Training and regression folds. In the training phase, the specific visual and audio is recorded, audio alignment is performed on each frame, visual content is processed by facial alignment and standardization, autoencoder features are learned on deformable parts, deep regressor model is also trained. In the regressor fold, phenome is obtained for the given audio, prediction is done by the regression network, maximal voting strategy is followed, votes are decoded to attain the video frames. It is evaluated on three different datasets namely GRID, SAVEE, and CCTV dataset. The dependency of this model on offline software and part-based features becomes the limitation and it is an open issue to be solved.

PERFORMANCE EVALUATION METRICS

In order to evaluate the lip-reading algorithm, it is mandatory to use appropriate evaluation metrics as follows:

I. **Word Error Rate (WER):** WER is defined as the ratio of sum of count of substitutions and deletions, insertions to total count of words in ground truth. WER denotes the number of operations needed to convert the predicted words as ground truth. WER can be mathematically represented as,

$$WER = \frac{\#\,Substitution + \#\,Deletions + \#\,Insertions}{\#\,words} \qquad (2) \qquad\qquad (2)$$

II. **Word per minute (WPM):** It is common evaluation metric that depicts the rate at the word entered. It is computed using the relation between recognized words, speaking and computational time. It is given by

$$WPM = \frac{\#\,words\,recognized - 1}{speaking\,time + computational\,time} \qquad (2) \qquad\qquad (3)$$

III. **Computational complexity (η):** The analysis of any algorithm or model developed for face- to-face translation and lip reading usually include a determination factor called computational complexity. As it includes both audio and visual data, computational complexity must be included as performance metric. The complexity involves storage, time and algorithm complexity. The algorithm complexity ix computed using big O notation.

IV. **Computational time (T):** The time taken by the algorithm or model to complete the lip- reading task refers to time complexity. A better trade off should be maintained between accuracy, time and resource complexity.

V. **Accuracy (A):** Accuracy refers to the percentage of correctly dubbed words with proper synchronization according to the ground truth. It is mathematically represented as, Accuracy=#correctly dubbed words with synchronization/#dubbed words in ground truth

VI. **Precision (P):** Precision denotes the ability of the model/algorithm to correctly dub the relevant data. In mathematical terms, it is defined as the ratio of #true positives to the sum of #true positives and #false positives.

VII. **Recall (R):** Recall denotes the parameter that identifies the false alarm occurred based on the model. It is mathematically represented by the ratio #true positives to the sum of #true positives and false negatives.

VIII. **F1Score (F):** F1score represents the harmonic average of precision and recall metric. F1score will be high when both precision and recall are high. Table 1 lists out the required states of any model developed to perform lip reading in Tamil.

Table 1. Performance metrics and its state

Metrics	WER	WPM	η	T	A	P	R	F
State	Low	High	Low	Low	High	High	High	High

APPLICATIONS OF AUTOMATED DUBBING

The automated lip synchronization will be very much useful in higher level applications like News reading, infotainment interviews, film dubbing and education related videos:

- **Entertainment:** In recent days, pan India movies are released by the film industry. Lip synchronization pipeline will aid the film makers to create movies in different languages in a cost-effective manner. The basic process for any dubbing is that the recorded/dubbed voice will be embedded over the captured video. This process will definitely suffer from the issue of non-sync of lip movements. Thus, automated framework for lip synchronization will alleviate the problem. The automate pipeline will generate a lip model and synchronize the lip movements over the captured video. The non-synchronization errors can be reduced by the automated lip synchronization framework. Given a movie clip, the automated dubbing system will do translation of the audio to the desired language. Hence, speech-speech translation also plays a crucial part in this framework. It makes the automated dubbing process a complex one.

- **Education:** It is one of the vital backbones to aid the growth of a nation in all aspects. Owing to the pandemic situation, most of the education systems have transformed its content towards e-content. Among the available educational contents, a quantum number of videos were delivered through English. Though these videos provide subtitle in native languages, it rises burden to the listener. The solution is to generate the dubbed videos based on speech-to-speech synthesis. The crucial issue that arises is the inconvenient visualization because of the non-synchronization of lip movement and the dubbed speech. This hindrance is alleviated by the proliferation of lip reading. It includes two folded processes: face-to-face translation and lip synchronization.

- **Infotainment:** Apart from educational and entertainment videos, so many contents are there to view like news, interviews, demos, cooking recipes and so on. The lip synchronization framework will potentially allow the users to access these infotainment videos and they can view the useful contents over the globe regardless of their nation, race, language. Hence, Lip reading and Face-to face translation provides a boon for wide variety of applications related to natural language processing.

Advantages of Face-To-Face Translation and Lip Synchronization

- The problem of lip reading in natural language should focus on both the audio and visual content in the video. It shows that the high-level image and signal processing plays a good role in solving this issue. It involves machine translation which uses the generation module for creating talking faces.
- It provides suitable solution for most of the resource-constrained natural languages. Owing to the advancements in computer vision, multimedia, machine learning and deep learning, the audio-visual contents can be easily translated according to the user requirements.
- The framework for lip reading will aid the hearing-impaired people and it works on the part-based model especially lip. The part would be extracted and the lip model is generated for different words. It follows the translation module and the speech signal will be converted into text.
- The automated dubbing process based on lip reading will hugely reduce tedious the manual labour involved in the traditional process. The accuracy will also be enhanced when compared with traditional dubbing process
- The automated lip reading and dubbing process helps the user to concentrate on the interesting scene rather than moving their heads up and down to read the subtitles. Also, the core meaning of any dialogue will be delivered to the audience in their language itself.
- There is no need for the dubbing panel to search people for different person to portray the voice of different characters. The automated lip reading and dubbing process works for all gender and ages.
- This automated framework helps the business domain massively through one time investment and assured quality through computer vision and machine learning techniques.

Challenges Faced by Lip Reading and Synchronization

- Till date, most of the industries rely on non-automated techniques to attain lip synchronization. The major cause is the high cost of the existing highly sophisticated software to accomplish this task.
- It requires the designed system to maintain a huge dictionary of words to be stored in memory for automated speech-text synthesis and translation module. It forces a huge burden on the memory and computational resources to be allocated for the automated process.
- The computational complexity involved in the real time process to manipulate both the visual data in three-dimensional space simultaneously with the audio data is one of the major challenges to be solved the automated lip-reading algorithm.

CONCLUSION AND FUTURE DIRECTIONS

This article discussed various deep architectures proposed so far to provide an efficient automatic dubbed speech. The necessity of these architectures which lead the research in dubbing domain, especially lip synchronization is reported. Followed by, the evaluation metrics required to validate the performance of different architectures was elaborated. Different domains that will get benefits due to the enhancement of automated dubbing algorithm is detailed. The research gaps to be filled in order to attain a benchmark performance in automated dubbing process in natural language is also elaborated. The challenges faced by the existing methodologies includes high cost, huge computational resources and memory complexity. Hence it is fruitful if the future research in dubbing domain concentrate on these challenges. Also, optimization of the network parameters, parallel processing of both audio and video data and computational complexity analysis will pave a fine enhancement in the research on automated dubbing process in natural languages. Dual stream and dual domain based deep network is not yet completely analysed for the automated dubbing process and there is a good scope. The automated dubbing process is a growing domain in the field of computer vision and the enhancements in deep learning provides a long term promise for the further improvement.

REFERENCES

Akman, N. P., Sivri, T. T., Berkol, A., & Erdem, H. (2022, July). Lip Reading Multiclass Classification by Using Dilated CNN with Turkish Dataset. In *2022 International Conference on Electrical, Computer and Energy Technologies (ICECET)* (pp. 1-6). 10.1109/ICECET55527.2022.9873011

Kumar, R., Sotelo, J., Kumar, K., de Brébisson, A., & Bengio, Y. (2017). *Obamanet: Photo-realistic lip-sync from text.* arXiv preprint arXiv:1801.01442.

Kunchukuttan, A., Mehta, P., & Bhattacharyya, P. (2017). *The iit bombay english-hindi parallel corpus.* arXiv preprint arXiv:1710.02855.

Federico, M., Enyedi, R., Barra-Chicote, R., Giri, R., Isik, U., Krishnaswamy, A., & Sawaf, H. (2020a). *From speech-to-speech translation to automatic dubbing.* arXiv preprint arXiv:2001.06785. doi:10.18653/v1/2020.iwslt-1.31

Federico, M., Virkar, Y., Enyedi, R., & Barra-Chicote, R. (2020b). Evaluating and Optimizing Prosodic Alignment for Automatic Dubbing. In INTERSPEECH (pp. 1481-1485). doi:10.21437/Interspeech.2020-2983

Öktem, A., Farrús, M., & Bonafonte, A. (2019). *Prosodic phrase alignment for machine dubbing.* arXiv preprint arXiv:1908.07226.

Matoušek, J., & Vít, J. (2012, March). Improving automatic dubbing with subtitle timing optimisation using video cut detection. In *2012 IEEE International Conference on Acoustics, Speech and Signal Processing (ICASSP)* (pp. 2385-2388). IEEE. 10.1109/ICASSP.2012.6288395

Liu, N., Zhou, T., Ji, Y., Zhao, Z., & Wan, L. (2020). Synthesizing talking faces from text and audio: An autoencoder and sequence-to-sequence convolutional neural network. *Pattern Recognition*, *102*, 107231. doi:10.1016/j.patcog.2020.107231

Taylor, S., Kim, T., Yue, Y., Mahler, M., Krahe, J., Rodriguez, A. G., Hodgins, J., & Matthews, I. (2017). A deep learning approach for generalized speech animation. *ACM Transactions on Graphics*, *36*(4), 1–11. doi:10.1145/3072959.3073699

Yuan, J., & Liberman, M. (2008). Speaker identification on the SCOTUS corpus. *The Journal of the Acoustical Society of America*, *123*(5), 3878. doi:10.1121/1.2935783

Cooke, M., Barker, J., Cunningham, S., & Shao, X. (2006). An audio-visual corpus for speech perception and automatic speech recognition. *The Journal of the Acoustical Society of America*, *120*(5), 2421–2424. doi:10.1121/1.2229005 PMID:17139705

Aharon, M., & Kimmel, R. (2006). Representation analysis and synthesis of lip images using dimensionality reduction. *International Journal of Computer Vision*, *67*(3), 297–312. doi:10.100711263-006-5166-3

KR, P., Mukhopadhyay, R., Philip, J., Jha, A., Namboodiri, V., & Jawahar, C. V. (2019, October). Towards automatic face-to-face translation. In *Proceedings of the 27th ACM international conference on multimedia* (pp. 1428-1436). ACM.

Chapter 10
Tamil Question Answering System Using Machine Learning

Ashok Kumar L.
PSG College of Technology, India

Karthika Renuka D.
PSG College of Technology, India

Shunmugapriya M. C.
PSG College of Technology, India

ABSTRACT

Tamil question answering system (QAS) is aimed to find relevant answers in in the native language. The system will help farmers to get information in Tamil related to the agriculture domain. Tamil is one of the morphologically rich languages. As a result, developing such systems that process Tamil words is a difficult task. The list of stop words in Tamil has to be collected manually. Parts of speech (POS) tagging is used to identify suitable POS tag for a sequence of Tamil words. The system employs Hidden Markov Model (HMM)-based viterbi algorithm, a machine learning technique for parts of speech tagging of Tamil words. The analyzed question is given to the Google search to obtain relevant documents. On top of Google search, locality sensitive hashing technique (LSH) is utilized to retrieve the five relevant items for the input Tamil question. Jaccard similarity is used to obtain the response from the retrieved document items. The proposed system is modelled using a dataset of 1000 sentences in the agriculture domain.

INTRODUCTION

Internet provides high source of data but English is the dominant language. Though the people get information from search engine it may or may not be useful and relevant. They spend much of time to get the relevant answer. The key idea of this work is to find and represent the exact answer to the user's query. The difficulty of finding and validating the right answer makes a QAS complex than the general information retrieval task.

DOI: 10.4018/978-1-6684-6001-6.ch010

The system processes Tamil questions and provides answers in Tamil to the user in the agriculture domain. Uzhavan mobile application for agriculture domain in Tamil provides information regarding agriculture schemes and subsidy. But it does not give concise answers to the farmer queries. To address such problems Tamil QAS system gives exact answers to user queries.

Table 1 shows the different type of questions in Tamil. In this work, the user queries in the agriculture domain is processed by the proposed model to get answer in Tamil. The key idea of this system is to find agriculture domain based question answering system in Tamil language. Stop words in Tamil are collected manually and the Tamil words are POS tagged. Locality sensitive hashing is used to retrieve relevant documents. Finally the answers are ranked using Jaccard similarity.

Table 2 shows the different types of QASs. QAS are classified based on application domain, analysis done and techniques used. Based on application domain it is classified as open and closed domain. Based on analysis QAS is further classified as semantic QAS, syntactic QAS and morphological QAS. Based on technique used it is classified as web based and ontology based.

Table 1. Types of Question

Question Type	Description	Sample Question (In Tamil)
Factoid Question	Description and definition type of questions	வறண்ட லத்திற்கு எவ்வாறான பழப்பயிர்களை தேர்ந்தெடுக்க வேண்டும்?
Listing Question	Types and list of questions	நெற்பயிரைத் தாக்கும் பூச்சிகள்?
Affirmative Question	Yes or No questions	கிழங்கு சாகுபடிக்கு 20 செ.மீ இடைவெளி இருப்பது சரியா?

Table 2. Types of Question Answering System

Types of QAS	Description	Example
Open Domain QAS	Users can ask questions in any domain and get relevant answers from the system.	IBM Watson
Closed Domain QAS	Users can ask question in one particular domain such as medical, science domain.	QAPD (physics domain)
Ontology Based QAS	The system makes use of ontology such as DBPedia Ontology and SparQL query to answer users questions as a knowledge source.	AquaLog and DeepQA IBM Watson System
Web Based QAS	The system exploits web resources such as Google, Wikipedia as knowledge repository to answers the users.	WEBQA
Semantic Analysis based QAS	The system conceptually analyzes the user questions and provides exact answers.	QUERIX and PANTO
Syntactic Analysis based QAS	Keyword based analysis is done by the system to answer queries.	ASKME
Morphological Analysis based QAS	The Morphological analyzer breaks the word (பயிர்கள்) into root word (பயிர்) and associated morpheme features (கள்).	TamilQAS

LITERATURE REVIEW

The information retrieval system does not give the exact answer but instead it gives a set of documents related to the query. So, there is a high demand for tools to extract answers in Indian languages.

Viterbi algorithm is a popular approach employed for sequence labelling. Another extensively used machine learning approach for sequence labelling in natural language processing is conditional random field (CRF). CRF based parts of speech tagging for Tamil sequence is introduced by (Pandian, 2009).

Conditional Random Field a machine learning approach is used by (Lakshmana Pandian, 2008) to develop a system on "Tamil Question Classification using morpheme features". The paper discusses different types of questions in Tamil using morpheme features. The system developed Condition Random Field (CRF) model to train tagged question corpus. Various CRF such as morpheme based CRF and generic CRF were compared. The comparison results showed that morpheme based CRF overwhelm generic CRF.

(Thenmozhi, 2018) has introduced a system on "Ontology based Tamil-English cross lingual information retrieval system". In this the user asks question in Tamil and gets answers in English. Ontology is defined as relationship between various concepts. They have also analyzed word sense disambiguation for Tamil words. After translating to English, the query is searched in the internet to retrieve the matching documents.

Parts of Speech Tags for Tamil words was done by (Dhanalakshmi, 2009). They suggested thirty two parts of speech tags and nine tags for chunking. They have used Tamil corpus of size two hundred and twenty five thousand words for training and testing the model.

Tamil parts of speech tagger based on the morpheme features was developed by (Pandian, 2008). They achieved high performance with an f-measure of 96%. They have compared various methods such as rule based tagging, hidden markov model (HMM) taggin and transformation based learning tagger.

Spell checking is an important step in question answering system which highly impacts the performance of the system. This system helps to identify the spelling errors in Tamil. They have developed morphological analyzer for analyzing Tamil words. In this system each word is compared against the dictionary word. If the spelling of the word is incorrect suggestion and spelling correction are given. Named entity recognition (NER) in Tamil was done by (Pandian, 2008). Named entity recognition is a process to identify the entity names such as place, organization, and person. NER is one of the preprocessing steps used in all natural language processing systems.

More recently, the research works focused on deep learning based approaches such as LSTM, attention based models for developing BOT based QA applications

TAMIL QUESTION ANSWERING SYSTEM ARCHITECTURE

Question answering system in native language helps the user to get answers in a well understandable and convenient way. The users input question is given to the system through a user interface. Figure 1 shows the architecture of the proposed system. Tamil question answering system have three main components and they are listed below.

- Preprocessing
- LSH based document retrieval
- Answer ranking and validation

Figure 1. Tamil QA System Architecture

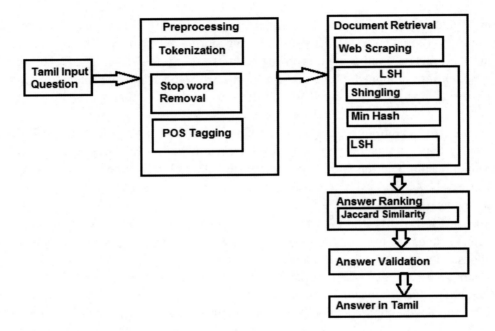

Pre-Processing

First step in pre-processing is tokenizing followed by stop word removal as shown in figure 2. Stop words are words without meaning or noisy terms such as conjunctions for example அல்லது, ஏனெனில், அதுவரையில். So, stop word removal have a great impact on the system performance. Few Tamil stop words are listed below in figure 3.

Parts-of-Speech Tagging in Tamil (தமிழ் சொ·எல்வகை கூறுகள்)

It is used to identify the most suitable POS tag for a sequence of words. A Viterbi algorithm is a dynamic programming method which finds the most probable tag sequence for the input sentence. Given a word sequence $w_1, w_2, .., w_n$ it identifies the corresponding tag sequence $t_1, t_2, .., t_n$. The probability view is given below in equation. Table 3 shows the few tag for Tamil words.

$$argmax_{t_1..t_n} P(t_1..t_n \mid w_1..w_n) = argmax_{t_1..t_n} P\left(t_1..t_n\right) P(w_1..w_n \mid t_1..t_n) \tag{1}$$

Figure 2. Pre-processing Tamil Words

Figure 3. Tamil Stop words

Tamil Stop words
ஒரு,என்று,மற்றும்,இந்த,இது,என்ற,கொண்டு,என்பது,பல,ஆகும்,அல் லது,அவர்,நான்,உள்ள,அந்த,இவர்,என,இருந்து,சில,என்,போன்ற,வே ண்டும்,வந்து,இதன்,அது,அவன்,தான்,பலரும்,என்னும்,மேலும்,பின்ன ர்,கொண்ட,எல்லாம்,மட்டுமே,இங்கே,அங்கே,அதில்,நாம்,எனவே,பிற, சிறு,மற்ற,எந்த,எனவும்

Table 3. Tamil POS Tag Set

S.No	English POS Tag	தமிழ் சொல்வகை குறிகள்
1	Adjective<ADJ>	பெயரடை
2	Adverb<ADV>	வினையுரிச்சொல்
3	Conjunction<CNJ>	இடைச்சொல்
4	Noun<NN>	பெயர்ச்சொல்
5	Proper Noun<NNP>	சிறப்பு பெயர்ச்சொல்
6	Verb<V>	வினைச் சொல்
7	Question Word<QW>	கேள்வி கேட்கும் போது பயன்படுத்தும் வார்த்தைகள்

Figure 4 describes the POS tagging using Viterbi algorithm for the Tamil sentence. The best POS path for the input sequence is given in bold lines.

Figure 4. POS Tagging Using Viterbi Algorithm

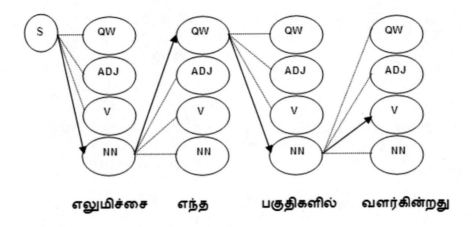

Figure 5. POS Tagging Tamil Words

LOCALITY SENSITIVE HASHING (LSH)

Use of LSH reduces the search space and improves the performance of the system. The 3 steps in LSH are listed as follows.

- Shingling

  Shingles are unigrams after removing punctuations and stop words
  ['எலுமிச்சை', 'எந்த', 'பகுதிகளில்', 'வளர்கின்றது']

- Min Hash

  Signature matrix is created by permutating the rows randomly Eg. 1234 → 2413.
  Figure 6 shows the step by step process in creating the signature matrix.

- LSH

  The signature matrix is divided into 2 bands of 2 rows each. And then each band is hashed separately.

Figure 6. Forming Signature Matrix

Shingles	Doc1	Doc2	Doc3
எலுமிச்சை	1	0	0
எந்த	0	1	0
பகுதிகளில்	1	1	1
வளர்கின்றது	1	0	1

→

Permutations	Doc1	Doc2	Doc3
1	1	2	3

Shingles	Doc1	Doc2	Doc3
பகுதிகளில்	1	1	1
வளர்கின்றது	1	0	1
எலுமிச்சை	1	0	0
எந்த	0	1	0

→

Permutations	Doc1	Doc2	Doc3
1	1	2	3
2	1	1	1

Shingles	Doc1	Doc2	Doc3
எந்த	0	1	0
எலுமிச்சை	1	0	0
வளர்கின்றது	1	1	1
பகுதிகளில்	1	0	1

→

Permutations	Doc1	Doc2	Doc3
1	1	2	3
2	1	1	1
3	2	1	3

Shingles	Doc1	Doc2	Doc3
வளர்கின்றது	1	1	1
பகுதிகளில்	1	0	1
எந்த	0	1	0
எலுமிச்சை	1	0	0

→

Permutations	Doc1	Doc2	Doc3
1	1	2	3
2	1	1	1
3	2	1	3
4	1	1	1

ANSWER RANKING USING JACCARD SIMILARITY

Jaccard similarity measure is used for ranking answers. The equation 2 is finds the Jaccard similarity for question-and-answer set.

$$J(Q,A) = \left| \frac{Q \cap A}{Q \cup A} \right| \qquad (2)$$

Where J(Q,A) is the Jaccard similarity of Q and A, Q is question set and A is answer set.

Figure 7. Forming Buckets in LSH

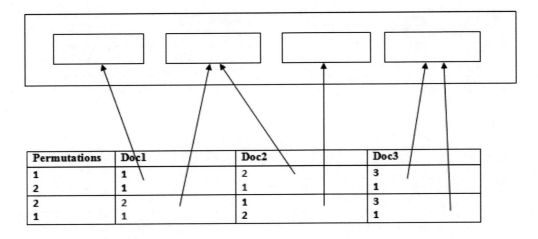

Permutations	Doc1	Doc2	Doc3
1 2	1 1	2 1	3 1
2 1	2 1	1 2	3 1

Figure 8. Jaccard Similarity

Question
Answer
எலுமிச்சை
எந்த
பகுதிகளில்
வளர்கின்றது
வெப்ப
மிதவெப்ப
மண்டல

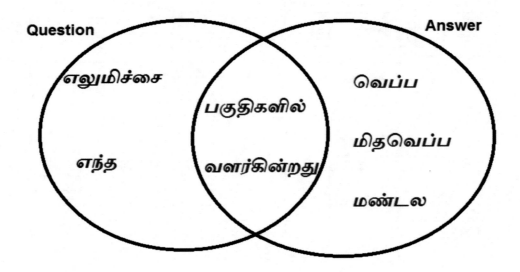

Figure 9. A nswer Retrieval

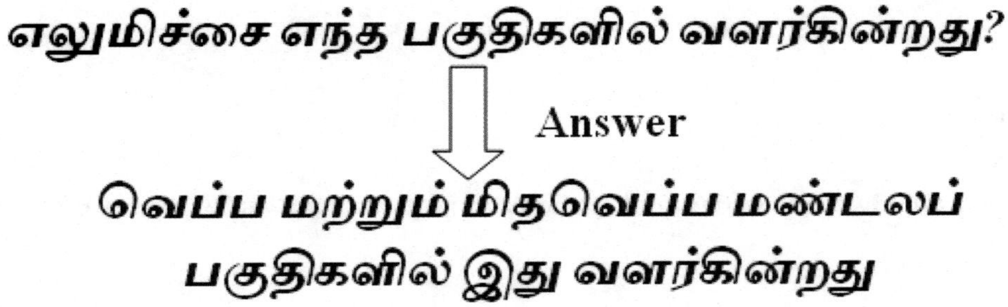

எலுமிச்சை எந்த பகுதிகளில் வளர்கின்றது?
Answer
வெப்ப மற்றும் மிதவெப்ப மண்டலப்
பகுதிகளில் இது வளர்கின்றது

RESULT ANALYSIS OF TAMIL QAS

The dataset is composed of 1000 sentences in Tamil was utilized for experimental analysis. The corpus is available at the Indian Language Technology Proliferation and Development Center. Dataset is divided into 80% training and 20% testing. The model was trained using Viterbi algorithm.

Tamil question answer dataset was created manually which consists of 85 Tamil questions and answers in agricultural domain.

To evaluate the performance of the system, we utilized four measures namely precision, recall, F-measure and accuracy. The dataset of 85 questions 43 questions are answered correctly by the system and 42 questions are not answered correctly by the system as shown in table 4. The equations 3-6 are used to calculate the performance metrics.

$$Accuracy = \frac{No\ of\ correctly\ answered\ questions}{Total\ No\ of\ testing\ samples} \tag{3}$$

$$Precision = \frac{No\ of\ correct\ answers}{Total\ no\ of\ related\ answers} \tag{4}$$

$$Recall = \frac{No\ of\ related\ record\ retrieved}{Total\ no\ of\ questions} \tag{5}$$

$$F - measure = \frac{2 * Precision * Recall}{Precision + Recall} \tag{6}$$

Table 4. Evaluation Metrics and Score

Evaluation	Score
Precision(P)	0.63
Recall(R)	0.65
F score	0.64
Accuracy	0.50

CONCLUSION

This paper presents a Tamil QAS for the agricultural domain. Locality Sensitive Hashing (LSH) based technique is used for extraction of the most relevant documents. Jaccard similarity measure is used for calculating sentence similarity. The system was analyzed using a Tamil corpus and the performance metrics were evaluated. The proposed system employs a keyword based search and cannot provide answer for listing type of questions like நெற்பயிரைத் தாக்கும் பூச்சிகள்? This effect influence the performance of the developed system. The future work is to improve by semantically analyzing Tamil words using Long Short Term Memory (LSTM).

REFERENCES

Dhanalakshmi, V., Kumar, M.A., Soman, K.P., & Rajendran, S. (2009). *POS Tagger and Chunker for Tamil Language*. Academic Press.

Lakshmana Pandian, S., & Geetha, T. V. (2008). Tamil Question Classification Using Morpheme Features. In B. Nordström & A. Ranta (Eds.), Lecture Notes in Computer Science: Vol. 5221. *Advances in Natural Language Processing. GoTAL 2008*. Springer. doi:10.1007/978-3-540-85287-2_26

Pandian, S., & Geetha, T. V. (2008). Morpheme based Language Model for Tamil Part-of-Speech Tagging. *Polibits*, *38*, 19–25. doi:10.17562/PB-38-2

Pandian, S. L., & Geetha, T. V. (2009). CRF Models for Tamil Part of Speech Tagging and Chunking. In W. Li & D. Mollá-Aliod (Eds.), Lecture Notes in Computer Science: Vol. 5459. *Computer Processing of Oriental Languages. Language Technology for the Knowledge-based Economy. ICCPOL 2009*. Springer. doi:10.1007/978-3-642-00831-3_2

Pandian, S. L., & Pavithra, K. A. (2008). Hybrid, Three-stage Named Entity Recognizer for Tamil. *Info*, S2008.

Thenmozhi, D., & Aravindan, C. (2018). Ontology-based Tamil–English cross-lingual information retrieval system. *Sadhana*, *43*(10), 157. doi:10.100712046-018-0942-7

Chapter 11
Abstractive Turkish Text Summarization and Cross-Lingual Summarization Using Transformer

Eymen Kagan Taspinar
https://orcid.org/0000-0002-2653-6482
Marmara University, Turkey

Yusuf Burak Yetis
https://orcid.org/0000-0003-0056-7309
Marmara University, Turkey

Onur Cihan
https://orcid.org/0000-0002-5729-2417
Marmara University, Turkey

ABSTRACT

Abstractive summarization aims to comprehend texts semantically and reconstruct them briefly and concisely where the summary may consist of words that do not exist in the original text. This chapter studies the abstractive Turkish text summarization problem by a transformer attention-based mechanism. Moreover, this study examines the differences between transformer architecture and other architectures as well as the attention block, which is the heart of this architecture, in detail. Three summarization datasets were generated from the available text data on various news websites for training abstractive summarization models. It is shown that the trained model has higher or comparable ROUGE scores than existing studies, and the summaries generated by models have better structural properties. English-to-Turkish translation model has been created and used in a cross-lingual summarization model which has a ROUGE score that is comparable to the existing studies. The summarization structure proposed in this study is the first example of cross-lingual English-to-Turkish text summarization.

DOI: 10.4018/978-1-6684-6001-6.ch011

INTRODUCTION

Due to the rapid growth of the web, the amount of text data is increasing exponentially which suggests a need for effective techniques and tools to manage this data. Reducing the length of texts while retaining the core meaning, referred to as summarization, has drawn significant attention from researchers in the recent past. There are two main classes of summarization methods: extractive and abstractive. The primary goal of extractive summarization, which uses identical sentences from the original text as part of the summary, is to identify the text's most essential phrases and clauses. In abstractive summarization, however, the aim is to create novel sentences by generating new words or rephrasing the existing ones. To achieve this, the text's semantic content should be examined using deep analysis and reasoning (Rachabathuni, 2017). Abstractive summarization methods provide concise and coherent summaries that are rich in information, short in length, and different from the original text.

Abstractive summarization of English text became a popular research topic thanks to the recent advances in natural language processing (NLP) algorithms. Performance evaluation of the summarization algorithms is done by comparing their ROUGE scores, which is a measure that compares obtained summaries against a reference summary set or translation (Lin, 2004). For English texts, the summarization algorithms in the current literature have ROUGE scores of around 40 which corresponds to a very successful summarization. As a result of the success of summarizing English texts, the authors of this chapter examine the problem of abstractive Turkish text summarization.

BACKGROUND

For abstractive summarization, a number of models utilizing sequence-to-sequence architecture have been presented recently. The transformer model, which exclusively relies on the attention process, was introduced by Vaswani et al. (2017). The attention mechanism was further utilized by the researchers to provide promising results in summarization (Lewis et al., 2019; Raffel et al., 2020). Lewis et al. (2019) proposed the BART model which contains both a bidirectional encoder and an autoregressive decoder. In the BART model, random noise is added to the text data and the original text is reconstructed using a sequence-to-sequence architecture. Raffel et al. (2020) introduced the T5 model which is a text-to-text framework based on an attention mechanism that can be used for various text processing tasks including translation, classification, and summarization. These models are remarkably successful in making sense of sentences since they consist of both the encoder and decoder structures of the Transformer language model, which makes them preferred for translation and summarization problems.

English text summarization problem has been examined by many authors in the literature (Rush et al., 2015; Chopra et al., 2016; Lin et al., 2018). Rush et al. (2015) used a convolutional and attention-based encoder for summarization. Chopra et al. (2016) utilized RNN cells to create a decoder block. Nallapati et al. (2016) suggested an abstractive summarization system for English texts using RNN cells in both encoder and decoder blocks. However, these attention-based structures lead to grammatical errors, semantic irrelevance, and repetition. Lin et al. (2018) provided a solution to this problem using CNN filters and LSTM cells. The studies containing both encoder and decoder structures of the Transformer architecture show higher performances in perceiving text and produce better texts (Raffel et al., 2020; Lewis et al., 2019). Zhang et al. (2019) performed a pre-trained model for English with the C4 corpus that is proposed by Raffel et al. (2020). The fine-tuning stage is performed with ready-to-use datasets such as XSum, CNN, NEWSROOM, and Multi-News. Researchers have recently concentrated on cross-lingual text summarization as a result of the popularity of English text summarization models. Wan et al. (2010) applied the "first summarize then translate" principle to summarize Chinese texts. While they stated that the advantage of this method is translating less text, the results were not very satisfactory. Zhu et al. (2020) utilized Transformer and translation layer together in their model. Most of the cross-lingual summarization studies in the literature have been conducted to summarize Chinese texts.

The studies involving Turkish text summarization are explained as follows. Extractive summarization of Turkish text is studied by Kutlu et al. (2010) where the authors assign scores to the sentences that are based on training the weights of parameters such as frequency of words, keywords, and sentence positions. Karakoc and Yilmaz (2019) considered abstractive summarization of Turkish text using LSTM cells and beam search structures. In another abstractive summarization study, the authors created a Turkish dataset and proposed an abstractive summarization model with an architecture consisting of LSTM cells (Ertam & Aydin, 2021). The absence of a Turkish abstractive summarization study using the latest models and architectures and the absence of any cross-lingual summarization studies involving the Turkish language constitute the research gap of this study. The main reason for this is that there is a far less amount of Turkish data than there is English data.

The main contributions of this chapter can be summarized as follows.

1) The authors create 3 Turkish text summarization datasets from the data of 3 news websites. These datasets consist of *216458, 218717,* and *7663* Turkish texts and their summaries. To the best of authors' knowledge, it is the largest Turkish summarization dataset currently available.
2) Since this study is carried out with the use of the latest architectures in the literature and very large datasets, the performances of obtained abstractive Turkish text summarization models are comparable to the existing English summarization models in the literature.
3) The authors propose an English-Turkish translation model and train it with a novel dataset consisting of English and Turkish subtitles of TV series and movies. It is shown that the results of the proposed translation model are promising, and the model can be utilized to summarize English text when used together with Turkish summarization algorithms. This is the first study to summarize English text in Turkish using a cross-lingual summarization model in the literature.

The remainder of the chapter is organized as follows. The next section provides the details of the models utilized in the chapter and explains the datasets created for training and testing. The results are presented and compared with the existing ones in the literature in the Solutions and Recommendations section. Finally, future research directions and concluding remarks are given in the last section.

MAIN FOCUS OF THE CHAPTER

The lengths of the texts to be summarized are flexible in text summarization, and the placement of words in a phrase affects its meaning. These reasons make sequential architecture (such as RNN and LSTM) suitable for abstractive text summarization. Since the result of the previous computation is required for the current computation, it is not possible to take full advantage of parallel processing using graphical processing units (GPUs). However, unlike RNN and LSTM, the transformer model does not require sequential processing of the sequential data in the training phase. The transformer model proposed by

Vaswani et al. (2017) has a higher BLEU score (which is a metric that Papineni et al. (2002) developed to assess the quality of the translation) and less training cost (FLOPs) for English to German and English to French translation models, compared to the previous state-of-the-art models.

Long-distance dependency plays a key role in many sequence-transformation tasks (Vaswani et al., 2017). The greatest path length between the inputs and outputs is negatively correlated with the learning capacity of models with such dependencies. The shorter the maximum path length between inputs and outputs, the easier to learn the dependencies between long distances. Since the maximum path length for the self-attention layer type is minimum, the attention mechanism is advantageous in text summarization problems. Furthermore, while the complexity of the transformer model is $O\left(N^2\right)$ (Vaswani et al., 2017), parallelization brings an important advantage in terms of speed once a computer with parallel processing capability is used. In the light of the above discussion, the researchers utilize an attention-based model in this study.

Design

Language processing models consist of two training phases: pre-training and fine-tuning. A base model is created in the first phase using large amounts of raw text data. It helps the model to understand the grammar and how words connect to generate sentences. During this phase, the model is trained in an unsupervised manner. This training phase differs from model to model. This distinction may be based on how the words are masked in the text. For example, in the BERT model (Devlin et al., 2019), the words are masked randomly whereas, in the GPT model (Radford et al., 2018), the next word is masked. BART (Lewis et al., 2019) and MBART (Liu et al., 2020) models use both masking methods. In addition, removing the noise created by changing the order of the sentences and masking the word groups is carried out in this training phase. It is expected that the tokenizer structure, which provides indexing of the words and sub-words, and the input embedding layer, which will create word vectors representing words in the semantic space, will be optimized during the pre-training phase. Training of these layers continues in the fine-tuning phase. The model may be utilized as a basis model in more complex language tasks if it understands the language's structure and content awareness. This base model goes through a fine-tuning stage. At this stage, the model is trained directly for a particular task. Note that the pre-training phase is computationally more expensive than the fine-tuning phase and requires a larger amount of text data.

To represent a word in a vector form, models utilize an input embedding or word embedding layer in which the words are processed for the first time. Words are disassembled and called tokens, then vectors corresponding to the tokens are created in this layer. The disassembling process is performed algorithmically by the embedding layer. There are various disassembling algorithms; WordPiece is used in BERT (Schuster and Nakajima, 2012), SentencePiece is utilized in T5 and MBART (Kudo & Richardson, 2018) and Byte level BPE is used in BART and GPT models (Radford et al., 2018). The process of disassembling words provides a great advantage, especially for agglutinative languages such as Turkish. If two words or subwords share similar semantic features or similar meanings, their embedding value vector comes closer. The attention mechanism is based on this convergence principle.

The word embedding layer is followed by the positional embedding. Positional embedding is used to indicate the positions of words in the text. It detects the positions of words with sinusoidal functions of different wavelengths. Since the variables for the positional embedding layer are the positions, the concept of wavelength is used instead of period. This layer represents the position in a space of the same dimension as the word vector. Sinusoidal functions with different wavelengths allow the model to have information about the relative position. Detecting the position of serial data is of vital importance for parallel processing.

The last indices of the positional embedding vector denote more distant word dependencies. With positional embedding, the position of the words can be exactly determined. Furthermore, the range of position detection goes well beyond the wavelength of the sinusoidal function with the longest wavelength. When the sinusoidal functions in all wavelengths are taken into account, the repeat range of the vector increases much more. Limitation in the model's handling of long texts stems from the inability of the model's linear layers to respond to these lengths, rather than the positional embedding's ability to address the position.

Figure 1 illustrates how the attention layer works. Multiple heads (attention heads) are used inside the transformer encoder and decoder blocks. Each head has a particular query, key, and value layers. Each head's attention filter may then concentrate on a separate section of the text in this way. Query, key, and value layers in all heads take the same matrix from input and positional embedding layers. The projection of this matrix to different spaces is the responsibility of these linear layers. The purpose of this projection is to manipulate matrices for their objectives and also reduce the processing cost.

Once the query and key matrices are passed through the matrix multiplication layer, the query matrix is multiplied by the transpose of the key matrix. The result is a square matrix with a dimension equal to the number of words or subwords in the input text. The objective of matrix multiplication is to determine the words which describe others based on the semantic similarity between them, as mentioned earlier.

The square matrix is then sent to the scale layer in order to reduce the dimension. In this layer, all elements of the matrix are divided by the square root of the matrix dimension.

The only difference between the masked and unmasked multi-head attention blocks is the masking layer between the softmax and the scale layer. Therefore, the masking layer depicted in Figure 1 is optional. If the attention block contains a masking layer, square matrix is passed through the masking layer at this stage and the name of the block becomes the masked multi-head attention block. While the encoder part of the model proposed by Vaswani et al. (2016) includes only the multi-head attention block, the decoder part includes both the masked and unmasked multi-head attention blocks.

Only the previous words are taken into account by the decoder which is made possible by the masking layer. The masking layer sets the upper triangular part of the square matrix to minus infinity. In the training phase, the masked multi-head attention block is used since the words expected to be produced in the training phase need to be masked. The training process has both source and target texts. Therefore, the resulting attention matrix can only deal with the words before the current word and cannot direct attention to the next ones.

In the softmax layer, the softmax operation is performed within all rows and columns of the matrix to normalize the square matrix. The output of this layer is the attention filter of the text. This matrix expresses how much attention each word pays to other. In the next matrix multiplication layer, the square matrix generated in the softmax layer and the matrix obtained from the value linear layer are multiplied. When the attention filter is multiplied by the value matrix, the result will be an attention filter applied value matrix that assigns high focus to more important phrases. The attention layer illustrated in Figure 1 forms the basis of this architecture. In the remaining parts, there are other linear and feed-forward layers where learning takes place.

Figure 1. Single masked attention block with word and positional embedding layers

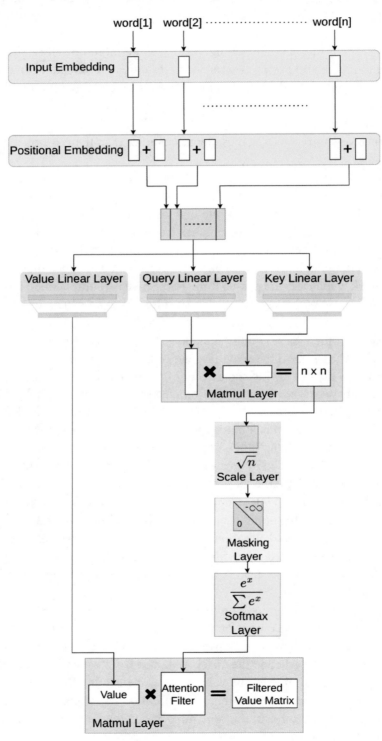

MODELS

The BART Model

In the literature, there is no Turkish BART model that can be used for Turkish language tasks. The BART model, which was proposed by Lewis et al. (2019), takes the advantages of the BERT (Devlin et al., 2019) and GPT (Radford et al., 2018) since it has a left-to-right decoder similar to GPT and a bidirectional encoder similar to BERT. The encoder and decoder parts of the model are connected to cross-attention logic, i.e., the decoder pays attention to the last hidden state of the encoder. Moreover, BART uses the GeLU activation function instead of ReLU (Hendrycks and Gimpel, 2016).

Figure 2. Pre-training of the BART model

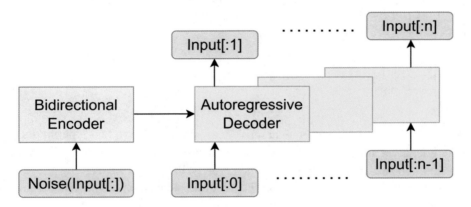

The pre-training phase of the BART model is performed by optimizing the encoder and decoder layers with the denoising method as illustrated in Figure 2. The input illustrated in the figure corresponds to the unlabeled raw text used in the pre-training phase. The pre-training phase is completed in an unsupervised manner since the model is aimed to generate the original text from a noisy text. Noisy texts are automatically generated by various methods such as token masking/deletion and sentence permutation during the pre-training phase.

In Figure 2, the autoregressive decoder layers try to predict the next word similar to the GPT model, with the casual masking and teacher forcing methods. The number of decoder layers shown in parallel is one less than the number of tokens of the input text. In this way, the model can perform decoder training in parallel with the help of the positional embedding layer. In the BART model, the bidirectional encoder is used to understand the text whereas the autoregressive decoder is utilized to generate the text.

The MBART Model

MBART model, which stands for Multilingual BART, is proposed by Liu et al. (2020) and provides multilingual support. The MBART architecture is pre-trained separately for each language it supports. The model uses the encoder-decoder structure proposed by Vaswani et al. (2016) and in the pre-train phase, it is trained according to the denoising principle. For the encoder inputs, sentences can be relocated, and some words can be masked. On the decoder side, there are noiseless versions of the text, therefore the model is aimed to raise awareness about the structure of the language and the connections between the sentences and the words. Figure 3 illustrates the fine-tuning phase of the MBART model for abstractive text summarization.

Figure 3. Fine-tuning of the MBART model for the task of abstractive summarization

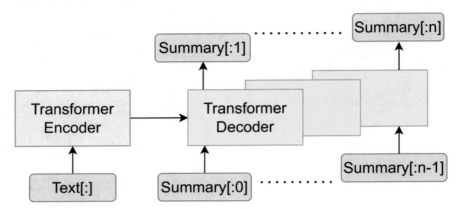

As can be seen from Figure 3, for an abstractive text summarization task, the inputs of the encoder layer and the decoder layer are the original texts and their summaries, respectively. For a translation task, these inputs are English and Turkish sentences, respectively. Similar to the training phase of BART, what is expected from each decoder layer is to create the next token based on the previous tokens. Parallelism in the training phase is provided by the parallel decoder layers and the token masking method.

Datasets

CNN/DailyMail and XSum datasets are two of the most popular datasets used in summarization studies. In the CNN/DailyMail dataset, summaries frequently match source phrases. As reported by Lewis et al. (2019), the models trained with this dataset tend to be more extractive. In contrast, XSum dataset consists of more abstractive sentences and shorter summaries. Scialom et al. (2020) created a dataset containing 1.5 million news and their summaries in five languages. The summaries generated by their model are extractive, i.e., exact words and sentences of the original text appear in the summary. Motivated by the above work, in this study, the authors generate datasets by extracting the information from 3 Turkish news websites:

- News Website 1 (NW1) dataset consists of *216458* news texts and their summaries. The summaries in NW1 dataset are longer than those in other datasets.
- News Website 2 (NW2) dataset consists of *218717* news texts and their summaries.
- News Website 3 (NW3) dataset consists of *7663* news texts and their summaries.

The data extracted from news websites are useful for training the abstractive summarization models. On the other hand, to create an English-Turkish translation model, the researchers obtained the data from

English and Turkish subtitles of TV series and movies. Note that the subtitles in different languages displayed at a particular time slot are translations of each other. By this means, the authors have created a list containing *2.4 million* English sentences and their Turkish translations.

Training Parameters

For the choice of epoch number equal to 8 and the number of batches equal to 18, the training phase is completed in 16 hours for the dataset consisting of more than 200 thousand input/output pairs. When the fine-tuned model was retrained to examine the effect of increasing the epoch number further, no decrease in the minimum loss value was observed. The learning rate has been fixed at 3×10^{-5} for all trainings. Note that floating-point numbers can be expressed in 32 bits (full precision) or 16 bits (half-precision). In half-precision representation the range of the floating-point number is preserved, and the space used in GPU memory per instance used for model training decreases, which consequently brings more processing capability in the same GPU bandwidth.

In this study, fine-tuning is done by updating the weight and bias matrices in the decoder layer. It is assumed that the encoder layer, which has undergone pre-training, is sufficiently optimized. With this assumption, it was possible to decrease the memory usage per batch and increase the number of batches during training. In addition, there has been a significant decrease in the total training cost. Updating the encoder layer may provide better results, as the basic model used by the researchers supports multiple languages. However, in this case, the extra training cost must be taken into account. On the other hand, the authors did not update the input embedding layer in the fine-tuning phase. Many words are addressed to a vector according to their meaning in the semantic space in the pre-trained model. Since the MBART model can address Turkish words very well, there was no need for updating in this layer.

Table 1 shows the effect of freezing some layers and using half-precision on the training costs. In the simulations, the dataset length is 40.000 and the number of epochs is chosen as 8.

Table 1. The effect of freezing some layers and using half-precision on the training time

Variables				Training Time
Freeze Encoder	**Freeze Embedding**	**FP16**	**Maximum Batch Size**	
✓	✓	✓	18	≈3 hours
✓	✓	✗	16	≈6 hours
✓	✗	✓	4	≈11 hours
✗	✓	✓	2	≈22 hours

The table shows that the shortest training time is achieved when the encoder and embedding layers are frozen and the floating-point numbers are expressed with half-precision. It can be noted from the table that updating the encoder layer during fine-tuning increases the training cost approximately by 600% and updating the input embedding layer increases the training cost approximately by 250%. Furthermore, while the floating-point precision does not have a direct effect on the batch size, the training cost is reduced by half.

SOLUTIONS AND RECOMMENDATIONS

In the scope of this research, three different summarization datasets they created, and summarization models are built. Furthermore, a translation dataset and a translation model from English to Turkish are obtained. These models are further combined to establish a cross-lingual summarization structure from English to Turkish. In this section, the researchers provide the results obtained from their abstractive summarization model, translation model, and cross-lingual summarization model; and discuss their performances with the existing results in the literature. The raw results of all models are given in a public GitHub repository (Taspinar et al., 2022).

Results from the NW1 Dataset

The ROUGE scores of the abstractive summarization model trained by NW1 dataset are given in Table 2.

Table 2. ROUGE scores of the model trained by NW1

Measure	Score
ROUGE-1	43.0229
ROUGE-2	29.2944
ROUGE-L	37.6815
ROUGE-LSUM	39.4936

As shown in Table 2, the ROUGE scores obtained in Turkish text summarization in this research are comparable to those in English text summarization models in the literature which is about 40 (Celikyilmaz et al., 2018; Zhang et al., 2019; Gehrmann et al., 2018; Liu & Lapata, 2019; Liu & Lapata, 2019).

Results from the NW2 Dataset

The ROUGE scores of the abstractive summarization model trained by the dataset NW2 are given in Table 3.

Table 3. ROUGE scores of the model trained by NW2

Measure	Score
ROUGE-1	44.0878
ROUGE-2	29.4983
ROUGE-L	37.5922
ROUGE-LSUM	39.6545

Despite the fact that the ROUGE scores are greater than those obtained using the NW1 dataset, the summary lacked sufficient abstraction.

Results from the NW3 Dataset

The amount of data in NW3 dataset was far less than those in NW1 and NW2 which lead to the ROUGE scores given in Table 4.

Table 4. ROUGE scores of the model trained by NW3

Measure	Score
ROUGE-1	31.8452
ROUGE-2	15.7560
ROUGE-L	26.5829
ROUGE-LSUM	26.6588

As listed in Table 4, the ROUGE scores are 25% less than the scores of the models trained using other datasets. Summaries, on the other hand, are abstractive as they incorporate phrases and words that are absent from the original text.

Results from the Combined Dataset

The curriculum learning structure proposed by Bengio et al. (2009) was used while combining the data sets and creating a new data set. With this structure, it is aimed to maximize the optimization process by training the model with the first simple examples followed by more difficult examples. While creating the dataset, the authors combined some parts of the NW1 and NW2 datasets, and all the data in the NW3 dataset. The combined dataset consists of 224188 Turkish texts and their summaries. NW1 and NW2 datasets are firstly utilized to extend the summaries and NW3 dataset is used to obtain more abstractive summaries. Table 5 provides a summary of the model's performance metrics after it was trained by the combined dataset.

Table 5. ROUGE scores of the model trained by NW1, NW2, and NW3

Measure	Score
ROUGE-1	38.9724
ROUGE-2	22.1475
ROUGE-L	32.4833
ROUGE-LSUM	34.3262

According to Table 5, the model obtained in this study is not the best in terms of ROUGE score, but the most abstractive summaries are obtained from this model. When the findings are analyzed, it is clear that the transitions between words and meaning integrity is well provided. On the other hand, some of the summaries consist of incorrect abbreviations and country names. The reasoning behind this may be due to dataset characteristics. Since datasets are created with news highlights and corresponding full texts, highlights may contain full versions of the abbreviations and country names although they do not exist in the full text.

Performance Comparison

In this section, the performances of the proposed models are compared with those in the literature. To this end, the ROUGE scores of the current research (summarization of Turkish text) and the studies in the English text summarization literature are given in Table 6.

Table 6. Comparison of the ROUGE scores of the English summarization models in the current literature and Turkish summarization model

Reference	Model	ROUGE-1	ROUGE-2	ROUGE-L
Celikyilmaz et al., 2018	DCA	41.69	19.47	37.92
Zhang et al., 2019	PEGASUS	45.07	33.39	41.28
Gehrmann et al., 2018	BOTTOMUP	41.22	18.68	38.34
Liu & Lapata, 2019	TransformerABS	40.21	17.76	37.09
Liu & Lapata, 2019	BERTSUMABS	41.72	19.39	38.76
Current study	Model trained with NW2	44.08	29.49	37.59

Celikyilmaz et al. (2018) used an LSTM-based model whereas a standard Transformer encoder-decoder structure was used in the PEGASUS model (Zhang et al., 2019). BOTTOMUP model use standard bidirectional LSTM (Gehrmann et al., 2018), and a bidirectional encoder-based architecture is used in the TransformerABS model and the BERTSUMABS model (Liu & Lapata, 2019). However, BERTSUMABS model was evaluated with the CNN/DailyMail dataset, which contains extractive summaries. As can be seen from Table 6, the Turkish text summarization model proposed in this chapter is 10% better than the DCA, BOTTOMUP, TransformerABS and BERTSUMABS models in terms of ROUGE-1 score while this difference is up to 50% in terms of ROUGE-2 score.

The ROUGE scores obtained for Turkish text summarization in the literature are summarized in Table 7.

Table 7. ROUGE-1 scores of Turkish text summarization studies in the current literature

Reference	ROUGE-1
Ertam and Aydin (2021)	43.17
Karakoc and Yilmaz (2019)	20
Model trained with NW2	44.09

As shown in Table 7, the ROUGE 1 score obtained with the model trained with NW2 is higher than the scores of the models in the current literature. Furthermore, the summaries obtained by the model proposed in Ertam and Aydin (2021) have word repetition, which is one of the main problems of the LSTM architecture. While the same problem occurred in the model trained with NW3 dataset, the other two models (trained with NW1 and NW2 datasets) do not have such problems. Furthermore, Ertam and Aydin (2021) obtained shorter summaries compared to those obtained in this study due to the lack of LSTM architecture's long-distance dependency capability. For a better performance comparison, the ROUGE-1, 2, and L scores of the current research and the research of Ertam and Aydin (2021) are given in Table 8.

Table 8. ROUGE scores of Ertam and Aydin (2021) and the model trained with NW2 dataset

Measure	Model of Ertam and Aydin (2021)	Model trained with NW2
ROUGE-1	43.17	44.09
ROUGE-2	21.94	29.50
ROUGE-L	43.34	37.59

Table 8 verifies that there is a small difference between the ROUGE-1 scores. This difference is in favor of the current research for ROUGE-1 and 2 scores whereas Ertam and Aydin (2021) obtained a better ROUGE-L score. In addition, the sentences generated by the model proposed in this study have a better structure and more abstractive. Karakoc and Yilmaz (2019) generated their summary dataset by rearranging an existing dataset created for the classification of news. Since the headlines were taken into account as the news summaries throughout the training phase, the summaries produced by their model were brief. Karakoc and Yilmaz (2019) have achieved a maximum ROUGE score of 20, which is far less than what is obtained in this study.

In the literature on Turkish text summarization, there are several important shortcomings. For instance, summaries generated by the model proposed in Ertam and Aydin (2021) do not contain Turkish characters and the results obtained by Karakoc and Yilmaz (2019) do not include punctuation and capital letters. On the other hand, the models obtained in this study generate summaries with Turkish characters, punctuation, and proper capitalization.

Translation Results from Subtitle Website Dataset

The BLEU score obtained in the translation model is 29.57 whereas Vaswani et al. (2017) obtained a BLEU score of 28.4 for their English to German translation model which corresponds to a 4% difference. This verifies that obtained English to Turkish translation model performs higher performance to the work of Vaswani et al., (2017). The BLEU scores of the current study and English-Turkish translation models in the literature are shown in Table 9.

As shown in Table 9, the BLEU score of the model proposed in this research is higher than the English-Turkish translation models in the literature.

Table 9. BLEU scores of the work in the current literature

Reference	BLEU Score
Oflazer and Durgar (2007)	25.08
Yeniterzi and Oflazer (2010)	23.78
Gorgun et al. (2016)	16.3
Bakay et al. (2019)	21.4
Obtained translation model	29.57

Summarize English Text into Turkish

From the discussions in the previous sections, the authors conclude that their models perform well in abstractive Turkish text summarization and English-Turkish translation. English texts are broken up into sentences and given to the translation model to create Turkish sentences since the translation model is trained on tiny texts. Subsequently, Turkish sentences are combined into a larger text and passed to the Turkish abstractive summarization model. The ROUGE scores obtained from the cross-lingual structure are shown in Table 10.

Table 10. ROUGE scores that are obtained using a cross-lingual framework

Measure	Score
ROUGE-1	21.6799
ROUGE-2	6.2554
ROUGE-L	11.8766
ROUGE-LSUM	12.6229

A small evaluation dataset was created with English texts and corresponding Turkish summaries to obtain the ROUGE scores of the models. Note here that the difference between the scores obtained in Table 10 and the scores obtained from the other summarization models in this study may be due to two reasons. The first reason is that due to the use of the translation and summarization model in the cascade structure, the summarization model amplifies the noise in the translation model. The second reason is that the cross-language summary structure is not created with a single dataset. Therefore, an evaluation dataset had to be created to evaluate the model. The evaluation dataset was created in the form of English texts and corresponding Turkish summaries. As a result, both translation and abstractive summarization have increased the possible textual differences between the results and the evaluation dataset. While Fikri et al. (2021) stated that the ROUGE score is inadequate in evaluating abstractive summarization models, the authors of this chapter believe that it is even more inadequate to evaluate cross-lingual summarization models due to the reasons stated above.

FUTURE RESEARCH DIRECTIONS

Since the size of the filter used in the attention mechanism is directly proportional to the length of the array, longer texts bring additional costs in terms of both computational power and model size. To overcome this problem, one can use the structure Beltagy et al. (2020) created to summarize longer Turkish texts.

In search engines, it has become important to focus on the meaning of the searched words as a whole rather than the individual meaning of each word. Since abstractive summarization models proposed in this research relies on the meanings of the texts, it has the potential to be integrated into search algorithms in further studies. Furthermore, attention-based models can be used not only for language tasks but also for solving many other sequential operations as stated by Jumper et al. (2021).

CONCLUSION

In this study, the authors investigate the abstractive summarization problem for Turkish text using a transformer attention-based mechanism. They have created three datasets for summarization from various news websites by crawling corresponding websites and they have shown that the model of their study performs better than the existing studies in the literature in terms of ROUGE scores and the structural properties of the summaries. Furthermore, the researchers have built an English to Turkish translation model and utilized it to obtain a cross-lingual summarization model. In future investigations, the authors plan to include a pre-train phase to their model using BART and T5 architectures which will help them to obtain a more abstractive summary and better performance.

ACKNOWLEDGMENT

This work was supported by The Scientific and Technological Research Council of Turkey (TUBITAK) grant number 1919B012003590 under the 2209-A Program.

REFERENCES

Bakay, O., Avar, B., & Yildiz, O. T. (2019). A tree-based approach for English-to-Turkish translation. *Turkish Journal of Electrical Engineering and Computer Sciences*, 27(1), 437–452. doi:10.3906/elk-1807-341

Beltagy, I., Peters, M., & Cohan, A. (2020). *Longformer: The Long-Document Transformer.* Arxiv:2004.05150.

Bengio, Y., Louradour, J., Collobert, R., & Weston, J. (2009). Curriculum Learning. *ICML '09: Proceedings of the 26th Annual International Conference on Machine Learning*, 41–48.

Celikyilmaz, A., Bosselut, A., He, X., & Choi, Y. (2018). *Deep Communicating Agents for Abstractive Summarization.* Arxiv: 1803.10357.

Taspinar, E. K., Yetis, Y. B., & Cihan, O. (2022). *Abstractive Turkish Text Summarization Using Transformer and Cross-Lingual Summarization.* https://eymenkagantaspinar.github.io/Abstractive-Turkish-Text-Summarization-Using-Transformer-and-Cross-Lingual-Summarization/

Chopra, S., Auli, M., & Rush, A. (2016). Abstractive sentence summarization with attentive recurrent neural networks. *Proceedings of the 2016 Conference of the North American Chapter of the Association for Computational Linguistics: Human Language Technologies*, 93–98. 10.18653/v1/N16-1012

Devlin, J., Chang, M., Lee, K., & Toutanova, K. (2018). *BERT: Pre-training of Deep Bidirectional Transformers for Language Understanding.* Arxiv:1810.04805.

Ertam, F., & Aydin, G. (2021). Abstractive text summarization using deep learning with a new Turkish summarization benchmark dataset. *Concurrency and Computation*, *34*(9). doi:10.1002/cpe.6482

Fikri, F., Oflazer, K., & Yanıkoglu, B. (2021). Semantic Similarity Based Evaluation for Abstractive News Summarization. *Proceedings of the 1st Workshop on Natural Language Generation, Evaluation, and Metrics*, 24–33. 10.18653/v1/2021.gem-1.3

Gehrmann, S., Deng, Y., & Rush, A. M. (2018). *Bottom-Up Abstractive Summarization.* Arxiv: 1808.10792. doi:10.18653/v1/D18-1443

Gorgun, O., Yildiz, O. T., Solak, E., & Ehsani, R. (2016). English-Turkish parallel treebank with morphological annotations and its use in tree-based smt. *International Conference on Pattern Recognition and Methods*, 510-516. 10.5220/0005653905100516

Hendrycks, D., & Gimpel, K. (2016). *Gaussian error linear units (gelus).* Arxiv:1606.08415.

Jumper, J., Evans, R., Pritzel, A., Green, T., Figurnov, M., Ronneberger, O., Tunyasuvunakool, K., Bates, R., Žídek, A., Potapenko, A., Bridgland, A., Meyer, C., Kohl, S. A. A., Ballard, A. J., Cowie, A., Romera-Paredes, B., Nikolov, S., Jain, R., Adler, J., & Hassabis, D. (2021). Highly accurate protein structure prediction with AlphaFold. *Nature*, *596*(7873), 583–589. doi:10.103841586-021-03819-2 PMID:34265844

Karakoc, E., & Yilmaz, B. (2019). Deep learning based abstractive Turkish news summarization. *2019 27th Signal Processing and Communications Applications Conference (SIU).*

Kudo, T., & Richardson, J. (2018). SentencePiece: A simple and language independent subword tokenizer and detokenizer for neural text processing. *Proceedings of the 2018 Conference on Empirical Methods in Natural Language Processing: System Demonstrations*, 66–71. 10.18653/v1/D18-2012

Kutlu, M., Cığır, C., & Cicekli, I. (2010). Generic Text Summarization for Turkish. *24th International Symposium on Computer and Information Sciences*, 224-229.

Lewis, M., Liu, Y., Goyal, N., Ghazvininejad, M., Mohamed, A., Levy, O., Stoyanov, V., & Zettlemoyer, L. (2019). BART: Denoising Sequence-to-Sequence Pre-training for Natural Language Generation. *Translation, and Comprehension. Proceedings of the 58th Annual Meeting of the Association for Computational Linguistics*, 7871–7880.

Lin, C. Y. (2004). ROUGE: A package for automatic evaluation of summaries. *Workshop on Text Summarization Branches Out*, 74-81.

Lin, J., Sun, X., Ma, S., & Su, Q. (2018). Global Encoding for Abstractive Summarization. In *Proceedings of the 56th Annual Meeting of the Association for Computational Linguistics* (*vol 2*: Short Papers, pp. 163–169). Academic Press.

Liu, Y., Gu, J., Goyal, N., Li, X., Edunov, S., Ghazvininejad, M., Lewis, M., & Zettlemoyer, L. (2020). Multilingual Denoising Pre-training for Neural Machine Translation. *Transactions of the Association for Computational Linguistics*, 8, 726–742. doi:10.1162/tacl_a_00343

Liu, Y., & Lapata, M. (2019). *Text Summarization with Pretrained Encoders.* Arxiv: 1908.08345

Nallapati, R., Zhou, B., Nogueira, C., Gulcehre, C., & Xiang, B. (2016). Abstractive text summarization using sequence-to-sequence RNNs and beyond. *Proceedings of the 20th SIGNLL Conference on Computational Natural Language Learning*, 280–290.

Oflazer, K., & Durgar, I. (2007). Exploring Different Representational Units in English-to-Turkish Statistical Machine Translation. *Proceedings of the Second Workshop on Statistical Machine Translation*, 25-32. 10.3115/1626355.1626359

Papineni, K., Roukos, S., Ward, T., & Zhu, W. (2002). Bleu: a method for automatic evaluation of machine translation. *Proceedings of the 40th Annual Meeting of the Association for Computational Linguistics (ACL)*, 311-318.

Rachabathuni, P. K. (2017). A survey on abstractive summarization techniques. In *Inventive computing and informatics* (pp. 762–765). ICICI.

Radford, A., Narasimhan, K., Salimans, T., & Sutskever, I. (2018). *Improving language understanding by generative pre-training.* Academic Press.

Raffel, C., Shazeer, N., Roberts, A., Lee, K., Narang, S., Matena, M., Zhou, Y., Li, W., & Liu, P. (2020). Exploring the Limits of Transfer Learning with a Unified Text-to-Text Transformer. *Journal of Machine Learning Research*, 1–67.

Rush, A., Chopra, S., & Weston, J. (2015). A neural attention model for abstractive sentence summarization. *Proceedings of the 2015 Conference on Empirical Methods in Natural Language Processing*, 379–389. 10.18653/v1/D15-1044

Schuster, M., & Nakajima, K. (2012). Japanese and Korean voice search. *2012 IEEE International Conference on Acoustics, Speech and Signal Processing (ICASSP).* 10.1109/ICASSP.2012.6289079

Scialom, T., Dray, P., Lamprier, S., Piwowarski, B., & Staiano, J. (2020). MLSUM: The Multilingual Summarization Corpus. *Proceedings of the 2020 Conference on Empirical Methods in Natural Language Processing*, 8051–8067. 10.18653/v1/2020.emnlp-main.647

Vaswani, A., Shazeer, N., Parmar, N., Uszkoreit, J., Jones, L., Gomez, A., Kaiser, L., & Polosukhin, I. (2017). Attention Is All You Need. *Advances in Neural Information Processing Systems*, 5998–6008.

Wan, X., Li, H., & Xiao, J. (2010). Cross-language document summarization based on machine translation quality prediction. *Proceedings of the 48th Annual Meeting of the Association for Computational Linguistics*, 917–926.

Yeniterzi, R., & Oflazer, K. (2010). Syntax-to-Morphology Mapping in Factored Phrase-Based Statistical Machine Translation from English to Turkish. *Proceedings of the 48th Annual Meeting of the Association for Computational Linguistics*, 454–464.

Zhang, J., Zhao, Y., Saleh, M., & Liu, P. (2019). *Zhang: Pretraining with Extracted Gap-sentences for Abstractive Summarization.* Arxiv:1912.08777.

Zhu, J., Zhou, Y., Zhang, J., & Zong, C. (2020). Attend, Translate and Summarize: An Efficient Method for Neural Cross-Lingual Summarization. *Proceedings of the 58th Annual Meeting of the Association for Computational Linguistics*, 1309–1321. 10.18653/v1/2020.acl-main.121

KEY TERMS AND DEFINITIONS

BLEU: Bilingual Evaluation Understudy Score is a scoring algorithm for comparing a target translation of the text to a reference translation.

FLOPS: Floating Point Operations is the unit that expresses the computational cost. It can also be used to evaluate the cost of training and expresses how many basic mathematical operations will be applied to the floating-point number while performing the algorithm.

ROUGE: Recall-Oriented Understudy for Gisting Evaluation is a scoring algorithm that evaluates the similarities of the texts. It is used for summarization and translation. References are compared to the text, generated summary, or translation. Different ROUGE measures are defined based on the comparison mechanism.

ROUGE-1: Determine the overlap of a single word between generated and reference text.

ROUGE-2: Determine the overlap of a pair of words between generated and reference text.

ROUGE-L: Refers to the scoring of the longest common subtext between texts.

Self-Attention Mechanism: It is the mechanism that expresses the amount of attention that words show to each other within the encoder and decoder layers. Basically, after the multiplication process is applied to the matrices created by the Query, Key, and Value linear layers, the amount of attention the words pay to each other is determined. The created attention map is used when transforming.

Chapter 12
Systematic Literature Survey on Sign Language Recognition Systems

Ashok Kumar L.
PSG College of Technology, India

Karthika Renuka D.
PSG College of Technology, India

Raajkumar G.
PSG College of Technology, India

ABSTRACT

Recently, communication via signing acknowledgment has received a lot of attention in personal computer vision. Sign language is a method of conveying messages by using the hand, arm, body, and face to convey considerations and implications. Communication through gestures, like communication in languages, arises and develops naturally within hearing-impaired networks. All the same, gesture-based communication is uncommon. There is no universally perceived and accepted gesture-based communication for all deaf and hard-of-hearing people. Each nation has its own communication via gestures with a significant level of syntactic variety, just as it does when communicating in language. The gesture-based communication utilized is usually known as sign language.

INTRODUCTION

Two approaches to dealing with sign language recognition acknowledgment are disconnected sign acknowledgment and persistent communication through signing acknowledgment. Another type of gesture acknowledgment is disconnected sign acknowledgment. Signal acknowledgement frameworks are typically designed to detect bogus motions. To communicate with the framework, the client must become familiar with these motions. To have a thought about the best methodology expected to assemble

DOI: 10.4018/978-1-6684-6001-6.ch012

a gesture-based communication acknowledgment framework, it is critical to review the frameworks that have already been created. As a result, the exploration of electronic data sets and investigation of a few papers that were broadly applicable to the framework was carried out. An examination and correlation of the techniques used for comparative framework improvement would aid in the application of the appropriate way to deal with foster the framework. The writings discussed are summarized below. A variety of procedures have been used to set up Sign Language Recognition Systems.

LITERATURE SURVEY

Acquisition Using Wearable Computing

Wearable registration approaches to gesture-based communication information security provide a precise method for separating data about the underwriters' hand developments and hand shape. Each detecting innovation differs in a few ways, including precision, goal and range of movement, client comfort, and cost.

(Berman, 2011) proposed a reasonable visual movement information glove with high acknowledgment precision. In place of the more widely used development separating fibres or multi-channel accounting, the glove device employed a single - carrier video, with a repeating estimate to make up for the deficiencies of single-channel accounts. The growth of the hand was captured using a monocular camera, and after that, a visual analyser estimation identified the optical markings and reconstructed the 3D locations of the joints and fingers. In MATLAB, three different circumstances (left/right snaps, numerals, and the OK symbol) were dealt with and made into 3D graphics.

(Madeo, 2013) used the KHU-l information glove to create a 3D hand movement following and motion recognition framework. A Bluetooth device was used to connect the information glove to a PC. It was capable of performing hand movements such as clench hand grasping, hand extending, and bowing. For 50 preliminary trials, three signals (scissor, rock, and paper) were tried with 100% precision. Although 3D recognition and remote transmission were significant advancements, they resulted in time lag.

(Witt, 2007) devised a method for integrating glove-based devices into various applications using a setting system. The hand glove synchronised with electronic device may be used in three different ways, as demonstrated: to move, zoom, and choose parts of an assistant; to study a regulator in display; and to control a toy robot's left and right movements. Backwards/advances One issue was that, while this device could detect movement in the X and Y hatchets, it couldn't detect movement in the Z centre, such as the claimed "yaw." Furthermore, the precision of acknowledgment was sacrificed in order to achieve wear capacity, light weight, and a cool appearance.

Spatiotemporal Gesture Recognition: Sign Language Recognition

(Spolaor, 2021) proposed and implemented a hand stance and motion demonstrating and acknowledgment framework. The framework altered the information obtained from the hands after handling to foster a component model, which was a fluffy deduction hand arrangement used as a contribution to a fluffy neural organisation, determines the actual hand pose based on the fluffy derivation model produced. Then, deciding the request for the information hand signals the completion of the motion. It presented another fluffy hand-act model as an element model (FHPM). An altered Circular Fuzzy Neural Network (CFNN) design was proposed for hand-pose recognition, along with a reduced time preparing system.

To prevent the susceptibility brought on by hand, lower arm, and upper arm impediment, each pixel was allocated to either the limb model or the establishment model during the identification process. Following the arm setups, specific, unambiguous casings were identified and linked together. This framework was tested on BBC broadcast film with a consistent grouping of 6,000 edges performed by three endorsers. When there was little arm cross-over, the outcome exactness was over 91 percent, and it was around 59 percent when there was a lot of cross-over.

(Liu, 2018) proposed a gesture-based system for view invariant communication. The affirmation task in their proposed structure was changed to an affirmation task due to the numerical requirement that the significant organisation associate with in two viewpoints be exceptional when the discernment and arrangement signs are procured concurrently under the virtual sound framework vision and the opposite way around. Tests on a language of 100 signs revealed that their strategy was 92 percent accurate, with five disconnected instances of each sign recorded.

(Zhang, 2011) extracted movement directions from ASL recordings and arranged signs using a period defer neural organisation. In testing based on a set of 40 signs, the average classification performance of disguised test directives was 93.4%.

(Fang, 2004) proposed a mix of identity feature space, HMMs, and a decision tree, all with cheap computing costs, for the classification of withdrawal signs in order to overcome the problem of huge language sign recognition. A data set containing 61365 disengaged occurrences of 5113 different signals served as the basis for the experiments. The findings showed a 91.6 percent average recognition rate.

Two imagination SLR structures that make use of hidden information were proposed by (Seim, 2022). The first Markov model employed a first-person perspective with a security camera on the client's cap, whereas the second SVM classifier used a camera viewfinder with a camera attached on the work area. The planning and development took up the whole region. For hand following, the two structures employed a skin coloring matching computation. During testing, the crucial evaluating system had to have a word correctness of 98 percent compared to the second-person view structure's 92 percent. The great accuracy showed that HMM is excellent for careful development monitoring.

(Bhavana, 2021) proposed an SVM classifier along with hand sign recognition system with eight stages, including image acquisition, skin concealment division, and establishment removal, cautious edge finding, and PCA feature extraction. Pictures were taken with a web camera, and then a picture concealment test was run in MATLAB. The concealing image was changed to look like a picture with RGB values, and all of the complexions were converted to high differentiation pixels. Unwanted images were dealt with by utilizing the request between districts, and then by utilizing extraordinary edge revelation. Help vector machine classifiers will be used to train the dataset. The SVM recognizes each of the various signs; the Support Vector Machine recognizes the image's class and plan as shown by it. The accuracy of the focus test is 94%.

(Shenoy, 2018) demonstrated a technique for distinguishing proof tolerating Convolutional Neural Networks (CNN) letters are generated from extraordinary images captured by Microsoft Kinect through multi-view development and expected combination. An exceptional image's 3D information is initially recovered by the multi-view development, which then creates more data for a variety of understanding viewpoints. The results demonstrated that it outperforms standard imaging systems because it can duplicate suitable varieties in settings where standard procedures cannot. The induction mix duplicates the problems with interclass assessment caused by differences in setting and finger end. It incorporates data from all individuals' perspectives and after that creates a final gauge, which was confirmed to be viable in further improving model execution. In the half and left-off tests, the useful results show a recognition precision of 100 and 93 percent, respectively. (Lakhotiya, 2021) proposed a front camera video-based language ID system based on predictable Indian signs. Selfie video captured in signal language is handled by limiting its handling ability to a high-level cell. Gaussian sifting is used in conjunction with Sobel's versatile square limit and construction deduction, as well as pre-filtration, form location, and division. Because of a discrete cosine change, the hand and head shape force arrangement qualities. The investigation of the primary parts speeds up the execution by removing the unnecessary parts. Sign attributes are defined by Euclid and Mahalanobis normalized region measurements. The most difficult test, not withstanding, was to precisely eliminate the endorsers' hand shapes. The signs should ideally be held in one hand, and the video configuration changes depending on the selfie stick's development and the available light.

Using Depth Data to Recognize Gestures

(Bogaerts, 2022) improved recognition by using a ToF camera rather than stereoscopic cameras. A Colour camera with a high definition of 640 × 480 pixels was paired with a ToF camera with a different resolution of 176 x 144 pictures to record depth pictures for division. A pre-planned, adjustable skin concealing model that was powered by concealing information obtained from the face was employed to choose the countenance used for revelation. Three instances called for the employment of near identification: when the hand was intimate to the face, whenever the face obscured the hand, and when a person was standing behind the analyser. In all three situations, significance-based disclosure was executed with higher than 98 percent accuracy, whereas concealing-based ID fell sharply from 92 percent in the first example to 19.8 percent.

A stereoscopic game plan of two video moves for 3D hand-following. It could constantly run and incorporated suppression and 3D hands following. Each camera recorded pictures, and the hand movements in both video feeds were divided into hand masses using 2D concealing hand trackers and afterwards matched by an organization review. Following that, hand shapes were altered and reproduced in 3D space. The ability to manage dynamically is advantageous, however, the monocular structure's evaluated importance data is actually raucous, and the system's need for modification creates its varied nature.

A method for tracking hands in extremely muddled conditions by utilising 3D significance data provided by a sensor that used the hour-of-flight (ToF) method to obtain concealment and significance data concurrently. Three calculations were utilised to calculate the typical fields of anticipated hand or face shapes: obtaining possible fields by utilising distance modification, k-parts based probably fields, and weights. Furthermore, a bowl of enchantment. The framework was tested on ten people in both head following and hand following, with excellent results. It could follow hands with impediment and perceive simple movements like "venture back" and "stop."

A Speaking skill mediator sign was developed to serve as a movement validation along each fingertip length using flex sensors connected to a fast hand glove. The fundamental result voltages first from flex sensors are transported to the microprocessor and transferred over to the forefront of technology, which informs the microcontroller. The result of the vibration sensor change based on the amount that each finger is twisted. The Arduino nano has three press buttons, one of which can be read from the LCD, to make it more versatile for the client. The software engineer stored in the microcontroller converts the perceived sign to its literary representation. The RF Tran authority is linked to for automated signal transmission far from transmission.

An Android application that ensures extraordinary correspondence with clients who have inadequacies, as well as the opposite way around. The application is used as a medium to understand all movement tongues in Arabic. In order to communicate with target persons who are unfamiliar with motion-based messaging, normal people must do it in two different ways. This is the most obvious manifestation of the application's control. This can be done by hearing spoken Arabic or by creating Arabic words. Additionally, those who have hearing loss and a penchant for risk-taking interact with the general public by choosing sign pictures from a variety of classes in the databases that represent their ideas and analyses on their phones. The movement in the images is changed into a passage of text. Preliminary findings show that 96% of the calm and almost deaf have been satisfied.

(Hikawa, 2021) proposed the stance acknowledgment equipment framework utilizing a combination organization. A SOM plus a Hebbian framework make comprise a hybrid approach. In order to create a more subdued neuron guidance in the SOM, stress vectors are eliminated from data station pictures. A single-layer neural structure called the Hebbian approach is used to differentiate configurations using Hebbian learning calculations. The inclusion of disturbances in the SOMHebb characterization arrangement data improved its progressive and scaling power. The entire structure has been updated with a field-modified door cluster that uses a different video plan. The system was expected to see 24 correspondence hand signals in view of American hand signals and to actually take a look at their validity through both amusement re-enactment and tests.

Signal Recognition Using Kinect

Recently, evolved profundity sensors, such as the Kinect sensor, have gained ubiquity in the field of human-PC connection (HCI). The Kinect sensor has made enormous progress in the fields of human activity recognition, human body tracking, and face recognition, among other things. Even with the elements acquired by the Kinect sensors, hand motion recognition is still a time-consuming task. When two degrees of classifiers are used for a large vocabulary, the hand appears to grow even more.

A detached gesture-based communication using the aforementioned combinational methodologies, they perceived independent confined signs. They used chosen variation strategies from discourse acknowledgment to work on their framework's exhibition while performing client autonomous acknowledgment. While perceiving 153 disconnected signs, an acknowledgment rate of 78.6 percent was accounted for.

(Low, 2020) presented yet another methodology for following hands, they used a supported classifier course to recognise hand shapes in dark-scale images. The K-implies bunching calculation was used to collect these images. Then, at that point, a tree structure with two layers of "powerless" hand locators was framed. All of the candidate images that could include hand forms were selected by the assessors in the first layer, and they were then forwarded to the second layer so they could be differentiated from all of the images in the distinguishing groups. Weak classifiers were found with the use of the Float Boost estimation. In a test using 5,013 hand photos, the first layer distinguished hands with an accuracy of 98 percent, while the second layer distinguished shapes in the immediate vicinity with an accuracy of 97.4 percent.

According to (Gupta, 2019) the first signal language is delegated one-gave or two-gave in this technique. Furthermore, in order to obtain a specified state of central pictures and link them in a single organisation, two types of characteristics, namely HOG and SIFT, are dropped from the two designs. Then, using the ready set's cross sections (HOG) and SIFT, histograms of histograms of oriented and spectrum feature transform capabilities for the data test picture are generated. The channel can function as both a descriptor and a limit finder. The information is then given to a K-Nearest Classifier to finish the final organization of the modelling picture because the overarching organisations are not entirely set. HOG and SIFT, two different types of descriptors, worked together to give an accuracy of 90% and Microsoft are among those who have contributed to this work. Kinect is a 3D somatosensory camera delivered by Microsoft that captures shading, profundity, and skeleton casings and helps with signal perception. The SVM calculation removes the hoard highlights from these images and orders them. Kinect programming libraries propose differentiating communication through signing by detecting hand position, hand activity, and hand shape. An exceptional 3D motion language dataset is gathered for Kinect programming to do this technique and behavior examinations to assess the strategy. The trial results show that utilizing histogram arranged inclination (HOG) and SVM calculations fundamentally improves the exactness of Kinect acknowledgment and is unconcerned about foundation and other elements. The typical recognizable proof rate is 88.8 percent; the Kinect technique eliminates the significant expense of information gadgets like smart gloves while achieving a similarly high genuine-time recognition rate.

CONCLUSION

This paper discusses the various calculations and strategies used for perceiving the hand signal, as well as the various voice acknowledgment procedures and record methods available for people who are tragically unable to communicate with the converser. Hand motion recognition framework is thought to be a more natural and capable human PC communication instrument. The range of applications includes virtual prototyping, communication via signing investigation, and clinical preparation. Gesture-based communication is one method of communication for people who are deaf, hard of hearing, or unable to speak. According to the preceding thought, vision-based hand signal recognition has made tremendous progress in the field of hand motion recognition. C, C++, and Java are programming languages that are used to implement the signal recognition framework. MATLAB with a picture handling tool stash is used to improve the work, especially when picture handling activities are required.

SUMMARY

In general, 10 billion people on the planet are hearing-impaired and confused, with many people experiencing hearing impedance (deafness) and confused states (awkwardness) that may have existed since their birth or during their lifetime later. Correspondence between people with special needs and the general population has always been difficult. This is due to the fact that not everyone understands gesture-based communication. This complicates their lives because one of the arrangements is correspondence. Furthermore, this will have an impact on their interest in human advancement. To address this issue, a gesture-based communication articulation framework should be developed with a specific goal in mind: to bridge the gap between impaired and ordinary people.

Gesture-based communication is a method of correspondence between people who are deaf or hard of hearing and those who live in a quiet neighbourhood. Correspondence via signals emerges and grows normally within the meeting's hampered environment. Both physical and non-manual signs are employed in motion-based correspondence; the former include the fingers, hands, and arms, while the latter include the face, head, eyes, and torso. A highly organised language called signal correspondence uses phonology, morphology, accentuation, and punctuation. A full customary language that recalls several methods for elucidating letters in daily life is correspondence via movements. The gesture-based architecture for communication acknowledgment moves the connection from human-human to human-PC relationship. The goal of the gesture-based communication acknowledgment framework is to introduce a capable and precise system for deciphering text or discourse, allowing for smooth "exchange correspondence" between hard of hearing and hearing individuals. There is no universally accepted form of communication through signing for all deaf people around the world. In any case, correspondence through marking isn't universal; just like correspondence in lingos, these vary from one area to the next. A person who can talk and hear normally (customary individual) cannot communicate with a nearly deaf or dumb person unless the person in question is aware of motion correspondence. When an ear and deafeningly. Thus, there are two primary approaches used in gesture-based communication acknowledgment: sensor-based and vision-based approaches.

Despite the fact that it is famously taken on by the public who have hearing or correspondence challenges, motion language is a critical method for discussion between hearing impaired and dumbfounded networks. The greater number of people are interested in motion language; regardless of whether the signal language exists, communication between people with disabilities and normal people is still difficult.

A dominant hand, head and hand eye coordination, head and hand recognition, an unambiguous state of the hand, the mark of a thumb and head bound by environment, and a hand movement are the five basic ideas that make up the movement language system. Two frameworks among all these five designs stand out: the head and hand positions. Drugs cannot be used to treat hearing loss (deafness) or confusion (idiocy), as these conditions are not brought on by an illness or a stressful situation. In order to discover an answer that would enable them to live better lives, those people need have trust in science and progress. The advancement practises in the acknowledgment of signal-based correspondence are deficient, yet correspondence through motions has a certified arrangement of flaws, for example, a limited informational index and the inability to talk as frequently as commonplace people. Regardless of how people are attempting to create an answer that can successfully communicate with ordinary people, the investigation is being carried out to create new contraptions and strategies such as magnificent gloves, Android applications, and so on.

In this review, different gesture-based communication acknowledgment, voice-to-communication via gestures interpretation, and the other way around procedures outperform other more experienced strategies in terms of preserving the discourse flags completely. The paper provides a composing outline of the new developments that have occurred in decreasing the correspondence boundary between people experiencing exceptional needs and the general population. It has been noted that ongoing improvements are being developed to close the gap between people's particular demands and those of everyone else. This document explains new devices and technological advancements.

REFERENCES

Berman, S., & Stern, H. (2011). Sensors for gesture recognition systems. *IEEE Transactions on Systems, Man and Cybernetics. Part C, Applications and Reviews*, 42(3), 277–290. doi:10.1109/TSMCC.2011.2161077

Madeo, R. C. B., Wagner, P. K., & Peres, S. M. (2013). *A review of temporal aspects of hand gesture analysis applied to discourse analysis and natural conversation.* arXiv preprint arXiv:1312.4640.

Witt, H., Nicolai, T., & Kenn, H. (2007, June). The WUI-Toolkit: A model-driven UI development framework for wearable user interfaces. In *27th International Conference on Distributed Computing Systems Workshops (ICDCSW'07)* (pp. 43-43). IEEE. 10.1109/ICDCSW.2007.80

Spolaor, F., Romanato, M., Annamaria, G., Peppe, A., Bakdounes, L., To, D. K., Volpe, D., & Sawacha, Z. (2021). Relationship between muscular activity and postural control changes after proprioceptive focal stimulation (Equistasi®) in middle-moderate Parkinson's disease patients: An explorative study. *Sensors (Basel)*, *21*(2), 560. doi:10.339021020560 PMID:33466838

Liu, H., & Wang, L. (2018). Gesture recognition for human-robot collaboration: A review. *International Journal of Industrial Ergonomics*, *68*, 355–367. doi:10.1016/j.ergon.2017.02.004

Zhang, X., Chen, X., Li, Y., Lantz, V., Wang, K., & Yang, J. (2011). A framework for hand gesture recognition based on accelerometer and EMG sensors. *IEEE Transactions on Systems, Man, and Cybernetics. Part A, Systems and Humans*, *41*(6), 1064–1076. doi:10.1109/TSMCA.2011.2116004

Fang, G., Gao, W., & Zhao, D. (2004). Large vocabulary sign language recognition based on fuzzy decision trees. *IEEE Transactions on Systems, Man, and Cybernetics. Part A, Systems and Humans*, *34*(3), 305–314. doi:10.1109/TSMCA.2004.824852

Seim, C. E., Ritter, B., Starner, T. E., Flavin, K., Lansberg, M. G., & Okamura, A. M. (2022). Design of a wearable vibrotactile stimulation device for individuals with upper-limb hemiparesis and spasticity. *IEEE Transactions on Neural Systems and Rehabilitation Engineering*, *30*, 1277–1287. doi:10.1109/TNSRE.2022.3174808 PMID:35552152

Bhavana, D., Kumar, K. K., Chandra, M. B., Bhargav, P. S. K., Sanjanaa, D. J., & Gopi, G. M. (2021). Hand sign recognition using CNN. *International Journal of Performability Engineering*, *17*(3), 314–321. doi:10.23940/ijpe.21.03.p7.314321

Shenoy, K., Dastane, T., Rao, V., & Vyavaharkar, D. (2018, July). Real-time Indian sign language (ISL) recognition. In *2018 9th international conference on computing, communication and networking technologies (ICCCNT)* (pp. 1-9). IEEE.

Lakhotiya, H., Pandita, H. S., & Shankarmani, R. (2021, May). Real Time Sign Language Recognition Using Image Classification. In *2021 2nd International Conference for Emerging Technology (INCET)* (pp. 1-4). IEEE. 10.1109/INCET51464.2021.9456432

Bogaerts, T., Watelet, S., De Bruyne, N., Thoen, C., Coopman, T., Van den Bergh, J., Reyniers, M., Seynaeve, D., Casteels, W., Latré, S., & Hellinckx, P. (2022). Leveraging Artificial Intelligence and Fleet Sensor Data towards a Higher Resolution Road Weather Model. *Sensors (Basel)*, *22*(7), 2732. doi:10.339022072732 PMID:35408346

Hikawa, H., Ichikawa, Y., Ito, H., & Maeda, Y. (2021). Dynamic gesture recognition system with gesture spotting based on self-organizing maps. *Applied Sciences (Basel, Switzerland)*, *11*(4), 1933. doi:10.3390/app11041933

Low, C. C., Ong, L. Y., Koo, V. C., & Leow, M. C. (2020). Multi-audience tracking with RGB-D camera on digital signage. *Heliyon*, *6*(9), e05107. doi:10.1016/j.heliyon.2020.e05107 PMID:33024875

Gupta, A., Zhang, P., Lalwani, G., & Diab, M. (2019). *Casa-nlu: Context-aware self-attentive natural language understanding for task-oriented chatbots.* arXiv preprint arXiv:1909.08705. doi:10.18653/v1/D19-1127

Chapter 13
Sign Language Recognition for Daily Activites Using Deep Learning

Shoba S.
Centre for Advanced Data Science, Vellore Institute of Technology, Chennai, India

Chanthini B.
Vellore Institute of Technology, Chennai, India

Sasithradevi A.
Centre for Advanced Data Science, Vellore Institute of Technology, Chennai, India

Manikandan E.
Centre for Innovation and Product Development, Vellore Institute of Technology, Chennai, India

ABSTRACT

Sign language recognition has become a critical research in the field of computer vision as the need of disability solutions grow. Sign language acts as a bridge to reduce the communication gap between normal people and deaf and dumb people. Current sign language identification systems, on the other hand, lack essential characteristics such as accessibility and cost, which are critical for people with speech disabilities to interact with their daily settings. The successful attractive solution is to initiate the sign languages in terms of words and common expressions for daily activities. This will interact the deaf and dumb people by connecting to the outside world more quickly and easily. The sign gestures obtained are processed through popular machine learning and deep learning models for classification accuracy. This chapter discusses the word sign recognition, image processing algorithms for separating the signs from the background, machine learning algorithms, and the complete model set up for sign recognition.

DOI: 10.4018/978-1-6684-6001-6.ch013

INTRODUCTION

The conversation is a key mechanism by which information sharing is being done among the people. People with disabilities need some way of communication to deal with normal and disabled people. But this is a challenging and difficult process when normal and deaf and mute people try to communicate. The best and most effective way of communication for deaf and dumb persons is sign language. Sign language communication not only benefits the communication between the deaf and dumb. But also benefits the communication between normal and deaf and dumb people. A deaf and mute person uses hand gestures for communication. Also, for normal people understanding their gestures is a complicated task. Hence, there is a need for a proper system which could resolve this problem and thereby make communication easier. Many systems have been developed for this process and still finding a complete solution is in research (Tolentino, 2019). The primary goal of this chapter is to find the gap between the current sign language identification system in the aspect of accessibility, cost and problem to apply in day-to-day activities. The first and primary challenge is collecting the real-time dataset. In the real scenario, capturing the images contains various backgrounds with noises. So, an efficient pre-processing step is required for accurate prediction. After pre-processing, the next step is segmentation which separates the background from the target signs. Multiple image processing algorithms are used to segment the image. The image after the segmentation process is modelled through machine learning algorithms and deep learning algorithms.

For disabled persons, the most popular language used is the American Sign Language (ASL). The pre-processed images are readily available as a dataset for ASL languages. But most of the existing datasets are of the alphabet. The current existing dataset is not suitable for recognizing words and day-to-day activities. Few of the datasets available in Indian sign languages are collected for words but the signs cannot be considered universal which differs with each country. The developed systems for sign language detection involve two basic approaches.

The first is contact-based i.e. using sensors and gloves hardware for gesture understanding and the second one is a non-contact vision-based system. The vision-based system can be categorized either as static or dynamic. The static system uses two-dimensional images for the analysis whereas the dynamic system uses proper cameras for capturing the real-time movements (Ismail et al, 2021). The hardware glove-based method is not comfortable for the users. But, the vision-based system is easier to implement than the hardware-based contact system and no physical contact is needed with the users. But the major issues to be addressed in vision-based are the accuracy of the detection and the recognition time. This accuracy of detection and recognition time can be improved by using proper machine/deep learning algorithms.

Related Work

The recent technological advancements made in machine learning and artificial intelligence-enabled the researchers to utilize AI for sign language prediction and thereby ease the process. Many excellent works are reported for an intelligent system for sign language recognition. A detailed and critical review on sign language prediction using ML techniques is reported. It is very clear and evident that the number of works reported for journals increased from 10s to 100s between 2001 and 2021 respectively. In this, the country-wise rank is also reported based on the number of publications with the particular affiliation where India is ranked top worldwide in sign language research. At present, more than 100s of sign languages are in use and automatic prediction of each is a challenging one facing as of now. The automatic sign language prediction with the help of AI could help and will be helpful to society in resolving this problem (Adeyanju et al, 2021).

A human-to-computer system was developed for sign language recognition which does not use any hardware components such as gloves, sensors (Punsara et al, 2020) etc. The advantage was it can be used for deaf and dumb as well as normal people. The segmentation was done from the LAB component of the image and for feature extraction, a Hough transform was utilized. The system was able to predict 31 Tamil sign languages (Jayanthi, P et al, 2013). In sign language prediction, accessing the depth information with the help of a 3D camera was difficult. So a convolutional and deep neural network was employed for re-sizing and pre-processing the obtained RGB images during the training period. These developed models were tested for American sign language recognition and obtained an accuracy level of nearly 83% and 90% for deep and convolutional neural networks respectively (Kasukurthi et al, 2018; Dasl, 2019). A sign language to speech conversion nothing but a synthesizer for Tamil has been developed by using Hidden Markov Model (HMM). In this system, the hardware components such as sensors were used for capturing the hand gestures and those are converted into Tamil phrases using HMM. This model used both the testing and synthesizing phase for the automatic signs-to-speech conversion process. In real-time, the developed system has achieved an accuracy of 87.5% and the dataset is able to achieve nearly 100%. It has been suggested that the hardware-based system should consume low power and at the same time the weight of the module to be kept minimum for making it wearable (Aiswarya et al, 2018).

Indian sign language recognition in real-time model was developed using the computer vision technique. A camera was used for capturing the real-time videos in the background and OpenCV was utilized for extracting the features and classification process. This system used fuzzy c-means algorithm for the prediction and was able to predict basic words and a few sentences based on the given dataset (Muthu Mariappan et al, 2019). Though the accuracy obtained was less than 80 it was an attempt to utilise videos for sign language recognition. Many well-known companies are working on augmented and virtual reality AR/VR, interactive computers and so on. So developing an automated sign language system is become mandatory for satisfying these applications. Processing with a low memory footprint is another direction of research. With this objective, a system was developed using the ARM process with 496 KB of RAM for automatic sign language recognition. The aspect here was to use a generalized and efficient CNN algorithm for the recognition of finger spelling (Paul et al, 2019). In addition to the flex sensors used for hand gesture identification, ANN was adopted for converting the signs into letters, numbers and sentences. But this will not give any meaning to the users. So, Natural Language Processing (NLP) has been utilized and a mobile application has also been developed for the end user. This system eases the process flow and helps the users with sign recognition. Recently, a combination of a deep learning network and singular value decomposition (SVD) is being utilized for sign language prediction which could be able to achieve more than 90% accuracy in real-time.

Challenges in the Existing System

- Sign language recognition system developed by researchers is for recognizing alphabets and words
- The Recognition system developed does not rely on universal language and grammatical skills
- The glove-based recognition system is not comfortable for users and a person needs to wear additional hardware.

- The non-contact vision system relies on the light intensity, climatic conditions and also people's skin colour while capturing the photo.

General Overview

Each acquisition method has its advantages and disadvantages. For example, in a vision-based system using cameras, the environmental factor such as light intensity, climatic conditions and also the skin colour of the people play a vital role in the capturing. So proper pre-processing is to be done based on the process environment. But the advantage can be seen as no need to wear any additional hardware for sign language recognition. On the other hand, a gloves-based system makes the users uncomfortable. But the glove-based system does not get affected by environmental conditions. So selection of the system and the other pre-processing technique should be thoroughly studied before developing the system.

The generalized schematic representation of the sign language detection system is depicted in Figure 1.

Figure 1. Schematic representation of Vision-based Sign Language Detection

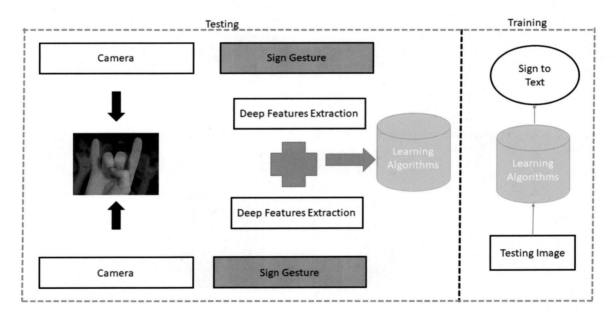

In the testing phase, the camera is used for capturing the real-time movements where both the top and bottom views are collected for improving the detection. The extracted images will be stored in the database and pre-processing will be done as required. The feature extraction is done and input is given to the learning algorithms. In the training phase, the testing image is fed to the algorithms and compared with the standard database. Finally, the sign-to-text conversion is done for the user's understanding.

The following section is as follows. Section 2 explains sign language recognition and how to segregate target images using image processing algorithms. Section 3 explains the machine learning models used for sign language and finally, section 4 is about the advantage, disadvantages and conclusion of this chapter.

SIGN LANGUAGE RECOGNITION

Recognizing the signs through hand gestures is the proper way of identifying the sign language. Recognizing the sign can be done through different approaches. The basic and easiest (Hills et al, 2021) approach is to classify the gesture using the hand manually through human vision as shown in Figure 2. Later, researchers paved attention by applying machine learning models to the pre-processed dataset and recognizing the hand gesture signs as depicted in Figure 3(Jafari et al, 2020).

Figure 2. Human sign language through man-made approach (Hills et al, 2021)

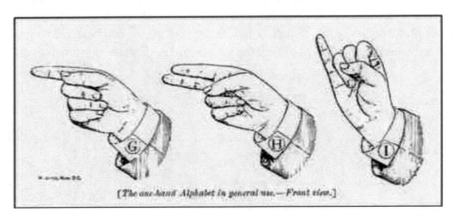

Figure 3. Classification done through machine learning approach (Jafari et al, 2020)

Various machine learning approaches like KNN, Random forest, SVM and Artificial neural networks are applied to the images and classified with the accuracy level. Later, the attention focused on the technology aspect and used infrared sensor technology via LeapMotion (Koul et al, 2016). Kinect (Yang et al, 2016), etc. In another way, wearing hand gloves and applying gestures increase the accuracy of the classification. Recent publications on sign language recognition focused on the real-time capture of images through smart devices of cameras and video (Jafari et al, 2020). Another challenge in sign language recognition as it's not been universally recognised a single language. As per the countries and states, different signs are used for the same alphabet or word. So it's difficult for the deaf and dumb disabled to understand the sign while travelling between countries and states. The types of sign language used in countries and states are America, India, Tamil, Australia, Persian, Taiwan, Vietnam, Ukrainian, Brazilian and Sri Lankan sign languages. Most of the research papers used ASL as depicted in Figure 4. The steps for sign language recognition are pre-processing, feature extraction, segmentation, modelling and classification.

Figure 4. American sign language alphabets

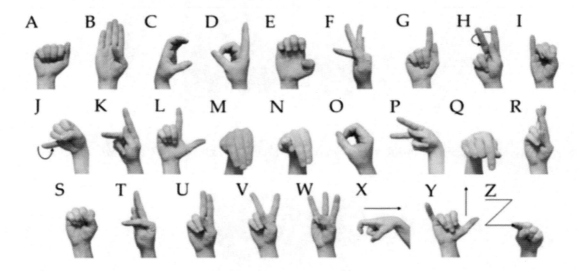

Pre-Processing Methods

Initially, the input data is gathered through various approaches like Kinect in Figure 5 (Yang et al, 2014), leap motion in Figure 4 (Koul et al, 2016), machine learning in Figure 3 (Jafari et al, 2020) and video camera method in Figure 6 (Jafari et al, 2020; Kuznetsova et al, 2013) as discussed in the previous section. Pre-processing is an important step and each approach has to be pre-processed before segmentation for noise removal. The role of the pre-processing method is to filter the noise from the input image captured and done through various methods. The initial stage of pre-processing is filtering the image through the median or average filtering method. This method removes the noise from the captured images (Mendes Junior et al, 2020). The spectral subtraction method is applied as the next step in the pre-processing block. As the spectral subtraction is computational and produces a less efficient method. To reduce the computation cost and time, the Gaussian average method (Philippe et al, 2008) is proposed which increases the accuracy level.

Segmentation – Image Processing Algorithms

The most important step of sign language is segmentation which segregates the image into two divisions. The first is to segment the target image from the background image. Some of the successful methods are bounding box, ostu threshold segmentation and canny edge detection. Each technique is explained as follows

Figure 5. Sign language recognition by infrared sensor technology using Kinect sensor (Yang et al, 2014)

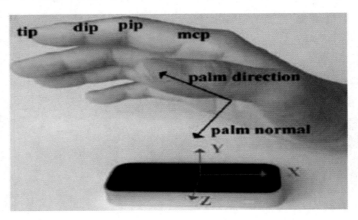

Figure 6. Sign language recognition through a real-time camera/video (Jafari et al, 2020; Kuznetsova et al, 2013)

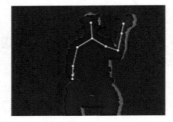

Bounding Box Technique

The bounding box technique is a remarkable one in the field of image processing and computer vision. The idea of using a bounding box is to identify the local target object in the input image. The bounding box is to locate the boundaries in the shape of a box which surrounds the local target image with single/ multiple regions of interest (ROI). In (Pariwat et al, 2021), segmentation is done in the form of a hand segmentation library where the hand signs are picked from the database and processed initially using semantic segmentation. Then RGB image is converted to a grayscale image. Applying a gaussian filter to the image will filter the noise and remove most of the background parts from the image. After the noise removal, the bounding box technique is applied to find the ROI of the target image. The final image shown in Figure 7 shows the hand segmented image after the bounding extraction process. Some of the sample images are depicted in Figure 8.

Canny Edge Detection

In this type of detection, first, the input image in RGB form is converted to grayscale image. The effective technique to detect the edges from the image is canny edge detection. This technique is applied to the grayscale image and detects the edges of the gesture position of the hand. In this work (Sharma et al, 2020), candy edge detection is applied as the first stage in Figure 9 (a) which focuses on the edges.

It is observed from Figure 9(b), that some of the background noises are also considered the edges. To make the detection more accurate, Oriented fast and rotated brief (ORB) feature detection is applied which projects only on the target image. This technique is similar to SIFT or SURF (*Rublee* et al, 2011). ORB calculate the key points in different angles to locate the points at the centroid patches by the approach names FAST (Viswanathan et al, 2009) key point detector. The features from accelerated and segments test (FAST) and binary robust independent elementary features (BRIEF) (Calonder et al) are two descriptors used for boosting the performance. ORB detects the points with patches as shown in Figure 9(c) forms a dimensional vector of features

Figure 7. Segmentation process using bounding box technique (Pariwat et al, 2021)

Figure 8. Sample segmented image after bounding box processing (Pariwat et al, 2021)

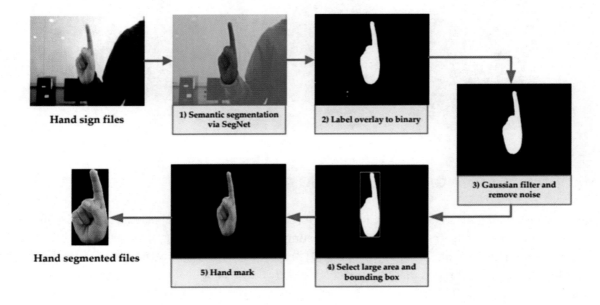

Otsu Thresholding Segmentation

The most popular and successful approach for thresholding the image in sign language applications is the ostu thresholding (Yang et al, 2020). This is popular because of its simple calculation and efficiency. This work (Sharma et al, 2013) selects the threshold value at an optimum level which maximizes the target image from the background images as in Figure 10(a). The maximum number of iterations occurs until it reaches the optimum value between the background and the target images as shown in Figure 10 (b). Due to its simplicity, it is considered the global thresholding technique which applies only to grayscale images.

Figure 9. Segmentation concept using Canny edge detection

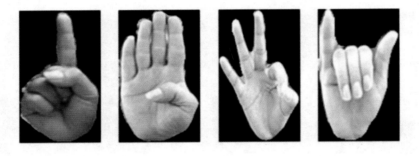

Figure 10. Segmentation using Otsu Thresholding technique (Sharma et al, 2013)

MACHINE LEARNING/DEEP LEARNING ALGORITHMS

Some of the existing machine learning models (Grobel et al, 1997; Nagarajan et al, 2013; Zafrulla et al, 2011) are evaluated in the form of training and testing (Grobel et al, 1997). There are some other small-scale datasets (Huang et al, 2015; Pigou et al, 2017) which use machine learning models and becomes overfitting model. The hidden markov model (HMM) (Starner et al, 2011) is used in sign language for temporal relationships. To label the signs (Nagarajan et al, 2013), a support vector machine (SVM) is used to classify the letters or words. The American sign language alphabets (ASL) are recognised by the K nearest neighbour algorithm and proposed by (Chuan et al, 2014). In this algorithm, the nearest gesture patterns are collected and their Euclidean distance is measured to find the gesture. K is a positive integer which determines the no of nearest distance points. The machine learning algorithms are suitable for small-scale dataset and the level of efficiency would be high as the number of samples is less. The current trend in many applications is deep learning architecture which benefits the large-scale dataset. Also, the classification and prediction can be done in various aspects.

Result Analysis

Most of the research work deals with the performance level as accuracy in sign language recognition. An increase in the value of accuracy determines accurate recognition and a decrease in the accuracy value shows the misclassification in the recognition of gestures. The sign language gestures are recognised by training and testing the samples using different deep learning and machine learning algorithms. Research findings for sign language recognition use various deep learning models and classify the gesture signs as shown in Table 1. The model classifies the sign in terms of alphabets, action words, numerals, letters and greeting sentences. Support vector machines (SVM) used in (Lee et al, 2018) are used to recognize the 26 alphabets in signs with the help of flex and IMU sensors. The work published in 2020 uses the isogsd (Sajanraj et al, 2018) dataset which classifies the letters using the deep neural network model of SSD, CNN and LSTM and produces an accuracy of 86.32%. Inertial motion units (IMU) sensors are used to create a dataset for the action words provided. The bidirectional LSTM model is applied in the encoder-decoder architecture to classify the gesture (Kavarthapu et al, 2017). To increase the accuracy of the system, Recurrent Neural Network (RNN) in combination with LSTM recognised the greeting words with 6 IMU sensors and achieved 99.81% (Lee et al, 2020). Sign language recognition models not only concentrate on alphabets and words but also on numbers. A convolutional neural network (CNN) is used to recognize the number using an IMU sensor and achieved 99.56% accuracy in (Rastgoo et al, 2020). Sign language recognition has to be focused on the speech impaired people for their daily activities concerning words and sentences. In future, an android app can be developed or a device can be made which makes the impaired life easy to communicate with normal people.

Table 1. Comparative analysis of the sign language recognition deep learning models

Reference	Year	Dataset	Sensor	Model	Accuracy	Classification
[33]	2020	ISOGD	IMU	SSD, CNN, LSTM	86.32%	Letter
[34]	2017	ASLLRP	IMU	Bidirectional LSTM	97.7%	Action Word
[35]	2018	26 finger spelling ASL	1IMU & flex sensors	SVM	98.20%	Alphabets
[36]	2020	27 word-based ASL gestures	6 IMU sensors	RNN-LSTM	99.81%	Word
[37]	2018	0-8 numbers	IMU	CNN	99.56%	Numbers

DISCUSSION

Advantages

Communication can be done efficiently and easier for deaf and dumb people who know and use them frequently. Educating the sign language to the deaf and dumb community will benefit them to have to communicate with normal human beings. Some of the points discussed are as follows

- A blend of text communication, lip-reading and signs will help the deaf community to ease their daily activities.
- An increase in a language known to the normal or deaf and dumb community will increase their creative thinking skill.
- Sign language skills of disability will increase problem-solving skills.
- The language barrier is reduced and increases the flexibility level between normal and deaf/dumb people.
- As the university/college is encouraging sign language recognition courses in recent years, people with disabilities achieve in the field of academics.
- The listening skill of the people will show a drastic improvement as signs are more focused to find out the deliverable words.
- The deaf/dumb people will be intellectual and strong in the literacy part as sign language becomes a need for society.

Disadvantages

Many sign language recognition applications developed are of commercial use and also costly. The applications developed for sign language by the researchers are of the alphabet and some are words. Mostly of the apps are developed for a specific need and don't help the deaf and dumb community to a greater extent.

Another demerit is the sign language developed does not rely on universal language and grammatical skills. Most of the sign language developed is in the form of the abstraction stage. Also, the sign differs as per country and state. So people with disabilities find it difficult when they travel across countries. It is also difficult to understand like a normal human being in the form of hearing different environmental noises and languages spoken by other people.

Applications of Algorithms

Nowadays, Sign language recognition becomes popular one is most universities and colleges due to its demand. The universities are educating with excellent services that satisfy the community of Deaf and Dumb people. Developing an app and training the teachers to educate the community.

CONCLUSION

This chapter guides us through the challenges faced by deaf and dumb community people. The communication gaps are also identified between normal people and deaf and dumb people. The current existing methods were processed with machine learning algorithms and their classification. Various image processing algorithms were investigated, evaluated and deployed to know more knowledge about sign language signs. Initially, the alphabets were classified and later, words were given as a dataset to recognise the words with the machine learning methods. Finally, the merits and demerits were discussed and the solutions were given.

REFERENCES

Adeyanju, I. A., Bello, O. O., & Adegboye, M. A. (2021). Machine learning methods for sign language recognition: A critical review and analysis. *Intell. Syst. with Appl.*, *12*, 200056. doi:10.1016/j.iswa.2021.200056

Aiswarya, V., Naren Raju, N., Johanan Joy, S. S., Nagarajan, T., & Vijayalakshmi, P. (2018). Hidden markov model-based sign language to speech conversion system in Tamil. *Proceedings of the 4th International Conference Biosignals, Images Instrumentation*, 206–212. 10.1109/ICBSII.2018.8524802

Calonder, M., Lepetit, V., Strecha, C., & Brief, F. P. (n.d.). Binary robust independent elementary features. *Proceedings of the European Conference on Computer Vision*, 778–792.

Chuan, C. H., Regina, E., & Guardino, C. (2014, December). American sign language recognition using leap motion sensor. In *13th International Conference on Machine Learning and Application, 2014* (pp. 541–544). IEEE Publications. 10.1109/ICMLA.2014.110

Dasl, A., Gawde, S., Suratwala, K., & Kalbande, D. (2018). Sign language recognition using deep learning on custom processed static gesture images. *Int. Conf. Smart City Emerg. Technol. ICSCET 2018*. 10.1109/ICSCET.2018.8537248

Grobel, K., & Assan, M. (1997). Isolated sign language recognition using hidden markov models. In *Computational Cybernetics and Simulation IEEE International Conference on Systems, Man, and Cybernetics*, 1 (pp. 162–167). IEEE Publications. 10.1109/ICSMC.1997.625742

Hills, R., Renner, D., Lott, P. S., & Valli, C. (2021). *The Gallaudet dictionary of American sign language.* Gallaudet University Press.

Huang, W. Z., Li, H., & Li, W. (2015). Sign language recognition using 3d convolutional neural networks. In *IEEE international conference on multimedia and expo (ICME)* (pp. 1–6). IEEE Publications.

Ismail, M. H., Dawwd, S. A., & Ali, F. H. (2021, December). Arabic Sign Language Detection Using Deep Learning Based Pose Estimation. In 2021 2nd Information Technology To Enhance e-learning and Other Application (IT-ELA) (pp. 161-166). IEEE. doi:10.1109/IT-ELA52201.2021.9773404

Jafari, M. R. (2020). *Persian sign gesture translation to English spoken language on smartphone* [Doctoral Dissertation]. Delhi Technological University.

Jafari, M. R. (2020). *Persian sign gesture translation to English spoken language on smartphone* [Doctoral Dissertation]. Delhi Technological University.

Jayanthi, P., & Thyagharajan, K. K. (2013). Tamil alphabets sign language translator. *5th Int. Conf. Adv. Comput. ICoAC 2013*, 383–388. 10.1109/ICoAC.2013.6921981

Kasukurthi, N., Rokad, B., Bidani, S., & Dennisan, D. A. (2019). *American sign language alphabet recognition using deep learning.* Academic Press.

Kavarthapu, D. C., & Mitra, K. (2017). Hand gesture sequence recognition using inertial motion units (IMUs). *Proceedings of the 4th IAPR Asian Conference. Pattern Recognition (ACPR)*, 953–957. 10.1109/ACPR.2017.159

Koul, M., Patil, P., Nandurkar, V., & Patil, S. (2016). Sign language recognition using leap motion sensor. *International Research Journal of Engineering and Technology, 3*(11), 322–325.

Kuznetsova, A., Leal-Taixé, L., & Rosenhahn, B. (2013). Real-time sign language recognition using a consumer depth camera. In *Proceedings of the IEEE International Conference on Computer Vision Workshops* (pp. 83–90). 10.1109/ICCVW.2013.18

Lee, B. G., Chong, T. W., & Chung, W. Y. (2020). Sensor fusion of motion-based sign language interpretation with deep learning. *Sensors (Basel), 20*(21), 6256. doi:10.339020216256 PMID:33147891

Lee, B. G., & Lee, S. M. (2018). Smart wearable hand device for sign language interpretation system with sensors fusion. *IEEE Sensors Journal, 18*(3), 1224–1232. doi:10.1109/JSEN.2017.2779466

Mendes, J. J. A. Junior, Freitas, M. B., Campos, D. P., Farinelli, F. A., Stevan, S. L., & Pichorim, S. F. (2020). Analysis of influence of segmentation, features, and classification in sEMG processing: A case study of recognition of Brazilian sign language alphabet. *Sensors (Basel), 20*(16), 4359. doi:10.339020164359 PMID:32764286

Muthu Mariappan, H., & Gomathi, V. (2019). Real-time recognition of Indian sign language. *ICCIDS - 2nd Int. Conf. Comput. Intell. Data Sci. Proc.,* 1–6. 10.1109/ICCIDS.2019.8862125

Nagarajan, S., & Subashini, T. (2013). Static hand gesture recognition for sign language alphabets using edge oriented histogram and multi class svm. *International Journal of Computers and Applications, 82*(4), 28–35. doi:10.5120/14106-2145

Pariwat, T., & Seresangtakul, P. (2021). Multi-stroke Thai finger-spelling sign language recognition system with deep learning. *Symmetry, 13*(2), 262. doi:10.3390ym13020262

Paul, A. J., Mohan, P., & Sehgal, S. (2020). Rethinking generalization in American sign language prediction for edge devices with extremely low memory footprint. 2020 IEEE recent Adv. *Intell. Comput. Syst. RAICS, 2020,* 147–152. doi:10.1109/RAICS51191.2020.9332480

Philippe, D., & Hermann, N. (2008). Visual modeling and feature adaptation in sign language recognition. *Voice communication (SprachKommunikation) ITG Conference on,* 1–4.

Pigou, Van Herreweghe, & Dambre. (2017). Gesture and sign language recognition with temporal residual networks. *IEEE International Conference on Computer Vision (ICCV) Workshops.*

Punsara, K. K. T. (2020). IoT based sign language recognition system. *ICAC - 2nd Int. Conf. Adv. Comput. Proc., 162–167.* 10.1109/ICAC51239.2020.9357267

Rastgoo, R., Kiani, K., & Escalera, S. (2020). Video-based isolated hand sign language recognition using a deep cascaded model. *Multimedia Tools and Applications, 79*(31–32), 22965–22987. doi:10.100711042-020-09048-5

Rublee, Rabaud, & Konolige. (2011). ORB: An efficient alternative to SIFT or SURF. *Proceedings of the IEEE International Conference on Computer Vision.*

Sajanraj, T. D., & Beena, M. (2018). Indian sign language numeral recognition using region of interest convolutional neural network. In *Proceedings of the 2nd International Conference Inventive Commun. Comput. Technol. (ICICCT)* (pp. 636–640). 10.1109/ICICCT.2018.8473141

Sharma, A., Mittal, A., Singh, S., & Awatramani, V. (2020). Hand gesture recognition using image processing and feature extraction techniques. *Procedia Computer Science, 173*, 181–190. doi:10.1016/j. procs.2020.06.022

Sharma, R., Nemani, Y., Kumar, S., Kane, L., & Khanna, P. (2013, July). Recognition of single handed sign language gestures using contour tracing descriptor. *Proceedings of the World Congress on Engineering, 2*.

Starner, T. E. (n.d.). *Visual recognition of American sign language using hidden markov models* [Technical report]. Massachusetts Institute of Tech Cambridge Department of Brain and Cognitive Sciences.

Tolentino, L. K. S., Juan, R. S., Thio-ac, A. C., Pamahoy, M. A. B., Forteza, J. R. R., & Garcia, X. J. O. (2019). Static sign language recognition using deep learning. *International Journal of Machine Learning and Computing, 9*(6), 821–827. doi:10.18178/ijmlc.2019.9.6.879

Viswanathan, D. G. (2009, May). Features from accelerated segment test (fast). *Proceedings of the 10th Workshop on Image Analysis for Multimedia Interactive Services, 6*–8.

Yang, H. D. (2014). Sign language recognition with the kinect sensor based on conditional random fields. *Sensors (Basel), 15*(1), 135–147. doi:10.3390150100135 PMID:25609039

Yang, P., Song, W., Zhao, X., Zheng, R., & Qingge, L. (2020). An improved Otsu threshold segmentation algorithm. *International Journal on Computer Science and Engineering, 22*(1), 146–153. doi:10.1504/ IJCSE.2020.107266

Zafrulla, Z., Brashear, H., Starner, T., Hamilton, H., & Presti, P. (2011). American sign language recognition with the kinect. *Proceedings of the 13th international conference on multimodal interfaces, Academic Medicine*, 279–286. 10.1145/2070481.2070532

Chapter 14

MorseEx:
A Communication Application for the Deaf-Blind

Suresh Kumar Nagarajan
Presidency University, India

Geetha N.
Vellore Institute of Technology, Vellore, India

Raghav Talwar
Vellore Institute of Technology, Vellore, India

Shivoma Ahuja
Vellore Institute of Technology, Vellore, India

ABSTRACT

MorseEx uses Morse code, which allows partially visually impaired and hard of hearing people to chat with others. In Morse code, letters are represented as a combination of dots and dashes. The person inputs a dot by tapping on the left of the screen, dash by tapping on the center of the screen to form a message, and tapping on the right will separate letters of the message, and tapping it twice sends the message. This message will be saved to the database and then converted to a normal text message to receive by people who do not have any impairments. On the other hand, people with no impairments have to type and send text messages. For this message to be understood by the visually and partially impaired, a dot will be produced as short vibration and a dash will be produced as long vibration. The model will be developing an Android mobile application using Android studio and Firebase database to store user information. The aim is to contribute to society in any way possible.

DOI: 10.4018/978-1-6684-6001-6.ch014

INTRODUCTION

Communication is an extremely vital part of everyday life. Being able to communicate effectively is one of the most important life skills. But something as trivial as communication seems very difficult for people who are visually or hearing impaired. They face multiple challenges every day of their lives and one of them is communicating their thoughts and opinions effectively. When people with good intentions convert to a slow manner of speaking, instead of assisting the hearing challenged, they make it more difficult for them to read lips. Hearing challenged persons have learned to understand words when others talk normally over time, thus purposely slowing things down can lead to misinterpretation. The absence of light makes it difficult for the hearing impaired to engage with people, whether in a poorly lit room or a boisterous dark club. They rely on visual stimuli to communicate, such as lip reading or sign language, therefore darkness is a problem. Various studies have found that deaf persons are roughly twice as likely to suffer from psychological issues as hearing ones. Here's where you'll find the appropriate financing source. If there are none, delete this. despair and anxiety, for example. This, according to research, stems from emotions of isolation. Worse, talking with a therapist is usually the most effective solution for these types of difficulties. Of course, finding a doctor or therapist who has the skills and experience to work effectively with people who have hearing problems is not straightforward. When it comes to the visually impaired, it is easy for them to read braille but when it comes to expressing their thoughts without verbal communication, not every person can understand braille. Even though technology is extremely advanced these days and speech-to-text conversion solves a lot of problems, it is not always possible to do it depending on the circumstances and the environment the person is in. This is where Morse Code comes in.

Morse code is indeed a telecommunications method for encoding characters as two-second signal sequences in the form of dots and dashes, or dits and dahs. The initial Morse Code is known as the American Morse Code since it was invented in America. The International Morse Code for languages that also utilize the Latin Alphabet, the Japanese Wabun Code, and the Korean Morse Code are only a few of the current Morse Code variants (SKATS). It was created by Samuel Finley Breese Morse. No distinction is made between capital and lowercase letters. A series of dots and dashes make up each Morse code symbol. The basic unit of time measurement in Morse code transmission is the duration of a dot, while the duration of a dash is three times that of a dot. Each dot or dash in a character is followed by a gap, which denotes a period of silence equal to the length of the dot. A space of duration equal to three dots separates a word's letters, and space of duration equal to seven dots separates words. Morse code is frequently delivered at the fastest rate the recipient can decode since its elements are proportionately stated rather than having set time lengths. The Morse code transmission rate is a unit of measurement that is expressed in groups per minute. An information-carrying medium that is switched on and off, such as electrical current, radio waves, visible light, or sound waves, is commonly used to transmit Morse code. It is simpler to differentiate between dots and dashes since the current or wave is present throughout the duration of the dot or dash but not in between.

People who have received the necessary training can directly decipher Morse code signals in a format that is perceptible to human senses, such as sound waves or visible light, and they can also directly analyze Morse code signals in a format that is perceptible to sensory organs, such as vibrations or visible light (Landicho, 2016). Morse code usually works with vibrations which are divided into short vibrations and long vibrations. The short vibration is used to indicate that the Morse code of a particular letter is finished whereas the long vibrations suggest that the whole world is completed and the next word will be followed. It makes it easy for disabled people to understand what message the other wants to convey. The objective of the project is to bridge the gap between people who are partially visually or hearing impaired and people with no impairments. MorseEx is an app, which empowers them to communicate with family, friends, or anyone else through their smartphones without any hesitation.

BACKGROUND

(Arato, 2014) conduct study on deaf-blind people, mainly from the standpoint of their behavior and communication. Inclusion in the deaf-blind population is based on the description of a range of subgroups and genetically based disorders connected with deaf-blindness. The methods of sensory assessment are examined, with a focus on residual capacities. The implications for everyday life are briefly discussed. No sensory, different classificatory schemes and techniques are utilized to describe the results of behavior modification interventions employed to address maladaptive behaviors. The use of tactile communication is discussed and evaluated. There are also some suggestions for learning alphabetic codes and sign acquisition.

In this paper, (Kumar et al., 2020) developed a complete framework based on three key current technologies: mobile devices, cloud resources, and social networks, to enable seamless communication between the blind and deaf, particularly in Arabic-speaking countries. Furthermore, by leveraging cutting-edge technologies such as time-of-flight cameras and social media, it is designed to facilitate connections with regular people in several ways. The majority of the framework's modules and components, as well as potential scenarios, are thoroughly investigated and defined. Information systems, with their modern approaches such as mobile and cloud computing, plays a significant role in improving intercommunication between persons with various disabilities and non-disabled people, as well as among handicapped people with similar or distinct impairments. However, the number of suggested systems for the Arabic Region is rather restricted. Furthermore, no mechanism for connecting the blind and deaf in direct Arabic language-based interactions was developed. In (Saranya et al., 2019) explores challenges of communication, independence, and isolation for a group of deaf people who also have vision impairments. The conversation is based on the experiences of 28 deafblind people from six different nations, which were gathered through interviews conducted as part of a larger study project on travel concerns. The disparities in experiences between countries, on the other hand, were not as strong as the commonalities. Barriers to communication and poor support were reported throughout the countries, resulting in problems of isolation and sadness. Similarly, deaf-blind persons in all countries were interested in participating in and contributing to society, as well as assisting others, particularly through organizations for blind and deafblind people. This goes against the trend of portraying deafblind and other disabled individuals solely as beneficiaries of assistance rather than being active members of society. However, there were some variances in the kind of assistance available in different countries.

In this study, researchers (Dushyant & Sanjay, 2017) suggested the SHAROJAN BRIDGE as a replacement system prototype to close the gap in the interaction between the deaf and the blind Wearable technology, Texas Instruments circuitry, and Arduino circuit boards will be used by the SHAROJAN BRIDGE to communicate to those with one or more of the limitations listed above. It is sometimes considered that someone who is deaf is also dumb, however, this is not the case. Cases involving three types of disabilities are considered, making it easier for impaired people and non-disabled people to converse with one another. The individual can communicate and convey messages according to his or her desires and needs. The stupid can use their Sign language to communicate, while those who are unable to comprehend Sign Language can utilize the gadget to get the message in audio format for normal or blind people, and Braille format for blind and deaf people. For Deaf persons, the message can be presented on the screen in written form, and it can even be transmitted over long distances via GSM Wireless Networks. As a result, this technique can address any challenges that may arise throughout the process of communication between differently-abled people and the general public.

The following paper (El-Gayyar et al., 2013) states how to teach Deaf-blind people Morse language so that they can communicate among themselves. This paper informs us about the advantages of Over portable braille lines, which are quite expensive, Morse code is used. They used an Android smartphone with a built-in vibrating motor to build a low-cost solution for reading and writing SMS messages with a Hungarian deaf-blind person. The vibrating Braille dots and Morse words are then created from the words and symbols. This research paper has also helped us to get an idea of how to use the vibrating feature of phones and Morse code to make a communication medium.

The authors of paper (Rastogi et al., 2015) use Bluetooth technology along with vibration-based communication. Cell phones are routinely utilized through the display; but sometimes users' clients might need to exchange pieces of information with adjacent associates, without moving their focus from the current task. Furthermore, this aids communication in situations where there is no visual or audible interaction. As a result, they created a one-of-a-kind Bluetooth communication program called Hand-to-Hand (H2B-Com). They sent a Morse-coded message over a Bluetooth channel using ordinary tapping and touching actions on the mobile display. The Morse-coded message is given to the receiver as a vibration on the Smartphone. They demonstrated the configuration of H2BCom on Android phones, including design, implementation, and evaluation. They discovered that using the Morse code was difficult for novices in the user research, but that after taking a Morse code teaching exercise, the users' skills improved. In this paper (Bidve et al., 2016) has created Voice Communicator which is a Smartphone messaging service built and developed for effective communication between two challenged people, particularly those who are deaf or blind. With the robust and intelligent Eclipse IDE, and thus the availability of several built-in Java libraries, particularly speech, Speech-to-text, and speech are two different things. Custom voice command functionality has been created using Recognizer Intent. Creating, replying to, sending, and forwarding messages are only a few of the study's first and most basic capabilities. The authors reviewed the results of the test survey and evaluation form and concluded that the appliance is user-friendly, efficient, and accurate in sending messages to its intended recipients, as well as having the key features that consumers expected.

This paper (Saranya et al., 2019) is aimed at presenting the main needs of deaf-blind people, their demands, and a proposal of a mobile solution to facilitate and expand interpersonal communication with deafblind people, including those people that don't have familiarity with the methods of communicating with deaf-blind people by specific signing. This proposal was created using inexpensive resources such as Arduino and other devices and therefore the Android app allowed the facilitation of the socialization of those disabled people. However, this prototype isn't intended for commercial use. The goal is to assist the institute where the initial demand was identified. However, this can be easily implemented in other institutions and will be an initiative that will motivate the creation of the latest solutions for multisensory disabled people.

This paper (Hersh, 2013) pro- posed android application supported Morse providing tactile assistance to the visually impaired the primary goal of this Android app was to provide a flexible and convenient approach to texting and navigation. Furthermore, the primary goal of this program is to make the Blind person feel inferior and independent. Because the Android operating system is well-documented and widely used for mobile phones, it will give the proposed project more versatility. Programming and mobile phones have been popular for use in training, guiding, learning, teaching, and computer-assisted instructions. Regardless, many programs are created for normal and healthy people, but they will be difficult to use by persons with disabilities until more adaptable gadgets and platforms are designed for use. Multiple trials are being conducted on blind persons to provide them with an easy and convenient form of correspondence. There are several programs available for both hearing and visually impaired people that can assist them in communicating in their daily lives; however, these applications aren't ideal and have limitations. [9] research looks at the issues that people with deaf blindness face when using computers and how these issues can be addressed through the redesign of a communication tool. With 12 participants, a qualitative interview and observation research was done. Future systems will need to improve in terms of simplicity, adaptability, and feedback, according to the findings. This re-design uses a screen reader use flow that provides precursor cues for reading on a Braille display. This is frequently done to assist users in gaining a quick overview of the application and its features. The benefits and issues that arise when applying this idea to work on both a visible and a Braille display are highlighted. This study by (Rutgersson, & Arvola, 2007) uses Whistle Morse technology to improve communication with the deaf and dumb. A gadget was created that could interpret various signs, including Indian signing, into text and audio format. The people that are communicating with the deaf and dumb might not understand their signs and expressions. Hence, an approach has been created and modified to listen to the Whistle based communication. The authors believed that this would make it easier for disabled people to convey their thoughts to others. Within the proposed system, an RF module is employed for transmitting and receiving the information, and raspberry pi as a processor and a memory card are additionally used for blind people to spot their location. The entire framework has been tried and tested and the outcomes have been positive.

MAIN FOCUS OF THE CHAPTER

Problem Statement

After going through these research papers, we have been able to study how deafblind people live, and their way of interacting with everything is very different compared to normal people. We also learn about different hardware solutions which were made for deafblind people but are not as feasible as they should be. We also get to know about the user interfaces that deafblind people are comfortable with. We learn about the practical usage of Morse code to enhance the lives of these people and give them a better communication medium. Our motive is to create an application that does not require any hardware unlike any other solutions and just uses Morse code and phone vibrations and provides a suitable user interface as we learned and taught deafblind people Morse code so that they can use it efficiently and easily.

A. Architecture

As the above architecture Figure 1 shows we have various modules which are interlinked together to work as a whole application. The architecture works as follows:

Figure 1. Architecture of the model

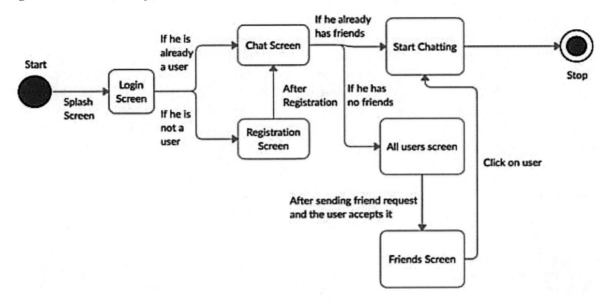

B. **Methodology**

First, when the user clicks on the application, he will be shown a splash screen and then he will be redirected to a login screen. This is where the user has to enter his credentials and then he will be taken to the main screen. If the user has not yet registered to our application, he has to do that first by going to the registration screen. After registering he will be taken to the main screen. On the Main Screen (Chat Screen) the user will be shown a list of people he is friends with and can chat with them. If there is no name shown that means the user has to make new friends and start chatting with them. To add friends, the user has to click on the All-user screen where the list of all the users registered to the application will be shown. Here the user has to click on a name and then send a friend request to the person. The friend request needs to be accepted by the user who has received it. After this process, both will be friends and can start chatting by clicking on each other's names.

C. **Functionality**

The main functionality is the chatting functionality which is not like normal chatting because it involves deafblind people. We will be using Morse code. We will be creating a customized keyboard for deafblind people which will have only 3 buttons. The three buttons will be a Dot(.), Dash (-), and Spacebar (). This Morse code will only be for deafblind people and for normal people it will be a normal keyboard with English letters.

D. **Algorithm**

The above flowchart Figure 2 explains how our algorithm will work when a deafblind person sends a message to a normal person. First, the deafblind person will write a message with a combination of dots, dashes, and spaces. That message will be then stored in the database and then we will send that message to the user where it will be converted into English from Morse code for a normal person to understand.

The above flowchart Figure 3 explains how our algorithm will work when a normal person sends a message to a deafblind person. First, the normal person will send the message. That message will be saved in the database. Then the message will be sent to the deafblind user. The message will be displayed in English but in the background, it will get converted to Morse code, that is dots and dashes. The conversion to dots and dashes is important because then the algorithm will make the phone vibrate according to the pattern of dots and dashes. The deafblind user can sense the vibrating pattern and can understand what the normal person is trying to convey.

Figure 2. Algorithm when a deaf-blind person sends a message

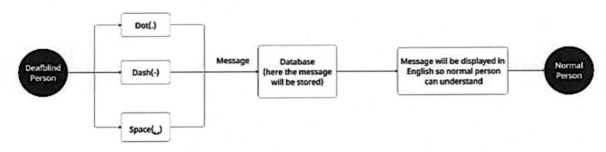

Figure 3. Algorithm when a normal person sends a message

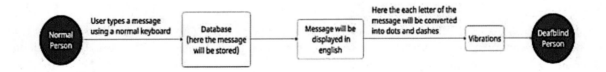

E.   **Technology to be Used**

To develop this application, we will be using Android studio as the IDE and the code will be written in Java language. We will also be using the online database Firebase database because it helps us to access the data in a JSON format and can save the user information in a secure way

TESTING

After testing our algorithm, the results, we get are very good. Our algorithm is successful in converting English words to Morse code and similarly Morse code to English words. Even the vibration through which the user gets to know what the other person is trying to convey set by us is perfectly working the way it should in the algorithm. Our method is a big improvement to the existing work because as mentioned in our literature survey most of the work done in this field is hardware-based, either it's a wearable technology or a special communication device. Hardware solutions are not feasible in every aspect it can be financially or even the transportation of devices hence we came up with a software-based solution with our rithm which is working perfectly acceptable.

SOLUTIONS AND RECOMMENDATIONS

After the successful design and implementation of the application, the below-mentioned functionalities run smoothly which aims to bridge the gap between the deaf-blind, and nondisabled people and help them communicate with each other effectively. Registering a new user

Discussion

From the above screenshots Figure 4,5,6,7 we can assure you that the application we proposed is ready with all the functionalities. After deep research, we can also concur there is no such application or software solution currently available which can solve the problem of long-distance communication between deaf-blind and normal people with the ease of access that our application provides. The existing applications mainly focus on blind people and make use of braille and sound technology rather than deaf-blind people who are unable to use sound technology without any barriers. Few researchers introduced Morse code in their solution but they focused on wearable hardware rather than software. Wearable hardware technology is not energy and cost-efficient as these devices are very expensive. Our application solves the purpose of our problem statement which was to bridge the gap between normal and deaf-blind people

Figure 4. Registering a new user

Figure 5. Logging into the app

Figure 6. Making New Friends chatting with and accepting the request

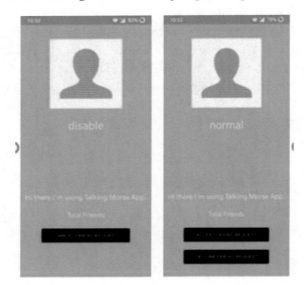

CONCLUSION

The research has been in the field of making a communication medium between deafblind people and individuals with no incapacities using the Morse code. The message is an extremely significant part of our day-to-day lives. Being able to communicate effectively is one of the most important life skills. But something as trivial as communication seems very difficult for people who are visually or hearing impaired. They face multiple challenges every day of their lives and one of them is communicating their thoughts and opinions effectively. Morse code can be memorized easily by the use of certain tricks and Persons skilled in the talent can directly decode Morse code communications in a manner observable

Figure 7. Special Keyboard for disabled people so they can chat

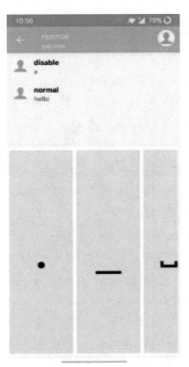

to the human senses, such as sound waves or visible light. Morse code usually works with vibrations which are divided into short vibrations and long vibrations. The short vibration is used to indicate that the Morse code of a particular letter is finished whereas the long vibrations suggest that the whole world is completed and the next word will be followed. It makes it easy for disabled people to understand what message the other wants to convey. There have been multiple types of research in the field of communication aid for the deaf and blind but most of them consist of the use of expensive hardware. The aim was to make an application that is easy to use as well as inexpensive as a person's inability to buy expensive hardware should not hinder their ability to communicate. This paper is an application that bridges the communication gap between deafblind people and normal people. Also, successful implementation of the application which is ready to use in the real world. The results achieved have been quite good. In the future, this application can further be expanded to teach Morse code to deaf-blind people, making it even easier to use.

REFERENCES

Arato, A., Markus, N., & Juhasz, Z. (2014, July). Teaching Morse language to a deaf-blind person for reading and writing SMS on an ordinary vibrating smartphone. In *International Conference on Computers for Handicapped Persons* (pp. 393-396). Springer. 10.1007/978-3-319-08599-9_59

Bidve, D. M., Shewale, T. D., Gaikwad, S. S., Murmure, A. R., & Pawar, S. (2016). Hand-to-Hand Instant Message Communication: Revisiting Morse Code. *FIRST–International Journal for Innovative Research in Science & Technology, 2*(12).

El-Gayyar, M., ElYamany, H. F., Gaber, T., & Hassanien, A. E. (2013, September). Social network framework for deaf and blind people based on cloud computing. In *2013 Federated Conference on Computer Science and Information Systems* (pp. 1313-1319). IEEE.

Hersh, M. (2013). Deafblind people, communication, independence, and isolation. *Journal of Deaf Studies and Deaf Education, 18*(4), 446–463. doi:10.1093/deafed/ent022 PMID:23749484

Kumar, K., Srikar, V. S., Swapnika, Y., Sravani, V. S., & Aditya, N. (2020). A novel approach for Morse code detection from eye blinks and decoding using OpenCV. *International Journal for Research in Applied Science and Engineering Technology*, 8. doi:10.22214/ijraset.2020.30811

Landicho, J. A. (2016). Voice Communicator: An Android Mobile Application for Hearing-impaired and Blind Communications. *Int. J. Interact. Mob. Technol., 10*(4), 26–31. doi:10.3991/ijim.v10i4.5859

Rastogi, R., Mittal, S., & Agarwal, S. (2015, March). A novel approach for communication among Blind, Deaf, and Dumb people. In *2015 2nd International Conference on Computing for Sustainable Global Development (INDIACom)* (pp. 605-610). IEEE.

Rönnberg, J., & Borg, E. (2001). A review and evaluation of research on the deaf-blind from perceptual, communicative, social, and rehabilitative perspectives. *Scandinavian Audiology, 30*(2), 67–77. doi:10.1080/010503901300112176 PMID:11409790

Rutgersson, S., & Arvola, M. (2007). User interfaces for persons with deafblindness. In *Universal Access in Ambient Intelligence Environments* (pp. 317–334). Springer. doi:10.1007/978-3-540-71025-7_21

Saranya, M., Abinaya, A., Dhanesh Priya, K. S., Kowsalya, G., & Madhumitha, B. (2019). Design And Implementation of Raspberry Pibased Whistle to Voice Translation Usingmorse Code for Dumb and Blind People. *International Journal of Innovative Research in Advanced Engineering, 3*(6), 2349–2163.

Singh, D., & Agarwal, S. (2017). Advanced Human- Smartphone Interface for the Blind Using Morse Code. *International Journal of Advances in Electronics and Computer Science, 4*(5).

Vieira, A. L. N., Novaes, F. F., Silva, D. M., Santos, L., Belozi, S., & Castro, T. (2016). A Mobile Solution for Linguistic Communication with Deaf-Blind People Using Arduino and Android. In INC (pp. 177-180). Academic Press.

Chapter 15
Cloud Hosted Ensemble Learning–Based Rental Apartment Price Prediction Model Using Stacking Technique

Rajkumar S.
Vellore Institute of Technology, Vellore, India

Ramanathan L.
Vellore Institute of Technology, Vellore, India

Mary Nikitha K.
Vellore Institute of Technology, Vellore, India

Rajasekar Ramalingam
University of Technology and Applied Sciences, Sur, Oman

Mudit Jantwal
Vellore Institute of Technology, Vellore, India

ABSTRACT

In this chapter, online rental listings of the city of Hyderabad are used as a data source for mapping house rent. Data points were scraped from one of the popular Indian rental websites www.nobroker.in. With the collected information, models of rental market dynamics were developed and evaluated using regression and boosting algorithms such as AdaBoost, CatBoost, LightGBM, XGBoost, KRR, ENet, and Lasso regression. An ensemble machine learning algorithm of the best combination of the aforementioned algorithms was also implemented using the stacking technique. The results of these algorithms were compared using several performance metrics such as coefficient of determination (R2 score), mean squared error (MSE), root mean squared error (RMSE), mean absolute error (MAE), and accuracy in order to determine the most effective model. According to further examination of results, it is clear that the ensemble machine learning algorithm does outperform the others in terms of better accuracy and reduced errors.

DOI: 10.4018/978-1-6684-6001-6.ch015

INTRODUCTION

Rent is always a key variable when it comes to explaining urban phenomena, whether theoretically or empirically. Many real estate market participants, including investors, regulators, and policymakers, rely on accurate rental price forecasting. Rent predictions, for example, are critical in the property valuation used in discounted cash-flow models. The imputed rent is a significant component of the estimate of gross domestic income. For public housing policy, a thorough understanding of the structure and evolution of rents in local and national housing markets is also essential. Furthermore, a general idea of the features of a piece of real estate that were most likely to affect the price during the pandemic can play a major role in the real estate market (Grybauskas, 2021). The parties involved in the real estate industry often tend to depend on external valuation or various other internal approaches. Due to the large number of parameters involved, these metrics are unreliable and imperfect because they do not take into account all of the property's unique qualities during calculations (Viriato, 2019).

The real estate industry is growing by the minute and hence advanced and accurate predictions of prices of listings are the need of the hour. The market is changing all the time, and today many software juggernauts are turning to artificial intelligence for improved decisions and resolving certain complex real-world problems using large amounts of data. Machine learning has now become interdisciplinary and can be incorporated into a variety of industries including real estate so that it can aid not only investors to increase their business throughput but also give individuals access to accurate information about properties within their financial limits. As a result, the ML models have the potential to take into account a wide range of criteria while analyzing patterns in order to provide efficient results in terms of complexity and accuracy (Reddy, 2018).

The main difference between unsupervised learning and supervised learning is that in unsupervised learning, the learner has no prior information about the purpose of learning, and is left to make its conclusion just based on the information provided, while in supervised learning, there must be data present on the target, using which it makes further predictions. Regression, a type of supervised learning is employed to tackle this problem since our goal is to anticipate real estate pricing based on previously collected, relevant information (Dataken, 2018). The dataset is obtained by scraping a popular Indian rental listing website with 18 variables including the number of rooms, bathrooms, amenities available, and size among others which are factors that can influence the price of a house. Based on seven regression algorithms and boosting methods the data is preconditioned (pre-processed) and trained. The boosting algorithms include AdaBoost, CatBoost, LightGBM, XGBoost, KRR, ENet Lasso regression, and Stacked Regressor. And then the ensemble model is generated using the best combination of the aforementioned algorithms to increase the accuracy.

RELATED WORKS

A few studies have raised a query that what attributes or variables of apartments influence their price. Swarali M. Pathak et al (Swarali, 2021) explored the correlation between house price and a number of attributes and came to the conclusion that Location and size of the apartment had strong links with the house price. On the other hand, Andrius, G et al (Grybauskas, 2021) concluded that the TOM (Time on the market) attribute is the predominant and constant variable for price prediction.

Next, studies focusing on using machine learning for predicting the prices of houses and apartments were explored. The datasets usually have a lot of nonlinearity. Mu, J. et al (Mu, 2014) aiming at tackling this problem of nonlinearity effectively concluded that SVM and LSSVM were the most effective models in terms of prediction effect and learning ability. Addressing the same issue, Čeh, M. et al (Ceh, 2018) established that in complicated urban forms, the random forest method can detect and predict the fluctuation in apartment values more successfully than multiple regression.

Ming, Y. et al (Ming, 2020) in their research used RandomForestRegressor, XGBoost, and LightGBM to predict and fit 12 key features and a comparative analysis was done based on the results provided by all three models. According to the results, the XGBoost model had a greater prediction effect than that of the other two models, making a valuable addition to Chengdu's housing rent prediction study. Satish, G. N et al (Satish, 2019) in their paper proposed that machine learning could also be expandable to sectors like real estate to effectively predict housing prices. The machine algorithms used were Linear Regression, Lasso Regression, and Gradient Boosting. From the results, it could be concluded that the best performing algorithm is Gradient Boosting with an accuracy of 91.14% while the Lasso and Linear Regression algorithms have almost the same results with an accuracy of 76.14% and 76.15% each. For further work, they suggested incorporating parallel computation to decrease processing time.

Lu, S. et al (Lu, 2017) in their study used a hybrid regression technique for house prices prediction. For the implementation, the machine learning algorithms taken into consideration were Ridge, Lasso, and Gradient Boosting. They decided to implement a hybrid algorithm of Lasso and Gradient Boosting. Among all the combinations of the hybrid regression model, 65% Lasso and 35% Gradient Boosting performed the best, and hence they concluded that a hybrid regression algorithm is better than a regression algorithm applied separately. Modi Modi et al (Modi, 2020) proposed to make use of ensemble machine learning methods for house price prediction. The dataset used in this application was from Kaggle.com which has 22 attributes and upon which a number of algorithms have been trained and tested. The algorithms used were Logistic Regression, SVM, Naive Bayes, Stochastic Gradient Descent, Extra Tree, K nearest Neighbors, and an ensemble machine learning algorithm that uses all the above-listed algorithms as weak learners. The performance of these algorithms was compared using various performance metrics, which concluded that the ensemble ML algorithm performed best overall followed by Extra Tree, Logistic Regression, and Naive Bayes.

Kansara, D. et al (Kansara, 2018) in their paper used a stacked regressor formed by integrating regression techniquessuch as Multiple Linear Regression, Random Forest Regressor, and XGBoost. The stacked regressor takes into account each algorithm's weaknesses and strengths and balances them out to produce the final output, thus also improving the total accuracy. Because of rigorous cross-validation in action, shortcomings coming from one model are balanced out by strengths exhibited by another model, reducing error rates and balancing error rates (Güneş, 2017).

METHODOLOGY

The methodology of this project consisted of four steps: (1) data mining, (2) data cleaning and preparation (3) machine learning methods and (4) Performance analysis. For better understanding, the entire research framework is depicted as above.

Figure 1. Research framework

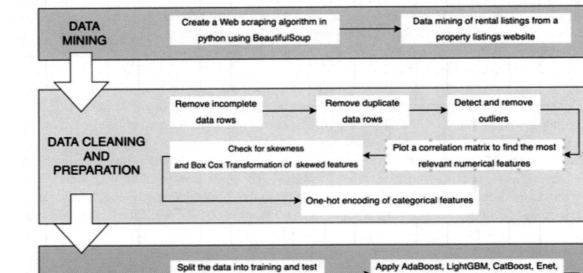

Data Mining

For data collection, we have made use of the web scraping technique. In this project, the Beautiful Soup package of the Python programming language was used to write an algorithm to collect data about apartment listings in the city of Hyderabad, from the popular rental website www.nobroker.in.The data was obtained from scraping over 150 pages of the website and ultimately stored in a CSV file.

Data Cleaning and Preparation

After extensive data collection, a total of 737107 apartment listings with at most 18 features (such as number of rooms, number of bathrooms, square feet, age, total floors of the building, floor on which apartment is located, lift availability, deposit required, negotiability, maintenance availability, Longitude, Latitude, Gym availability, furnishing status, parking availability, facing direction, locality and rent were collected.

The data cleaning and preparation process is as follows:

- The rows with duplicate data are dropped.
- The rows with incomplete information are dropped
- Outliers are detected and removed using bivariate analysis of Rent with square feet
- A correlation matrix is plotted to find the most relevant numerical features and the irrelevant columns are dropped
- Some categorical features are label encoded
- The skewness of all numerical features is checked and Box-Cox Transformation is applied to (highly) skewed features
- The remaining categorical features are one hot encoded

After the cleaning and preparation to use for subsequent stages, the resultant data frame had a shape of (4165, 1169)

Machine Learning Methods

The ML procedure we have taken has three stages.

1.   Applying ML algorithms individually

Initially,80% of the dataset is considered as a training dataset, and the remaining as test dataset. The 7 regression algorithms and boosting methods applied are AdaBoost, CatBoost, LightGBM, Lasso Regression, Elastic Net Regression, Kernel Ridge Regression and XGBoost.

The **AdaBoost** algorithm combines a lot of weak learners, sequentially. These weak learners are called "stumps" and are very short (one-level) decision trees. Each new model in the series is constructed by taking into account the mistakes made by the model preceding it. This is accomplished by each subsequent stump taking into account the previous stump's mistakes (Bhweshgaur,2022)

The key distinction between the two frameworks is that **XGBoost** grows trees depth-wise, whereas **LightGBM** grows trees leaf-wise. **Catboost** cultivates a well-balanced tree. In each level of such a tree, the feature-split pair with the lowest loss (as determined by a penalty function) is chosen and applied to all nodes in that level (Neptune, 2022)

The addition of penalties with the loss function gives simpler models having minuscule coefficient values that is an extension of **conventional linear regression**.Regularized linear regression and penalized linear regression are terms used to describe these expansions (Jason, 2022).

Lasso regression is when the L1 penalty, which is using the sum of absolute values, is incorporated into the least-squares linear regression (Jason, 2022). If instead, the L2 norm, which is the sum of the squares of the weights is used, we get a procedure known as ridge regression. This combined with the kernel trick is what gives rise to the **Kernel ridge regression** (Math, 2022).

Elastic net combines both the aforementioned penalty functions L1 and L2 (Carvadia, 2022) as regularised linear regression.

2.   Hyperparameter tuning

After primarily fitting these algorithms to the data, hyperparameter tuning is applied to the algorithms wherever applicable. Hyperparameter tuning is the task of identifying the perfect model architecture, with **hyperparameters** referring to the parameters that form the model architecture.

There are a number of hyperparameter tuning methods. We make use of the GridSearch method, one of the most popular tuning methods used. Using this method, a model is created for each conceivable combination of the hyperparameter values provided. Following that, each model is examined, with the best findings being considered as the parameters for the ideal architecture.

Hyperparameter tuning forAdaboost - For getting better scores we try to tune the hyperparameters – number of estimators and learning rate using GridsearchCV. After hyperparameter tuning the algorithm provides better scores

Hyperparameter tuning forLasso - The main purpose of tuning the hyperparameters for Lasso is to find the appropriate value of alpha for our dataset. We defined a *search space* of possible alpha values in the range of 0.0001 to 1 and maximum iterations within which the hyperparameters will be chosen based on its effective minimization of error using the GridSearchCV method.

Hyperparameter tuning for ENet - The hyperparameter tuning of ENet is very similar to the Lasso regression. We defined a *search space* of possible alpha values in the range of 0.0001 to 1, maximum iterations, and l1_ratio within which the hyperparameters will be chosen based on its effective minimization of error using the GridSearchCV method.

3.   Creating an ensemble model using stacking technique

In the second stage, we seek to implement a model assembling technique called stacking. Ensemble learning is a machine learning paradigm in which several models (commonly referred to as "weak learners") are trained to handle the same problem and then integrated to improve results. The main idea is that by correctly combining weak models, we can get more accurate and/or resilient models. Learning several weak learners and then combining them by training a meta-model to output predictions based on the various predictions provided by these weak models is known as stacking (Rocca, 2022).

Due to its smoothing nature and its ability to highlight and balance out each of the models' strengths and weaknesses, the stacked model (also known as the 2nd-level model) often outperforms each of the separate models. As a result, stacking works best when the base models are drastically different.

Steps involved in Ensemble stacking technique:

1.   Divide the data for training into two folds
2.   Choose L weak learners and fit them to first-fold data
3.   For each of them, produce predictions for observations in the second fold
4.   Fit the meta-model on the second fold using predictions made by the weak learners as inputs (Rocca, 2022).

We implemented this technique for a number of combinations from the 7 algorithms. After evaluating the results, the combination of CatBoost, XGBoost and LightGBM was the one that performed the best.

Application

This code is hosted on the cloud and can be accessible by anyone, no matter the location. Other developers of similar projects can use this code to make suitable conclusions about their personal datasets. An ideal dataset would consist of many real time variables such as square feet, total floors of the building, floor on which apartment is located, amenities availability, furnishing status, parking availability, locality and rent. As stated previously, our results can be integrated with additional information to be used in various urban studies and can also serve as practical references for homeowners and renters.

Using this dataset, the code can be tweaked accordingly to either predict the rent based on the other available real time factors or vice versa to predict any of the factors such as square feet, amenities availability, furnishing status or parking availability based on the rent and other factors (Manish, 2022).

RESULTS AND DISCUSSION

Seven algorithms are used in the prediction to determine which model has the best accuracy and so construct a system for speedier prediction (Mehta, 2022). The following metrics are used to evaluate the regression model: **Coefficient of determination (R^2 score), Mean Squared Error** (MSE), **Root Mean Squared Error** (RMSE), **Mean Absolute Error** (MAE), and **Accuracy** (Manickam, 2019), (Sonal, 2022).

The coefficient of determination, Mean Squared Error (MSE), Root Mean Squared Error (RMSE), Mean Absolute Error (MAE), and Accuracy (Mishra, 2022) of the test datasets are presented below.

Table 1. Results of trained model on testing data

Algorithm	R^2	MAE	MSE	RMSE	Accuracy (%)
AdaBoost	0.830	0.69	0.98	0.99	96.71
LightGBM	0.906	0.49	0.54	0.73	97.69
CatBoost	0.909	0.5	0.52	0.72	97.64
Lasso Regression	0.898	0.57	0.58	0.76	97.3
Kernel Ridge Regression	0.894	0.58	0.6	0.78	97.23
ElasticNet Regression	0.899	0.57	0.58	0.76	97.31
XGBoost	0.907	0.5	0.53	0.73	97.64
Stacking algorithm (Catboost + LightGBM + XGBoost)	0.912	0.48	0.5	0.73	97.72

A higher value of R^2 is desirable as it indicates better results. Hence, the stacking algorithm performs the best with the lowest R^2 value of 0.912, closely followed by XGBoost and CatBoost.

A low MAE value indicates better performance of the model. Hence Stacking algorithm performs the best, closely followed by LightGBM, the CatBoost algorithm

For MSE, a lower value is better and 0 indicates a perfect model. Hence, the stacking algorithm performs the best with the lowest MSE value of 0.5.

A lower value of RMSE is desirable as it indicates better results. Hence CatBoost performs the best, closely followed by LightGBM, XGBoost and the stacking algorithm

The greater the accuracy, the better the model. Hence Stacking algorithm performs the best with an accuracy of 97.72%

In conclusion, taking into consideration the seven individual algorithms implemented, it can be seen that all algorithms have an accuracy of above 95%, with the best being LightGBM closely followed by Catboost and XGboost. Coincidentally, these algorithms proved to be the best combination to be used in the ensemble machine learning algorithm using the stacking technique, giving an increased accuracy of 97.72%. Another observation is that AdaBoost has the worst performance in terms of MSE, RMSE, and MAE but the stacking algorithm outperforms all the others in terms of error metrics having an MSE of 0.5, RMSE of 0.73 and MAE of 0.4 and R^2 score of 0.912

Table 2. Comparison of Execution Time

Model	Execution Time
AdaBoost	6.8 s
LightGBM	290 ms
CatBoost	9.18 s
Lasso Regression	381 ms
Kernel Ridge Regression	811 ms
ElasticNet Regression	709 ms
XGBoost	3.92 s
Stacking algorithm	58.9 s

Regarding the model's performance, there are significant differences in the model execution times. While LightGBM, Lasso, KRR, and Enet have considerably short run times while the other models could take longer, which are indicated in the table above. It is also underlined that the stacking algorithm spends more training time than any of the individual algorithms. Therefore, there is a trade-off between modes' runtime and prediction accuracy.

CONCLUSION

To sum up, this paper executes different machine learning models and boosting methods for house price prediction that have several applications in the real estate industry. Firstly, the original data which is scraped from a rental listings website is prepared and transformed into a cleaned dataset ready for analysis using various techniques. Seven different machine learning algorithms and boosting methods are applied and evaluated. In addition, the best combination of the aforementioned algorithms using stacking technique is sought after. From the results, it is concluded that the combination of XGBoost, CatBoost and Light GBM provides the most optimal solution in terms of accuracy but its runtime could be an area of improvement. Therefore, it could be used for further deployment.

REFERENCES

Bhweshgaur. (n.d.). https://github.com/bhweshgaur/Health-Insurance-Cross-Sell-Prediction/

Carvadia. (n.d.). https://carvadia.com/what-is-partitioned-regression/

Čeh, M., Kilibarda, M., Lisec, A., & Bajat, B. (2018). Estimating the performance of random forest versus multiple regression for predicting prices of the apartments. *ISPRS International Journal of Geo-Information, 7*(5), 168. doi:10.3390/ijgi7050168

Dodan, M. E., Vien, Q. T., & Nguyen, T. T. (2022). Internet traffic prediction using recurrent neural networks. *EAI Endorsed Transactions on Industrial Networks and Intelligent Systems, 9*(4), e1–e1. doi:10.4108/eetinis.v9i4.1415

Grybauskas, A., Pilinkienė, V., & Stundžienė, A. (2021). Predictive analytics using Big Data for the real estate market during the COVID-19 pandemic. *Journal of Big Data, 8*(1), 1–20. doi:10.118640537-021-00476-0 PMID:34367876

Güneş, F., Wolfinger, R., & Tan, P. Y. (2017, April). Stacked ensemble models for improved prediction accuracy. *Proc. Static Anal. Symp.*, 1-19.

Jason. (n.d.). https://machinelearningmastery.com/ridge-regression-with-python/

Kansara, D., Singh, R., Sanghvi, D., & Kanani, P. (2018). Improving accuracy of real estate valuation using stacked regression. *Int. J. Eng. Dev. Res., 6*(3), 571–577.

Lu, S., Li, Z., Qin, Z., Yang, X., & Goh, R. S. M. (2017, December). A hybrid regression technique for house prices prediction. In 2017 IEEE international conference on industrial engineering and engineering management (IEEM) (pp. 319-323). IEEE. doi:10.1109/IEEM.2017.8289904

Machine learning algorithms in human language. (2018, August 13). Datakeen. Available: https://www.datakeen.co/en/8-machine-learning-algorithms-explained-in-human-language/

Manickam, A., Haldar, R., Saqlain, S. M., Sellam, V., & Soundrapandiyan, R. (2019). Fingerprint image classification using local diagonal and directional extrema patterns. *Journal of Electronic Imaging, 28*(3), 033027. doi:10.1117/1.JEI.28.3.033027

ManishK. S. (n.d.). https://manish-ks.medium.com/advantages-and-disadvantages-of-linear-regression-its-assumptions-evaluation-and-implementation-61437fc551ad/

Math. (n.d.). https://www.mathworks.com/matlabcentral/fileexchange/63122-kernel-ridge-regression/

MehtaD. (n.d.). https://github.com/dhruv-mehta2604/housePricePrediction/

Ming, Y., Zhang, J., Qi, J., Liao, T., Wang, M., & Zhang, L. (2020, September). Prediction and analysis of chengdu housing rent based on xgboost algorithm. In *Proceedings of the 2020 3rd International Conference on Big Data Technologies* (pp. 1-5). 10.1145/3422713.3422720

MishraD. (n.d.). https://towardsdatascience.com/regression-an-explanation-of-regression-metrics-and-what-can-go-wrong-a39a9793d914

Modi, M., Sharma, A., & Madhavan, D. P. (2020). Applied research on house price prediction using diverse machine learning techniques. *International Journal of Scientific & Technology Research*, *9*(04).

Mu, J., Wu, F., & Zhang, A. (2014, August). Housing value forecasting based on machine learning methods. In *Abstract and Applied Analysis* (Vol. 2014). Hindawi.

Neptune. (n.d.). https://neptune.ai/blog/xgboost-vs-lightgbm

Pathak & Chaudhari. (2021). Comparison of Machine Learning Algorithms for House Price Prediction using Real Time Data. *International Journal of Engineering Research & Technology, 10*(12).

Reddy, T., Sanghvi, J., Vora, D., & Kanani, P. (2018). Wanderlust: A Personalised Travel Itinerary Recommender. *International Journal Of Engineering Development And Research IJEDR*, *6*(3), 78–83.

RoccaJ. (n.d.). https://towardsdatascience.com/ensemble-methods-bagging-boosting-and-stacking-c9214a10a205

Satish, G. N., Raghavendran, C. V., Rao, M. S., & Srinivasulu, C. (2019). House price prediction using machine learning. *Journal of Innovative Technology and Exploring Engineering*, *8*(9), 717–722. doi:10.35940/ijitee.I7849.078919

SinghA. (n.d.). https://medium.com/@amanbamrah/how-to-evaluate-the-accuracy-of-regression-results-b38e5512afd3

Sonal. (n.d.). https://sonalsart.com/how-do-you-evaluate-a-regression-model//

Viriato, J. C. (2019). AI and machine learning in real estate investment. *Journal of Portfolio Management*, *45*(7), 43–54. doi:10.3905/jpm.2019.45.7.043

Chapter 16
DL–EDAD Deep Learning Approach to Early Detection for Alzheimer's Disease Using E–GKFCM

Sanjay V.
School of Computer Science and Engineering, Vellore Institute of Technology, Vellore, India

Swarnalatha P.
School of Computer Science and Engineering, Vellore Institute of Technology, Vellore, India

ABSTRACT

In Alzheimer's disease (AD), memory and cognitive abilities deteriorate, affecting the capacity to do basic activities. In and around brain cells, aberrant amyloid and tau protein accumulation is believed to cause it. Amyloid deposits create plaques surrounding brain cells, whereas tau deposits form tangles inside brain cells. The plagues and tangles harm healthy brain cells, causing shrinkage. This damage seems to be occurring in the hippocampus, a brain region involved in memory formation. There are presently no methods that provide the most accurate outcomes. The current techniques do not identify AD early. The proposed DL-EDAD method achieves excellent clustering using CNN with E-GKFCM (enhanced gaussian kernel fuzzy c-means clustering). The E-GKFCM utilizes an elbow method to determine the number of clusters in a dataset. Unlike other medical pictures, brain scans are extremely sensitive.

INTRODUCTION

One of the most essential parts of the body is the brain. The brain controls and facilitates all the actions and reactions that allow individuals to speculate and perceive. It also helps to reinforce the memory, and concepts are also strengthened due to it (Armstrong, Nugent & Moore, 2009). AD is an unrepairable and progressive brain dysfunction. Every four seconds, a new case of Alzheimer's disease is discovered throughout the globe. The memory cells are ripped apart gradually, causing people to lose their ability

DOI: 10.4018/978-1-6684-6001-6.ch016

to think clearly. It's a neurodegenerative disorder that may lead to neuronal dysfunction or even death. After an Alzheimer's diagnosis, the usual life expectancy is between four and eight years (Coppola, Kowtko, Yamagata, Joyce, 2013).

One in ten individuals over the age of 65 has this disease on average, although it may strike at any age and is seen in various young age individuals. Alzheimer's disease is the most common form of dementia among the elderly. Cognitive abilities crucial for everyday activities are diminished in patients with Alzheimer's disease (AD). Plaques and tangles form in the brain due to this condition, and cells in the brain are damaged or killed. After her death, several clumps were found in her brain, which the doctor discovered when examining her brain. These were shown to be the primary cause of this disease (Khan & Usman, 2015). In doing so, they disrupted the brain's ability to communicate with other parts of the body. As a result, regular duties like driving, cooking, and cleaning are difficult for those with this condition. A person who has Alzheimer's disease may have difficulty remembering names, misplacing important possessions, and difficulty organizing their daily activities (Sandhya, Babu Kande & Savithri, 2017). Alzheimer's disease's intermediate stage lasts the longest and is exemplified by disposition shifts, confusion, impulsiveness, little attention periods, and difficulty identifying objects. At this point, things are at their worst (Udupa & Herman, 2000).

Figure 1. Representation of a Normal Brain and. Alzheimer affected Brain

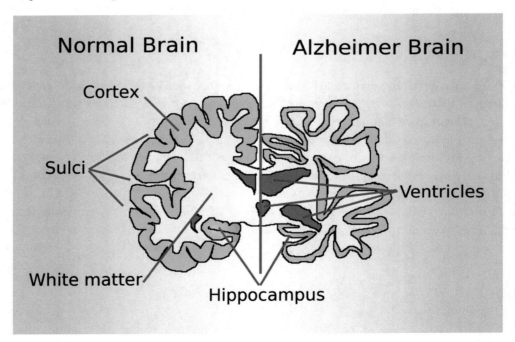

Artificial Intelligence (AI) comprises a wide range of algorithms and approaches, including genetic algorithms (Gordillo, Montseny & Sobrevilla, 2013; Jean, Kowtko, Yamagata & Joyce, 2013), neural networks (Khan & Usman, 2015), and evolutionary algorithms (Thakare & Pawar, 2016). Computers may "learn" from recorded data sets with the help of machine learning (ML), a branch of artificial intelligence. Deep learning (DL) is a subcategory of ML). DL is a multi-parameter, multi-layer neural network. Convolutional neural networks (CNNs), a kind of conventional neural network that has been enlarged spatially by shared weights, are one of the numerous fundamental network topologies.

A convolutional neural network (CNN) is utilized to distinguish the boundary of a recognized object on the image to identify images (Yousuf & Nobi, 2010). A subcategory of artificial neural networks known as recurrent neural networks (RNNs) consists of connections between nodes laid out in a time-ordered graph. Instead of processing input sequences in a feedforward manner, RNNs use their internal state. To distinguish sequences, such as speech or text, RNNs are used (Udupa, & Herman, 2000). The input sequence is not time-dependent, distinguishing recursive neural networks from hierarchical ones. As a result, the input must be processed via a tree. Different external inputs correlate to diverse brain activity, and distinct brain activity produces various functional brain images (Wang, Tsai, Liu JW-S & Zao, 2009). As a result, image classification is crucial in determining the varied brain activities. Classifying images of diverse brain processes using DL methods have been the subject of several DL techniques (Zhao, Ma, Jiang, Zeng, Wang & Li, 2020).

Short-term memory loss and vision impairments are the most noticeable symptoms. Other indicators include a lack of efficient communication and increased susceptibility to infection. Alzheimer's disease affects an estimated 50 million people worldwide. Scientists and clinicians have a major challenge today since cognitive disorders are often ascribed to aging, which sometimes goes undiagnosed until it is too late. Until more effective therapies are discovered, this illness will pose a threat. As a result, the elderly is the most likely to get this illness. Even though there is no known treatment for this condition, early diagnosis may help to reduce Alzheimer. A nutritious diet, frequent exercising, social engagement, headgear, learning, live band, and other cognitive hobbies have all been linked to a reduced likelihood of Alzheimer's disease. In conclusion, similar kind of activity can enhance one's general mental well-being and cognitive abilities.

Figure 2. Stages of AD

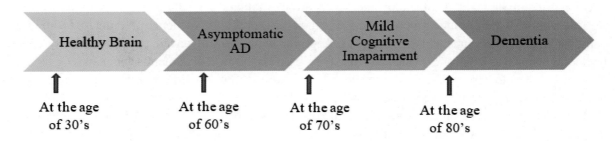

In diagnosing Dementia, neuroscientists may use various ML techniques to process the medical images (MRI). Alzheimer's disease is a long-term neurotoxic condition that destroys tissue throughout the entire brain. Dopaminergic neurons death typically begins gradually and progresses over time. It is predicted that several people will have AD within the decade 2050. The chapter is organized as follows. In the Related works section, previous researchers discuss a range of Alzheimer's diagnosis methods. The Main Focus Section includes a diagram of the DL-EDAD model. The investigation's findings are summed up in the solution and recommendations. The section's conclusion includes a discussion of the findings and directions for future research.

RELATED WORKS

Armstrong, Nugent, Moore & Finlay (2009) suggested how cell telephone devices should be incorporated for people with Alzheimer's disease. This work has proposed how a cell phone may control blood pressure and heart rate, particularly for Alzheimer's patients. There are currently no devices allowing the unlimited usage of cell phones in the wellness tracking scheme.

Babalola et al. (2009) proposed four completely automatic segmentation assessments for subcortical portion forms such as volumetric, intersecting, distance-centered, and spatial procedures. The approaches include profile active appearance models, regular segmentation, the classifier's atlas-based fusion, and Bayesian appearance models. It was emphasized that it is usually more difficult to segment subcortical structures, including the hippocampus, thalamus, putamen, and caudate. However, the signal amplitude is insufficient to differentiate between different structures of subcortical gray matter. The subcortical arrangements include typical forms and spatial interactions. Therefore, the segmentation procedures for these constructs typically provide details with a priori regarding their predicted shape and position from the brain atlas. In 270 participants, any approach tried to divide 18 subcortical structures, and the results were identical.

Coppola et. al., (2013) proposed audio, and pictures play a vital function in Alzheimer's disease. This research explores intellectual capacity and the condition of people's life together with a scientific analysis of Alzheimer's disease. Researchers created a hand-held device program for early detection of disease in old-aged adults having disabilities via service-knowledge classes. This study explores mobile apps created by researchers to enhance the identification accuracy of Alzheimer's disease patients.

Gordillo et al. (2013) proposed various kinds of segmenting brain cancers from MRI photographs depending on the extent of necessary individual involvement. Dissection methods for a brain tumor may be differentiated widely into labor-intensive, partial-automatic, and completely automatic methods.

Jean et al. (2013) presented a report addressing the operational and excellence of living for technologically diagnosed individuals with dementia. The research focuses on advanced, popular, and easy-to-use technologies such as iPads and tablets, which may help assess the level of dementia and boost cognizance. The study hopes to explore the newly developed applications. Current aid software may reduce symptoms and enhance memory in older adults who have AD or other disorders associated with dementia.

Khan et al. (2015) presented an analysis, which compares and assesses recent work on the prediction/diagnosis of Alzheimer by implementing ML approaches. The suggested ML approach (three general algorithms for function selection, filter methods, wrapper, and embedded methods) deals with pathologically validated data. It resolves class differences and problems in overtraining. The precision is 96.6%.

Sandhya et al. (2017) proposed an optimization approach on finding the right answer for a particular problem. Traditional optimization techniques were initially employed for engineering challenges but only for a single objective purpose. And there were meta-heuristic methods added. These methods are focused on nature or on swarming. These methods are mostly focused on swarm intelligence and solving optimization problems.

MAIN FOCUS OF THE CHAPTER

DL-EDAD Model

The main goal of the proposed approach is the early detection of AD. An important consideration in the identification of AD is brain deterioration. Brain deterioration is detected mostly by the MRI image segmentation method using E-GKFCM (Enhanced Gaussian Kernel Fuzzy C-means). Employing image gradients, the brain cavity's deterioration was confirmed. A gradient in an image is a change in the color or intensity of the MRI image. This earlier approach uses a simple process and a low level of visual intricacy. The DL-EDAD approach accomplishes 99% of the recommended process without the requirement for early identification and prevents brain injury. The patient is classified as stable, first stage AD, second stage AD, or moderate cognitive dysfunction using Convolutional Neural Networks. The DL-EDAD system is a contribution to the field of medical imaging. It showed higher accuracy over performance when compared to other existing ones, in addition to E-GKFCM, a dimensionality reduction technique known as LDA (Linear Discriminant Analysis). It decreases the number of parameters or dimensionality inside a dataset while keeping the pertinent data. Optimization techniques are also used in the DL-EDAD work to get the best solution without compromising the quality. The early detection and classification of AD are more accurate in the DL-EDAD system.

Dataset

The goal of the DL-EDAD effort is to identify AD early. The training dataset has a significant impact. To train the model to take the required actions, training information is necessary. The majority 80% of the data is used for training the model and 20% of the dataset is used for testing. The DL-EDAD system uses datasets related to Alzheimer's that were downloaded from Kaggle.com to run the process.

Pre-Processing Step

Noise reduction on the MRI's is performed in the pre-processing step to improve the classification accuracy. Brain imaging requires less noise while retaining optimal visibility since it is more responsive than other diagnostic imaging. Image processing techniques include converting images from color to monochromatic, scaling, contouring, filtering, etc.

MRI DENOISING - ANT COLONY OPTIMIZATION (ACO)

Pre-processing methods for MRI images improve the detection of problematic areas. Two phases involved are the pre-processing and augmentation technique. To begin with, a positioning system removes MRI film artifacts such as labels and X-ray tags. Second, the Ant Colony Optimization (ACO) technique is used to get rid of high-frequency components. Comparing the results of the DL-EDAD technique to those of the median, adaptive, and spatial filter systems. Before extensive data interpretation and separation, pre-processing including tracking functions that include noise removal is frequently necessary. This pre-processing is frequently characterized as radiological or geometrical improvements.

The pheromone concentration of the paths and an intuitive assessment are the only criteria used to choose high-frequency segments. A specific ant, k, choose which node to move to next throughout the construction process using a probabilistic action selection rule that calculates the likelihood that ant, k, will move from the current node, i, to the following node, j.:

$$p_{ij}^k \frac{[T_{ij}]^\alpha [n_{ij}]^\beta}{\sum_{Ni}^k [T_{ij}]^\alpha [n_{ij}]^\beta} \ if \ j \in N_i^k \tag{1}$$

Here T_{ij} is the arc or edge from node i to j. N_i^k implies the neighboring nodules for a specific ant k, considering node i as start node. The constants correspond to the subject and intuitive changes, respectively. Finally, n_{ij} indicates the heuristics movements from node i to j.

In the proposed DL-EDAD approach, all of the images were focused on the sensory receptors and the brain. Various fields can be found inside a photograph. The images were taken from the Kaggle dataset repository, which in this case included a variety of images. For the assessment of pixel intensities in various sectors, there are significant factors. There were captured about 50 images of the multiple patients. The actions and performance of the patient are ensured to be normal and accurate by the approach.

Figure 3. MRI image

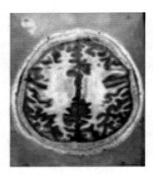

The crude input MRI image presented in Figure 3 is instantly employed for pre-processing step to remove noise and sharpen it.

Segmentation Process

The subject of interest is located in its planned place, and the chosen area is potted and focused in. The pixels' intensity is changed using this image. In the image, pixels are considered as either white or black relying on how brilliant they are. While the Black Region symbolizes damaged tissue, the White Area indicates living cells. On calculating the quantity of white and black pixels, it is determined that the patient is fine if there are very few black pixels. The patient either has a mild reading disability, Alzheimer or is in good health, as determined by the Black Pixels ratio. A popular technique for image segmentation is thresholding. With the help of this image segmentation approach, the grayscale or pixel power segmentation is produced. It's indeed two-tier thresholding, which divides pixels in a picture into two groups according to their brightness.

The Image segmentation is displayed in figure 4, in which an MRI image is segregated into several provinces. The segmented sections are need to be processed after segmentation.

Figure 4. Segmentation on MRI

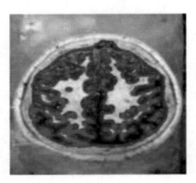

The morphological image is shown in figure 5. Here the images are processed based on shapes. Basic morphological operations are erosion, dilation, etc.

Figure 5. Morphological Image

Figure 6 displays the pre-processed binary image identification, identifying the binary trends and modes of higher-level characteristics.

Figure 6. Efficient LBP Features

Clustering

Clustering methods are uncontrolled segmentation techniques that separate an image into comparable intensity pixel/voxel clusters without training images. Clustering algorithms make use of accessible picture data for self-practice. The segmentation and planning were conducted in two steps: Data clustering and tissue sort estimation features.

$$j_m = \sum_{i=1}^{c}\sum_{j=1}^{N} u_{ijD_{ij}}^{m} \tag{2}$$

Each region is lighted independently, depending on the cluster's position. It is processed at a high rate of noise cancellation with poor homogeneity figures and a high rate of morphologic image filtering.

Figure 7 separates each area between localizations and distinguishes the normal and benign portions. Separately.

Figure 7. Cluster Region Separately

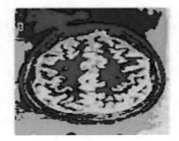

Feature Description

The points, edges, objects, etc., are the most common features seen in an image. A feature may be thought of as a piece of information about the content of a picture; the information shows whether or not a certain portion of the image has specific attributes. The classification of the feature details based on generated and formulated information is registered with the binary texture pattern. The DL-EDAD method has many data fields that base the average data on the complete data for the classified part.

Optimization

A swarm-based optimization technique is used in the DL-EDAD system. An optimization technique is needed if the needed area is not identified properly. Using this optimization technique, the area can be identified clearly and accurately.

E-GKFCM SYSTEM

The proposed E-GKFCM (Enhanced Gaussian Kernel Fuzzy C-Means Clustering) detects AD early. Vascular and brain atrophy are exacerbated. The implementation is accomplished by using picture segmentation to identify larger Vascular. The extent of enlargement will determine whether the patient is classified as healthy, in the first stage of AD, in the second stage of AD, or has mild cognitive impairment. Another critical element in the identification of AD is brain shrinkage. Brain atrophy is detected using the E-GKFCM image segmentation technique. The image's gradient is used to assess Cavity in Brain atrophy. This automated approach employs a straightforward process and produces images with minimal time complexity. This solves the issue of early detection while causing no harm to the brain. This will bolster medical imaging research.

Algorithm Steps-E-GKFCM

Given, E= {x1, ...xn}$\subset R^p$ The E-GKFCM partitions E into cl-fuzzy divisions by reducing the subsequent formula

$$J(U,V) = \sum_{i=1}^{cl}\sum_{k=1}^{n} U_i^m \left\| X - V_i \right\|^2 \tag{3}$$

Where cl is the total clusters and chosen the same as particular quantity in this work, n is the number of data-points, Uik is the participation of Xk in a class t, fulfilling the $\sum_{i=1}^{c} u_{ik} = 1, m$ measure controls clustering fuzziness and v the set of cluster centers or prototype (vi$\in$ Rp).

Now consider the proposed E-GKFCM algorithm. A nonlinear mapping is described as $\varnothing x \rightarrow \varnothing(x) \in feature\,space$, where x $\in$ X, X illustrates the data space, boundless dimension. E-GKFCM reduces the subsequent empirical formula.

$$J(U,V) = \sum_{i=1}^{c} \sum_{k=1}^{n} U_i^m \left\| \varnothing(X) - \varnothing(V_i) \right\|^2 \tag{4}$$

$$\| \varnothing(X_K) - \varnothing(V_i) \|^2 = K(X_K, X_K) + K(V_i, V_i) - 2K(X_K, V_i) \tag{5}$$

Where $Kr(x,y) = \varnothing(x)^T \varnothing(y)$ is an internal produce kernel function.

$KR(x,y) = \exp(-\| x - y \|^2 / \sigma^2)$, then $KR(x,x) = 1$, according to equation (4), equation (5) can be modified as

$$J(U,V) = 2 \sum_{i=1}^{c} \sum_{Kr=1}^{n} U_i^m (1 - KR(X_{Kr}, V_i)) \tag{6}$$

Minimizing equation (6) beneath the restriction of μ_{ik},

$$\mu_{ik} = \frac{(1 / (1 - K(x_K, v_i)))^{\frac{1}{m-1}}}{\sum_{j=1}^{c} (1 / (1 - K(x_K, v_i)))^{\frac{1}{m-1}}} \tag{7}$$

$$V_i = \frac{\sum_{Kr=1}^{n} U_{iKr}^m KR(x_{KR}, v_i) x_{Kr}}{\sum_{Kr=1}^{A} U_{iKr}^m KR(x_{KR}, v_i)} \tag{8}$$

For simplicity, we employ the Gaussian Kernel function (GKF) here. If various kernel functions are utilized, Equations (7) and (8) will be modified accordingly (8). Equation (4) is a kernel-stimulated latest metric, as follows.

$$d(x,y) = \| \varnothing(x_k) - \varnothing(v_i) \| = \sqrt{2(1 - k(x,y))} \tag{9}$$

It is possible to demonstrate that d(x,y) in equation (9) is a metric in the unique space if Kr(x,y) is the GKF.

Convolutional Shape Local Binary Texture using CNN

In this method, a normal image is classified as grayscale and sharpened scaled of the image, making the image a reshaped scaled one to have all scales as the same pixel length and intensity, and magnitude of the image throughout the image. This is the same data starting with local binary bit pattern and texture classification. Then, the formulated data of an image again is pre-processed with the grouped region so that every part of the image is clustered into such a matrix format, where every piece of data on the matrix structure will have a local and global cluster head, which means it is the average of all data from the whole cycle. Overall, many local and cluster heads will be generated based on the region displaced.

SOLUTIONS AND RECOMMENDATIONS

The performance of the DL-EDAD model needs to be analyzed. The accuracy, precision, etc., were used for classification result evaluation. The E-GKFCM algorithm was chosen to solve the problem. MATLAB 2018 was used for the implementation of the DL-EDAD work. The test utilizes neuroimaging data to diagnose AD to assess brain atrophy, hippocampal shrinkage, and vascular expansion. This is accomplished via several pixel intensity segmentation algorithms and the color gradient. The procedure was carried out on 12 MRI samples.

The resulting feature map is shown in Figure 8. The x-axis represents the number of feature rates, while the y-axis represents the feature's dimension rate. Feature maps are formed by applying feature detectors or filters to the input picture or previous layer output.

Figure 8. Proposed Feature Map

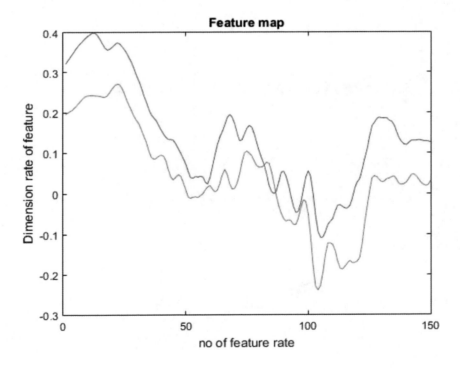

The Local Binary Pattern (LBP) histogram is shown in figure 9. LBP is a texture operator. Its function is to label the pixel images. The labeling is done by thresholding. The result will be a binary number.

The best validation performance is computed using 31 Epochs, shown in figure 10. The performance is checked at every stage. This is done to check whether the performance is at the desired level.

Figure 9. Histogram LBP

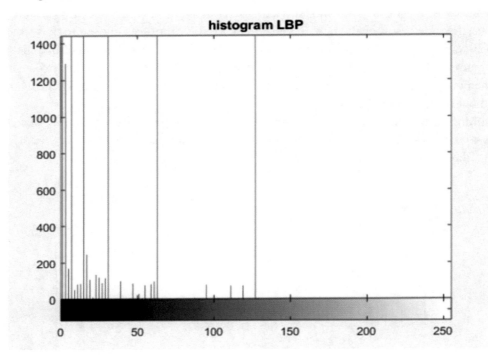

Figure 10. Validation Performance

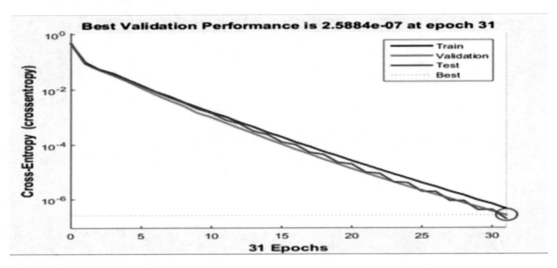

The error histogram with 20 binary values is represented in figure 11. This histogram shows the error between target values and predicted values. This diagram makes it easy to understand whether the predicted value is the same as the target value. The 20 bins indicate the number of vertical bars observed in the graph.

The overall performance and accuracy of E-GKFCM are better than other algorithms. Figures 12 given illustrates various comparisons on accuracy of different algorithms.

Figure 11. Error Histogram with 20 Bins

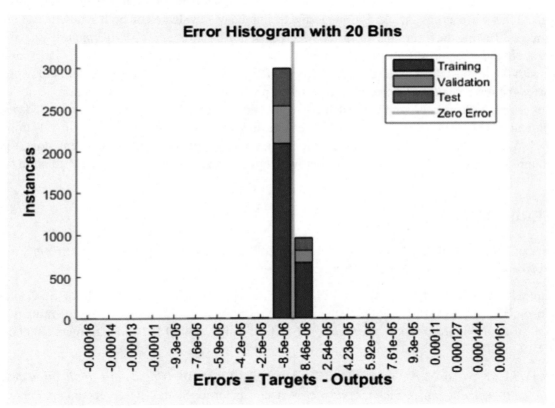

Figure 12. Proposed Algorithm Comparison of Accuracy

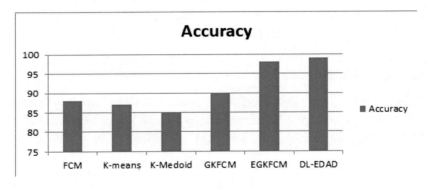

CONCLUSION

Worldwide, research is underway to detect and diagnose Alzheimer's. The study's goal is to detect and diagnose this disease early. We proposed the DL-EDAD model for Early Prediction for AD using E-GKFCM. The performance of E-GKFCM is compared to K-Means, K-Medoid, FCM, and GKFCM. This model is the fastest and most accurate at 99%. In particular, the purported connection between MRI volume decreases and gravity is elusive. Textural characteristics of amyloid-beta and tau may be derived from MRI images. The study shows how to utilize wavelet, wave atom, and E-GKFCM in MRI images. This improves categorization accuracy. Correct MRI image segmentation requires pre-processing. It is suggested that wave atoms shrink. The suggested technique was evaluated on both synthetic and clinical MR images. Testing the technique on various degrees of noise validates it. An MRI picture is segmented to extract textural features. Labeling the lateral ventricles locates the MRI seed site. a Gaussian histogram with the highest third peak. Level separates MRI images. The DL-EDAD segmentation approach enhances the resemblance and spatial intersect. Pre-processing pictures using wave atom shrinking increases accuracy. An early Alzheimer's detection objective Cerebral and vascular. The extended vascular is segmented in pictures. The patient is classified as healthy, early-stage AD, or mild cognitively impaired. Brain shrinkage is another indicator of AD. It identifies brain atrophy via picture segmentation. A gradient picture shows brain shrinkage. For Further, we improve the accuracy of the Early Prediction of AD.

REFERENCES

Armstrong, N., Nugent, C., Moore, G., & Finlay, D. (2009). Article. In *International Conference on Smart Homes and Health Telematics*. Springer.

Babalola, K. O., Patenaude, B., Aljabar, P., Schnabel, J., Kennedy, D., Crum, W., Smith, S., Cootes, T., Jenkinson, M., & Rueckert, D. (2009). An evaluation of four automatic methods of segmenting the subcortical structures in the brain. *NeuroImage, 47*(4), 1435–1447. doi:10.1016/j.neuroimage.2009.05.029 PMID:19463960

Coppola, J.F., Kowtko, M.A., Yamagata, C., & Joyce, S. (2013). *Applying mobile application development to help dementia and Alzheimer patients*. Wilson Center for Social Entrepreneurship. Paper 16.

Gordillo, N. C., Montseny, E., & Sobrevilla, P. (2013). State of the art survey on MRI brain tumor segment. *Magnetic Resonance Imaging, 31*(8), 1426–1438. doi:10.1016/j.mri.2013.05.002 PMID:23790354

Jean, F., Kowtko, M.A., Yamagata, C., & Joyce, S. (2013). *Applying Mobile Application Development to Help Dementia and Alzheimer Patients*. Academic Press.

Khan, A., & Usman, M. (2015). Article. In *2015 7th International Joint Conference on Knowledge Discovery, Knowledge Engineering and Knowledge Management (IC3K)*. IEEE.

Sandhya, G., Babu Kande, G., & Savithri, T. S. (2017). Multilevel Thresholding Method Based on Electromagnetism for Accurate Brain MRI Segmentation to Detect White Matter, Gray Matter, and CSF. *BioMed Research International, 2017*, 1–17. doi:10.1155/2017/6783209 PMID:29250547

Thakare, P., & Pawar, V. (2016). Article. In *2016 International Conference on Inventive Computation Technologies (ICICT)*. IEEE.

Udupa, J. K., & Herman, G. T. (2000). *3D Imaging in Medicine*. CRC Press.

Wang, M.-Y., Tsai, P., Liu, J. W.-S., & Zao, J. K. (2009). Article. In *2009 Ninth IEEE International Conference on Bioinformatics and BioEngineering*. IEEE.

Yousuf, M.A., & Nobi, M.N. (2010). A new method to remove noise in magnetic resonance and ultrasound images. *Journal of Scientific Research, 3*(1), 81-89.

Zhao, Y., Ma, B., Jiang, P., Zeng, D., Wang, X., & Li, S. (2020). Prediction of Alzheimer's Disease Progression with Multi-Information Generative Adversarial Network. *IEEE Journal of Biomedical and Health Informatics*, 1–1. doi:10.1109/JBHI.2020.3006925 PMID:32750952

Compilation of References

Abadi, M., Agarwal, A., Barham, P., Brevdo, E., & Chen, Z. (2016). *Tensorflow: Large-scale machine learning on heterogeneous distributed systems.* https://arxiv.org/abs/1603.04467

Abdel-Hamid, O., Abdel-rahman, M., Jiang, H., Deng, L., Penn, G., & Yu, D. (2014). Convolutional neural networks for speech recognition. *IEEE/ACM Transactions on Audio, Speech, and Language Processing, 22*(10), 1533–1545. doi:10.1109/TASLP.2014.2339736

Abel, J., & Fingscheidt, T. (2017). A DNN regression approach to speech enhancement by artificial band- width extension. In *IEEE Workshop on Applications of Signal Processing to Audio and Acoustics.* IEEE.

Abu-El-Haija, Kothari, Lee, Natsev, Toderici, Varadarajan, & Vijayanarasimhan. (2016). *YouTube-8M: A large-scale video classification benchmark.* https://arxiv.org/abs/1609.08675.

Adeyanju, I. A., Bello, O. O., & Adegboye, M. A. (2021). Machine learning methods for sign language recognition: A critical review and analysis. *Intell. Syst. with Appl., 12,* 200056. doi:10.1016/j.iswa.2021.200056

Aghakhani, H., Machiry, A., Nilizadeh, S., Krügel, C., & Vigna, G. (2018). Detecting Deceptive Reviews Using Generative Adversarial Networks. *2018 IEEE Security and Privacy Workshops (SPW),* 89-95.

Agnese, J., Herrera, J., Tao, H., & Zhu, X. (2020). A survey and taxonomy of adversarial neural networks for text-to-image synthesis. *Wiley Interdisciplinary Reviews. Data Mining and Knowledge Discovery, 10*(4), e1345. doi:10.1002/widm.1345

Agrawal, S. (2019). *Reading between the layers (LSTM Network).* Retrieved 31 March 2020, from https://towardsdatascience.com/reading-between-the-layers-lstm-network-7956ad192e58

Aharon, M., & Kimmel, R. (2006). Representation analysis and synthesis of lip images using dimensionality reduction. *International Journal of Computer Vision, 67*(3), 297–312. doi:10.100711263-006-5166-3

Aiswarya, V., Naren Raju, N., Johanan Joy, S. S., Nagarajan, T., & Vijayalakshmi, P. (2018). Hidden markov model-based sign language to speech conversion system in Tamil. *Proceedings of the 4th International Conference Biosignals, Images Instrumentation,* 206–212. 10.1109/ICBSII.2018.8524802

Akman, N. P., Sivri, T. T., Berkol, A., & Erdem, H. (2022, July). Lip Reading Multiclass Classification by Using Dilated CNN with Turkish Dataset. In *2022 International Conference on Electrical, Computer and Energy Technologies (ICECET)* (pp. 1-6). 10.1109/ICECET55527.2022.9873011

Alexa Voice Service Overview (v20160207) | Alexa Voice Service. (n.d.). Retrieved May 15, 2022, from https://developer.amazon.com/docs/alexa-voice-service/api-overview.html

Alom, M. Z., Taha, T. M., Yakopcic, C., Westberg, S., Sidike, P., Nasrin, M. S., Hasan, M., Van Essen, B. C., Awwal, A. A. S., & Asari, V. K. (2019). A State-of-the-Art Survey on Deep Learning Theory and Architectures. *Electronics (Basel), 8*(3), 292. doi:10.3390/electronics8030292

Al-Sabahi, K., Zuping, Z., & Kang, Y. (2018). *Bidirectional attentional encoder-decoder model and bidirectional beam search for abstractive summarization.* arXiv preprint arXiv:1809.06662.

Alvarez, S., Oliver, A., & Badia, T. (2020, November). Quantitative Analysis of Post-Editing Effort Indicators for NMT. In *Proceedings of the 22nd Annual Conference of the European Association for Machine Translation* (pp. 411-420). Academic Press.

Aneja, J., Deshpande, A., & Schwing, A. G. (2018). Convolutional image captioning. In *Proceedings of the IEEE conference on computer vision and pattern recognition* (pp. 5561-5570). IEEE.

Antony Vijay, J., Anwar Basha, H., & Arun Nehru, J. (2021). A Dynamic Approach For Detecting The Fake News Using Random Forest Classifier And Nlp. In *Computational Methods And Data Engineering* (pp. 331–341). Springer. doi:10.1007/978-981-15-7907-3_25

Arato, A., Markus, N., & Juhasz, Z. (2014, July). Teaching Morse language to a deaf-blind person for reading and writing SMS on an ordinary vibrating smartphone. In *International Conference on Computers for Handicapped Persons* (pp. 393-396). Springer. 10.1007/978-3-319-08599-9_59

Armstrong, N., Nugent, C., Moore, G., & Finlay, D. (2009). Article. In *International Conference on Smart Homes and Health Telematics.* Springer.

Artetxe, M., Labaka, G., Agirre, E., & Cho, K. (2017). *Unsupervised neural machine translation.* arXiv preprint arXiv:1710.11041.

Atal, B., & Remde, J. (1982, May). A new model of LPC excitation for producing natural-sounding speech at low bit rates. In *Proceedings of the IEEE International Conference on Acoustics, Speech, and Signal Processing (ICASSP'82)* (vol. 7, pp. 614-617). IEEE. 10.1109/ICASSP.1982.1171649

Averbuch, A., Bahl, L., Bakis, R., Brown, P., Cole, A., Daggett, A. G., Das, S., Davies, K., DeGennaro, S., DeSouza, P., Epstein, E., Fraleigh, D., Jelinek, F., Katz, S., Lewis, B., Mercer, R., Nadas, A., Nahamoo, D., Picheny, M., ... Spinelli, P. (1986). An IBM PC based large-vocabulary isolated-utterance speech recognizer. In *Proceedings of the IEEE International Conference on Acoustics, Speech, and Signal Processing (ICASSP'86)* (vol. 11, pp. 53-56). IEEE. 10.1109/ICASSP.1986.1169169

Azhar, I., Afyouni, I., & Elnagar, A. (2021, March). Facilitated Deep Learning Models for Image Captioning. In *2021 55th Annual Conference on Information Sciences and Systems (CISS)* (pp. 1-6). IEEE. 10.1109/CISS50987.2021.9400209

Babalola, K. O., Patenaude, B., Aljabar, P., Schnabel, J., Kennedy, D., Crum, W., Smith, S., Cootes, T., Jenkinson, M., & Rueckert, D. (2009). An evaluation of four automatic methods of segmenting the subcortical structures in the brain. *NeuroImage, 47*(4), 1435–1447. doi:10.1016/j.neuroimage.2009.05.029 PMID:19463960

Bagui, S. C., Mehra, K. L., & Vaughn, B. K. (1997). An M-stage version of the k-RNN rule in statistical discrimination. *Journal of Statistical Planning and Inference, 65*(2), 323–333. doi:10.1016/S0378-3758(97)00055-4

Bahl, L. R., Jelinek, F., & Mercer, R. L. (1983). A maximum likelihood approach to continuous speech recognition. *IEEE Transactions on Pattern Analysis and Machine Intelligence, PAMI-5*(2), 179–190. doi:10.1109/TPAMI.1983.4767370 PMID:21869099

Bakay, O., Avar, B., & Yildiz, O. T. (2019). A tree-based approach for English-to-Turkish translation. *Turkish Journal of Electrical Engineering and Computer Sciences, 27*(1), 437–452. doi:10.3906/elk-1807-341

Baker, J. (1973). Machine-Aided Labeling of Connected Speech. In *Working Papers in Speech Recognition--II.* Computer Science Department, Carnegie Mellon University. Retrieved from https://apps.dtic.mil/docs/citations/AD0770633

Baker, J. M. (1989). DragonDictate (TM)-30K: Natural Language Speech Recognition with 30,000 Words. In *Proceedings of the First European Conference on Speech Communication and Technology* (pp. 2161-2163). Academic Press.

Beim Graben, P., & Blutner, R. (2019). Quantum approaches to music cognition. *Journal of Mathematical Psychology*, *91*, 38–50. doi:10.1016/j.jmp.2019.03.002

Beltagy, I., Peters, M., & Cohan, A. (2020). *Longformer: The Long-Document Transformer.* Arxiv:2004.05150.

Benamira, A., Devillers, B., Lesot, E., Ray, A. K., Saadi, M., & Malliaros, F. D. (2019, August). Semi-supervised learning and graph neural networks for fake news detection. In *2019 IEEE/ACM International Conference on Advances in Social Networks Analysis and Mining (ASONAM)* (pp. 568-569). IEEE. 10.1145/3341161.3342958

Bengio, Y., Louradour, J., Collobert, R., & Weston, J. (2009). Curriculum Learning. *ICML '09: Proceedings of the 26th Annual International Conference on Machine Learning*, 41–48.

Benzeghiba, M., DeMori, R., Deroo, O., Dupont, S., Erbes, T., Jouvet, D., Fissore, L., Laface, P., Mertins, A., Ris, C., Rose, R., Tyagi, V., & Wellekens, C. (2007). Automatic speech recognition and speech variability: A review. *Speech Communication*, *49*(10-11), 763–786. doi:10.1016/j.specom.2007.02.006

Berant, J., Chou, A., Frostig, R., & Liang, P. (2013). Semantic parsing on freebase from question- answer pairs. In Empirical Methods in Natural Language Processing (Vol. 2). Association for Computational Linguistics.

Berman, S., & Stern, H. (2011). Sensors for gesture recognition systems. *IEEE Transactions on Systems, Man and Cybernetics. Part C, Applications and Reviews*, *42*(3), 277–290. doi:10.1109/TSMCC.2011.2161077

Besacier, L., Barnard, E., Karpov, A., & Schultz, T. (2014). Automatic speech recognition for under-resourced languages: A survey. *Speech Communication*, *56*, 85–100. doi:10.1016/j.specom.2013.07.008

Bharath, M., & Prakash, S., & Chinnasamy. (2021). Detecting Fake News Using Machine Learning Algorithms. *2021 International Conference on Computer Communication and Informatics (ICCCI)*, 1-5. doi: 10.1109/ICCCI50826.2021.9402470

Bhavana, D., Kumar, K. K., Chandra, M. B., Bhargav, P. S. K., Sanjanaa, D. J., & Gopi, G. M. (2021). Hand sign recognition using CNN. *International Journal of Performability Engineering*, *17*(3), 314–321. doi:10.23940/ijpe.21.03.p7.314321

Bhweshgaur. (n.d.). https://github.com/bhweshgaur/Health-Insurance-Cross-Sell-Prediction/

Bidve, D. M., Shewale, T. D., Gaikwad, S. S., Murmure, A. R., & Pawar, S. (2016). Hand-to-Hand Instant Message Communication: Revisiting Morse Code. *FIRST–International Journal for Innovative Research in Science & Technology, 2*(12).

Bilmes, J. A., & Kirchhoff, K. (2003, May). Factored language models and generalized parallel backoff. In *Proceedings of the 2003 Conference of the North American Chapter of the Association for Computational Linguistics on Human Language Technology: companion volume of the Proceedings of HLT-NAACL 2003—short papers-Volume 2* (pp. 4-6). Association for Computational Linguistics. 10.3115/1073483.1073485

Bogaerts, T., Watelet, S., De Bruyne, N., Thoen, C., Coopman, T., Van den Bergh, J., Reyniers, M., Seynaeve, D., Casteels, W., Latré, S., & Hellinckx, P. (2022). Leveraging Artificial Intelligence and Fleet Sensor Data towards a Higher Resolution Road Weather Model. *Sensors (Basel)*, *22*(7), 2732. doi:10.339022072732 PMID:35408346

Bogert, B. P., Healy, M. J. R., & Tukey, J. W. (1963, June). The quefrency analysis of time series for echoes; Cepstrum, pseudo-autocovariance, cross-cepstrum and saphe cracking. In *Proceedings of the Symposium on Time Series Analysis* (pp. 209-243). Academic Press.

Borges, L., Martins, B., & Calado, P. (2019). Combining similarity features and deep representation learning for stance detection in the context of checking fake news. *Journal of Data and Information Quality*, *11*(3), 1–26. doi:10.1145/3287763

Borji, A. (2019). Pros and cons of gan evaluation measures. *Computer Vision and Image Understanding, 179*, 41–65. doi:10.1016/j.cviu.2018.10.009

Borji, A. (2022). Pros and cons of GAN evaluation measures: New developments. *Computer Vision and Image Understanding, 215*, 103329. doi:10.1016/j.cviu.2021.103329

Braşoveanu, A. M., & Andonie, R. (2019). *Semantic fake news detection: a machine learning perspective*. International Work-Conference on Artificial Neural Networks.

Breiman, L. (2003). Statistical modeling: The two cultures. *Quality Control and Applied Statistics, 48*(1), 81–82.

Bringert, B. (2007, June). Speech recognition grammar compilation in Grammatical Framework. In *Proceedings of the workshop on grammar-based approaches to spoken language processing* (pp. 1-8). 10.3115/1626333.1626335

Brown, P. F., DellaPietra, V. J., deSouza, P. V., Lai, J. C., & Mercer, R. L. (1992). Class-Based n-gram Models of Natural Language. *Computational Linguistics, 18*(4), 467–479.

Budak, C., Agrawal, D., & El Abbadi, A. (2011). Limiting The Spread Of Misinformation In Social Networks. *Proceedings Of The 20th International Conference On World Wide Web*, 665–674. 10.1145/1963405.1963499

Calleja, J., & Mendez, A. (2021). SQYQP@ Vaxxstance: Stance detection for the antivaxxers movement. In *Proceedings of the International Conference of the Spanish Society for Natural Language Processing (IberLEF 2021)* (pp. 202-209). Academic Press.

Calonder, M., Lepetit, V., Strecha, C., & Brief, F. P. (n.d.). Binary robust independent elementary features. *Proceedings of the European Conference on Computer Vision*, 778–792.

Carton, S., Mei, Q., & Resnick, P. (2018). *Extractive Adversarial Networks: High-Recall Explanations For Identifying Personal Attacks In Social Media Posts*. doi:10.18653/v1/D18-1386

Carvadia. (n.d.). https://carvadia.com/what-is-partitioned-regression/

Castelvecchi, D. (2016). Can we open the black box of AI? *Nature, 538*(7623), 20–23. doi:10.1038/538020a PMID:27708329

Čeh, M., Kilibarda, M., Lisec, A., & Bajat, B. (2018). Estimating the performance of random forest versus multiple regression for predicting prices of the apartments. *ISPRS International Journal of Geo-Information, 7*(5), 168. doi:10.3390/ijgi7050168

Celikyilmaz, A., Bosselut, A., He, X., & Choi, Y. (2018). *Deep Communicating Agents for Abstractive Summarization*. Arxiv: 1803.10357.

Chang, J. R., Ling, T. T., & Li, T. C. (2020, November). A Research on Image Captioning by Different Encoder Networks. In *2020 International Symposium on Computer, Consumer and Control (IS3C)* (pp. 68-71). IEEE. 10.1109/IS3C50286.2020.00025

Chaudhary, J. R., & Patel, A. C. (2018). Bilingual machine translation using RNN based deep learning. *International Journal of Scientific Research in Science, Engineering and Technology, 4*(4), 1480–1484.

Chaudhary, J. R., & Patel, A. C. (2018). Machine translation using deep learning: A survey. *International Journal of Scientific Research in Science, Engineering and Technology, 4*(2), 145–150.

Chen, T., & Chefd'hotel, C. (2014). Deep learning based automatic immune cell detection for immuno- histochemistry images. In *International Workshop on Machine Learning in Medical Imaging*. Springer. 10.1007/978-3-319-10581-9_3

Chen, T., Li, M., Li, Y., Lin, M., Wang, N., Wang, M., Xiao, T., Xu, B., Zhang, C., & Zhang, Z. (2015). *MXNet: A flexible and efficient machine learning library for heterogeneous distributed systems.* https://arxiv.org/abs/1512.01274

Chen, C., Seff, A., Kornhauser, A., & Xiao, J. (2015). Deepdriving: Learning affordance for direct perception in autonomous driving. In *IEEE International Conference on Computer Vision.* IEEE. 10.1109/ICCV.2015.312

Cheng, H., Devlin, J., Fang, H., Gupta, S., Deng, L., He, X., & Mitchell, M. (2015). *Language models for image captioning: The quirks and what works.* arXiv preprint arXiv:1505.01809.

Cheng, Y. (2019). Semi-supervised learning for neural machine translation. In *Joint Training for Neural Machine Translation* (pp. 25–40). Springer. doi:10.1007/978-981-32-9748-7_3

Chen, K., Zhao, T., Yang, M., Liu, L., Tamura, A., Wang, R., Utiyama, M., & Sumita, E. (2017). A neural approach to source dependence based context model for statistical machine translation. *IEEE/ACM Transactions on Audio, Speech, and Language Processing, 26*(2), 266–280. doi:10.1109/TASLP.2017.2772846

Chetlur, S., Woolley, C., Vandermersch, P., Cohen, J., Tran, J., Catanzaro, B., & Shelhamer, E. (2014). *cuDNN: Efficient primitives for deep learning.* http:// arxiv.org/abs/1410.0759

Chien, J.-T., & Hsieh, H.-L. (2013). Nonstationary source separation using sequential and variational Bayesian learning. *IEEE Transactions on Neural Networks and Learning Systems, 24*(5), 681–694. doi:10.1109/TNNLS.2013.2242090 PMID:24808420

Cho, K., Van Merriënboer, B., Bahdanau, D., & Bengio, Y. (2014). *On the properties of neural machine translation: Encoder-decoder approaches.* arXiv preprint arXiv:1409.1259. doi:10.3115/v1/W14-4012

Cho, K., Van Merriënboer, B., Gulcehre, C., Bahdanau, D., Bougares, F., Schwenk, H., & Bengio, Y. (2014). *Learning phrase representations using RNN encoder-decoder for statistical machine translation.* arXiv preprint arXiv:1406.1078. doi:10.3115/v1/D14-1179

Choi, K., Fazekas, G., Cho, K., & Sandler, M. (2018). The effects of noisy labels on deep convolutional neural networks for music tagging. *IEEE Transactions on Emerging Topics in Computational Intelligence, 2*(2), 139–149. doi:10.1109/TETCI.2017.2771298

Chopra, S., Auli, M., & Rush, A. (2016). Abstractive sentence summarization with attentive recurrent neural networks. *Proceedings of the 2016 Conference of the North American Chapter of the Association for Computational Linguistics: Human Language Technologies*, 93–98. 10.18653/v1/N16-1012

Chou, W., & Juang, B. H. (2003). *Pattern recognition in speech and language processing.* CRC Press. doi:10.1201/9780203010525

Chuan, C. H., Regina, E., & Guardino, C. (2014, December). American sign language recognition using leap motion sensor. In *13th International Conference on Machine Learning and Application, 2014* (pp. 541–544). IEEE Publications. 10.1109/ICMLA.2014.110

Cignarella, A. T., Lai, M., Bosco, C., Patti, V., & Paolo, R. (2020). Sardistance@EVALITA2020: Overview of the task on stance detection in Italian tweets. In *Proceedings of the Seventh Evaluation Campaign of Natural Language Processing and Speech Tools for Italian (EVALITA 2020)*. 10.4000/books.aaccademia.7084

CMU Sphinx download | SourceForge.net. (n.d.). Retrieved May 15, 2022, from https://sourceforge.net/projects/cmusphinx/

Conneau, A., Khandelwal, K., Goyal, N., Chaudhary, V., Wenzek, G., Guzmán, F., . . . Stoyanov, V. (2019). *Unsupervised cross-lingual representation learning at scale.* arXiv preprint arXiv:1911.02116.

Cooke, M., Barker, J., Cunningham, S., & Shao, X. (2006). An audio-visual corpus for speech perception and automatic speech recognition. *The Journal of the Acoustical Society of America, 120*(5), 2421–2424. doi:10.1121/1.2229005 PMID:17139705

Coppola, J.F., Kowtko, M.A., Yamagata, C., & Joyce, S. (2013). *Applying mobile application development to help dementia and Alzheimer patients*. Wilson Center for Social Entrepreneurship. Paper 16.

Cremelie, N., & Martens, J. P. (1999). In search of better pronunciation models for speech recognition. *Speech Communication, 29*(2-4), 115–136. doi:10.1016/S0167-6393(99)00034-5

Dasl, A., Gawde, S., Suratwala, K., & Kalbande, D. (2018). Sign language recognition using deep learning on custom processed static gesture images. *Int. Conf. Smart City Emerg. Technol. ICSCET 2018*. 10.1109/ICSCET.2018.8537248

Datta, D., David, P. E., Mittal, D., & Jain, A. (2020). Neural Machine Translation using Recurrent Neural Network. *Regular Issue, 9*(4), 1395–1400. doi:10.35940/ijeat.D7637.049420

Davis, K. H., Biddulph, R., & Balashek, S. (1952). Automatic recognition of spoken digits. *The Journal of the Acoustical Society of America, 24*(6), 637–642. doi:10.1121/1.1906946

Deepak, S., & Chitturi, B. (2020). Deep neural approach to Fake-News identification. *Procedia Computer Science, 167*, 2236–2243. doi:10.1016/j.procs.2020.03.276

Dempster, A. P., Laird, N. M., & Rubin, D. B. (1977). Maximum Likelihood from Incomplete Data via the EM Algorithm. *Journal of the Royal Statistical Society. Series B. Methodological, 39*(1), 1–38. doi:10.1111/j.2517-6161.1977.tb01600.x

Devlin, J., Chang, M. W., Lee, K., & Toutanova, K. (2018). *BERT: Pre-training of deep bidirectional transformers for language understanding*. arXiv preprint arXiv:1810.04805.

Devlin, J., Chang, M., Lee, K., & Toutanova, K. (2018). *BERT: Pre-training of Deep Bidirectional Transformers for Language Understanding*. Arxiv:1810.04805.

Devlin, J., Gupta, S., Girshick, R., Mitchell, M., & Zitnick, C. L. (2015). *Exploring nearest neighbour approaches for image captioning*. arXiv preprint arXiv:1505.04467.

Dhanalakshmi, V., Kumar, M.A., Soman, K.P., & Rajendran, S. (2009). *POS Tagger and Chunker for Tamil Language*. Academic Press.

Dodan, M. E., Vien, Q. T., & Nguyen, T. T. (2022). Internet traffic prediction using recurrent neural networks. *EAI Endorsed Transactions on Industrial Networks and Intelligent Systems, 9*(4), e1–e1. doi:10.4108/eetinis.v9i4.1415

Dong, S., & Ni, N. (2021). A method for representing periodic functions and enforcing exactly periodic boundary conditions with deep neural networks. *Journal of Computational Physics, 435*, 110242. doi:10.1016/j.jcp.2021.110242

Dozat, T. (2016). Incorporating Nesterov momentum into Adam. *International Conference on Learning Representations Workshop*, 1–4.

Dragon Speech Recognition - Get More Done by Voice | Nuance. (n.d.). Retrieved May 15, 2022, from https://www.nuance.com/dragon.html

DragonDictate® 2.5. Computer software. (1997). Dragon Systems.

Duchi, J. C., Hazan, E., & Singer, Y. (2010). Adaptive subgradient methods for online learning and stochastic optimization. In *Conference on Learning Theory*. Omnipress.

Dulhanty, C., Deglint, J. L., Daya, I. B., & Wong, A. (2019). *Taking a stance on fake news: Towards automatic disinformation assessment via deep bidirectional transformer language models for stance detection.* arXiv preprint arXiv:1911.11951.

El Ayadi, M., Kamel, M. S., & Karray, F. (2011). Survey on speech emotion recognition: Features, classification schemes, and databases. *Pattern Recognition, 44*(3), 572–587. doi:10.1016/j.patcog.2010.09.020

El-Gayyar, M., ElYamany, H. F., Gaber, T., & Hassanien, A. E. (2013, September). Social network framework for deaf and blind people based on cloud computing. In *2013 Federated Conference on Computer Science and Information Systems* (pp. 1313-1319). IEEE.

Elmer, S. (2016). Relationships between music training, neural networks, and speech processing. *International Journal of Psychophysiology, 100*(108), 46. doi:10.1016/j.ijpsycho.2016.07.152

Elsherief, M., Sumner, S. A., Jones, C. M., Law, R. K., Kacha-Ochana, A., Shieber, L., Cordier, L., Holton, K., & De Choudhury, M. (2021). Characterizing And Identifying The Prevalence Of Web-Based Misinformation Relating To Medication For Opioid Use Disorder: Machine Learning Approach. *Journal of Medical Internet Research, 23*(12), E30753. doi:10.2196/30753 PMID:34941555

Ertam, F., & Aydin, G. (2021). Abstractive text summarization using deep learning with a new Turkish summarization benchmark dataset. *Concurrency and Computation, 34*(9). doi:10.1002/cpe.6482

European Telecommunications Standards Institute. (2003). *Speech Processing, Transmission and Quality Aspects (STQ); Distributed speech recognition; Front-end feature extraction algorithm; Compression algorithms.* ETSI ES 202 050 V1.1.5 (2007-01). Retrieved May 15, 2022, from: https://www.etsi.org/deliver/etsi_es/202000_202099/ 202050/01.01.05_60/ es_202050v010105p.pdf

Fajcik, M., Burget, L., & Smrz, P. (2019). *BUT-FIT at SemEval-2019 task 7: Determining the rumour stance with pretrained deep bidirectional transformers.* arXiv preprint arXiv:1902.10126. doi:10.18653/v1/S19-2192

Fakoor, R., Ladhak, F., Nazi, A., & Huber, M. (2013). Using deep learning to enhance cancer diag- nosis and classification. In *International Conference on Machine Learning.* Omnipress.

Fang, G., Gao, W., & Zhao, D. (2004). Large vocabulary sign language recognition based on fuzzy decision trees. *IEEE Transactions on Systems, Man, and Cybernetics. Part A, Systems and Humans, 34*(3), 305–314. doi:10.1109/TSMCA.2004.824852

Federico, M., Enyedi, R., Barra-Chicote, R., Giri, R., Isik, U., Krishnaswamy, A., & Sawaf, H. (2020a). *From speech-to-speech translation to automatic dubbing.* arXiv preprint arXiv:2001.06785. doi:10.18653/v1/2020.iwslt-1.31

Federico, M., Virkar, Y., Enyedi, R., & Barra-Chicote, R. (2020b). Evaluating and Optimizing Prosodic Alignment for Automatic Dubbing. In INTERSPEECH (pp. 1481-1485). doi:10.21437/Interspeech.2020-2983

Feichtenhofer, C., Pinz, A., & Zisserman, A. (2016). Convolutional two-stream network fusion for video action recognition. In *IEEE Conference on Computer Vision and Pattern Recognition.* IEEE. 10.1109/CVPR.2016.213

Feng, J., Chai, Y., & Xu, C. (2021). A novel neural network to nonlinear complex-variable constrained nonconvex optimization. *Journal of the Franklin Institute, 358*(8), 4435–4457. doi:10.1016/j.jfranklin.2021.02.029

Feng, M., Xiang, B., Glass, M. R., Wang, L., & Zhou, B. (2015). Applying deep learning to answer selection: A study and an open task. In *IEEE Workshop on Automatic Speech Recognition and Understanding.* IEEE. 10.1109/ASRU.2015.7404872

Fikri, F., Oflazer, K., & Yanıkoglu, B. (2021). Semantic Similarity Based Evaluation for Abstractive News Summarization. *Proceedings of the 1st Workshop on Natural Language Generation, Evaluation, and Metrics,* 24–33. 10.18653/v1/2021.gem-1.3

Fisher, R. A. (1936). The Use of Multiple Measurements in Taxonomic Problems. *Annals of Eugenics*, *7*(2), 179–188. doi:10.1111/j.1469-1809.1936.tb02137.x

Fosler-Lussier, E. (2003). A tutorial on pronunciation modeling for large vocabulary speech recognition. In *Text-and Speech-Triggered Information Access* (pp. 38–77). Springer. doi:10.1007/978-3-540-45115-0_3

Freitas, J., Calado, A., Barros, M. J., & Dias, M. S. (2009). Spoken language interface for mobile devices. In *Proceedings of the Language and Technology Conference* (pp. 24-35). Springer.

Fukushima, K. (1980). Neocognitron: A self-organizing neural network model for a mechanism of pattern recognition unaffected by shift in position. *Biological Cybernetics*, *36*(4), 193–202. doi:10.1007/BF00344251 PMID:7370364

Galatolo, F., Cimino, M., & Vaglini, G. (2021) Generating Images from Caption and Vice Versa via CLIP-Guided Generative Latent Space Search. *International Conference on Image Processing and Vision Engineering*. 10.5220/0010503701660174

Ganesan, K., Zhai, C. X., & Han, J. (2010). Opinosis: A graph-based approach to abstractive summarization of highly redundant opinions. In *23rd International Conference on Computational Linguistics*. Association for Computational Linguistics.

Gao, S., Huang, Y., Zhang, S., Han, J., Wang, G., Zhang, M., & Lin, Q. (2020). Short-term runoff prediction with GRU and LSTM networks without requiring time step optimization during sample generation. *Journal of Hydrology (Amsterdam)*, *589*, 125188. doi:10.1016/j.jhydrol.2020.125188

Garofolo, J. S., Lamel, L. F., Fisher, W. M., Fiscus, J. G., & Pallett, D. S. (1993). *DARPA TIMIT acoustic-phonetic continuous speech corpus*. NIST speech disc 1-1.1. NASA STI/Recon Technical Report N 93.

Gehrmann, S., Deng, Y., & Rush, A. M. (2018). *Bottom-Up Abstractive Summarization*. Arxiv: 1808.10792. doi:10.18653/v1/D18-1443

Georgila, K., Fakotakis, N., & Kokkinakis, G. (2004). A Graphical Tool for Handling Rule Grammars in Java Speech Grammar Format. In *Proceedings of the 4th International Conference on Language Resources and Evaluation (LREC)* (pp. 615-618). Academic Press.

Gers, F. A., Schmidhuber, J., & Cummins, F. (2000). Learning to forget: Continual prediction with LSTM. *Neural Computation*, *12*(10), 2451–2471. doi:10.1162/089976600300015015 PMID:11032042

Ghafari, S. M., Joshi, A., Beheshti, A., Paris, C., Yakhchi, S., & Orgun, M. (2019). Dcat: A Deep Context-Aware Trust Prediction Approach For Online Social Networks. *Proceedings Of The 17th International Conference On Advances In Mobile Computing & Multimedia*, 20–27. 10.1145/3365921.3365940

Ghayoomi, M., & Mousavian, M. (2022). Deep Transfer Learning For Covid-19 Fake News Detection In Persian. *Expert Systems: International Journal of Knowledge Engineering and Neural Networks*, *39*(8), E13008. doi:10.1111/exsy.13008 PMID:35599852

Ghosh, S., Singhania, P., Singh, S., Rudra, K., & Ghosh, S. (2019). Stance detection in web and social media: A comparative study. In *Proceedings of the International Conference of the Cross-Language Evaluation Forum for European Languages* (pp. 75-87). Springer. 10.1007/978-3-030-28577-7_4

Gidado, U. M., Chiroma, H., Aljojo, N., Abubakar, S., Popoola, S. I., & Al-Garadi, M. A. (2020). A Survey on Deep Learning for Steering Angle Prediction in Autonomous Vehicles. *IEEE Access: Practical Innovations, Open Solutions*, *8*, 163797–163817. doi:10.1109/ACCESS.2020.3017883

Giorgioni, S., Politi, M., Salman, S., Basili, R., & Croce, D. (2020). UNITOR@Sardistance2020: Combining transformer-based architectures and transfer learning for robust stance detection. In *Proceedings of the Seventh Evaluation Campaign of Natural Language Processing and Speech Tools for Italian (EVALITA 2020).* 10.4000/books.aaccademia.7092

Gokhale, M. Y., & Khanduja, D. K. (2010). Time Domain Signal Analysis Using Wavelet Packet Decomposition Approach. *International Journal of Communications, Network and Systems Sciences, 3*(03), 321–329. doi:10.4236/ijcns.2010.33041

Goldani, M. H., Momtazi, S., & Safabakhsh, R. (2021). Detecting fake news with capsule neural networks. *Applied Soft Computing, 101,* 106991. doi:10.1016/j.asoc.2020.106991

Gordillo, N. C., Montseny, E., & Sobrevilla, P. (2013). State of the art survey on MRI brain tumor segment. *Magnetic Resonance Imaging, 31*(8), 1426–1438. doi:10.1016/j.mri.2013.05.002 PMID:23790354

Gorgun, O., Yildiz, O. T., Solak, E., & Ehsani, R. (2016). English-Turkish parallel treebank with morphological annotations and its use in tree-based smt. *International Conference on Pattern Recognition and Methods,* 510-516. 10.5220/0005653905100516

Grobel, K., & Assan, M. (1997). Isolated sign language recognition using hidden markov models. In *Computational Cybernetics and Simulation IEEE International Conference on Systems, Man, and Cybernetics,* 1 (pp. 162–167). IEEE Publications. 10.1109/ICSMC.1997.625742

Gruetzemacher, R., & Paradice, D. (2022). Deep transfer learning & beyond: Transformer language models in information systems research. *ACM Computing Surveys, 54*(10s), 1–35. Advance online publication. doi:10.1145/3505245

Grybauskas, A., Pilinkienė, V., & Stundžienė, A. (2021). Predictive analytics using Big Data for the real estate market during the COVID-19 pandemic. *Journal of Big Data, 8*(1), 1–20. doi:10.118640537-021-00476-0 PMID:34367876

Guderlei, M., & Aßenmacher, M. (2020, December). Evaluating unsupervised representation learning for detecting stances of fake news. In *Proceedings of the 28th International Conference on Computational Linguistics* (pp. 6339-6349). 10.18653/v1/2020.coling-main.558

Güneş, F., Wolfinger, R., & Tan, P. Y. (2017, April). Stacked ensemble models for improved prediction accuracy. *Proc. Static Anal. Symp.,* 1-19.

Gupta, A., Zhang, P., Lalwani, G., & Diab, M. (2019). *Casa-nlu: Context-aware self-attentive natural language understanding for task-oriented chatbots.* arXiv preprint arXiv:1909.08705. doi:10.18653/v1/D19-1127

Haeb-Umbach, R., & Ney, H. (1992, March). Linear discriminant analysis for improved large vocabulary continuous speech recognition. In *Proceedings of the 1992 IEEE International Conference on Acoustics, Speech, and Signal Processing (ICASSP-92)* (vol. 1, pp. 13-16). IEEE. 10.1109/ICASSP.1992.225984

Hakak, S., Alazab, M., Khan, S., Gadekallu, T. R., Maddikunta, P. K., & Khan, W. Z. (2021). An ensemble machine learning approach through effective feature extraction to classify fake news. *Future Generation Computer Systems, 117,* 47–58. doi:10.1016/j.future.2020.11.022

Hamilton, W., Ying, Z., & Leskovec, J. (2017). Inductive Representation Learning On Large Graphs. *Advances in Neural Information Processing Systems, 30.*

Han, Y., Kim, J., & Lee, K. (2016). Deep convolutional neural networks for predominant instrument recognition in polyphonic music. *IEEE/ACM Transactions on Audio, Speech, and Language Processing, 25*(1), 208–221. doi:10.1109/TASLP.2016.2632307

Hasani, R., Lechner, M., Amini, A., Rus, D., & Grosu, R. (2021). Liquid time-constant networks. *Proceedings of the AAAI Conference on Artificial Intelligence, 35*(9), 7657–7666. doi:10.1609/aaai.v35i9.16936

Hegelich, S., & Janetzko, D. (2016). Are Social Bots On Twitter Political Actors? Empirical Evidence From A Ukrainian Social Botnet. *Tenth International Aaai Conference On Web And Social Media.*

Hendrycks, D., & Gimpel, K. (2016). *Gaussian error linear units (gelus).* Arxiv:1606.08415.

He, Q., Lv, Y., Wang, X., Huang, M., & Cai, Y. (2022). Reinforcement Learning-Based Rumor Blocking Approach In Directed Social Networks. *IEEE Systems Journal*, 1–11. doi:10.1109/JSYST.2022.3159840

Hermansky, H. (1990). Perceptual linear predictive (PLP) analysis of speech. *Journal of Acoustica. Society of America*, *87*(4), 1738–1752. PMID:2341679

Hermansky, H., & Morgan, N. (1994). RASTA processing of speech. *IEEE Transactions on Speech and Audio Processing*, *2*(4), 578–589. doi:10.1109/89.326616

Herremans, D., & Chew, E. (2017). MorpheuS: Generating structured music with constrained patterns and tension. *IEEE Transactions on Affective Computing*, *10*(4), 510–523. doi:10.1109/TAFFC.2017.2737984

Hersh, M. (2013). Deafblind people, communication, independence, and isolation. *Journal of Deaf Studies and Deaf Education*, *18*(4), 446–463. doi:10.1093/deafed/ent022 PMID:23749484

Heusel, M., Ramsauer, H., Unterthiner, T., Nessler, B., & Hochreiter, S. (2017). Gans trained by a two time-scale update rule converge to a local nash equilibrium. *Advances in Neural Information Processing Systems*, 30.

Hikawa, H., Ichikawa, Y., Ito, H., & Maeda, Y. (2021). Dynamic gesture recognition system with gesture spotting based on self-organizing maps. *Applied Sciences (Basel, Switzerland)*, *11*(4), 1933. doi:10.3390/app11041933

Hills, R., Renner, D., Lott, P. S., & Valli, C. (2021). *The Gallaudet dictionary of American sign language.* Gallaudet University Press.

Hinton, G. E., Dayan, P., Frey, B. J., & Neal, R. (1995). The wake-sleep algorithm for unsupervised neural networks. *Science*, *268*(5214), 1158–1161. doi:10.1126cience.7761831 PMID:7761831

Hinz, T., Heinrich, S., & Wermter, S. (2018, September). Generating Multiple Objects at Spatially Distinct Locations. *International Conference on Learning Representations.*

Hinz, T., Heinrich, S., & Wermter, S. (2020). Semantic object accuracy for generative text-to-image synthesis. *IEEE Transactions on Pattern Analysis and Machine Intelligence.* PMID:32877332

Hizlisoy, S., Yildirim, S., & Tufekci, Z. (2021). Music emotion recognition using convolutional long short-term memory deep neural networks. *Engineering Science and Technology, an International Journal*, *24*(3), 760-767.

Home| Linguistic Data Consortium. (n.d.). Retrieved May 15, 2022, from https://www.ldc.upenn.edu/

Hossain, M. Z., Sohel, F., Shiratuddin, M. F., & Laga, H. (2019). A comprehensive survey of deep learning for image captioning. *ACM Computing Surveys*, *51*(6), 1–36. doi:10.1145/3295748

Hossain, M. Z., Sohel, F., Shiratuddin, M. F., Laga, H., & Bennamoun, M. (2021). Text to image synthesis for improved image captioning. *IEEE Access: Practical Innovations, Open Solutions*, *9*, 64918–64928. doi:10.1109/ACCESS.2021.3075579

HTK speech Recognition Toolkit. (n.d.). Retrieved May 15, 2022, from https://htk.eng.cam.ac.uk/

Huang, W. Z., Li, H., & Li, W. (2015). Sign language recognition using 3d convolutional neural networks. In *IEEE international conference on multimedia and expo (ICME)* (pp. 1–6). IEEE Publications.

Huang, J. X., Lee, K. S., & Kim, Y. K. (2020). Hybrid Translation with Classification: Revisiting Rule-Based and Neural Machine Translation. *Electronics (Basel)*, *9*(2), 201. doi:10.3390/electronics9020201

Huang, X. D., & Jack, M. A. (1988). Hidden Markov modelling of speech based on a semicontinuous model. *Electronics Letters*, *24*(1), 6–7. doi:10.1049/el:19880004

Huang, X. D., & Jack, M. A. (1989). Semi-continuous hidden Markov models for speech signals. *Computer Speech & Language*, *3*(3), 239–251. doi:10.1016/0885-2308(89)90020-X

Huh, M., Liu, A., Owens, A., & Efros, A. A. (2018). Fighting Fake News: Image Splice Detection Via Learned Self-Consistency. *Proceedings Of The European Conference On Computer Vision (Eccv)*, 101–117. 10.1007/978-3-030-01252-6_7

Hutchings, P. E., & McCormack, J. (2019). Adaptive music composition for games. *IEEE Transactions on Games*, *12*(3), 270–280. doi:10.1109/TG.2019.2921979

Ismail, M. H., Dawwd, S. A., & Ali, F. H. (2021, December). Arabic Sign Language Detection Using Deep Learning Based Pose Estimation. In 2021 2nd Information Technology To Enhance e-learning and Other Application (IT-ELA) (pp. 161-166). IEEE. doi:10.1109/IT-ELA52201.2021.9773404

Ivašić-Kos, M., & Hrga, I. (2019, May). Deep image captioning: An overview. In *2019 42nd International Convention on Information and Communication Technology, Electronics and Microelectronics (MIPRO)* (pp. 995-1000). IEEE.

Jafari, M. R. (2020). *Persian sign gesture translation to English spoken language on smartphone* [Doctoral Dissertation]. Delhi Technological University.

Jason. (n.d.). https://machinelearningmastery.com/ridge-regression-with-python/

Jayanthi, P., & Thyagharajan, K. K. (2013). Tamil alphabets sign language translator. *5th Int. Conf. Adv. Comput. ICoAC 2013*, 383–388. 10.1109/ICoAC.2013.6921981

Jean, F., Kowtko, M.A., Yamagata, C., & Joyce, S. (2013). *Applying Mobile Application Development to Help Dementia and Alzheimer Patients*. Academic Press.

Jiao, M., Wang, D., & Qiu, J. (2020). A GRU-RNN-based momentum optimized algorithm for SOC estimation. *Journal of Power Sources*, *459*, 228051. doi:10.1016/j.jpowsour.2020.228051

JSpeech Grammar Format. (2000). Retrieved May 15, 2022, from https://www.w3.org/TR/jsgf/

Juang, B. H., & Rabiner, L. R. (1991). Hidden Markov Models for Speech Recognition. *Technometrics*, *33*(3), 251–272. doi:10.1080/00401706.1991.10484833

Jumper, J., Evans, R., Pritzel, A., Green, T., Figurnov, M., Ronneberger, O., Tunyasuvunakool, K., Bates, R., Žídek, A., Potapenko, A., Bridgland, A., Meyer, C., Kohl, S. A. A., Ballard, A. J., Cowie, A., Romera-Paredes, B., Nikolov, S., Jain, R., Adler, J., & Hassabis, D. (2021). Highly accurate protein structure prediction with AlphaFold. *Nature*, *596*(7873), 583–589. doi:10.103841586-021-03819-2 PMID:34265844

Kalchbrenner, N., Espeholt, L., Simonyan, K., Oord, A. V. D., Graves, A., & Kavukcuoglu, K. (2016). *Neural machine translation in linear time*. arXiv preprint arXiv:1610.10099.

Kaldi-ASR. (n.d.). Retrieved May 15, 2022, from https://kaldi-asr.org/

Kansara, D., Singh, R., Sanghvi, D., & Kanani, P. (2018). Improving accuracy of real estate valuation using stacked regression. *Int. J. Eng. Dev. Res.*, *6*(3), 571–577.

Karakoc, E., & Yilmaz, B. (2019). Deep learning based abstractive Turkish news summarization. *2019 27th Signal Processing and Communications Applications Conference (SIU)*.

Karande, H., Walambe, R., Benjamin, V., Kotecha, K., & Raghu, T. S. (2021). Stance detection with BERT embeddings for credibility analysis of information on social media. *PeerJ. Computer Science*, 7, e467. doi:10.7717/peerj-cs.467 PMID:33954243

Karpe, V., Kabadi, S., Mutgekar, A., & Pokharkar, M. (2014). Controlling Device through Speech Recognition System. *International Journal of Advanced Research in Computer Science and Software Engineering*, 4(2), 1020–1024.

Karpov, I., & Glazkova, E. (2020). Detecting Automatically Managed Accounts In Online Social Networks: Graph Embeddings Approach. *International Conference On Analysis Of Images, Social Networks And Texts*, 11–21.

Karras, T., Laine, S., Aittala, M., Hellsten, J., Lehtinen, J., & Aila, T. (2020). Analyzing and improving the image quality of stylegan. In *Proceedings of the IEEE/CVF conference on computer vision and pattern recognition* (pp. 8110-8119). 10.1109/CVPR42600.2020.00813

Kasukurthi, N., Rokad, B., Bidani, S., & Dennisan, D. A. (2019). *American sign language alphabet recognition using deep learning*. Academic Press.

Kavarthapu, D. C., & Mitra, K. (2017). Hand gesture sequence recognition using inertial motion units (IMUs). *Proceedings of the 4th IAPR Asian Conference. Pattern Recognition (ACPR)*, 953–957. 10.1109/ACPR.2017.159

Khan, A., & Usman, M. (2015). Article. In *2015 7th International Joint Conference on Knowledge Discovery, Knowledge Engineering and Knowledge Management (IC3K)*. IEEE.

Kikel, C. (2022). A *Brief History of Voice Recognition Technology | Total Voice Technologies*. Retrieved May 15, 2022, from https://www.totalvoicetech.com/a-brief-history-of-voice-recognition-technology/

Kim, D. S., Jeong, J. H., Kim, J. W., & Lee, S. Y. (1996, May). Feature extraction based on zero-crossings with peak amplitudes for robust speech recognition in noisy environments. In *Proceedings of the 1996 IEEE International Conference on Acoustics, Speech, and Signal Processing* (vol. 1, pp. 61-64). IEEE. 10.1109/ICASSP.1996.540290

Klatt, D. (1987). A review of text-to-speech conversion for English. *The Journal of the Acoustical Society of America*, 3(3), 737–793. doi:10.1121/1.395275 PMID:2958525

Klatt, D. H. (1977). Review of the ARPA speech understanding project. *The Journal of the Acoustical Society of America*, 62(6), 1345–1366. doi:10.1121/1.381666

Koehn, P., & Knowles, R. (2017). *Six challenges for neural machine translation*. arXiv preprint arXiv:1706.03872. doi:10.18653/v1/W17-3204

Kohler, T. W., Fugen, C., Stüker, S., & Waibel, A. (2005). Rapid porting of ASR-systems to mobile devices. In *Proceedings of the Ninth European Conference on Speech Communication and Technology* (pp. 233-236). 10.21437/Interspeech.2005-116

Kolozali, Ş., Barthet, M., Fazekas, G., & Sandler, M. (2013). Automatic ontology generation for musical instruments based on audio analysis. *IEEE Transactions on Audio, Speech, and Language Processing*, 21(10), 2207–2220. doi:10.1109/TASL.2013.2263801

Koul, M., Patil, P., Nandurkar, V., & Patil, S. (2016). Sign language recognition using leap motion sensor. *International Research Journal of Engineering and Technology*, 3(11), 322–325.

Kozik, S., Kula, S., Choraś, M., & Woźniak, M. (2022). Technical Solution To Counter Potential Crime: Text Analysis To Detect Fake News And Disinformation. *Journal of Computational Science*, 60, 101576. doi:10.1016/j.jocs.2022.101576

KR, P., Mukhopadhyay, R., Philip, J., Jha, A., Namboodiri, V., & Jawahar, C. V. (2019, October). Towards automatic face-to-face translation. In *Proceedings of the 27th ACM international conference on multimedia* (pp. 1428-1436). ACM.

Küçük, D. (2021). *Stance quantification: Definition of the problem.* arXiv preprint arXiv:2112.13288.

Küçük, D., & Can, F. (2020). Stance detection: A survey. *ACM Computing Surveys, 53*(1), 1–37. doi:10.1145/3369026

Küçük, D., & Can, F. (2021). Stance detection: Concepts, approaches, resources, and outstanding issues. In *Proceedings of the 44th International ACM SIGIR Conference on Research and Development in Information Retrieval* (pp. 2673-2676). ACM.

Küçük, D., & Can, F. (2022). A tutorial on stance detection. In *Proceedings of the Fifteenth ACM International Conference on Web Search and Data Mining* (pp. 1626-1628). 10.1145/3488560.3501391

Kudo, T., & Richardson, J. (2018). SentencePiece: A simple and language independent subword tokenizer and detokenizer for neural text processing. *Proceedings of the 2018 Conference on Empirical Methods in Natural Language Processing: System Demonstrations*, 66–71. 10.18653/v1/D18-2012

Kudugunta, S., & Ferrara, E. (2018). Deep Neural Networks For Bot Detection. *Information Sciences, 467*, 312–322. doi:10.1016/j.ins.2018.08.019

Kumar, K. C., Aswale, S., Shetgaonkar, P., Pawar, V., Kale, D., & Kamat, S. (2020, February). A Survey of Machine Translation Approaches for Konkani to English. In *2020 International Conference on Emerging Trends in Information Technology and Engineering (ic-ETITE)* (pp. 1-6). IEEE.

Kumar, R., Sotelo, J., Kumar, K., de Brébisson, A., & Bengio, Y. (2017). *Obamanet: Photo-realistic lip-sync from text.* arXiv preprint arXiv:1801.01442.

Kumar, A., & Aggarwal, R. K. (2022). Hindi speech recognition using time delay neural network acoustic modeling with i-vector adaptation. *International Journal of Speech Technology, 25*(1), 67–78. doi:10.100710772-020-09757-0

Kumar, K., Srikar, V. S., Swapnika, Y., Sravani, V. S., & Aditya, N. (2020). A novel approach for Morse code detection from eye blinks and decoding using OpenCV. *International Journal for Research in Applied Science and Engineering Technology*, 8. doi:10.22214/ijraset.2020.30811

Kunchukuttan, A., Mehta, P., & Bhattacharyya, P. (2017). *The iit bombay english-hindi parallel corpus.* arXiv preprint arXiv:1710.02855.

Kutlu, M., Cığır, C., & Cicekli, I. (2010). Generic Text Summarization for Turkish. *24th International Symposium on Computer and Information Sciences*, 224-229.

Kuutti, S., Bowden, R., Jin, Y., Barber, P., & Fallah, S. (2021, February). A Survey of Deep Learning Applications to Autonomous Vehicle Control. *IEEE Transactions on Intelligent Transportation Systems, 22*(2), 712–733. doi:10.1109/TITS.2019.2962338

Kuznetsova, A., Leal-Taixé, L., & Rosenhahn, B. (2013). Real-time sign language recognition using a consumer depth camera. In *Proceedings of the IEEE International Conference on Computer Vision Workshops* (pp. 83–90). 10.1109/ICCVW.2013.18

Lakhotiya, H., Pandita, H. S., & Shankarmani, R. (2021, May). Real Time Sign Language Recognition Using Image Classification. In *2021 2nd International Conference for Emerging Technology (INCET)* (pp. 1-4). IEEE. 10.1109/INCET51464.2021.9456432

Lakshmana Pandian, S., & Geetha, T. V. (2008). Tamil Question Classification Using Morpheme Features. In B. Nordström & A. Ranta (Eds.), Lecture Notes in Computer Science: Vol. 5221. *Advances in Natural Language Processing. GoTAL 2008*. Springer. doi:10.1007/978-3-540-85287-2_26

Lample, G., Ott, M., Conneau, A., Denoyer, L., & Ranzato, M. A. (2018). *Phrase-based & neural unsupervised machine translation*. arXiv preprint arXiv:1804.07755. doi:10.18653/v1/D18-1549

Landicho, J. A. (2016). Voice Communicator: An Android Mobile Application for Hearing-impaired and Blind Communications. *Int. J. Interact. Mob. Technol.*, *10*(4), 26–31. doi:10.3991/ijim.v10i4.5859

LDC-IL. (n.d.). Retrieved May 15, 2022, from https://www.ldcil.org/resourcesSpeechCorp.aspx

Lee, B. G., Chong, T. W., & Chung, W. Y. (2020). Sensor fusion of motion-based sign language interpretation with deep learning. *Sensors (Basel)*, *20*(21), 6256. doi:10.339020216256 PMID:33147891

Lee, B. G., & Lee, S. M. (2018). Smart wearable hand device for sign language interpretation system with sensors fusion. *IEEE Sensors Journal*, *18*(3), 1224–1232. doi:10.1109/JSEN.2017.2779466

Lee, T. W. (1998). Independent component analysis. In *Independent component analysis* (pp. 27–66). Springer. doi:10.1007/978-1-4757-2851-4_2

Lewis, M., Liu, Y., Goyal, N., Ghazvininejad, M., Mohamed, A., Levy, O., Stoyanov, V., & Zettlemoyer, L. (2019). BART: Denoising Sequence-to-Sequence Pre-training for Natural Language Generation. *Translation, and Comprehension. Proceedings of the 58th Annual Meeting of the Association for Computational Linguistics*, 7871–7880.

Li, H. (2020). Piano automatic computer composition by deep learning and blockchain technology. *IEEE Access: Practical Innovations, Open Solutions*, *8*, 188951–188958. doi:10.1109/ACCESS.2020.3031155

Lin, J., Sun, X., Ma, S., & Su, Q. (2018). Global Encoding for Abstractive Summarization. In *Proceedings of the 56th Annual Meeting of the Association for Computational Linguistics* (*vol 2*: Short Papers, pp. 163–169). Academic Press.

Lin, C. Y. (2004). ROUGE: A package for automatic evaluation of summaries. *Workshop on Text Summarization Branches Out*, 74-81.

Lin, T. Y., Maire, M., Belongie, S., Hays, J., Perona, P., Ramanan, D., ... Zitnick, C. L. (2014, September). Microsoft coco: Common objects in context. In *European conference on computer vision* (pp. 740-755). Springer.

Liu, X., Gong, C., Wu, L., Zhang, S., Su, H., & Liu, Q. (2021). *Fusedream: Training-free text-to-image generation with improved clip+ gan space optimization*. arXiv preprint arXiv:2112.01573.

Liu, Y., & Fung, P. (2000). Rule-based word pronunciation networks generation for Mandarin speech recognition. In *Proceedings of the International Symposium of Chinese Spoken Language Processing (ISCSLP'00)* (pp. 35–38). Academic Press.

Liu, Y., & Lapata, M. (2019). *Text Summarization with Pretrained Encoders*. Arxiv: 1908.08345

Liu, Y., Ott, M., Goyal, N., Du, J., Joshi, M., Chen, D., . . . Stoyanov, V. (2019). *RoBERTa: A robustly optimized BERT pretraining approach*. arXiv preprint arXiv:1907.11692.

Liu, F., Zhang, L., & Jin, Z. (2020). Modeling programs hierarchically with stack-augmented LSTM. *Journal of Systems and Software*, *164*, 110547. doi:10.1016/j.jss.2020.110547

Liu, H., & Wang, L. (2018). Gesture recognition for human-robot collaboration: A review. *International Journal of Industrial Ergonomics*, *68*, 355–367. doi:10.1016/j.ergon.2017.02.004

Liu, N., Zhou, T., Ji, Y., Zhao, Z., & Wan, L. (2020). Synthesizing talking faces from text and audio: An autoencoder and sequence-to-sequence convolutional neural network. *Pattern Recognition*, *102*, 107231. doi:10.1016/j.patcog.2020.107231

Liu, Y., & Fung, P. (2004). State-dependent phonetic tied mixtures with pronunciation modeling for spontaneous speech recognition. *IEEE Transactions on Speech and Audio Processing*, *12*(4), 351–364. doi:10.1109/TSA.2004.828638

Liu, Y., Gu, J., Goyal, N., Li, X., Edunov, S., Ghazvininejad, M., Lewis, M., & Zettlemoyer, L. (2020). Multilingual Denoising Pre-training for Neural Machine Translation. *Transactions of the Association for Computational Linguistics*, *8*, 726–742. doi:10.1162/tacl_a_00343

Li, X., Lu, P., Hu, L., Wang, X., & Lu, L. (2022). A Novel Self-Learning Semi-Supervised Deep Learning Network To Detect Fake News On Social Media. *Multimedia Tools and Applications*, *81*(14), 19341–19349. doi:10.100711042-021-11065-x PMID:34093070

Lo, K.-C., Dai, S.-C., Xiong, A., Jiang, J., & Ku, L.-W. (2022). Victor: An Implicit Approach To Mitigate Misinformation Via Continuous Verification Reading. *Proceedings Of The Acm Web Conference 2022*, 3511–3519. 10.1145/3485447.3512246

Low, C. C., Ong, L. Y., Koo, V. C., & Leow, M. C. (2020). Multi-audience tracking with RGB-D camera on digital signage. *Heliyon*, *6*(9), e05107. doi:10.1016/j.heliyon.2020.e05107 PMID:33024875

Lowerre, B. T. (1976). *The Harpy Speech Recognition System* [Unpublished doctoral dissertation]. Carnegie Mellon University, Pittsburgh, PA, United States.

Lu, S., Li, Z., Qin, Z., Yang, X., & Goh, R. S. M. (2017, December). A hybrid regression technique for house prices prediction. In 2017 IEEE international conference on industrial engineering and engineering management (IEEM) (pp. 319-323). IEEE. doi:10.1109/IEEM.2017.8289904

Lucassen, J., & Mercer, R. (1984). An information theoretic approach to the automatic determination of phonemic baseforms. In *Proceedings of the IEEE International Conference on Acoustics, Speech, and Signal Processing (ICASSP'84)* (vol. 9, pp. 304-307). IEEE. 10.1109/ICASSP.1984.1172810

Luong, M. T., Pham, H., & Manning, C. D. (2015). *Effective approaches to attention-based neural machine translation.* arXiv preprint arXiv:1508.04025. doi:10.18653/v1/D15-1166

Lwowski, B., & Najafirad, P. (2020). *Covid-19 surveillance through twitter using self-supervised and few shot learning.* Academic Press.

Ma, Yu, Wang, & Wang. (2015). Large-scale transportation network congestion evolution prediction using deep learning theory. *PLoS ONE*, *10*(3), e0119044

Maas, A. L., Qi, P., Xie, Z., Hannun, A. Y., Lengerich, C. T., Jurafsky, D., & Ng, A. Y. (2017). Building DNN acoustic models for large vocabulary speech recognition. *Computer Speech & Language*, *41*, 195–213. doi:10.1016/j.csl.2016.06.007

Machine learning algorithms in human language. (2018, August 13). Datakeen. Available: https://www.datakeen.co/en/8-machine-learning-algorithms-explained-in-human-language/

Madeo, R. C. B., Wagner, P. K., & Peres, S. M. (2013). *A review of temporal aspects of hand gesture analysis applied to discourse analysis and natural conversation.* arXiv preprint arXiv:1312.4640.

Makhoul, J. (1975). Linear prediction: A tutorial review. *Proceedings of the IEEE*, *63*(4), 561–580. doi:10.1109/PROC.1975.9792

Manickam, A., Haldar, R., Saqlain, S. M., Sellam, V., & Soundrapandiyan, R. (2019). Fingerprint image classification using local diagonal and directional extrema patterns. *Journal of Electronic Imaging*, *28*(3), 033027. doi:10.1117/1.JEI.28.3.033027

ManishK. S. (n.d.). https://manish-ks.medium.com/advantages-and-disadvantages-of-linear-regression-its-assumptions-evaluation-and-implementation-61437fc551ad/

Marra, F., Gragnaniello, D., Cozzolino, D., & Verdoliva, L. (2018). Detection Of Gan-Generated Fake Images Over Social Networks. *2018 IEEE Conference On Multimedia Information Processing And Retrieval (Mipr),* 384–389.

Matero, M., Soni, N., Balasubramanian, N., & Schwartz, H. A. (2021). *MeLT: Message-level transformer with masked document representations as pre-training for stance detection.* arXiv preprint arXiv:2109.08113. doi:10.18653/v1/2021. findings-emnlp.253

Math. (n.d.). https://www.mathworks.com/matlabcentral/fileexchange/63122-kernel-ridge-regression/

Matoušek, J., & Vít, J. (2012, March). Improving automatic dubbing with subtitle timing optimisation using video cut detection. In *2012 IEEE International Conference on Acoustics, Speech and Signal Processing (ICASSP)* (pp. 2385-2388). IEEE. 10.1109/ICASSP.2012.6288395

Maučec, M. S., & Donaj, G. (2019). Machine Translation and the Evaluation of Its Quality. In Natural Language Processing-New Approaches and Recent Applications. IntechOpen.

MehtaD. (n.d.). https://github.com/dhruv-mehta2604/housePricePrediction/

Meisel, W. (2010). "Life on-the-Go": The Role of Speech Technology in Mobile Applications. In A. Neustein (Ed.), *Advances in Speech Recognition* (pp. 3–18). Springer. doi:10.1007/978-1-4419-5951-5_1

Mendes, J. J. A. Junior, Freitas, M. B., Campos, D. P., Farinelli, F. A., Stevan, S. L., & Pichorim, S. F. (2020). Analysis of influence of segmentation, features, and classification in sEMG processing: A case study of recognition of Brazilian sign language alphabet. *Sensors (Basel),* 20(16), 4359. doi:10.339020164359 PMID:32764286

Mikolov, T., Karafiát, M., Burget, L., Černocký, J., & Khudanpur, S. (2010). Recurrent neural network based language model. In *Proceedings of the Eleventh annual conference of the international speech communication association* (pp. 1045-1048). Academic Press.

Ming, Y., Zhang, J., Qi, J., Liao, T., Wang, M., & Zhang, L. (2020, September). Prediction and analysis of chengdu housing rent based on xgboost algorithm. In *Proceedings of the 2020 3rd International Conference on Big Data Technologies* (pp. 1-5). 10.1145/3422713.3422720

MishraD. (n.d.). https://towardsdatascience.com/regression-an-explanation-of-regression-metrics-and-what-can-go-wrong-a39a9793d914

Mittal, P., & Singh, N. (2020). Subword analysis of small vocabulary and large vocabulary ASR for Punjabi language. *International Journal of Speech Technology,* 23(1), 71–78. doi:10.100710772-020-09673-3

Mittal, S., & Umesh, S. (2021). A survey on hardware accelerators and optimization techniques for RNNs. *Journal of Systems Architecture,* 112, 101839. doi:10.1016/j.sysarc.2020.101839

Modi, M., Sharma, A., & Madhavan, D. P. (2020). Applied research on house price prediction using diverse machine learning techniques. *International Journal of Scientific & Technology Research,* 9(04).

Mohammad, S., Kiritchenko, S., Sobhani, P., Zhu, X., & Cherry, C. (2016). SemEval-2016 Task 6: Detecting stance in tweets. In *Proceedings of the 10th International Workshop on Semantic Evaluation (SemEval-2016)* (pp. 31-41). 10.18653/v1/S16-1003

Mondal, S. K., Sahoo, J. P., Wang, J., Mondal, K., & Rahman, M. (2022). Fake News Detection Exploiting Tf-Idf Vectorization With Ensemble Learning Models. In *Advances In Distributed Computing And Machine Learning* (pp. 261–270). Springer.

Mosallanezhad, A., Karami, M., Shu, K., Mancenido, M. V., & Liu, H. (2022). Domain Adaptive Fake News Detection Via Reinforcement Learning. *Proceedings Of The Acm Web Conference 2022*, 3632–3640. 10.1145/3485447.3512258

Mu, J., Wu, F., & Zhang, A. (2014, August). Housing value forecasting based on machine learning methods. In *Abstract and Applied Analysis* (Vol. 2014). Hindawi.

Mukherjee, H., Dhar, A., Ghosh, M., Obaidullah, S. M., Santosh, K. C., Phadikar, S., & Roy, K. (2020). Music chord inversion shape identification with LSTM-RNN. *Procedia Computer Science*, *167*, 607–615. doi:10.1016/j.procs.2020.03.327

Muthu Mariappan, H., & Gomathi, V. (2019). Real-time recognition of Indian sign language. *ICCIDS - 2nd Int. Conf. Comput. Intell. Data Sci. Proc.*, 1–6. 10.1109/ICCIDS.2019.8862125

Nagarajan, S., & Subashini, T. (2013). Static hand gesture recognition for sign language alphabets using edge oriented histogram and multi class svm. *International Journal of Computers and Applications*, *82*(4), 28–35. doi:10.5120/14106-2145

Nallapati, R., Zhou, B., Nogueira, C., Gulcehre, C., & Xiang, B. (2016). Abstractive text summarization using sequence-to-sequence RNNs and beyond. *Proceedings of the 20th SIGNLL Conference on Computational Natural Language Learning*, 280–290.

National Speech Corpus-Infocomm Media Development Authority. (n.d.). Retrieved May 15, 2022, from https://www.imda.gov.sg/programme-listing/digital-services-lab/national-speech-corpus

Neptune. (n.d.). https://neptune.ai/blog/xgboost-vs-lightgbm

Neustein, A. (2010). *Advances in speech recognition: mobile environments, call centers and clinics*. Springer Science & Business Media. doi:10.1007/978-1-4419-5951-5

Nishimura, Y., Sudoh, K., Neubig, G., & Nakamura, S. (2019). Multi-source neural machine translation with missing data. *IEEE/ACM Transactions on Audio, Speech, and Language Processing*, *28*, 569–580. doi:10.1109/TASLP.2019.2959224

Nkosi, M., Manamela, M., & Gasela, N. (2011). Creating a Pronunciation Dictionary for Automatic Speech Recognition - a Morphological approach. In *Proceedings of the Southern Africa Telecommunication Networks and Applications Conference (SATNAC)* (pp. 1-5). Academic Press.

O'Brien, K., Simek, O., & Waugh, F. (2019). *Collective Classification For Social Media Credibility Estimation*. Academic Press.

Oflazer, K., & Durgar, I. (2007). Exploring Different Representational Units in English-to-Turkish Statistical Machine Translation. *Proceedings of the Second Workshop on Statistical Machine Translation*, 25-32. 10.3115/1626355.1626359

Öktem, A., Farrús, M., & Bonafonte, A. (2019). *Prosodic phrase alignment for machine dubbing*. arXiv preprint arXiv:1908.07226.

Olah, C. (2018). *Understanding LSTM Networks-Colah's Blog*. https://colah. github. io/posts/2015-08-Understanding-LSTMs/

OpenSLR.org- LibriSpeech. (n.d.). Retrieved August 20, 2022 from https://www.openslr.org/12

OpenSLR.org- TED-LIUM. (n.d.). Retrieved August 20, 2022 from https://www.openslr.org/51

Ott, M., Edunov, S., Grangier, D., & Auli, M. (2018). *Scaling neural machine translation.* arXiv preprint arXiv:1806.00187. doi:10.18653/v1/W18-6301

Paka, W. S., Bansal, R., Kaushik, A., Sengupta, S., & Chakraborty, T. (2021). Cross-SEAN: A cross-stitch semi-supervised neural attention model for COVID-19 fake news detection. *Applied Soft Computing, 107,* 107393. doi:10.1016/j.asoc.2021.107393

Palani, B., Elango, S., & Viswanathan, K. (2022). Cb-Fake: A Multimodal Deep Learning Framework For Automatic Fake News Detection Using Capsule Neural Network And Bert. *Multimedia Tools and Applications, 81*(4), 5587–5620. doi:10.100711042-021-11782-3 PMID:34975284

Pandian, S. L., & Geetha, T. V. (2009). CRF Models for Tamil Part of Speech Tagging and Chunking. In W. Li & D. Mollá-Aliod (Eds.), Lecture Notes in Computer Science: Vol. 5459. *Computer Processing of Oriental Languages. Language Technology for the Knowledge-based Economy. ICCPOL 2009.* Springer. doi:10.1007/978-3-642-00831-3_2

Pandian, S. L., & Pavithra, K. A. (2008). Hybrid, Three-stage Named Entity Recognizer for Tamil. *Info,* S2008.

Pandian, S., & Geetha, T. V. (2008). Morpheme based Language Model for Tamil Part-of-Speech Tagging. *Polibits, 38,* 19–25. doi:10.17562/PB-38-2

Papineni, K., Roukos, S., Ward, T., & Zhu, W. (2002). Bleu: a method for automatic evaluation of machine translation. *Proceedings of the 40th Annual Meeting of the Association for Computational Linguistics (ACL),* 311-318.

Pariwat, T., & Seresangtakul, P. (2021). Multi-stroke Thai finger-spelling sign language recognition system with deep learning. *Symmetry, 13*(2), 262. doi:10.3390ym13020262

Park, H., Takiguchi, T., & Ariki, Y. (2009). Integrated phoneme subspace method for speech feature extraction. *EURASIP Journal on Audio, Speech, and Music Processing, 2009,* 1–6. doi:10.1155/2009/690451

Park, S., Kim, B., Kang, C. M., Chung, C. C., & Choi, J. W. (2018). Sequence-to-Sequence Prediction of Vehicle Trajectory via LSTM Encoder-Decoder Architecture. *2018 IEEE Intelligent Vehicles Symposium (IV),* 1672-1678. 10.1109/IVS.2018.8500658

Patel, A., & Meehan, K. (2021). Fake News Detection On Reddit Utilising Countvectorizer And Term Frequency-Inverse Document Frequency With Logistic Regression, Multinominalnb And Support Vector Machine. *2021 32nd Irish Signals And Systems Conference (Issc),* 1–6.

Pathak & Chaudhari. (2021). Comparison of Machine Learning Algorithms for House Price Prediction using Real Time Data. *International Journal of Engineering Research & Technology, 10*(12).

Patwari, N., & Naik, D. (2021, April). En-de-cap: An encoder decoder model for image captioning. In *2021 5th International Conference on Computing Methodologies and Communication (ICCMC)* (pp. 1192-1196). IEEE.

Paul, A. J., Mohan, P., & Sehgal, S. (2020). Rethinking generalization in American sign language prediction for edge devices with extremely low memory footprint. 2020 IEEE recent Adv. *Intell. Comput. Syst. RAICS, 2020,* 147–152. doi:10.1109/RAICS51191.2020.9332480

Pearson, K. (1901). On Lines and Planes of Closest Fit to Systems of Points in Space. *Philosophical Magazine, 2*(11), 559–572.

Pendyala, V. (2018). *Veracity of Big Data: Machine Learning and Other Approaches to Verifying Truthfulness.* Apress. doi:10.1007/978-1-4842-3633-8

Pendyala, V. S. (2019). Securing Trust In Online Social Networks. *International Conference On Secure Knowledge Management In Artificial Intelligence Era*, 194–201.

Pendyala, V. S., & Figueira, S. (2015, October). Towards a truthful world wide web from a humanitarian perspective. In *2015 IEEE Global Humanitarian Technology Conference (GHTC)* (pp. 137-143). IEEE. 10.1109/GHTC.2015.7343966

Pendyala, V. S., Liu, Y., & Figueira, S. M. (2018). A Framework For Detecting Injected Influence Attacks On Microblog Websites Using Change Detection Techniques. *Development Engineering, 3*, 218–233. doi:10.1016/j.deveng.2018.08.002

Philippe, D., & Hermann, N. (2008). Visual modeling and feature adaptation in sign language recognition. *Voice communication (SprachKommunikation) ITG Conference on*, 1–4.

Pigou, Van Herreweghe, & Dambre. (2017). Gesture and sign language recognition with temporal residual networks. *IEEE International Conference on Computer Vision (ICCV) Workshops*.

Pouyanfar, Sadiq, Yan, Tian, Tao, Reyes, Shyu, Chen, & Iyengar. (2018). A Survey on Deep Learning: Algorithms, Techniques, and Applications. *ACM Comput. Surv., 51*(5). doi:10.1145/3234150

Punsara, K. K. T. (2020). IoT based sign language recognition system. *ICAC - 2nd Int. Conf. Adv. Comput. Proc., 162–167*. 10.1109/ICAC51239.2020.9357267

Qiao, Y., Hashimoto, K., Eriguchi, A., Wang, H., Wang, D., Tsuruoka, Y., & Taura, K. (2020). Parallelizing and optimizing neural Encoder–Decoder models without padding on multi-core architecture. *Future Generation Computer Systems, 108*, 1206–1213. doi:10.1016/j.future.2018.04.070

Qi, Y., Liu, Y., & Sun, Q. (2019). Music-driven dance generation. *IEEE Access: Practical Innovations, Open Solutions, 7*, 166540–166550. doi:10.1109/ACCESS.2019.2953698

Quach, T., & Farooq, M. (1994). Maximum Likelihood Track Formation with the Viterbi Algorithm. In *Proceedings of the 33rd IEEE Conference on Decision and Control* (pp. 271–276). 10.1109/CDC.1994.410918

Rabiner, L. R. (1989). A tutorial on Hidden Markov models and selected applications in speech recognition. *Proceedings of the IEEE, 77*(2), 257–286. doi:10.1109/5.18626

Rachabathuni, P. K. (2017). A survey on abstractive summarization techniques. In *Inventive computing and informatics* (pp. 762–765). ICICI.

Radford, A., Narasimhan, K., Salimans, T., & Sutskever, I. (2018). *Improving language understanding by generative pre-training*. Academic Press.

Radford, A., Kim, J. W., Hallacy, C., Ramesh, A., Goh, G., Agarwal, S., ... Sutskever, I. (2021, July). Learning transferable visual models from natural language supervision. In *International Conference on Machine Learning* (pp. 8748-8763). PMLR.

Raffel, C., Shazeer, N., Roberts, A., Lee, K., Narang, S., Matena, M., Zhou, Y., Li, W., & Liu, P. (2020). Exploring the Limits of Transfer Learning with a Unified Text-to-Text Transformer. *Journal of Machine Learning Research*, 1–67.

Rajalaxmi, R., Narasimha Prasad, L., Janakiramaiah, B., Pavankumar, C., Neelima, N., & Sathishkumar, V. (2022). Optimizing Hyperparameters And Performance Analysis Of Lstm Model. In *Detecting Fake News On Social Media*. Transactions On Asian And Low-Resource Language Information Processing.

Ramesh, A., Pavlov, M., Goh, G., Gray, S., Voss, C., Radford, A., ... Sutskever, I. (2021, July). Zero-shot text-to-image generation. In *International Conference on Machine Learning* (pp. 8821-8831). PMLR.

Rao, K., Peng, F., & Beaufays, F. (2015, April). Automatic pronunciation verification for speech recognition. In *Proceedings of the 2015 IEEE International Conference on Acoustics, Speech and Signal Processing (ICASSP)* (pp. 5162-5166). IEEE. 10.1109/ICASSP.2015.7178955

Rastgoo, R., Kiani, K., & Escalera, S. (2020). Video-based isolated hand sign language recognition using a deep cascaded model. *Multimedia Tools and Applications*, *79*(31–32), 22965–22987. doi:10.100711042-020-09048-5

Rastogi, R., Mittal, S., & Agarwal, S. (2015, March). A novel approach for communication among Blind, Deaf, and Dumb people. In *2015 2nd International Conference on Computing for Sustainable Global Development (INDIACom)* (pp. 605-610). IEEE.

Rath, B., Salecha, A., & Srivastava, J. (2020, December). Detecting fake news spreaders in social networks using inductive representation learning. In *2020 IEEE/ACM International Conference on Advances in Social Networks Analysis and Mining (ASONAM)* (pp. 182-189). IEEE. 10.1109/ASONAM49781.2020.9381466

Reddy, T., Sanghvi, J., Vora, D., & Kanani, P. (2018). Wanderlust: A Personalised Travel Itinerary Recommender. *International Journal Of Engineering Development And Research IJEDR*, *6*(3), 78–83.

Reed, S., Akata, Z., Yan, X., Logeswaran, L., Schiele, B., & Lee, H. (2016). Generative adversarial text to image synthesis. *International conference on machine learning* (pp. 1060–1069). Academic Press.

Ren, Y., Zhang, Y., Zhang, M., & Ji, D. (2016). Context-sensitive Twitter sentiment classification using neural network. *Proceedings of the Thirtieth AAAI Conference on Artificial Intelligence*. 10.1609/aaai.v30i1.9974

Rizky, L. M. R., & Suyanto, S. (2021). Improving stance-based fake news detection using BERT model with synonym replacement and random swap data augmentation technique. In *Proceedings of the IEEE 7th Information Technology International Seminar (ITIS)* (pp. 1-6). 10.1109/ITIS53497.2021.9791600

RoccaJ. (n.d.). https://towardsdatascience.com/ensemble-methods-bagging-boosting-and-stacking-c9214a10a205

Rodgers, W., Yeung, F., Odindo, C., & Degbey, W. Y. (2021). Artificial intelligence-driven music biometrics influence customers' retail buying behavior. *Journal of Business Research*, *126*, 401–414. doi:10.1016/j.jbusres.2020.12.039

Rogers, A., Kovaleva, O., & Rumshisky, A. (2020). A primer in BERTology: What we know about how BERT works. *Transactions of the Association for Computational Linguistics*, *8*, 842–866. doi:10.1162/tacl_a_00349

Rönnberg, J., & Borg, E. (2001). A review and evaluation of research on the deaf-blind from perceptual, communicative, social, and rehabilitative perspectives. *Scandinavian Audiology*, *30*(2), 67–77. doi:10.1080/010503901300112176 PMID:11409790

Rublee, Rabaud, & Konolige. (2011). ORB: An efficient alternative to SIFT or SURF. *Proceedings of the IEEE International Conference on Computer Vision.*

Rush, A., Chopra, S., & Weston, J. (2015). A neural attention model for abstractive sentence summarization. *Proceedings of the 2015 Conference on Empirical Methods in Natural Language Processing*, 379–389. 10.18653/v1/D15-1044

Rutgersson, S., & Arvola, M. (2007). User interfaces for persons with deafblindness. In *Universal Access in Ambient Intelligence Environments* (pp. 317–334). Springer. doi:10.1007/978-3-540-71025-7_21

Saha, S. (2018). *A Comprehensive Guide to Convolutional Neural Networks — the ELI5 way.* Retrieved June 28, 2022, from https://towardsdatascience.com/a-comprehensive-guide-to-convolutional-neural-networks-the-eli5-way-3bd2b1164a53

Sahan, M., Smidl, V., & Marik, R. (2021). Active Learning For Text Classification And Fake News Detection. *2021 International Symposium On Computer Science And Intelligent Controls (Iscsic)*, 87–94. 10.1109/ISCSIC54682.2021.00027

Sajanraj, T. D., & Beena, M. (2018). Indian sign language numeral recognition using region of interest convolutional neural network. In *Proceedings of the 2nd International Conference Inventive Commun. Comput. Technol. (ICICCT)* (pp. 636–640). 10.1109/ICICCT.2018.8473141

Salem, F. K., Al Feel, R., Elbassuoni, S., Ghannam, H., Jaber, M., & Farah, M. (2021). Meta-learning for fake news detection surrounding the Syrian war. *Patterns*, 2(11), 100369. doi:10.1016/j.patter.2021.100369 PMID:34820650

Salimans, T., Goodfellow, I., Zaremba, W., Cheung, V., Radford, A., & Chen, X. (2016). Improved techniques for training gans. *Advances in Neural Information Processing Systems*, 29.

Samadi, M., Mousavian, M., & Momtazi, S. (2021). Deep contextualized text representation and learning for fake news detection. *Information Processing & Management*, 58(6), 102723. doi:10.1016/j.ipm.2021.102723

Sandhya, G., Babu Kande, G., & Savithri, T. S. (2017). Multilevel Thresholding Method Based on Electromagnetism for Accurate Brain MRI Segmentation to Detect White Matter, Gray Matter, and CSF. *BioMed Research International*, 2017, 1–17. doi:10.1155/2017/6783209 PMID:29250547

Saranya, M., Abinaya, A., Dhanesh Priya, K. S., Kowsalya, G., & Madhumitha, B. (2019). Design And Implementation of Raspberry Pibased Whistle to Voice Translation Usingmorse Code for Dumb and Blind People. *International Journal of Innovative Research in Advanced Engineering*, 3(6), 2349–2163.

Satish, G. N., Raghavendran, C. V., Rao, M. S., & Srinivasulu, C. (2019). House price prediction using machine learning. *Journal of Innovative Technology and Exploring Engineering*, 8(9), 717–722. doi:10.35940/ijitee.I7849.078919

Saxena, S. (2021). *Introduction to Long Short Term Memory (LSTM)*. Retrieved June 28, 2022, from https://www.analyticsvidhya.com/blog/2021/03/introduction-to-long-short-term-memory-lstm

Schalkwyk, J., Beeferman, D., Beaufays, F., Byrne, B., Chelba, C., Cohen, M., & Strope, B. (2010). Your word is my command. In *Google search by voice: A case study. Advances in speech recognition* (pp. 61–90). Springer. doi:10.1007/978-1-4419-5951-5_4

Schiller, I. S., Morsomme, D., & Remacle, A. (2018). Voice use among music theory teachers: Voice dosimetry and self-assessment study. *Journal of Voice*, 32(5), 578–584. doi:10.1016/j.jvoice.2017.06.020 PMID:28754577

Schuster, M., & Nakajima, K. (2012). Japanese and Korean voice search. *2012 IEEE International Conference on Acoustics, Speech and Signal Processing (ICASSP)*. 10.1109/ICASSP.2012.6289079

Scialom, T., Dray, P., Lamprier, S., Piwowarski, B., & Staiano, J. (2020). MLSUM: The Multilingual Summarization Corpus. *Proceedings of the 2020 Conference on Empirical Methods in Natural Language Processing*, 8051–8067. 10.18653/v1/2020.emnlp-main.647

Seim, C. E., Ritter, B., Starner, T. E., Flavin, K., Lansberg, M. G., & Okamura, A. M. (2022). Design of a wearable vibrotactile stimulation device for individuals with upper-limb hemiparesis and spasticity. *IEEE Transactions on Neural Systems and Rehabilitation Engineering*, 30, 1277–1287. doi:10.1109/TNSRE.2022.3174808 PMID:35552152

Sennrich, R., Haddow, B., & Birch, A. (2015). *Neural machine translation of rare words with subword units*. arXiv preprint arXiv:1508.07909.

Shambharkar, P. G., Kumari, P., Yadav, P., & Kumar, R. (2021, May). Generating Caption for Image using Beam Search and Analyzation with Unsupervised Image Captioning Algorithm. In *2021 5th International Conference on Intelligent Computing and Control Systems (ICICCS)* (pp. 857-864). IEEE. 10.1109/ICICCS51141.2021.9432245

Sharma, A., Mittal, A., Singh, S., & Awatramani, V. (2020). Hand gesture recognition using image processing and feature extraction techniques. *Procedia Computer Science*, 173, 181–190. doi:10.1016/j.procs.2020.06.022

Sharma, R., Nemani, Y., Kumar, S., Kane, L., & Khanna, P. (2013, July). Recognition of single handed sign language gestures using contour tracing descriptor. *Proceedings of the World Congress on Engineering*, 2.

Shen. (2022). Mdn: Meta-Transfer Learning Method For Fake News Detection. *Ccf Conference On Computer Supported Cooperative Work And Social Computing*, 228–237.

Shenoy, K., Dastane, T., Rao, V., & Vyavaharkar, D. (2018, July). Real-time Indian sign language (ISL) recognition. In *2018 9th international conference on computing, communication and networking technologies (ICCCNT)* (pp. 1-9). IEEE.

Shlens, J. (2014). *A tutorial on principal component analysis*. arXiv preprint arXiv:1404.1100.

Sigtia, S., Benetos, E., & Dixon, S. (2016). An end-to-end neural network for polyphonic piano music transcription. *IEEE/ACM Transactions on Audio, Speech, and Language Processing*, 24(5), 927–939. doi:10.1109/TASLP.2016.2533858

Singh, D., & Agarwal, S. (2017). Advanced Human- Smartphone Interface for the Blind Using Morse Code. *International Journal of Advances in Electronics and Computer Science, 4*(5).

SinghA. (n.d.). https://medium.com/@amanbamrah/how-to-evaluate-the-accuracy-of-regression-results-b38e5512afd3

Singh, S. P., Kumar, A., Darbari, H., Singh, L., Rastogi, A., & Jain, S. (2017, July). Machine translation using deep learning: An overview. In *2017 International Conference on Computer, Communications and Electronics (Comptelix)* (pp. 162-167). IEEE. 10.1109/COMPTELIX.2017.8003957

Siri - Apple (IN). (n.d.). Retrieved May 15, 2022, from https://www.apple.com/in/siri/

Slovikovskaya, V. (2019). *Transfer learning from transformers to fake news challenge stance detection (FNC-1) task.* arXiv preprint arXiv:1910.14353.

Smith, A., & Colton, S. (2021). Clip-guided gan image generation: An artistic exploration. *Evo, 2021*, 17.

Soltau, H., Liao, H., & Sak, H. (2016). *Neural speech recognizer: Acoustic-to-word LSTM model for large vocabulary speech recognition.* arXiv preprint arXiv:1610.09975.

Sonal. (n.d.). https://sonalsart.com/how-do-you-evaluate-a-regression-model//

Spoken corpora | Clarin ERIC. (n.d.). Retrieved May 15, 2022, from https://www.clarin.eu/resource-families/spoken-corpora

Spolaor, F., Romanato, M., Annamaria, G., Peppe, A., Bakdounes, L., To, D. K., Volpe, D., & Sawacha, Z. (2021). Relationship between muscular activity and postural control changes after proprioceptive focal stimulation (Equistasi®) in middle-moderate Parkinson's disease patients: An explorative study. *Sensors (Basel)*, 21(2), 560. doi:10.339021020560 PMID:33466838

Starner, T. E. (n.d.). *Visual recognition of American sign language using hidden markov models* [Technical report]. Massachusetts Institute of Tech Cambridge Department of Brain and Cognitive Sciences.

Sturm, B. L., Ben-Tal, O., Monaghan, Ú., Collins, N., Herremans, D., Chew, E., Hadjeres, G., Deruty, E., & Pachet, F. (2019). Machine learning research that matters for music creation: A case study. *Journal of New Music Research*, 48(1), 36–55. doi:10.1080/09298215.2018.1515233

Tan, B. T., Fu, M., Spray, A., & Dermody, P. (1996, October). The use of wavelet transforms in phoneme recognition. In *Proceeding of the Fourth International Conference on Spoken Language Processing (ICSLP'96)* (vol. 4, pp. 2431-2434). IEEE. 10.1109/ICSLP.1996.607300

Taspinar, E. K., Yetis, Y. B., & Cihan, O. (2022). *Abstractive Turkish Text Summarization Using Transformer and Cross-Lingual Summarization.* https://eymenkagantaspinar.github.io/Abstractive-Turkish-Text-Summarization-Using-Transformer-and-Cross-Lingual-Summarization/

Tay, Y., Dehghani, M., Bahri, D., & Metzler, D. (2020). *Efficient transformers: A survey.* arXiv preprint arXiv:2009.06732.

Taylor, S., Kim, T., Yue, Y., Mahler, M., Krahe, J., Rodriguez, A. G., Hodgins, J., & Matthews, I. (2017). A deep learning approach for generalized speech animation. *ACM Transactions on Graphics*, *36*(4), 1–11. doi:10.1145/3072959.3073699

Thakare, P., & Pawar, V. (2016). Article. In *2016 International Conference on Inventive Computation Technologies (ICICT)*. IEEE.

Thenmozhi, D., & Aravindan, C. (2018). Ontology-based Tamil–English cross-lingual information retrieval system. *Sadhana*, *43*(10), 157. doi:10.100712046-018-0942-7

Tian, L., Zhang, X., Wang, Y., & Liu, H. (2020). Early detection of rumours on twitter via stance transfer learning. In *Proceedings of the European Conference on Information Retrieval (ECIR)* (pp. 575-588). Springer. 10.1007/978-3-030-45439-5_38

Tolentino, L. K. S., Juan, R. S., Thio-ac, A. C., Pamahoy, M. A. B., Forteza, J. R. R., & Garcia, X. J. O. (2019). Static sign language recognition using deep learning. *International Journal of Machine Learning and Computing*, *9*(6), 821–827. doi:10.18178/ijmlc.2019.9.6.879

Tu, S. (2014). *Pattern Recognition and Machine Learning (Information Science and Statistics).* Retrieved May 15, 2022, from https://people.eecs.berkeley.edu/~stephentu/writeups/ hmm-baum-welch-derivation.pdf

Tu, Z., Lu, Z., Liu, Y., Liu, X., & Li, H. (2016). *Modeling coverage for neural machine translation.* arXiv preprint arXiv:1601.04811. doi:10.18653/v1/P16-1008

Tufano, M., Pantiuchina, J., Watson, C., Bavota, G., & Poshyvanyk, D. (2019, May). On learning meaningful code changes via neural machine translation. In *2019 IEEE/ACM 41st International Conference on Software Engineering (ICSE)* (pp. 25-36). IEEE. 10.1109/ICSE.2019.00021

Udupa, J. K., & Herman, G. T. (2000). *3D Imaging in Medicine.* CRC Press.

Umer, M., Imtiaz, Z., Ullah, S., Mehmood, A., Choi, G. S., & On, B. W. (2020). Fake news stance detection using deep learning architecture (CNN-LSTM). *IEEE Access: Practical Innovations, Open Solutions*, *8*, 156695–156706. doi:10.1109/ACCESS.2020.3019735

Urena, R., Chiclana, F., & Herrera-Viedma, E. (2020). Decitrustnet: A Graph Based Trust And Reputation Framework For Social Networks. *Information Fusion*, *61*, 101–112. doi:10.1016/j.inffus.2020.03.006

Vamvas, J., & Sennrich, R. (2020). X-stance: A multilingual multi-target dataset for stance detection. In *Proceedings of the 5th SwissText & 16th KONVENS Joint Conference* (p. 9). Academic Press.

Vaswani, A., Shazeer, N., Parmar, N., Uszkoreit, J., Jones, L., Gomez, A. N., ... Polosukhin, I. (2017). Attention is all you need. *Advances in Neural Information Processing Systems*, 30.

Vaswani, A., Shazeer, N., Parmar, N., Uszkoreit, J., Jones, L., Gomez, A., Kaiser, L., & Polosukhin, I. (2017). Attention Is All You Need. *Advances in Neural Information Processing Systems*, 5998–6008.

Vieira, A. L. N., Novaes, F. F., Silva, D. M., Santos, L., Belozi, S., & Castro, T. (2016). A Mobile Solution for Linguistic Communication with Deaf-Blind People Using Arduino and Android. In INC (pp. 177-180). Academic Press.

Vijayaprabakaran, K., & Sathiyamurthy, K. (2020). Towards activation function search for the long short-term model network: a differential evolution based approach. *Journal of King Saud University-Computer and Information Sciences.*

Viriato, J. C. (2019). AI and machine learning in real estate investment. *Journal of Portfolio Management*, *45*(7), 43–54. doi:10.3905/jpm.2019.45.7.043

Viswanathan, D. G. (2009, May). Features from accelerated segment test (fast). *Proceedings of the 10th Workshop on Image Analysis for Multimedia Interactive Services*, 6–8.

Voice Recognition Software | Speech Recognition Software | tazti. (n.d.). Retrieved May 15, 2022, from https://www.tazti.com/

Wah, C., Branson, S., Welinder, P., Perona, P., & Belongie, S. (2011). *The Caltech-UCSD Birds-200-2011 dataset*. Academic Press.

Wanda, P., & Jie, H. J. (2020). Deepprofile: Finding Fake Profile In Online Social Network Using Dynamic Cnn. *Journal Of Information Security And Applications*, *52*, 102465. doi:10.1016/j.jisa.2020.102465

Wang, M.-Y., Tsai, P., Liu, J. W.-S., & Zao, J. K. (2009). Article. In *2009 Ninth IEEE International Conference on Bioinformatics and BioEngineering*. IEEE.

Wang, C., Zhou, Z., & Xu, L. (2021). An integrative review of image captioning research. Journal of Physics: Conference Series.

Wang, H., Zhang, Y., & Yu, X. (2020). An overview of image caption generation methods. *Computational Intelligence and Neuroscience*. doi:10.1155/2020/3062706 PMID:32377178

Wang, R., Utiyama, M., Finch, A., Liu, L., Chen, K., & Sumita, E. (2018). Sentence selection and weighting for neural machine translation domain adaptation. *IEEE/ACM Transactions on Audio, Speech, and Language Processing*, *26*(10), 1727–1741. doi:10.1109/TASLP.2018.2837223

Wang, S., Zhao, J., Shao, C., Dong, C., & Yin, C. (2020). Truck traffic flow prediction based on LSTM and GRU methods with sampled GPS data. *IEEE Access: Practical Innovations, Open Solutions*, *8*, 208158–208169. doi:10.1109/ACCESS.2020.3038788

Wang, X., Feng, W., & Wang, F. (2021). Determining the rumour stance with ensemble method based on BSAF model. In *Proceedings of the 4th International Conference on Computer Science and Software Engineering (CSSE 2021)* (pp. 6-12). 10.1145/3494885.3494887

Wang, X., Tu, Z., & Zhang, M. (2018). Incorporating statistical machine translation word knowledge into neural machine translation. *IEEE/ACM Transactions on Audio, Speech, and Language Processing*, *26*(12), 2255–2266. doi:10.1109/TASLP.2018.2860287

Wang, Y., Yang, W., Ma, F., Xu, J., Zhong, B., Deng, Q., & Gao, J. (2020, April). Weak supervision for fake news detection via reinforcement learning. *Proceedings of the AAAI Conference on Artificial Intelligence*, *34*(01), 516–523. doi:10.1609/aaai.v34i01.5389

Wan, X., Li, H., & Xiao, J. (2010). Cross-language document summarization based on machine translation quality prediction. *Proceedings of the 48th Annual Meeting of the Association for Computational Linguistics*, 917–926.

Wei, X., Cucchiarini, C., van Hout, R., & Strik, H. (2022). Automatic Speech Recognition and Pronunciation Error Detection of Dutch Non-native Speech: Cumulating speech resources in a pluricentric language. *Speech Communication*, *144*, 1–9. doi:10.1016/j.specom.2022.08.004

Westendorf, C. M., & Jelitto, J. (1996, October). Learning pronunciation dictionary from speech data. In *Proceedings of the Fourth International Conference on Spoken Language Processing (ICSLP'96)* (vol. 2, pp. 1045-1048). IEEE. 10.1109/ICSLP.1996.607784

Witt, H., Nicolai, T., & Kenn, H. (2007, June). The WUI-Toolkit: A model-driven UI development framework for wearable user interfaces. In *27th International Conference on Distributed Computing Systems Workshops (ICDCSW'07)* (pp. 43-43). IEEE. 10.1109/ICDCSW.2007.80

Wu, Y., Schuster, M., Chen, Z., Le, Q. V., Norouzi, M., Macherey, W., . . . Klingner, J. (2016). *Google's neural machine translation system: Bridging the gap between human and machine translation.* arXiv preprint arXiv:1609.08144.

Wu, J., Hu, C., Wang, Y., Hu, X., & Zhu, J. (2019). A hierarchical recurrent neural network for symbolic melody generation. *IEEE Transactions on Cybernetics*, *50*(6), 2749–2757. doi:10.1109/TCYB.2019.2953194 PMID:31796422

Wu, J., Liu, X., Hu, X., & Zhu, J. (2020). PopMNet: Generating structured pop music melodies using neural networks. *Artificial Intelligence*, *286*, 103303. doi:10.1016/j.artint.2020.103303

Wu, W., Alvarez, J., Liu, C., & Sun, H.-M. (2018). Bot Detection Using Unsupervised Machine Learning. *Microsystem Technologies*, *24*(1), 209–217. doi:10.100700542-016-3237-0

Xia, P., Wu, S., & Van Durme, B. (2020). *Which* BERT? A survey organizing contextualized encoders.* arXiv preprint arXiv:2010.00854. doi:10.18653/v1/2020.emnlp-main.608

Xia, Y. (2020). Research on statistical machine translation model based on deep neural network. *Computing*, *102*(3), 643–661. doi:10.100700607-019-00752-1

Xia, Y., He, T., Tan, X., Tian, F., He, D., & Qin, T. (2019, July). Tied transformers: Neural machine translation with shared encoder and decoder. *Proceedings of the AAAI Conference on Artificial Intelligence*, *33*, 5466–5473. doi:10.1609/aaai.v33i01.33015466

Xie, J., Chai, Y., & Liu, X. (2022). An Interpretable Deep Learning Approach To Understand Health Misinformation Transmission On Youtube. *Proceedings Of The 55th Hawaii International Conference On System Sciences*. 10.24251/HICSS.2022.183

Xu, T., Zhang, P., Huang, Q., Zhang, H., Gan, Z., Huang, X., & He, X. (2018). Attngan: Fine-grained text to image generation with attentional generative adversarial networks. *Proceedings of the IEEE conference on computer vision and pattern recognition*, 1316–1324. 10.1109/CVPR.2018.00143

Yang, H. D. (2014). Sign language recognition with the kinect sensor based on conditional random fields. *Sensors (Basel)*, *15*(1), 135–147. doi:10.3390150100135 PMID:25609039

Yang, L., Zhang, M., Li, C., Bendersky, M., & Najork, M. (2020, October). Beyond 512 tokens: Siamese multi-depth transformer-based hierarchical encoder for long-form document matching. In *Proceedings of the 29th ACM International Conference on Information & Knowledge Management* (pp. 1725-1734). 10.1145/3340531.3411908

Yang, P., Song, W., Zhao, X., Zheng, R., & Qingge, L. (2020). An improved Otsu threshold segmentation algorithm. *International Journal on Computer Science and Engineering*, *22*(1), 146–153. doi:10.1504/IJCSE.2020.107266

Ycart, A., & Benetos, E. (2020). Learning and Evaluation Methodologies for Polyphonic Music Sequence Prediction With LSTMs. *IEEE/ACM Transactions on Audio, Speech, and Language Processing*, *28*, 1328–1341. doi:10.1109/TASLP.2020.2987130

Yeniterzi, R., & Oflazer, K. (2010). Syntax-to-Morphology Mapping in Factored Phrase-Based Statistical Machine Translation from English to Turkish. *Proceedings of the 48th Annual Meeting of the Association for Computational Linguistics*, 454–464.

Yousuf, M.A., & Nobi, M.N. (2010). A new method to remove noise in magnetic resonance and ultrasound images. *Journal of Scientific Research, 3*(1), 81-89.

Yu, D., Eversole, A., Seltzer, M. L., Yao, K., Guenter, B., Kuchaiev, O., Seide, F., Wang, H., Droppo, J., Huang, Z., Zweig, G., Rossbach, C. J., & Currey, J. (2014). An introduction to computational networks and the computational network toolkit. In *The 15th Annual Conference of the International Speech Communication Association*. ISCA.

Yuan, J., & Liberman, M. (2008). Speaker identification on the SCOTUS corpus. *The Journal of the Acoustical Society of America, 123*(5), 3878. doi:10.1121/1.2935783

Zafrulla, Z., Brashear, H., Starner, T., Hamilton, H., & Presti, P. (2011). American sign language recognition with the kinect. *Proceedings of the 13th international conference on multimodal interfaces, Academic Medicine*, 279–286. 10.1145/2070481.2070532

Zhang, J., Zhao, Y., Saleh, M., & Liu, P. (2019). *Zhang: Pretraining with Extracted Gap-sentences for Abstractive Summarization.* Arxiv:1912.08777.

Zhang, B., Xiong, D., Su, J., & Duan, H. (2017). A context-aware recurrent encoder for neural machine translation. *IEEE/ACM Transactions on Audio, Speech, and Language Processing, 25*(12), 2424–2432. doi:10.1109/TASLP.2017.2751420

Zhang, G., Tu, E., & Cui, D. (2017). Stable and improved generative adversarial nets (GANS): a constructive survey. *2017 IEEE International Conference on Image Processing (ICIP)*, 1871–1875. 10.1109/ICIP.2017.8296606

Zhang, H., Xu, T., Li, H., Zhang, S., Wang, X., Huang, X., & Metaxas, D. N. (2017). Stackgan: Text to photo-realistic image synthesis with stacked generative adversarial networks. *Proceedings of the IEEE international conference on computer vision*, 5907–5915. 10.1109/ICCV.2017.629

Zhang, H., Xu, T., Li, H., Zhang, S., Wang, X., Huang, X., & Metaxas, D. N. (2018). Stackgan++: Realistic image synthesis with stacked generative adversarial networks. *IEEE Transactions on Pattern Analysis and Machine Intelligence, 41*(8), 1947–1962. doi:10.1109/TPAMI.2018.2856256 PMID:30010548

Zhang, N. (2020). Learning adversarial transformer for symbolic music generation. *IEEE Transactions on Neural Networks and Learning Systems*, 1–10. doi:10.1109/TNNLS.2020.2990746 PMID:32614773

Zhang, X., Chen, X., Li, Y., Lantz, V., Wang, K., & Yang, J. (2011). A framework for hand gesture recognition based on accelerometer and EMG sensors. *IEEE Transactions on Systems, Man, and Cybernetics. Part A, Systems and Humans, 41*(6), 1064–1076. doi:10.1109/TSMCA.2011.2116004

Zhao, Y., Ma, B., Jiang, P., Zeng, D., Wang, X., & Li, S. (2020). Prediction of Alzheimer's Disease Progression with Multi-Information Generative Adversarial Network. *IEEE Journal of Biomedical and Health Informatics*, 1–1. doi:10.1109/JBHI.2020.3006925 PMID:32750952

Zhu, J., Zhou, Y., Zhang, J., & Zong, C. (2020). Attend, Translate and Summarize: An Efficient Method for Neural Cross-Lingual Summarization. *Proceedings of the 58th Annual Meeting of the Association for Computational Linguistics*, 1309–1321. 10.18653/v1/2020.acl-main.121

Zhu, M., Pan, P., Chen, W., & Yang, Y. (2019). Dm-gan: Dynamic memory generative adversarial networks for text-to-image synthesis. *Proceedings of the IEEE/CVF Conference on Computer Vision and Pattern Recognition*, 5802–5810. 10.1109/CVPR.2019.00595

Zubiaga, A., Aker, A., Bontcheva, K., Liakata, M., & Procter, R. (2018). Detection and resolution of rumours in social media: A survey. *ACM Computing Surveys, 51*(2), 1–36. doi:10.1145/3161603

Zwicker, E. (1961). Subdivision of the audible frequency range into critical bands. *The Journal of the Acoustical Society of America, 33*(2), 248. doi:10.1121/1.1908630

About the Contributors

L. Ashok Kumar was a Postdoctoral Research Fellow from San Diego State University, California. He was selected among seven scientists in India for the BHAVAN Fellowship from the Indo-US Science and Technology Forum and also, he received SYST Fellowship from DST, Govt of India. He has 3 years of industrial experience and 22 years of academic and research experience. He has published 173 technical papers in International and National journals and presented 167 papers in National and International Conferences, He has completed 26 Government of India funded projects worth about 15 Crores and currently 9 projects are in progress worth about 12 Crores. He has developed 27 products and out of that 23 products have been technology transferred to industries and for Government funding agencies, He has created Eight Centres of Excellence at PSG Tech in collaboration with Government agencies and Industries namely, Centre for Audio Visual Speech Recognition, Centre for Alternate Cooling Technologies, Centre for Industrial Cyber Physical Systems Research Centre for Excellence in LV Switchgear, Centre for Renewable Energy Systems, Centre for Excellence in Solar PV Systems. Centre for Excellence in Solar Thermal Systems. His PhD work on wearable electronics earned him a National Award from 1STE and he has received 26 awards in the National and in international level. He has guided 92 graduate and postgraduate projects. He has produced 6 PhD Scholars and 12 candidates are doing PhD under his supervision. He has visited many countries for institute industry collaboration and as a keynote speaker. He has been an invited speaker in 345 programs. Also, he has organized 102 events, including conferences, workshops, and seminars. He completed his graduate program in Electrical and Electronics Engineering from University of Madras and his post-graduate from PSG College of Technology, India, and Masters in Business Administration from IGNOU, New Delhi. After completion of his graduate degree he joined as project engineer for Serval Paper Boards Ltd. Coimbatore (now ITC Unit, Kova Presently he is working as a Professor in the Department of EEE, PSG College of Technology. He is also a Certified Chartered Engineer and BSI Certified ISO 50001 2008 Lead Auditor. He has authored 19 books in his areas of interest published by Springer, CRC Press, Elsevier, Nova Publishers. Cambridge University Press. Wiley. Lambert Publishing and IGI Global. He has 11 patents, one Design patent and two Copyrights to his credit and also contributed 18 chapters in various books. He is also the Chairman of Indian Association of Energy Management Professionals and Executive Member in institution of Engineers, Coimbatore Executive Council Member in Institute of Smart Structure and Systems. Bangalore, Associate Member in CODISSIA. He is also holding prestigious positions in various national and international forums and he is a Fellow Member in IET (UK), Fellow Member In IETE, Fellow Member IE and Senior Member in IEEE.

Dhanaraj Karthika Renuka is working as Professor in Department of Information Technology, PSG College of Technology. Her professional career of 19 years has been with PSG College of Technology since 2004. She is a recipient of Indo-U.S. Fellowship for Women in STEMM (WISTEMM)-Women Overseas Fellowship program supported by the Department of Science and Technology (DST), Govt. of India and implemented by the Indo-U.S. Science & Technology Forum (IUSSTF). She was a Post-doctoral Research Fellow from Wright State University, Ohio, USA. She has received "Women Scientist Award" under the category of Machine learning on May30th, 2021 from HUMCEN Awards. Her area of specializations includes Data Mining, Evolutionary Algorithms, Soft Computing, Machine Learning and Deep Learning, Affective Computing, Computer Vision. She is a reviewer for Computers and Electrical Engineering, Elsevier, Wiley Book chapter, Springer Book Chapters on "Knowledge Computing and its Applications". She has authored a book titled "Deep Learning using Python", Wiley India Pvt Ltd. She has published several papers in reputed National and International journals and conferences.

S. Geetha (Senior Member, IEEE) is currently a Professor and the Associate Dean, Research with the School of Computer Science and Engineering, Vellore Institute of Technology, Chennai Campus, India. She received the B.E. degree in Computer Science and Engineering from Madurai Kamaraj University, India, in 2000, and the M.E. degree in Computer Science and Engineering and the Ph.D. degree from Anna University, Chennai, India, in 2004 and 2011, respectively. Her research interests include steganography, steganalysis, multimedia security, intrusion detection systems, machine learning paradigms, computer vision and information forensics. She has more than 20 years of rich teaching and research experience. She has published more than 100 papers in reputed international conferences and refereed journals like IEEE, Springer, Elsevier publishers. She joins the Review Committee and the Editorial Advisory Board of reputed journals. She has given many expert lectures, keynote addresses at international and national conferences. She has organized many workshops, conferences, and FDPs. She was a recipient of the University Rank and Academic Topper Award in her B.E. and M.E. degrees, in 2000 and 2004, respectively. She was also the proud recipient of the ASDF Best Academic Researcher Award 2013, the ASDF Best Professor Award 2014, the Research Award in 2016, and the High Performer Award 2016, Best Women Researcher Award 2021.

* * *

Ankit Mishra, completed degree from the School of Computer Science & Engineering at VIT, Vellore. His area of interest is Machine Learning, Deep Learning, Soft Computing, Optimization, and Data mining.

Chanthini Baskar completed her Bachelor's degree in Electronics & Communication from Anna university Chennai in 2012. She received her postgraduate degree in Embedded systems from SASTRA Deemed university in 2014. She completed a doctoral degree in the field of Internet of Things from SASTRA Deemed university in 2020 and also received INSPIRE fellowship from the Department of Science & Technology for the same. Currently, she is working with the school of Electronics Engineering, Vellore Institute of Technology, Chennai. Her major research area includes Embedded system design, real-time data analytics and application of IoT.

Chinnasamy Ponnusamy received his Bachelor's in Computer Science and Engineering from Anna University, Chennai and Master's degree in Computer Science and Engineering from Kalasalingam University. He also received Doctor of Philosophy in computer science during the year 2019. He was an Associate Professor of Computer Science and Engineering at MLR Institute of Technology, Hyderabad. His research interest includes Cloud Security, Access control, Blockchain Technology and Cryptography. Moreover, he has also published 16 papers in International Journal, 18 papers in International Conferences and 7 book chapters.

Debajit Datta is a Bachelor of Technology degree holder with a Computer Science major, currently working as a Software Developer at JP Morgan Chase & Co., with experiences working in several non-profit organizations and software industries. He is skilled in Java, Spring Boot, ReactJS, Python, HTML, CSS, Javascript, NodeJS, MySQL, C++, C, Microsoft Office. He is a former inner circle member of two student chapters of VIT including Venturesity and Google's Developer Student Clubs and has volunteered as a Java mentor at C4 Projects, He has been appointed as Program Representative of B.Tech Computer Science at VIT University, for three consecutive years. He can execute team management really well and is good at writing content and corporate emails. He has published a total of 12 papers so far, including a conference paper, a book chapter, and several articles.

Dilek Küçük, Ph.D, is an associate professor and senior chief researcher at TÜBİTAK Marmara Research Center (MRC). She has obtained her B.S., M.S. and Ph.D. degrees all from Middle East Technical University in Ankara (Turkey), in 2003, 2005, and 2011, respectively. Between May 2013 and May 2014, she has studied as a post-doctoral researcher at European Commission's Joint Research Centre in Italy. Her research interests include energy informatics, data mining, social media analysis, natural language processing, and database applications in engineering domains. She is the author or co-author of 16 papers published at SCI-indexed journals, in addition to more than 40 papers presented at international conferences.

Eymen Kagan Taspinar received BS degree in Electrical and Electronics Engineering from Marmara University, Turkey, in 2021. His research interests include deep learning, embedded systems, and cryptography.

Fowjiya S. received the B.Tech. in Information Technology from Anna University, Chennai India, (2011) and the M.E. in Computer and Communication Engineering from Anna University of Technology, Chennai, India (2013). Her research interests include Artificial Intelligence, Machine Learning, Data science and Network security.

Geetha N, completed M. Tech in Computer Science & Engineering at VIT, Vellore and completed MCA at Sacred Heart College, Tirupattur. She is currently pursuing her Ph.D. at VIT, Vellore. She has 7 years of experience in the teaching field. Her area of interest is Machine Learning, Deep Learning, Soft Computing, Optimization, and Data mining.

Geraldine Amali received her Ph.D. and M.Tech. degrees in Computer Science and Engineering from Vellore Institute of Technology, India. She is working as an Assistant Professor at VIT and has more than 10 years' experience teaching computer science. Her research interests include machine learning and biologically inspired optimization algorithms.

Jency A. Jebamani B received the B.Tech. in Computer Science and Engineering from Kalasalingam Academy of Research Education, Krishnankovil, India, (2019) and the M.Tech. in Computer Science and Engineering from Kalasalingam Academy of Research Education, Krishnankovil, India, (2021). She is currently working as an assistant professor in Department of Computer Science and Engineering, KPR Institute of Engineering and Technology, Coimbatore, India. Her field of interest includes Machine Learning, Deep Learning and Computer Vision.

Mangayarkarasi Ramaiah received her Ph.D. Degree in Information Technology and Engineering from VIT University, M.E. Computer Science from Anna University. She is working as an Associate Professor in the School of Information Technology and Engineering at VIT University, Vellore Campus, India. She has published good number of papers in various journals. Her research interest includes Computer Vision, Image Processing, Machine Learning, Deep Learning, and Internet of Things.

Manikandan E. received the B.E. degree in electronics and communication engineering from the Anna University in 2010. He has received M.Tech. in Embedded System technologies and Ph.D. in Electrical Engineering from the Anna University in 2012 and 2019 respectively. respectively. Currently he is a Senior Assistant Professor in the School of Electronics Engineering at Vellore Institute of Technology, Chennai. His research interests are in the areas of sensors and micromachining. He has published over 60 journal and conference papers in these areas. He has also published three book chapters in the indexed publications. He has filed two papers in his credit. He is the recipient of a member of "Confederation of Elite Academician of IICDC". He received DST-ITS grant for visiting Japan in 2018 and also best researcher award from SSN College of Engineering in 2018. Dr Manikandan delivered many invited talks in prestigious institutions in the area micromachining and sensors. He has 7 years of teaching and 3 years of research experience. He has served as a reviewer for several journals.

Mary Nikitha K, graduated student from the computer science department at VIT Vellore (2022 Batch) and going to pursue a Master's degree in Data Science from New York University this fall.

Mathew Mithra Noel joined VIT in 2009 and is currently Professor (HAG) and Dean, School of Electrical Engineering at VIT, Vellore. He received his Ph.D. in Electrical and Computer Engineering from the University of Alabama-Birmingham, USA in 2005. He then served as an Assistant Professor in Electronics Engineering at Norfolk State University, USA from 2006 to 2009. He received his M.E. in Electronics and Control from BITS, Pilani and B.Tech. in Electrical and Electronics Engineering from Bharathidasan University. His current research interests are Machine Learning, Control and Global Optimization Algorithms. He works to develop new machine learning architectures, control strategies and optimization algorithms. He was the recipient of the Teaching Scholarship at BITS, Pilani, Graduate School Scholarship at the University of Alabama-Birmingham, USA, STARS research award 2006 & 2007, Summer Research Grant from Intelligence Community Center for Academic Excellence, Norfolk State University, USA, 2009 and Best Teacher Award for School of Engineering 2009 at Norfolk State University, USA.

Mudit Jantwal is a recently graduated student from the computer science department at VIT Vellore (2022 Batch) and am going to pursue a Masters degree in Data Science.

Nithyasri A. received the Bachelor Degree in Computer Science and Engineering from Anna University, Chennai India, (2009) and the Master Degree in Computer Science and Engineering from Anna University, Chennai, India (2012). She is currently working as an Assistant Professor in the Department of Artificial Intelligence and Data Science, M. Kumarsamy College of Engineering, Karur. Her research interests include Artificial Intelligence, Machine Learning, Deep Learning and Cloud Computing.

Onur Cihan received BS degrees in Control Engineering and Electrical Engineering from Istanbul Technical University, Turkey, in 2007. He received MS and PhD degrees in Electrical and Electronics Engineering from Bogazici University, Istanbul, Turkey in 2009 and 2014, respectively. He was a post-doctoral researcher at the Center for Systems Science, Yale University, New Haven, CT, before joining the Department of Electrical and Electronic Engineering, Marmara University, Istanbul, Turkey, where he is currently working as an Associate Professor. His research interests include mathematical systems theory, multi-agent systems, distributed control, data mining and deep learning.

Puneet Mittal received her PhD in Computer Engineering in Year 2020 from Punjabi University, Patiala. Currently, she is working as an Associate Professor in Department of Artificial Intelligence & Machine Learning at Mangalore Institute of Technology & Engineering, Mangalore. She has contributed more than 30 quality publications in indexed international journals, books and conferences. Her key areas of research are Software Engineering, Natural Language Processing, Machine Vision and Blockchain Technologies.

Raajkumar G is a Project Associate in PSG College of Technology.

Raghav Talwar, completed his degree from the School of Computer Science & Engineering at VIT, Vellore. His area of interest is Machine Learning, Deep Learning, Soft Computing, Optimization, and Data mining.

Rajasekar R. is currently working as Faculty in the Department of IT, the University of Technology and Applied Sciences (Sur Campus), Sultanate of Oman. He is currently pursuing his Ph.D. degree from Vellore Institute of Technology, India, in the Internet of Things Security area. His areas of expertise are computer networking, computer security, the Internet of Things, and Cyber Security. He is proficient in conveying conceptual knowledge, developing learning materials, and extensive participation in co-curricular and professional development activities.

Rajkumar S, is working as an Associate Professor in the school of Computer Science and Engineering (SCOPE) in Vellore Institute of Technology, Vellore. He earned his PhD in 2017 in the area of Digital Image Processing from Vellore Institute of Technology under the supervision of Dr. P.V.S.S.R. Chandra Mouli. He completed his M.E in CSE from Anna University in 2010 and completed his B.E in CSE from Anna University in 2008. Received fund from DHR-ICMR to conduct a workshop and got a consultancy project. He is a life member of Computer Society of India (CSI) and a senior member of IEEE.

Ramanathan L. has received his B.E. in Computer Science & Engineering from Bharathidasan University, Tiruchirappalli, India, and M.E in Computer Science from Sathyabama University, Chennai, India and a Ph.D. degree in Computer Science and Engineering from VIT University, Vellore, India. He is currently working as an Associate Professor in VIT, Vellore, India. His area of interest is Data Mining, Database Systems, Software Engg, Cloud Computing, and Virtualization. He is having 14+ years of teaching experiences. He has published more papers in International Journals and Conferences. He is an Editorial board member/reviewer of International/ National Journals and Conferences. His ongoing research is on Prediction, Classification, and Clustering for Educational systems. He is a member of IACSIT, CSI, ACM, IACSIT, IEEE (WIE), ACEEE.

Rishabh Kumar, completed his degree from the School of Computer Science & Engineering at VIT, Vellore. His area of interest is Machine Learning, Deep Learning, Soft Computing, Optimization, and Data mining.

Rishav Agarwal is currently pursuing the degree - Master of Science in Computer Science - from Columbia University, New York, USA. He completed the degree of Bachelor of Technology in Computer Science and Engineering from Vellore Institute of Technology, Vellore in 2021. He has been the co-author of 7 published research papers in the domain of Machine Learning, Artificial Intelligence and Software Development. As a graduate student, he has served as a Teaching Assistant at Columbia University for the Data Visualization course, while also serving as a Research Intern in the Data Science Institute of the University. Throughout his academia, he has been part of multiple projects involving Cloud Technologies, Machine Learning and Data Science techniques. He has also been an active part of various cultural and technical organisations serving as part of their governing bodies.

Ritwik Kundu is a final-year student currently majoring in Computer Science and Engineering from Vellore Institute of Technology. He is very enthusiastic about coding and design. His interest lies in Android Development, Machine Learning and IoT. He has a keen interest in design and digital art as well.

Sanjay V, is a Research Scholar in School of Computer Science and Engineering, Vellore Institute of Technology, Vellore, Tamilnadu, India.

Sasithradevi A. completed her Bachelor Degree in Electronics and Communication Engineering from Anna university. She completed her Post Graduate in Communication systems from Anna University. She completed Doctoral degree from Anna University in 2018. She is with School of Electronics Engineering, Vellore Institute of Technology, Chennai. Her research interest includes Video processing, Image processing, Machine Learning and Deep Learning. She has published her research articles in reputed journal and conferences.

Shaurya Singh is a final-year student currently pursuing his undergraduate degree in Computer Science and Engineering from Vellore Institute of Technology, Vellore. He is passionate about Artificial Intelligence and Machine Learning.

Shivoma Ahuja, completed her degree from the School of Computer Science & Engineering at VIT, Vellore. Her area of interest is Machine Learning, Deep Learning, Soft Computing, Optimization, and Data mining.

Shoba S. is working as an Assistant Professor (Senior) in the School of Electronics Engineering at VIT university, Chennai Campus. Before joining VIT University, she was a Post-Doctoral Researcher at the Department of Computer Science and Engineering at IIITDM Kancheepuram, Chennai. She worked as researcher in SSN College of Engineering from 2017 to 2019. She worked as an Assistant Professor in Anand Institute of Higher Technology, Anna University Chennai. (Sister concern of Kalasalingam University) from 2012 to 2016. In addition, she has 2 years of experience in industry from 2007 to 2009. She received her Ph.D from Anna University, Chennai and received her M.E from SSN college of Engineering, Chennai. She is an active member of a number of professional bodies such as IEEE and ISTE. She has published her papers in reputed journals like IET, Elsevier and Springer. She has more than 20 papers in peer-reviewed journals and conferences. Her research interests include speech signal processing, deep learning, Artificial Intelligence, machine learning and image processing with specific focus on enhancement, separation, modeling, and analysis.

Shunmugapriya MC is a Research scholar at PSG College of technology in the domain of machine learning, speech analytics.

Sri Sathya K. B. received the B.Tech. in Information Technology from Anna University, Chennai India, (2009) and the M.Tech. in Mainframe Technology from Anna University of Technology, Coimbatore, India (2011). She is currently working on her Ph.D. in Information and communication engineering at Anna University, Chennai. Her research interests include Artificial Intelligence, Machine Learning, Deep Learning and Computer Vision.

Sukhwinder Sharma received his PhD in Computer Science & Engineering in Year 2019. Currently, he is working as an Associate Professor in Department of Computer Science & Engineering at Mangalore Institute of Technology & Engineering, Mangalore. He has contributed more than 35 quality publications in indexed international journals, books and conferences. His key areas of research are Wireless Sensor Networks, Natural Language Processing, Internet of Things and Blockchain Technologies.

Suresh Kumar Nagarajan, is working as a professor at Presidency University, India. He have 20 years of experience in the field of teaching. He completed my Ph.D. in VIT. His area of interest is Image Processing, Machine Learning, Deep Learning, Soft Computing, Optimization, and Data mining.

Swarnalatha Purushotham is an Associate Professor, in the School of Computing Science and Engineering, Vellore Institute of Technology at Vellore, India. She pursued her Ph.D degree in Image Processing and Intelligent Systems. She has published more than 120 papers in International Journals/International Conference Proceedings/National Conferences. She is having 20+ years of teaching experiences. She has filed two Patents and also awarded with Dr. APJ Abdul Kalam Award for Teaching Excellence. She is a senior member of IACSIT, CSI, ACM, IACSIT, IEEE (WIE), ACEEE. She is an Editorial board member/reviewer of reputed International/ National Journals and Conferences. She had edited three IGI Global books. Her current research interest includes Image Processing, Remote Sensing, Artificial Intelligence.

Umadevi K. S.'s primary research interests are in the field of wireless network protocols as well as security and distributed systems. The current research interest includes 5G, Cloud Computing, Software defined networking, Internet of Things, Machine Learning, Cyber Security, Blockchain and Authentication mechanisms. An active member of several professional associations, journal editorial boards, national and international conferences. The impacts of publications and presentations are reflected in academics, research, and practices.

Vanmathi C. received her Ph.D. degree in Information Technology and Engineering from VIT University, M.Tech (IT) from Sathyabama University and B.E. Computer Science from Madras University. She is working as an Associate Professor in the School of Information Technology at VIT University, Vellore Campus, India. She is having 19 years of research experience. Her area of research includes Deep Learning, Computer Vision, Soft Computing, Cyber Physical Systems and Internet of Things. She is a member of Computer society of India and Soft Computing Research Society.

Vignesh Kumar Thangarajan is a Software Engineer with excellent skills in problem solving and programming, with more than 5 years of experience across the domains of Networking, Operating Systems, Application Development and Data Science.

Vishnu S. Pendyala is a faculty member of the Department of Applied Data Science at San Jose State University and the chair of IEEE Computer Society, Silicon Valley Chapter. He has over two decades of experience with software industry leaders like Cisco and Synopsys in the Silicon Valley, USA. Dr. Pendyala served on the Board of Directors, Silicon Valley Engineering Council during 2018-2019. During his recent 3-year term as an ACM Distinguished speaker and before that as a researcher and industry expert, he gave numerous (50+) invited talks. He holds MBA in Finance and PhD, MS, and BE degrees in Computer Engineering from US and Indian universities. Dr. Pendyala taught a one-week course sponsored by the Ministry of Human Resource Development (MHRD), Government of India, under the GIAN program in 2017 to Computer Science faculty from all over the country and delivered the keynote in a similar program sponsored by AICTE, Government of India in 2022. Dr. Pendyala's book, "Veracity of Big Data: Machine Learning and Other Approaches to Verifying Truthfulness" made it to several libraries, including those of MIT, Stanford, CMU, and internationally.

Yusuf Burak Yetis received BS degree in Electrical and Electronics Engineering from Marmara University, Turkey, in 2021. He is currently working as a software test engineer. His research interest is deep learning.

288

Index

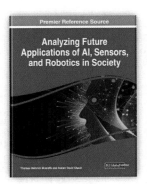

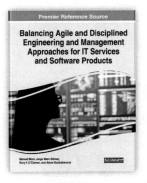

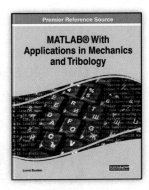

Ensure Quality Research is Introduced to the Academic Community

Become an Evaluator for IGI Global Authored Book Projects

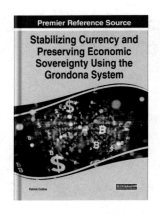

Premier Reference Source

Stabilizing Currency and Preserving Economic Sovereignty Using the Grondona System

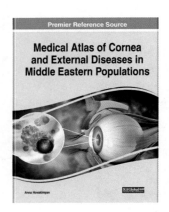

Premier Reference Source

Medical Atlas of Cornea and External Diseases in Middle Eastern Populations

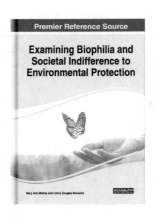

Premier Reference Source

Examining Biophilia and Societal Indifference to Environmental Protection

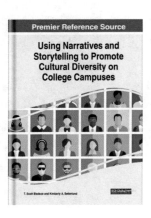

Premier Reference Source

Using Narratives and Storytelling to Promote Cultural Diversity on College Campuses

The overall success of an authored book project is dependent on quality and timely manuscript evaluations.

Applications and Inquiries may be sent to:
development@igi-global.com

Applicants must have a doctorate (or equivalent degree) as well as publishing, research, and reviewing experience. Authored Book Evaluators are appointed for one-year terms and are expected to complete at least three evaluations per term. Upon successful completion of this term, evaluators can be considered for an additional term.

If you have a colleague that may be interested in this opportunity, we encourage you to share this information with them.

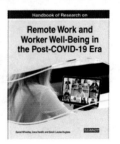
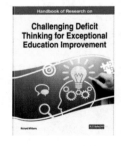

Printed in the United States
by Baker & Taylor Publisher Services